PRECISION SHOOTING
AT 1,000 YARDS

Edited by
Dave Brennan

Published by:
Precision Shooting, Inc.
222 McKee Street
Manchester, CT 06040

Cover photo courtesy of
Art Durham of Darien, Illinois

First Printing, October 2000
Second Printing, October 2002
Third Printing, February 2005

INTRODUCTION

There has long been a fascination with "the long shot", among both the skilled marksmen and the neophyte shooters of the world. Truly long range shooting traces its military history back to the snipers of both sides in the American Civil War. Billy Dixon's famed shot at the battle of Adobe Walls in Texas in 1874…at a measured distance in excess of 1,500 yards. The historic first Palma match at the Creedmoor range on Long Island in 1876. Then the snipers of World War I in the trench warfare that so ravaged Europe. The snipers of the Russian Front during World War II, and the Marine Scout-Snipers of Vietnam fame. The renaissance of long range highpower shooting in National and International competition. The remarkable growth of 1,000 yard benchrest shooting in the United States in recent years. The singular long range accomplishments of the groundhog and prairie dog varmint shooters of the US in current times. It's all here; for the dedicated lover of serious rifle accuracy it will prove to be a book like no other to be found today. All the writers are well known to the *Precision Shooting* readers. With the exception of parts of the McPherson and Hugel chapters, all are previously unpublished. A number of the chapters will likely come to be recognized as the definitive work on their respective subjects.

DEDICATION

The book is respectfully dedicated to the memory of the late Gunnery Sergeant Carlos N. Hathcock II, USMC...the nation's ultimate Scout Sniper.

To many of us, when we are talking about long range shooting among ourselves, there is Carlos Hathcock…and then there is everyone else.

It seems as if there ought to be more than two classes for a group that is potentially so large. But most of us are rather satisfied with just those two classes. Carlos Hathcock…and everyone else.

DISCLAIMER

Throughout this book are quoted a number of loads, used by the writers and other shooters who are the subjects of the writing, in their reloading of cartridges. Neither the writers nor the publisher makes any representation as to the safeness of these same loads in any other rifles. There are a myriad of factors, many of them minute and subtle, that could make these same loads dangerous in a different rifle on a different day. Always reduce quoted loads, and slowly work up to them, watching closely for signs of increasing pressure as you go.

TABLE OF CONTENTS

Chapter 1 The Tom Whitaker Interview: "The Road to 1,000 Yards Starts At 50 Feet"
by Tom Lintner.. 1

Chapter 2 A Short History of Long Range Shooting in the United States
by Hap Rocketto 17

Chapter 3 1000 Yard Military Sniping
by Norm & Rocky Chandler 31

Chapter 4 Live Varmint Shooting at 1,000 Yards and Beyond
by Steve Hanson... 43

Chapter 5 Ultra Long Range Shooting In Colorado (Parts 1-2-3)
by Steve Hugel 77

Chapter 6 Recipes For Success—The Ingredients For A Great Long Range Rifle
by Ian Cheeseman 95

Chapter 7 1000 Yard Benchrest—The Dawn Of A New Era
by Jacob Gottfredson 103

Chapter 8 1000 Yard Glass
by Jacob Gottfredson 127

Chapter 9 Conventional Long-Range Competition
by Randolph Constantine 149

Chapter 10 Replicating (?) Billy Dixon's Lengendary Long-Shot (Part I)
Billy Dixon Revisited (Part II)
by M.L. McPherson 171

Chapter 11 "Farky" Shooting F-Class
by Larry Bartholome 191

Chapter 12 Bill Shehan Zeroes In On 1,000-Yard Accuracy
by Dave Scott.. 213

Chapter 13 Handloading For Long Range Highpower Rifle Competition
by John Feamster 229

Chapter 1

The Tom Whitaker Interview:
"The Road to 1,000 Yards Starts At 50 Feet"

by Tom Lintner

Prologue

Generally, it's somewhat unusual to have an author's prolog with a short story. But then again, sometimes it's necessary to "set the stage" so the reader can enjoy it better. Such is the case here...

This particular chapter in the book is an interview with Tom Whitaker, one of the top competitive shooters in the world today. In deciding how to write the story I had two options: present it as the "classic" question and answer interview format or, tell a narrative story based on the interview. Since I have known Tom for a number of years, shot with him as an individual as well as team member, I choose the later. So, Good Reader, what you are about to embark on is a long short-story that is the culmination of several interview sessions, countless phone calls, too many emails, and a couple of wild rides on the shooting lines.

I think it's an interesting, and in many cases a very surprising story, of how a boy from southern California went from racing horses to becoming one of the best long range shooters in the world today. It's a story of transition from a smallbore shooter, to highpower, to the international world of the US Palma Team. We'll take a detailed look at what he's done, and examine how he does what he does. Of course we'll talk about equipment and reloading. We'll share a section where Tom describes what he sees when he looks through a sight and how he manages all those perfect shots.

For many people who "think" they know Tom

Whitaker based on his success in highpower and Palma, you will find yourself amazed at his "real roots."

For those of you who grew up shooting in the same time era it will allow you a trip "down memory lane." For those of you who are not of his

Leech Cup Win 1998.

generation, I offer this story as a look into the past to see how a champion shooter learned to shoot and how he developed his values.

Finally, this is a story of success. But it's also a warning call of what we can lose if we don't remember the lessons of the past and fail to invest in our future....

The First 10 Years

"Tom, you're going to drive me absolutely nuts! You just shot a long-range course of fire at Quantico with two Palma matches and an individual 1,000-yd match. You only dropped 3 lousy points, you set a national record with a score of 1097-71X out of a possible 1100, and you're trying to tell me you didn't know what was happening with your shots? You're telling me the flags were lying *AND* the mirage was lying.??? Fer cryin' out loud… come on, gimme a break!"

Honest, in May of 2000, I said that to Tom Whitaker following the long-range match at Quantico, Virginia. He was perfectly serious when he told me, since he hadn't shot on that range for twenty years, he was not comfortable with being able to completely read the conditions. At that time I could not for the life of me understand how he could shoot like that (I should be so lucky) and then say he wasn't sure of some of his shots. Well, several weeks later, after Tom and I finished our marathon interview, I finally began to understand a little of what makes him the shooter he is.

But, I'm already getting ahead of myself. To "set the stage" for this story we need to travel back in time to the quiet community of Orange, California circa 1947… where Tom Whitaker was born.

To hear Tom tell the story, it was the classic "growing up in America" story. He and his family had spent a lot of time traveling in New Mexico and Arizona racing horses. This is what Tom calls "the early years" and when he was in 6th grade the family settled back in California. In 1958 Tom joined the Boy Scouts and in the "summer of '59" (Gee, sounds like a good title for a movie), he went to a Boy Scout summer camp. There he had his first exposure to "target" shooting.

Although this was Tom's first time for a somewhat "formal" shooting experience, it was

not his first time behind a rifle. That actually started earlier since his father had been a WWII veteran from the South Pacific and taught him the basics while plinking at cans.

After that summer camp experience, he decided to try to get his Merit Badge for Marksmanship. But before he could do this he had to go through the California Hunter Safety Program. This was accomplished by attending class one Saturday a week for 8 weeks and included shooting standing at 25 yards with pistol targets. According to Tom, after eight weeks of shooting standing, the prone course of fire with the Boy Scouts was easy. So he dropped out of the Boy Scouts to concentrate on shooting and became associated with a junior rifle club sponsored by the VFW. According to Tom, the club was "somewhat disorganized" and his Dad took over to manage the shooting activities. At this point Tom is 12 years old and in seventh grade.

While shooting with the club he earned 9-bars for expert. It was all .22 rimfire and Tom described his life with Dad as, "a Little League father with a rifle…" and is quick to add that "we went through a lot of rifles." In fact, Tom said at the time, "the family didn't have any money and we didn't have any furniture….but we had a lot of rifles." I of course said to myself, "So, what's wrong with that?"

The first significant match came in the early '60's when the American VFW conducted a national postal match comprised of a 10 shot standing and 10 shot prone course of fire. He has no idea how many people were involved but suspects it was in the thousands. After all, the intra-club shooting that he was involved in had about 35-50 juniors *per club* so this estimate is reasonable.

Although he doesn't know the number of competitors, he does know that he won with a 195 out of a possible 200 and received an all expense paid hunting trip to Lubbock, Texas. There he met Millroy Powell, who owned the ranch and was the first "Marlboro Man." As a special note, this author was born and raised "in the shadow of The Empire State Building" so the idea of shooting this well, beating thousands of people, and getting a free trip to *Lubbock, Texas* didn't do a thing for me…However, Tom said he was really impressed.

Anyway, this is where Tom's shooting began to move to a more formal and structured level. They (Tom and his father) discovered another gun club in southern California called the South Coast Gun Club, which was located in Corona del Mar at that time, about 50 miles from where he lived. They had smallbore prone matches every Friday night. So, at the age of 14, and now shooting a Remington 40x, Tom started competing in open class NRA type smallbore matches against adults, the likes of Bill Grater, Dave Kimes, Tom Guerin, and Emmitt Duncan.

We can now look back in history and know what's going to happen. Tom recounts that "This was the "real thing" and I started to win some matches. My first classification card was an expert and the following month I was a master. Then they asked me to join the junior club and I started into junior competition. I guess I was kinda doing this backwards but I started shooting in the monthly Southern California Junior Rifle League matches with entries of 200+ people."

Clearly, for those of us who have been involved in competitive shooting, this focus in southern California is huge. Not only did they cultivate a large number of junior shooters but they established a network of inter and intra club competition that allowed the shooting community to flourish. This is one of the lessons we need to learn in today's world if the sport is to continue to grow.

Our story now takes an interesting twist and provides our first look at the mindset of Tom Whitaker. Tom's in High School and involved in track…he's running the 100 yard dash in the mid 9-second bracket. His time is under 22 seconds for the 220-yard dash and around 50 seconds for the 440 and he thought he might have been good enough to get a track scholarship. But he made a decision to give up track to concentrate on shooting.

When Tom told me that during the interview, I just about fell off the chair and asked, "Why pass up a college scholarship to shoot?" His answer was even more reflective of the attitudes of the time and his own competitive nature. He recounted that, "I looked at the longevity of each sport and asked myself what level could I get to in each. Track looked limited while shooting looked unlimited so I dropped out of track in my senior

year to focus on shooting." This was not to be the last time Tom put shooting first and it's a statement on his commitment to the sport.

On his first trip to Perry (by the way, Tom said the cost for Perry in 1964 was $35.00 per phase, which included housing in the huts and meals at the mess hall) he shot smallbore before the high-power phase and encountered another turning point in his shooting career.

This was the year that "Young Master Whitaker" met Lt. Lones Wigger, Gary Anderson and Jack Foster, who he described as "smallbore heroes." In talking to Tom, this event clearly made an impression on him and I suspect made him "raise his sights" even higher than they already were. "In 1963, Wigger won both the Smallbore Prone and Position Championships, the first time that feat had been accomplished" says Tom.

In 1964, Tom got his first, although limited, introduction to shooting highpower in conjunction with the DCM State Rifle Team. According to Tom, in 1963 only one junior shot the California Service Rifle Championships and since the DCM subsidized two juniors per State team, in 1964 a lot of juniors looked at the DCM State Rifle Team as an opportunity to go to Perry. So Tom borrowed a National Match M1, shot one match, went to the California State Championship, was high Junior, and went to Perry with the team. It was the beginning of a pattern he would follow for years to come. He recalled that, "The 30-06 M1 beat the living crap out of me. My lip was black and blue for two weeks afterwards, but I sure had fun."

Although he did not to shoot on "The Big Team" that year (it seemed that they didn't want to "burn him"), it was a successful first introduction to Perry. In 1965, after graduating from High School his smallbore club sent a team to Perry that Tom describes as "the blossoming of my career."

This trip was to be a total smallbore shooting trip focusing on the 4800 aggregate prone championship as well as the 1600, 4-position aggregate. When all the shooting was done and the dust settled Tom had won the National Junior Position Championship and lost the Junior Prone Championship by only 5 X's….almost matching Wigger's record in the junior category. Meanwhile, watching from the sidelines, the military teams started to take notice of a new young talent.

During the same period, the formal education phase of Tom's "growing up" takes a humorous twist, especially for those of us who have "been there and done that…"

Following graduation from High School, Tom was accepted at UC Berkley as an engineering major. Tom said, "I vividly remember the Dean of the school addressing the class on the first day and telling 3,000 freshmen, "By the end of the first semester half of you will be gone.' "

"Well, I came from a small High School where things were easy and I played too hard. So, guess who was not there after the first semester?"

Now having flunked out of college, finding himself with a "1A" draft classification and Vietnam in full swing, in 1966 Tom capitalizes on the opportunity to join the Air Force. It seems that he had met the U.S. Air Force International Team at an ISU 3-Position match in California where he set his first National Junior record with a 361 out of a possible 400 standing. Unbeknownst to him, the military had also been watching him at Camp Perry and this match turned out to be his "tryout" for the Air Force team. He had also been in touch with Tommy Pool and Bill Pullum, who were in charge of the Army International Team at the time. In an effort to recruit Whitaker, Pool was trying to get Tom's basic training switched to Ft. Benning so that the team could pick him up easier after Basic Training but it was not to be.

"I hadn't heard from Tommy for a couple of weeks and one day my 1A Draft Card came in the mail, so I panicked," Tom said. "Figuring four years in the Air Force on the shooting team was better than risking having to spend two years in a muddy foxhole, I joined the Air Force."

In the world of the Air Force teams, there are only two people who were put on permanent assignment to marksman school right out of Basic Training, Tom Whitaker and Mid Tompkins.

We need to pause in the story and look at "who was where" in history to see how other people are influencing Tom's shooting experience. The Army had Gary Anderson (in the Reserves), Lones Wigger, Jack Foster, Tommy Pool, Bill Krilling, Jack Writer, and a petite Lt. by the name of Margaret Thompson. Most notable from the Marines was a Warrant Officer named David (D.I.) Boyd. It was clearly a powerhouse of shooting talent that would interface with each other for

several years. However, Tom said, "I wasn't in their league, these people were the best of the best in International Shooting. But just to get the chance to train with them at times and learn from them was an honor."

So, Tom is now on the Air Force Team and in 1967 they won one of the smallbore team matches at the Nationals. This was his first experience with a winning military team and in 1968, Tom gained his first exposure to international shooting as a member of the "Council International du Sport Military" or CISM team. This is, according to Tom, "the international military Olympics for NATO countries."

Historically, these teams were selected from army shooters in Europe but in '68 they came to the US to look for additional competitors. The tryout was at Ft. Benning and consisted of a 60 shot slow fire (three position) course of fire. This was then followed by the same 3-Position course but rapid fire. Specifically, they had three minutes per position to fire 20 shots standing, kneeling, and prone with an M-14 rifle.

Tom was the only Air Force shooter (for rifle) to make the team and he was joined, in part, by Bill Krilling, Margaret Thompson (future Margaret Murdock, '76 Olympic 3-Position Silver medallist), Charlie Davis (who held the Wimbledon record on the 5V target with 63 consecutive V's) and others.

Camp Perry Smallbore 1968.

During the competition in France, involving teams from the NATO countries as well as Romania and Hungry, the US Team won the team championship as well as the combined rifle/pistol championship. Tom shot a 561 in the slow fire phase, which was two points over the existing I.S.U World Record of 559 for "Army Rifle" (now 300 meter Standard Rifle). But since the match was not sanctioned by I.S.U. it didn't count as a record. He went on to win four gold medals, one silver, and the overall individual championship. This was the start of a string of U.S victories that ran for over 25 years.

In fact, the US team was so successful that they were invited to the Netherlands to host a clinic for the Netherlands team. It seems that the US Team had elected to use M70 Winchester Sniper rifles cut down to 11 pounds for the competition and the Dutch were struggling with rack grade FN assault rifles. According to Tom, "They invited us to fly up for their National Championships and give a clinic to try to convince their superiors that they needed better rifles." The end result was the Dutch flying their version of Air Force 2 to pick up the America team and a certain Air Force Sergeant was "very impressed."

It's clear that Tom was developing into a "force to be reckoned with" in the world of smallbore and international shooting but he was not without a "human side." In fact, he readily admits that in 1968 during the Nationals at Perry, he had won the iron sight individual championship and was leading in the overall national championship when he says he "started thinking negative thoughts." He described it as "a mind game" and admits he "just blew it and took myself out of the running."

With this experience behind him he now began working more seriously on his own rifles. Previously, he had not done any "significant" work and he started his "gunsmithing" career by designing his own prone stock during the winter of 1968. The stock was built based on ideas Tom had along with some thoughts and suggestions from Herb Hollister and Dieter Anschutz, who Tom had met in Germany that year. The next season (1969), using his own stock he went on to shoot in 16 major matches winning 14 and taking second or third in the balance.

In 1969 in Shreveport, LA, Tom also shot his first 3200 (perfect) score in a prone match. At this time in history it was only the 5th 3200 score fired in a smallbore prone match and I asked him what he was using for a rifle/ammo combination. Tom said he was still using a 40X for prone with Eley Tenex ammo and an Anschutz for 3-Position with Remington ammo. Eley had just started to make its way onto the American market and Tom had only "dabbled" with Eley "Because it was hard to get the Air Force to buy a foreign product when a domestic equivalent (which there really wasn't) was available."

By this time, he had a total of only 10 years shooting experience.

The Road to the National Championship and The World of Palma

In 1969, the United States NRA sent a smallbore team to Bisley, England, to compete for the Field Marshall Earl Roberts Trophy, which is the British counterpart to our Pershing Trophy. With a significant amount of literary license, and if you really stretch things a bit, you *may* be able to say this is the smallbore world's version of the Palma match. This was the inaugural match for this competition, which was set up to provide a rotation for competition between North America and Great Britain and the U.S. team won over the British Team. Or, if you have a mischievous soul and enjoy taunting the Brits, you could say the British were last since there were only two teams competing.

In the individual competition, Tom placed third in the smallbore matches. To appreciate the significance of this you need to realize that competition at Bisley is much larger than Perry. According to Tom's estimate, over 1,000 shooters participated that year.

Returning to Perry following the Bisley match, and having improved his self-control at dealing with match pressure, he won the individual smallbore championship by two points!

However, all good things have to come to an end and in February 1970, Tom got out of the Air Force and began Phase II of his "What Am I Going To Do When I Grow Up" story.

After leaving the Air Force, Tom's first civilian job was a Park Ranger in San Mateo and, something that will not come as a surprise to any reader, a range officer for San Mateo. Later that year he found himself employed by F. Bob Chow's Gun Shop in San Francisco where he began a six-year apprenticeship with Bob Chow, who was an Olympic pistol shooter in 1948 and 1952.

Tom recounted that, "As a teaching tool, Bob had me build my own .22 and .45 competition pistols, so I dabbled at NRA Bullseye Pistol Competition." Tom earned his Master classification and was shooting in the mid to high 2500's before going back to rifle competition. But for the time he was with Bob, his main focus was building match grade .45 Colt pistols.

Although he was working on pistols, Tom was still shooting smallbore and in 1973, at the Western Wildcats 6400 match in Phoenix, he set another national record with a 6399-595X when he dropped his only point on the 2nd day's 50-meter iron sight match. I asked him, "what happened?" and, expecting a detailed analysis of whatever the situation was at the time, I was told (with a straight face), "It didn't go in the 10-ring."

"Yeah, OK Tom, sorry I asked….."

In 1975 at the same match, Tom fired the first 6400 score ever shot in competition with a 6400-574X's. I made the observation that this was categorical proof the a "6400 with none will beat a 6399 with 595X's…." Tom looked at me like I had lost my mind (did I mention he and I have some things in common), but he acknowledged that my observation was correct.

"Those two matches were probably my best shooting in smallbore" according to Tom. "Obviously, not losing a point over four days of shooting was great, but to average over 37 X's per match in the 1973 match still amazes me. To shoot both in the Western Wildcats Match at Black Canyon (now the Ben Avery Range near Phoenix) was pretty good too. In fact, in one 50 yard iron sight match I shot a 400 – 40x and went on to shoot an additional 65 X's before losing one and I believe that record still stands."

As an interesting side note to this facet of history, thanks to Ben Avery, Tom's accomplishment at shooting the first 6400 was reported by *Sports Illustrated*. There is a rumor that Tom was disappointed the story wasn't in the swimsuit issue but that rumor has yet to be confirmed.

At this point in the interview I remember we took a short break and I casually asked Tom, "what did you plan on doing then?" What I really meant was, having all that experience shooting rifles and then starting to shoot pistols, what was he planning on doing. The answer I got was, "Go to dental school," and I fell off the chair for the second time.

"Dental school? Where the heck did that come from, Tom?"

"Well," he explained, "I really didn't know what I wanted to do, so my shooting buddy, Dr. John Demas, thought I should look into Dentistry since I seemingly was detail oriented and could work with my hands. I knew engineering was not it and this was the "Golden Age" of dentistry before we had "K-Mart dentists." I thought it was a good way to make a living."

Western Smallbore "Big Guns" Circa 1979. Left to Right: Mary Stidworthy, Tom Whitaker, Alan Knowles, George Stidworthy, Vic Auer, Tom Guerin.

50 yd. Iron Sight Record 1973.

I asked Tom, "OK, so how did you go about that little effort?" and sat back to hear, what I was convinced was going to be an interesting story. I was not disappointed.

"I looked at this as another challenge," Tom said. "I had been out of school for a long time and I was in my mid 20's. I still had no idea what I wanted to do and between 1970 and 1974 I had been taking general courses at night. In 1974 I started to think about dental school."

"At the time I thought becoming a doctor was really something, which I guess it is, but as Dr. Demas once said, being a doctor just proves you are too pig-headed to quit. Bob Chow was nice enough to give me a work schedule which allowed me to work full time and go to school full time, so I transferred to San Francisco State University and finished up a BA degree in biology with a 4.0 average. I owe Bob a lot for the "life lessons" he taught me … ancient Chinese wisdom. So, after finishing up the undergraduate degree in 1976, I was accepted to USC School of Dentistry in Los Angeles and entered dental school at the ripe old age of 29."

He honestly said that as simply as when he explained he lost the one point at the Western Wildcats because "it didn't go in the 10-ring." I had mentioned earlier in the story that everything Tom has done has been focused on shooting and the next several years was to confirm that.

In the late '70's, after entering dental school, Tom joined the Army Reserve to allow him to continue shooting and also provide a financial

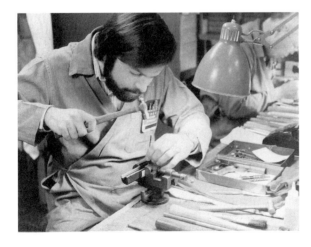

Working at the bench with Bob Chow, circa 1975.

source of income so he could continue to shoot.

This took Tom back into the world of international shooting where, in 1978, he just missed making the world championship and going to Korea. In 1979, he took a leave of absence from dental school to try out for the Pan American games shooting 3-Position. He successfully made the 3-position team that went on to win the Gold Medal in San Juan, Puerto Rico.

If we were to now look at a timeline, we are at a point where it's been 18 years since he started shooting and Tom has just started to shift from smallbore to highpower. This transition began in 1978 when, at the request of Al Coots, who was with the US Army team at Ft. Benning, he joined the Army Reserve team to go to Camp Perry. He ended up being the tyro on the team, shot a 495, and the USAR team won the National Trophy Team Match at Camp Perry.

As we move into the early '80's another major change took place. Tom has now effectively "retired from smallbore," came to the end of shooting with the Army Reserve team, and (finally) finished dental school after having lost a year due to shooting.

I asked Tom, "So, what was in store for you now?"

With something like a chuckle, he said, "Well, I was 35 years old and it was time to grow up and go to work." However, being the consummate competitor, he was quick to point out that this was also the start of a phase he called "flogging the golf ball."

By this time in our conversations I had gotten over being surprised by all the twists and turns in his story. I was now expecting to hear that he entered the "such and such championship" having never picked up a 9-iron before and won the championship. I really thought that was going to be the next statement... What he ended up saying was, "I stunk up the course at golf…" As I said, I was starting to get over surprises.

For those readers who are avid shooters, I suspect you have recognized the same time honored pattern that many of us have followed. Clearly not to the same degree but the basic transition seems to be the same. Plinking…smallbore…highpower…service rifle….match rifle, etc.

Tom continued his transitions as he moved

from the service rifle (after being 2nd to D.I. Boyd in the 1981 service rifle championship) to the NRA match rifle. He continued to shoot match rifle and eventually qualified for the 1985 Palma team.

However, for the very first time, he put shooting second to opening up a dental office and he did not participate with the 1985 Palma Team. From 1985 until 1991 Tom says he "retired from the shooting business" and concentrated on his practice and other endeavors.

In fact, because of the "self imposed retirement," Tom did not try out for the 1988 or the 1992 Palma Teams. According to Tom, at the time there wasn't a great interest in Palma shooting among U.S shooters. "I don't think many shooters understood the game, I certainly didn't."

As a side note, I was left with the thought that "We've come a long way" since the US Palma Team is now entering its third consecutive century of competition with a remarkable growth in the level of participation.

But in the fall of '91 he went to the Arizona State Championship because, according to Tom, "I missed the people and I was really crummy at golf."

This event was to be "the road back to the top" and in 1992 he came in 2nd in the Nationals behind Carl Bernowski. I asked Tom, "How could you do that after effectively laying off shooting for five years?"

"Well, I really think it had a lot to do with the long years of smallbore and international experience," Tom said. He also added that, "I seemed to be blessed with exceptional muscle memory and I can lay down and immediately know if my position is right."

Between 1992 and 1996 the old drive and focus was back. The sabbatical seemed to have worked and the early success in the '92 Nationals only fueled the competitive fire that was never really extinguished.

1993 saw Whitaker win the first stage of the Palma Team tryout against 200 competitors. Although he was to miss the 2nd phase to the shooting try-out due to a family crisis at the last minute, the late George Tubb explained the situation to the shooters trying out for the team and they voted to put him onto the 1995 team.

Tom remembered that, "George called me and

explained what he was going to propose and I told him I would only accept it if it was done before the tryouts were complete. I was not going to "bump" anyone after they had made the team. Being voted onto the team by my peers was one of my greatest honors. That was a great group to be part of … an experience of a lifetime. Unfortunately, we have since lost Rick Del Sesto and Richard Anthony, but they will always be in the hearts of the people who were on that team."

After the 1995 Palma Championship in New Zealand, the sport of Palma really began to grow in the United States. Tom continued his transition as he began to focus on long range shooting. When I asked him what was it about long range that intrigued him, he said, "I'd always been interested in long range shooting because it parallels smallbore prone so much. I just had not had too much success before because most of the shooting was done with magnums and they're really hard to get to shoot well." Personally, that made me feel better since I had always thought it was me who couldn't shoot that 300 Win Magnum that's collecting dust in the safe.

In 1996, Tom went to Perry and finally stopped being number 2 in highpower. With David Tubb hot on his heels, Tom won the Individual National Championship. That same year he also won the National Long Range Championship, which was only the third time the same person won both championships in the same year.

Missing the first day of shooting at Camp Perry in 1997 due to illness took him out of the running to be a repeat champion, but he did manage to recover and win the two remaining 800 sub aggregates in the championship.

Tom then turned to coaching and earned a spot as a coach on the 1999 U.S. Palma Team, and was subsequently named Vice-captain by Middleton Tompkins. With the World Championships and Palma Team Match being held in South Africa in 1999, Tom and several others involved with the team traveled to South Africa in April of 1998 on a "scouting mission." He narrowly missed winning the South African Championship placing fourth after experiencing a mysterious miss in one match. But he vowed "I'll be back".

The 1998 National Championships would bring Tom the individual trophy he coveted the most at Camp Perry. With a 200-12x on his relay and a 100-

8x in the shoot off, Tom won the Leech Cup. "I wanted it more than any other trophy because it is shot at 1000 yards with metallic sights."

Tom says he had three goals when he returned to Bloemfontein, South Africa in 1999: the U.S. Team winning the Palma Team Match; winning the World Individual Long Range Championship; and to win the South African Fullbore Championship. Tom admits those were lofty goals, but added "I wasn't going half way around the world to lose".

Well, the U.S. Team didn't win and Tom placed fifth in the Individual World Championship. However, he did make good on his goal to win the South African Fullbore Championship (with a record score) and became only the third non-South African and the second winner who did not come from the African continent.

Up until this point in the story, I have been careful to focus on Tom's shooting, not the mechanics of how Whitaker does what he does. When we got to this point in the interview, I told him I wanted to dive into the "nuts and bolts" of how he shoots.

I asked him questions from, "What do you see when you look through the sights?" to "How do you load winning ammo?"

It was not easy for him to describe what he

1999 South African Championship.

called "what I learned over 40 years of shooting." It was more difficult for me to put that experience down on paper. However, we're now going move into another area of the story. Specifically, the long answer to the very short question, "Tom, just exactly how do you do what you do?"

The Secrets of a Champion

Something Whitaker said reminded me of the TV show when the Chinese Shau-lin priest said to David Carradine, "Ah, Grasshopper… you have learned patience…. very good…" I think it was when he said, "practice… practice… practice… Grasshopper." Yeah, that was it.

All of which brings us to an important difference in perspective according to Tom. "I don't practice, I train," he said.

"OK, Tom, I'll bite. What do you see as the difference between "practice" and "training," I asked.

"Practice is something you do to learn a skill. Once you have learned it, you then need to train in order to become proficient at that skill. I stopped "practicing" over 30 years ago but have never stopped training."

I could see where he was coming from and decided to ask how he trains.

"Well, now I train by shooting in matches," Tom said. "First, it's hard to find someone to help pull targets while you train and besides, 90% or more of the game is mental. So to me, the best conditions to train under are during actual matches."

"Tom, for those people who are just starting their shooting career, when would you say that a person goes from "practicing" to "training?"

"As a general rule, my personal assessment would be when the person reaches the master classification they have learned all the basic skills. Now they must train to enhance their performance."

After thinking about this it made sense to me. Remembering back to my own shooting development, I recall a point, coincidentally after making master, where my confidence went up and it seemed like my shooting under adverse conditions improved. Perhaps I had simply stumbled onto something the experts like Whitaker had known for years.

"Tom, training and practice aside, lets start to talk about the basics of how you do what you do and then lets build from there to discuss how you make all those perfect shots."

"Well, if you want to talk about how to make the shot, it all starts with position," he said.

"No matter what position you are shooting, be it standing, sitting, kneeling, or prone, there is only one basic position. You build on that position (this is practice, not training), to develop a position that will work for you.

"Shooting can be painful enough," Tom said, "the position should not make it worse. You must stretch your muscles and work the body. Obviously you need to be able to breath while you're in position and look through the sights normally without any undue amount of pain."

"Tom, wait a minute....let's talk about pain," I said. "Do you experience that too?"

"Of course," he said, "But you learn to work through it. Name one competitive sport that does not involve pain of some sort. When I shoot in the United States my pain is in the left arm because that is where most of the pressure is. However, when we shoot outside the United States, as you know, they shoot two or sometimes three people on the same target. In that case the pain comes from the endurance of the amount of time you are on the mound and in position. You have to be in some sort of physical and mental shape to play this game."

Sometimes I find it amazing that we (individual shooters) think that we are the only people in the world who are having a problem with "such and such." I find it quite refreshing, as in this case when Tom told me about his experience, to realize we're all in the same boat. All that ibuprofen will not seem so bad anymore.

Anyway, getting back to the story, Tom continued by adding, "Let me clarify something about what I mean by a basic position. Much research has been done on shooting positions. Initially by the Russians and, in the past 20 years or so, by several U.S. Universities using modern scientific methods and equipment, stability platforms, and such. These studies have been directed to improve our International Shooting (Olympic style) Team performance just like what's been done in track, swimming, etc. They have shown that the basic

positions, mainly developed by the Russians and used by all Olympic shooters, to be the most stable and efficient positions. To stray from those basics has been shown to be a disaster for a shooter's performance. I believe these basics apply to all rifle shooting. When I was an instructor in the Long Range Firing school at Camp Perry, one class I taught was the Prone Position. This was the first course because it is the foundation for everything else. That class took almost three hours to cover the why's and wherefore's of the basic prone position. Once a shooter understands the basics of a position, transitioning from one discipline to another becomes much easier."

"For example," he added, "When someone transitions from a service rifle to a match rifle, they should measure the distance to the sling stop and make that the distance on the match rifle hand stop. They should measure the service rifle length of pull and set the butt plate to the same length."

"By doing that, they will have started with the same basic position. As adjustments need to be made, they can be small changes to compensate for specific requirements."

"The next part of your position is when the cheek goes onto the cheek-piece. Sight alignment should be immediate. Lining the sights up on the target and achieving the natural point of aim is achieved by pivoting your body around the left elbow. To change elevation, move your body back or forward to increase or decrease elevation. Don't muscle the gun into position."

"OK Tom, once you have the basics down, what do you do to enhance your position?"

With little hesitation, and not surprising considering his smallbore experience, Tom said, "One of the best ways to make the position better is to dry fire with a scope. Get into position and dry fire until you are comfortable with your position. Then try minute changes to see what happens to your position. Change sling tension and see what happens. Then play with the cheek piece height. In any event, all of this must be done on the garage floor or during a practice/training session, not in an important match. There your focus should be on shooting the shot. But if the need arises during a match you will already have an idea of the impact of these changes and be better prepared to use them if necessary."

"There are other tools you can use like cameras and videos. Go take a picture of a position and see if you can perfect it. Dry fire into a mirror and see how it looks from the front. But in all cases, the amount of time you spend on that garage floor training is worth its weight in gold. Know what you're capable of achieving. How many High Power shooters know how good they really hold? I believe it is a small percentage. So, go put a scope on the rifle (yes, a hard thing for Service rifle shooters) and see how much it moves on the target. Then try to improve it if you're not satisfied"

"Time," "practice," "training," "dry firing." I was starting to see a pattern. Tom was also quick to answer the question I had not yet asked.

"I can hold 1/4 minute in the prone position on a good day...sometimes it will be better, and sometimes it will be worse. It depends totally on my physical condition, level of fatigue and how much the wind buffets the position, but it will never be the same."

As I had mentioned, I was finding this interview fascinating. We were talking about "basic" shooting. Nothing anyone who has ever fired a shot has not heard already. The only difference was that Tom was raising the bar on the thought process behind the basics.

One of the things that has always intrigued me, as I'm sure it has with many other people, is how others "see" the target. Just remember how long it took you to envision what the instructor meant by "sight alignment." How long did it take you to explain to the new shooter what they should be seeing and what "focus on the front sight" meant?

Well, in my discussion with Tom, that's where we went next and it was another interesting perspective. All of it was to follow the simple question, "Tom, when you look through your sights, what do you see?" But first, for background I asked him how his vision is now.

Tom reported that the last time he had his vision checked it was 20/15 but he needs glasses for reading. This was due to the natural aging of the eye (presbiopia), in which the lens becomes less flexible and is therefore less able to keep many distances in focus at the same time. He shoots with a rear lens to bring his focal point back to the front sight. For those of you over the age of 40 who have already experienced this same thing, you will also be happy to know that Tom

sees "floaters." In his case all he does is blink and work around them. For those of you under 40 who don't have a clue what a floater is, just wait...you'll love them.

According to Tom, when he goes into position he will look through the rear sight and center the entire front sight in the rear aperture. The rear sight is a "blurry hole" and the front is relatively clear. He sees the entire front sight and the level and the rear sight is far enough away that he will see space about half the diameter of the front sight around the front sight. The inner ring, the actual aiming front sight, is *not crystal clear*. He describes it as simply, "pretty sharp, and the bull is fuzzy"

Since the statement that the front sight was not crystal clear flew in the face of "tradition" I asked him to expound on it.

Tom said that if he opens the rear aperture he can focus the front sight and make it clearer but then the bull gets worse. He elects to shoot with a darker picture and the edge of the front sight aperture will appear slightly fuzzy. "I rarely change the rear iris setting. I compensate for the differences in light by the color density of the glasses I use, sort of light neutral density filters on a camera."

"But Tom, just what does that mean? How do you see it?" I asked.

"I think most people expect, or try to see the classic sight picture you see in books. Everything sharp and centered. At 1000 yards it isn't going to happen. The human eye is a wonderful instrument but it does have limitations. You have to find a happy medium between the front sight and the bull with the front sight taking priority. Picture the "classic" book concept of the front sight picture as a circle of wire being held at arms length with a marble in the center. Now, make the circle out of wool yarn and the marble a cloud of dark gray smoke and that's about what I see."

Tom and I had started to develop a certain synergy during our conversation and he quickly added, "Before you ask, let me tell you about seeing and then executing the shot."

So, as Tom turned into an interviewer's dream subject, I simply sat back to listen.

"If you work at the sight picture too much, expecting the "perfect" sight picture, you will try to *make* the shot happen. This is not the way. What you should be trying to do is *let* the shot happen. "Letting the shot happen" means relying on having a good hold and trigger technique and follow through. The shot should go off as sort of a surprise … sound familiar? Basic Marksmanship 101."

"So lets talk about "execution," Tom said.

"As I get ready to fire the shot, I'm concentrating on the front sight. I align the sight, and center the bull. Maybe I see movement in the front sight, maybe I don't, but I don't pay attention to that. I squeeze the trigger, trying for a smooth let off. I want it to appear to be a surprise when it goes off but I NEVER think, "I want it to go off NOW." That would be making the shot happen vs. letting the shot happen."

"Now, we're not done yet and we still need to talk about "follow-through". The worst thing you could do is "quit the shot" and not pay attention to the follow-through and the call. Otherwise you will never know what happened."

As Tom went on he added, "A good hold is a great thing to have but the goal is actually to fire the shot without disturbing the hold. This is where smallbore or air rifle is a great aid because recoil masks many shooter errors."

"Controlling recoil, which starts when anything happens in the rifle, including the firing pin falling, means controlling your position so the recoil of the shot is the same everytime. All this put together is what I refer to as execution."

"When a shot goes off I see the front sight like a "freeze frame photo." When I shot a 300 yard rapid-fire national record of 200-19X, I remember seeing recoil of the 9th shot in the second string being different. The rifle recoiled to the 1 o'clock position and I knew it was there. I didn't know if it was a 10 or a 9 or an X but I knew it was at 1 o'clock."

Almost all of us have some ability to call our shots. Some are better than others. Here is Tom's thought process as he calls the shot.

"I see a freeze frame when the shot goes off because of my concentration on the front sight and not "quitting the shot." In the freeze frame I may see the front aperture *slightly* at 7 o'clock and the rifle recoils normally. The front sight was only slightly mis-aligned so the shot will probably be an "X." My call is "X at 7." If I see a centered shot, but the recoil is more towards 1 or 2 o'clock rather than more straight back, which is normal, I'm going to call the shot out of the X at 1-2 o'clock because I feel the control of recoil, or lack of control, has more influence on the shot. Now, if I see the sight mis-aligned and the recoil moving in the same direction…look out! I probably just shot a 9 because I think it takes at least two mistakes to take you out of the ten ring."

Now to put this in some kind of perspective, it has taken quite a number of paragraphs to explain how Tom breaks the shot. As we finished up this portion of the interview he told me that he will fire the shot and the next thing he realizes is that he's pulling the case out of the chamber. An amazing level of concentration….

A Good Break Doesn't Count If You Can't Read The Wind

At this point in the interview it dawned on me that no matter how much training goes into shooting a good shot, if you can't do it under all conditions, it's not worth too much. Needless to say, I was anxious to ask the next question.

"So Tom, tell me….what is the trick to reading wind?"

"You know," Tom said, "You really have a knack for asking a really short question that needs a really long answer…."

"I know. That's why I get paid the big bucks to do these interviews. Now, you talk and I'll type."

"First, there is no instant method to read the wind. It is done by the SWAG method … 'Scientific Wild Ass Guess.' The more times you guess and remember the consequences of that guess, the better your guesses become. Now, as to the scientific part..."

"There are three components of wind that will effect the bullet. Velocity, direction, and terrain. When you go look at a range, look at the terrain first. Does it have hills, trees, guillies? Will they effect the wind patterns? If your assessment is "Yes," start looking at how this will change the wind. Will it cause updrafts, downdrafts or block the wind in certain areas? This is where you first start thinking about the value of the winds being different from different directions. Look at prevailing direction. Is there a particular direction that the wind always comes from? If all the trees are growing sideways this may be a fair indication of a prevailing wind."

"Range conditions, even at the same range, can change and each day can be a new learning experience. The trick is to find out as quickly as possible which indicators are valuable and which are not."

"At 1000 yards (or any distance) your primary concern is to hit the target with your first shot. From there you have a chance at getting the shot to the center. But if you're off the target it's obviously much more difficult."

"When I look at a target I'm thinking that the target is 6' wide, or approximately 7 minutes across. I see the wind is blowing a fair amount and I think there may be 6 minutes of wind. I then ask myself, "Can I hit the target with 10 minutes? The answer is "No." Can I hit the target with 2 minutes? Maybe. Can I hit the target with 8 minutes? Yeah, that I can do so I shoot the first shot with 5¹/₂ minutes of wind."

"Basically, you're bracketing the target with this shot. The first goal is to get the shot on paper and use that as your key to the wind. Considering all the possible factors associated with 1,000 yard shooting, even after all these years I still get a kick out of seeing the target just go down on the first shot."

"Well Tom," I added, "You know all about the debate between reading flags and reading mirage. Is one indicator better than another?"

"Flags and mirage are simply another set of condition indicators that the shooter can use. In my opinion, one of the reasons we (the American shooters) are not as good at reading wind flags as other countries is that most of our shooting is done on military ranges. There, flags are used as safety indicators, not wind indicators. Add to this the varying types of flags, non-standard locations, etc., and it becomes almost impossible to learn consistent characteristics of flag reading. In the US, we may only have three flags on a 1,000 yard range while overseas the same range would have 20. However, our real weakness is high wind conditions when the wind is 18-20+mph. In the United States, we really don't see this too often. When it does happen, there is no mirage and generally, the flag system is not the best."

"First, you need to realize that all mirage is not the same. Every range has its own mirage and it's affected by the same things we talked about regarding the wind…complete with the same

pluses and minuses. Mirage is a "real-time" indication of what is happening "right now," between you and the target. This, by itself is important, but not of primary importance. What is important is knowing what the wind is when the gun goes off."

"Flags, on the other hand, are not "real time" indicators unless they are right next to your line of fire to the target. They are used to predict what is going to happen with the wind."

"Wind acts just like any other gases or fluids. Just go look at the ocean and a bunch of surfers waiting for a wave. The surfers are waiting for sets of waves to cycle through so they can find the "perfect wave" to ride. The wind is the same as those waves. It will pick up, pause, and cycle back just like a sine wave on a chart. Whether you are waiting for a wave to surf, or looking at wind or mirage, the characteristics are the same. What is important is knowing the cycle of the wind when you are shooting. Is it going up or down? So, if you look at mirage, you can estimate the wind is worth 3 minutes but you also need to factor for the up/downswing of the cycle. It's very possible that you would see 3 minutes in the scope but then, when the shot actually goes off, there is 6 minutes of wind."

According to Tom, everyone can learn to read the wind given enough time but what is really important is the person's ability to judge what the wind will be *as the shot is fired.* When I think about my own shooting style he's right. I'll estimate the wind, put X-minutes on the rifle, and then focus on getting a good shot off. In reality, I'm oblivious to the wind during the time I'm firing the shot. Then, I go through the famous "second-guessing that 8" process of saying to myself, "I never saw that change!"

I was still hoping to hear what "THE GREAT SECRET" was but I soon became disappointed as he continued with his answer.

"The only way to learn to judge the wind is to go out and do it. There is no instant cure and no pill you can take. However, there are some things that can help the learning process."

"If you're an individual trying to learn to read wind, your ability as a marksman will be a significant factor. If I were to ask the question, "How can an 8-ring shooter evaluate wind correctly?" the answer would be, "he can't," unless he can call the shot very, very accurately."

"The basic mistake better shooters make in this area is calling the shot a "9 at 9," having a "9 at 9" come up on the target, *and then making a sight correction.* This brings us to Rule Number 1: **"If it comes up on call there is no reason to make a change."**

"Now, in order for rule #1 to work," Tom continued, "the shooter has to be totally honest with himself. The shooter must accept the fact that if the call was a "9 at 9" and that's what the target shows, he shot it there. Nothing else did it and there's no "mysterious" wind to blame. You cannot say, "I didn't see that change."" Well, I said to myself, "So much for my time honored rationalization."

"That takes us to Rule Number 2: "The more you change your sights the bigger your group becomes," he said.

This rule, according to Tom, is based on the concept that, the wind is doing less than most people suspect. So, when we get ourselves convinced that "the wind is doing funny things," we start cranking the windage knob hither and yon and end up with a lower score than had we simply left it on the average wind and shot the string.

"Tom, I heard different stories about wind velocity vs. wind direction. Which is more important?" I asked.

"Either one can be the more important factor, it depends on the circumstances.

When I said, "OK, Tom, I suspect some folks may feel the same way intuitively but could you take a crack at explaining why?" I got that "eyes rolling in his head" look that indicated he realized he was just set up for another very long answer.

"Okay, you seem to be ready for the more "scientific" part of the SWAG method," he said.

"Velocity is linear given a constant angle. That means if the velocity doubles the correction change needed doubles. However, angle changes are logarithmic. This means that given a constant velocity, as the angle increases amount of correction change needed decreases exponentially."

"The most devastating effect takes place when there is a change in direction between 0 and 30 degrees in any quadrant, that is changes between 12 & 1; 5 & 6; 6 & 7; 11 & 12. The reason, if we can go off on a tangent (no pun intended), deals with force vectors."

"Here's a quick (approximate) Trig Table: The sine of 15° is .26; 30° is .50; 45° is .70; 60° is .86:

75° is .96, and 90° is 1.00."

"Let's set up the trig problem. First, we assume that at 1000 yards using a .308 with 155 grain bullets (@ 2950+ fps) the full value (90 degree) wind drift is approximately 1 MOA per 1 MPH of wind."

"Therefore, if we have a light wind of 4 MPH coming from 12 o'clock we shouldn't need any correction. But if that wind moves to 1 o'clock, we need to put on 2 minutes (4 mph x the sine of 30°, which is .50). The change from 1 o'clock to 3 o'clock (full value) only requires 2 *more* minutes. Therefore, the small angle changes from 0 to 30 (or 45) degrees will hurt you more (on a proportional basis) than a small velocity change. To put it another way, a 300% increase in the angle (from 30° to 90°) only resulted in a 100% increase in the correction (from 2 minutes to 4 minutes). So, I pay more attention to angle changes from 0 to about 45 degrees, which make up 70% of the full value correction, then I shift concentration more to velocity changes from 45 to 90 degrees. As I said at the start of this discussion, either one could be the more important factor, it depends on the circumstances. This is how I put a priority on the circumstances, which is going to hurt you more if you miss it."

"This is why people complain about "fishtail winds." That little 4 mph wind changing from 1 to 11 will move the bullet about 4 minutes, or from 9 ring to 9 ring. Think about what an 8 or 12 mph fishtail wind will do! In the 1995 Palma Match in New Zealand, on the second day we had a fishtail wind as high as 20 mph. The wind was changing from 10 minutes right to 10 minutes left (or more) in 30 seconds or less ... I was happy I was not a coach that day!"

Tom was quick to add that this was something a shooter should understand but not get too "detail oriented" as to lose focus on shooting a good shot. Not everyone has a knack for doing the math quickly in their head. It is something that the shooter should consider and study during training exercises.

So, I guess we'll never have that pill to take to make us all the greatest wind readers on the planet but perhaps we now have a series of things to look at and study. If we can combine them together, as Tom apparently can, this can only serve to improve our skills at shooting. Especially long-range.

Thoughts on Equipment and Reloading

Everytime I have ever interviewed someone in the shooting community I have had mixed feeling about these subjects. Generally, they are highly opinionated, sometimes controversial, and occasionally boring. This session was to prove pleasantly different and again reflected Tom's experience in the shooting sports and his ability not only to recognize what is important but the ability to realize *when* it's important.

"OK, Tom, by this time in the book we will hopefully have a number of readers who have stuck it out with us, page after page, and are still awaiting that "magic secret" of how you've done what you've done. Are we going to find that in "equipment and reloading?"

"Listen, I already told you there are no secrets or pills you can take to do this. But, there are some things that can help. Earlier, you had asked me, "What makes a good rifle," so let me start with equipment."

"Generally, there is too much of a premium placed on equipment. No matter what the sport, it has always been true that you should invest in the best equipment you can afford and shooting is no different. However, the key to shooting is the *delivery system* and the biggest area for improvement in this area is the physical skills of the shooter. For example, you will never be able to go from a 7-ring hold to a 10-ring hold by upgrading from a 2 MOA rifle to a 1 MOA rifle. It will never happen. In this case, to improve the *delivery system* you need to go out and train. A lot. Additionally, most people really do not know how good their hold actually is. Go out and put a scope on the rifle, either smallbore or highpower, and see for yourself. Then, when you get the physical skills of the delivery system as best that they can be, the upgrade to that 1 MOA rifle will become more critical and timely."

I knew that Tom builds his own rifles and I asked him who he thought were some of the best gunsmiths around today.

"There are a lot of people out there who can put a barrel on and true up an action but you really need someone who is familiar with the sport. They have a feel for "what's right." There's really no mystery in building a rifle but it does call for absolutely zero

tolerance and a focused drive to build the gun perfectly. In that area a couple of people come to mind. Alan Warner because he's a tool and die maker and is used to working in terms of ten-thousandths of an inch and understands this game. Jim Borden and Bruce Baer also come to mind. I'd have to go with Alan since he's familiar with Palma shooting. But if I were going to go outside the game and have a rifle built for me I'd go to Borden. Mainly because of his reputation and his benchrest experience."

"The bottom line in building rifles is the willingness to do it right without shortcuts. That ain't fast and it certainly ain't cheap."

"Tom, after 40 years of shooting experience, if money was no object, what would you consider the best components to use to build a long-range prone rifle," I asked.

"If money was no object, I would use a Panda gunsmithed by Alan Warner, a Krieger barrel, Anschutz trigger, McMillan prone stock, Warner #2 rear sight, and an RPA ladder type front sight. In fact, guess what my two primary long range rifles are?"

"Finally, I do not believe that accuracy is a linear function, I think it's hyperbolic. Specifically, just because a rifle may group 0.5 MOA at 100 yards doesn't mean it's a 0.5 MOA rifle at 1,000 yards. I have owned and have seen rifles (.308's) that shoot great to 800 yards, pretty good at 900, but you couldn't hit your butt with them at 1000 yards. You *HAVE* to test the rifle at the distance you are going to be shooting at to be sure it will work."

"Well Tom, based on your concept term *"delivery system,"* I think we have covered 2/3's of the system; the shooter's skills and the rifle equipment. In my mind that leaves the last part, the ammo. What are your thoughts about that?" I asked.

"First, I'm going to talk about ammo from a Palma focus but I need to acknowledge that the best measure of accurate ammo comes from the benchrest game. It just doesn't get better than that and some of their experience will bleed over to how I load ammo."

"When I first started loading for highpower, I honestly thought all I had to do was get the components, read the instructions in the book, weigh the powder real carefully, put everything together and presto, I'd have good ammo. Well, it didn't turn out that way and it all shot like crap. So to begin learning I started copying what winners like Mid Tompkins and Bob Jensen were doing."

"I've been learning to load long range ammo for 15-20 years and still I'm learning. Right now, this is what I do…"

"I try to eliminate as many factors as possible that I have physical control over. I don't know if it really helps but it does make me feel better. Remember the Yogi Bera statement that, "50% of this game is 90% mental," and you can see the importance of not having to worry about your ammo."

"Anyway, I uniform all primer pockets and de-bur the flash holes. For a long time I did not neck turn the cases but I do now. In all honestly, I don't know if it makes a significant difference but again, it makes me feel better. I then segregate cases by weight, keeping them all within 0.5 grains. I weigh the bullets and have found the occasional "off weight" bullet."

"All cases are hand primed with the Sinclair priming tool. I just recently switched to Lapua cases from Winchester, mainly due to peer pressure, but the jury is still out on the differences between the two."

"I full length size all ammo with the die set just enough to bump the case back .001 in the chamber. I don't neck size because I don't think any chamber is perfectly round and I also use a custom die or a bushing die to avoid an expander ball."

"I weigh all charges within 0.1 grain, not +/- 0.1. I have also found that neck tension is extremely important. Not so much as how much tension but the uniformity of the tension. I try to segregate ammo in boxes based on the feel of how the bullet is seated since I really think this has an effect at long range."

Well, I sat back and tried to assess all this and consider the workload associated with the individual who may be shooting 2,000 to 3,000 rounds a year. The thought of all this work was mind numbing and I asked Tom, "When does this really make a difference?"

His reply helped put a focus on this when he said, "Generally, a lot of these things will not begin to make a difference until you are able to shoot in the 440 to 445 range in a Palma match on a calm day. I'm looking for everything I can get

out of myself, the rifle and ammo. Nobody has shot a 450 x 45 with any rifle much less a .308 Winchester and I sure would like to be the first."

For me that put it into a nice balance so that the individual shooter could gauge their stage of training and allow them to concentrate on the right things at the right time. It dovetailed into the concept that it makes little sense to neck turn cases when you're still focusing on developing a 10-ring hold.

As we finished up the interview I was happy with how it turned out. Clearly, there is a wealth of experience Tom has accumulated over the course of 40 years. There are many lessons to learn and hopefully, some of the knowledge he shared during this exercise can pay off for the individual shooter who, like all of us, aspire to higher scores.

Epilogue

As I mentioned in the prolog, part of this story is a warning call of how we can lose this sport. Go back to the first couple of pages where we talked about Tom's early years. Reread about the Boy Scouts and Junior shooting. Look at the clubs with 30-50 junior shooters and competitions where there were hundreds of competitors.

This is the lesson we must heed. In spite of all of our denials, we are not getting any younger. There will be a limit to how long we can shoot and, unless we allow this sport to grow and we find and train our replacements, we will end up being more successful than any anti-gun movement.

F-class has made important inroads at keeping the "older" shooters involved in the sport and that is a very good thing. But we cannot afford to forget the very basics of smallbore, air rifle and the junior shooter.

Not too long ago I went to a State Smallbore Championship. There were four shooters and no juniors. I was not a happy person. Think about it.

Chapter 2

A Short History of Long Range Shooting in the United States

by Hap Rocketto

Long range is, by definition, a relative term. When the earliest European settlers arrived on the east coast of what would become the United States of America they were armed with a collection of match, wheel lock, and snaphaunce actuated firearms that were, occasionally, more dangerous to the user than the intended victim. Among the immigrants were gentlemen adventurers on the prowl for quick riches, families looking to build a new life, and others who sought religious freedom; all who drilled with these firearms under the leadership of the likes of Captain John Smith, in the Virginias, and Captain Myles Standish, in the Plymouth Colony.

The separatist Puritans came from England and, with the possible exception of one or two men, had never used firearms. Firearms were a tool of the soldier and a plaything of the aristocracy, hunting being forbidden the common man. As much as the Pilgrims might have impressed the natives with the flames, explosive sounds and rolling smoke, they were far from effective marksmen. Even with a generous supply of powder, ball, and time to exercise themselves with their 16th and 17th century firearms, it took almost two years for the Pilgrims to become proficient. However, by the time they learned to hit what they aimed at, a hunting party of four could bring home enough game to feed the village for a week. Whether this is a comment upon the developing skill of the Pilgrim marksman or the quantity of game is left to the reader. In the early

days of settlement, long range might mean a distance of as much as 50 yards. The enduring myth that every American boy can drill out a gnat's eye at 100 paces was in the making.

As time passed, gunsmiths from continental Europe immigrated to the New World and set up shop. They brought a tradition of manufacture and knowledge that was soon adapted to the technical and economic realities of the colonies. The somewhat clumsy and large caliber rifles of Germany, Austria, and Switzerland underwent evolutionary changes in the Lancaster region of Pennsylvania in the early 1700s at the hands of French Huguenot, Swiss and German craftsmen. The first American made rifles were manufactured in smaller calibers than its European antecedents to save precious lead and powder. The spherical bullet, between .32 and .45, weighed about 160 grains. The powder charge, of about 60 or 70 grains, left a minimum amount of fouling. The long barrel, about 40 inches, increased velocity, making efficient use of powder and ball, as well as dampening the sound of the shot that might attract uninvited attention from four footed quarry or two footed enemy.

The rifle was equipped with what was the most reliable ignition system of the time-the flintlock. It had brass furniture and a recess built into the butt to hold a supply of grease or greased patches. Called a patch box, this is a distinguishing feature of the Kentucky rifle. Provided with a small, sometimes brass, blade front sight and a hickory ramrod, its graceful and comely shape, pleasing to the eye, made it easy to carry and employ in the forest.

A distinct disadvantage of the rifle, as opposed to the more common smooth bore musket, was that loading was slow and required a short metal rod and mallet to start the bullet into the bore. At some point in time an unknown marksman thought up the idea of using a slightly undersized ball and a greased patch to ease the loading of the powder fouled rifle while insuring the tight fit necessary for the ball to engage the rifling. The American marksman now had a firearm that was capable at a range of 300 yards and deadly accurate at 100 yards. The technological advance of the patched ball made rifles capable of equaling the feat of James Fenimore Cooper's fictional Hawkeye, *La Longue Carabine*, who with his rifle 'Killdeer' boasted an astounding firing rate of three rounds a minute standing or two prone.

A good shooting rifle, hand made by a Pennsylvania craftsman, might cost a man half a year's wages. It earned its keep and repaid its owner by its daily use in hunting and, if need be, defense. Horace Kephart describes the so-called Kentucky Rifle as "...remarkable for its precision and the distance it shot. It was generally three feet six inches long, weight about seven pounds, and ran about seventy bullets to the pound of lead." The artist's belief that form follows function reached one of its highest evolutionary points with the development of this distinctly American firearm.

Oddly enough the rifle seemed to be almost solely a development of the Allegheny frontier and its German influence. That hotbed of colonial industry, the Connecticut River valley of New England, boasted firearms manufacturing but it was almost exclusively devoted to smoothbore muskets. It wasn't until just prior to the Revolutionary War that rifles became more widely used and manufactured in what would become the center of the American firearms industry.

The rifle gained its fame and name from its use in what Native Americans called the "Dark and Bloody Ground". The land west of the Allegheny Mountains, populated by the Iroquois and Cherokee, was the site of continuous warfare, the ground stained dark by the blood shed in battle between these two tribes for possession of these rich hunting lands. In the years leading up to the Revolutionary War frontiersmen thought of the region as a hunter's paradise. John Findley traveled the Ohio River documenting the valley's beauty and abundance of game. A young adventurer and skilled marksman named Daniel Boone, explored the passage now known as the "Cumberland Gap" and followed Findley, rifle in hand, into what is modern day Kentucky.

Boone's rifle, and its cousins, is more correctly known as a Pennsylvania Rifle. The more popular appellation, Kentucky Rifle, became permanent on January 8, 1815, two weeks after the Peace of Christmas Eve was signed at Ghent. The War of 1812 was already over when five thousand American soldiers and militiamen, including two thousand Kentucky and Tennessee frontiersmen armed with long barreled rifles, under the command of General Andrew Jackson, engaged 7,500 British troops along a drainage canal just south of New Orleans. The British forces grimly advanced into the fire of cannon manned by Jean Lafitte's pirates. As the orderly lines of troops came into rifle range, Jackson ordered the cannons to lift their fire so that the billowing powder smoke would not obscure the Redcoats. In just a few minutes British General Edward Pakenham and 2,000 of his Redcoats were cut down by American riflemen hidden in trenches and behind cotton bales in the pointless Battle of New Orleans. A popular song called "The Hunters of Kentucky" or "The Battle of New Orleans" was soon ringing throughout the nation's taverns hailing Jackson's victory. One couplet proclaiming "But Jackson he was wide awake, and wasn't scar'd at trifles, for well he knew what aim we take, with our Kentucky Rifles" was a public relations coup of gigantic proportions. To this day, few ever refer to this quintessential American flintlock as the Pennsylvania Rifle.

The Battle of New Orleans may have raised public consciousness about the rifle but it was not the first conflict on American soil where the long-range capabilities of the colonial marksmen played an important part. Between 1689 and 1763, England and France fought a series of four wars on the continent that were mirrored in the colonies. The final conflict was The French and

Indian War, known as the Seven Years' War in Europe, fought between 1754 and 1763. Among the young colonials blooded in the conflict was a young teamster by the name of Daniel Morgan. Morgan, Daniel Boone's cousin, survived the disastrous rout of General Edward Braddock's expeditionary force in July of 1755 along with two young lieutenant colonels who would have much to do with each other two decades later—British regular Thomas Gage and Virginia militiaman George Washington.

Twenty years after serving with the British the tables turned. In July of 1775 Washington found himself in command of the newly formed Continental Army and with it, ten companies of riflemen. In command of the company from Virginia was Captain Morgan. As proof of their capabilities the Virginians marched from Winchester, Virginia to Boston, 300 miles away, in just three weeks. New England was treated to displays of marksmanship that amazed the locals who were unfamiliar with the rifle. Morgan's men would demonstrate their skill by regularly hitting targets at twice the maximum range of the Yankee's muskets and fowling pieces.

Over the next several years Morgan would command troops under Benedict Arnold in his abortive expedition to Quebec and in the Hudson River Valley. One lesson he would learn was that, as good as the rifle was, it was still slower than the musket, and rifleman could not engage the enemy without support. Morgan's riflemen would prove their worth at Saratoga where they functioned as skirmishers, going out in front of the main battle lines to use their skills with the rifle to disable gun crews, kill officers, and generally harass the enemy. The constant rain of accurate long-range rifle fire hampered the fighting efficiency and mettle of the British troops under the command of Braddock's Defeat *alumnus* General Thomas Gates.

It was here that one of the more famous long range shots of the war took place. The most celebrated of Morgan's riflemen was Pennsylvania rifleman Tim Murphy. Tradition has it that Murphy was ordered to kill a British officer astride a gray horse. Perched in a tree and steadying his aim on a strong limb he missed with his first shot. With his second he mortally wounded General Burgoyne's *Aide de Camp*, Captain Sir Francis Clerke, at a range of some 300 yards. Reloading, he next drew a bead and downed General Simon Fraser. Clerke and Fraser lingered for hours in agony before succumbing and were buried on the battlefield. In the end the British losses were twice that of the Colonial forces with rifle fire contributing greatly to the American dominance of the battlefield.

The British made several halfhearted attempts to establish a corps of rifleman to counter the colonial marksmen. The most noteworthy unit was under Major Patrick Ferguson of the Second Battalion of the 71st Highlanders, one of the finest marksman of his day and the developer of a breech loading flintlock rifle. Ferguson raised a company for deployment in North America to test his rifle. A colonial bullet shattered his right elbow on September 11, 1777 at Brandywine Creek, a battle where his riflemen contributed significantly to the British victory. After a lengthy convalescence he returned to active service but, ironically, before he could definitely prove the effectiveness of either his rifle or his troops, one of Morgan's riflemen killed "The British Morgan" at the Battle of King's Mountain, North Carolina on October 7, 1780.

After the war was won the rifle continued to prove its worth as the new nation pushed westward. As a tool, it both protected and fed the immigrants. On the occasional holiday it provided entertainment in the form of a riflemen's frolic or turkey or beef shoot. These matches were fired standing, or from a rest, at 100 yards, or so. The target might be an X drawn with the fire-blackened end of a piece of wood from a campfire on a blazed tree side or a trussed turkey partially hidden behind a downed log. As the condemned bird's head bobbed up and down the frontiersmen took turns trying to hit the moving mark. A successful shot earned the marksman the unlucky bird. If the prize were a beef then it might well be awarded in quarters, with each marksman taking his selection in the order of finish. Nothing went to waste with the "fifth quarter"—the hide, entrails, and bones—presented to the least successful of the five best riflemen.

The Revolution and the War of 1812 hinted that the rifle was the firearm of the future despite the disadvantage of slow rate of fire and cost. The new nation created two armories, one at Springfield, Massachusetts, and another at Harper's Ferry, Virginia, that produced both muskets and rifles for the Army. Harper's Ferry produced about 15,000 Model 1803 U.S. Flintlock Rifles while private contractors manufactured the Model 1817 U.S. Flintlock Rifle, often known as "The Common Rifle", under license from Harper's Ferry. John Hall's design of a breech loading flintlock rifle was adopted and produced at Harper's Ferry as the Model 1819 Hall U.S. Breechloading Flintlock Rifle. The Hall rifle bears several distinctions: it was the first regulation breechloader manufactured in significant numbers, over 19,000 rifles being made and it was the first firearm manufactured with totally interchangeable parts.

Noted firearms historian Norm Flayderman reports that it is also the only firearm every presented in lieu of a medal or citation for gallantry. By Act of Congress fifteen were taken from the production of 1824 and prepared for presentation to schoolboys who had volunteered and, much like Horatius, bravely defended a bridge during the siege of Plattsburgh, New York in 1814. The rifles were furnished with engraved silver plaques that commemorated the event.

As the new nation moved westward, the rifle would begin to replace the smoothbore musket. Technological advances would begin to redefine long range beyond the 200-300 yard distance that seemed to be the limit of the Kentucky rifle. The first major employment of rifles by the United States was the Model 1841 U.S. Percussion Rifle. This muzzle loading 54 caliber rifle was used by Jefferson Davis' Mounted Mississippi Rifles in the Mexican War, hence its nickname, "The Mississippi Rifle". This rifle is historically important because it was one of the first massed produced military rifles that employed the percussion ignition system, which had been perfected by Joshua Shaw around 1825. The percussion cap was a great improvement over the venerable flintlock. The new improvement was unaffected by wet weather and provided a quicker and more certain ignition under all circumstances. This innovation brought the round ball muzzle-loading rifle to its apogee.

All that was left was to improve the bullet. The round ball had limited efficiency because of its small bearing surface's inability to fully engage the rifling. Claude Etienne Minié, a captain in the French Army, made a major innovative step in firearms technology in 1853 with the creation of the bullet that bears his name. The misnamed Minié ball is actually a conical cylinder made of soft lead with an iron cup at the base. When fired the force of the rapidly burning powder forces an iron cup against the base of the bullet expanding it against the rifling causing a tight seal. The aerodynamically shaped Minié ball had a spin imparted upon it by the rifling making the bullet more stable in flight. The Minié ball was manufactured slightly smaller than the caliber of the rifle in which it was used and, as such, made it easier to load, overcoming the most important objection to muzzle loading rifles. It was a great improvement on the patched rifle ball used by earlier rifles.

The new bullet was more accurate and capable of flying further than the traditional spherical ball it replaced. Such was the impact of the new bullet that Secretary of War Jefferson Davis, ordered all Springfield muskets returned to the armories to have their barrels rifled. However, tradition dies hard in the world of firearms and, to this day, any cartridge with a solid bullet is still referred to as ball ammunition.

The definition of long range was about to be rewritten for the first time since the introduction of the Kentucky Rifle. The Minié ball ammunition consisted of a bullet wrapped in a paper pouch filled with powder. The soldier only had to tear open the base of the cartridge with his teeth to begin loading. Incidentally this brought about the first serious medical examination of infantry recruits and with it a physically disqualifying condition for a new soldier. Up to this time about the only physical requirement for a recruit was that he be breathing. Now he was required to have two fully usable opposing teeth, for without teeth with which to tear open the paper cartridges he was useless as an infantryman.

The paper cartridge was torn open and the powder charge poured down the barrel. A steel ramrod then seated the bullet and the paper, which formed a wad between powder and ball. The last step was to place a percussion cap on the nipple of the lock and the rifle was ready to be fired. Each soldier was now armed with a rifle that was accurate to about three times the distance of previous rifles, and had a maximum range of 1,000 to 1,200 yards. An additional advantage was that the speed of reloading with paper cartridges was much faster than with ball and powder flask thereby increasing the volume of fire that might be delivered in a period of time.

As military rifles developed, the recreational use of firearms also progressed. Around the beginning of the 19th Century some gunsmiths had begun to produce a rifle used for competition. These flintlocks were heavy, mounting octagon barrels of 38 to 40 inches in length, had full stocks, double set triggers, and used metallic tube sights. The competition rifle would continue to develop with such innovations as the addition of cap locks; pinhead front sights coupled with adjustable micrometer rear sights, and improved types of rifling such as gain twist. The later match rifles were equipped with false muzzles and bullet starters to allow a paper patched bullet to be loaded without deformation. Attention to this small detail could double the accurate range of a particular rifle. After about 1840, according to no less an authority than Captain Ned Roberts, matches began to be fired at ranges of 100 to 200 rods, a rod being 16.5 feet, or 550 to 1100 yards with some regularity. When the Civil War began these rifles, and riflemen, would figure prominently in the selection of sharpshooters to serve under Colonel Hiram Berdan in the Union Army.

As the smoke in Charleston Harbor cleared and the defeated Union garrison of Fort Sumter marched out of the battered fortress, thousands of men flocked to the colors, be they the 'Stars and Bars' or 'Stars and Stripes'. Of all the men, just a small proportion were skilled marksmen, experienced at hunting or competition, and willing to put their particular skills at the service of their respective governments.

The Confederacy, while long on martial spirit and outdoor and hunting skills, lacked manufacturing capability and the rifles used by southern sharpshooters were largely Whitworth and Kerr rifles that were slipped past the Federal naval blockade. The soldiers designated to use the expensive British rifles were chosen from those who had demonstrated superior marksmanship skills. They were not organized into bodies, as

were the sharpshooters of the Union. By early November of 1863 the *Richmond Daily Examiner* would boast "We have a wonderful gun in our Army, the Whitworth rifle. It kills at 2,000 yards, more than a mile." Hundreds of the British target rifles found their way into the hands of Confederate troops.

Originally designed as a 45-caliber rifle, with a polygon bore, the Whitworths were rifled at a rate of one turn in 20 inches and shot a hexagonal bullet. However, the Confederate troops used a 530-grain cylindrical bullet. The British Government never adopted the percussion cap muzzle-loading rifle for military purposes but 40 of them were manufactured for use in the 1860 meeting of the British National Rifle Association where they proved their worth. The rifle was equipped with a metallic leaf sight that was graduated to 1200 yards and many were fitted with a 14.5-inch low power Davidson telescopic sight mounted on the left side of the rifle. Rifles similar to these were manufactured and shipped to the Confederacy where the sharpshooters generally relied on the globe sights, as the telescopic sights were easily damaged.

Confederate snipers and their Whitworth rifles accounted for a large number of Federal troops and officers. Perhaps the most famous long-range sniping incident of the Civil War occurred at the Battle of Spotsylvania on May 9, 1864. With his troops ducking for cover because of sporadic small arms fire, Union General John Sedgwick, demonstrated his bravery by remaining standing as he rallied his men by gently chiding them. 'Uncle John', as he was fondly known to his troops because of his unselfish and warmhearted character, called out, "They couldn't hit an elephant at this distance!" They would be his final words. Sergeant Charlie Grace of the Fourth Georgia, some 800 yards away, had Sedgwick in his sights and squeezed the trigger of his Whitworth rifle. The dead general, shot in the head, fell into the arms of an aide

The Confederate sharpshooters proved to be a valuable and potent asset. While picking off Federal officers and troops at long range was good for the morale of the southern troops, the real worth of the sharpshooters was in keeping opposing troops under the constant threat of well aimed fire. The southerners often used its limited assets of skilled marksmen to try to neutralize the overwhelming strength of northern artillery by harrying the Federal gun crews with well aimed rifle fire.

While the south employed its sharpshooters in small independent teams the north took a more traditional approach in application but an innovative view of equipment. With the advantage of its industrial might the Federal forces formed two large units, the 1st and 2nd United States Sharpshooters under the command of Colonel Hiram Berdan. Berdan's Sharpshooters were armed with mass produced rapid fire breech loading rifles and placed as skirmishers ahead of the main line of battle.

Just as the southerners had issued its precious Whitworth and Kerr rifles only to shooters of known quality, the requirements of the United States Sharpshooters required a man to demonstrate a high level of skill. The prospective sharpshooter had to be capable of shooting, "...a string of 50 inches in 10 consecutive shots at 200 yards with globe or telescope sights from a rest....". Shooting a string was a traditional scoring method by which a wooden peg was inserted into each bullet hole on the target. A string was then stretched from the center of the aiming point around each peg and back again, each shot in turn, with its total length determining the winner of a match. A group meeting the 50-inch standard would be about five inches across, some two inches larger than the X-ring on the present National Rifle Association short-range target. When a company of 100 New Hampshire sharpshooters under a Captain Jones reported for duty the best string recorded was a phenomenal ten inches, shot by Jones, while the average string was 30 inches.

Many of Berdan's men came with their own competition rifles and were paid a bounty for bringing them. These personal rifles, along with some purchased by the government, would be used for special sniping activities that required long range accuracy. The troops would be issued a standard shoulder arm for day-to-day work, their favorite being the Sharps Model 1859.

Berdan's command became one of the most famous units of the war. They were effective as both skirmishers and sharpshooters, feared by the enemy, and established the primacy of breechloading small arms. Berdan's men boasted they were responsible for killing more of the enemy than any other unit in the Federal army.

By the time of Lee's surrender of the Army of Northern Virginia at Appomatox Courthouse the definition of long range had been altered by technological advancements. From the early 1700s until the Civil War, a shot at 200, perhaps 300 yards, was the ultimate in long-range accuracy. As the states were reunified and began its westward expansion, a successful shot of 600 yards, or more, was the new standard. The first to take advantage of the advancement in firearms technology were the competitor and the hunter.

For the better part of the first half of the 19th Century the hunters and trappers who began the economic exploitation of the far west needed a reliable firearm and a good knife. If one were to believe popular fiction, not one of those hearty souls that ventured into the vast expanses of Indian country went without a Green River knife on his hip and a 50-caliber rifle made by Saint Louis Gunsmith Jake Hawken in the crook of his arm. True as we may wish it to be, it seems that Hawken Rifles, fine pieces that they were, were usually sighted in for 125 yards and fiction has far outstripped fact in the case of the knife and rifle of choice for that breed of adventurers that would become generically known as "Mountain Men".

The true long-range rifles of the old west were those used by the generation of hunters to follow the Mountain Men, the buffalo runners. Using carefully handloaded ammunition, both for accuracy and economy, and a telescopic sight mounted on a Sharps or Remington rifle, these professional hunters were consistently deadly out to 500 yards. In several documented cases these rifles were capable of hitting a target in excess of 1,000 yards. This seems to be no small feat for a rifle with a bullet size in the range of 40 to 50 caliber. Experts of the time swore by the .45-120-550 Sharps with paper patched bullets. A .45 rifle with a black powder charge of 120 grains was capable of pushing a 550-grain lead slug with good accuracy. The Ballard, in .40-70 and .40-90, was also held in high regard.

Noted buffalo runner Frank H. Mayer recorded that a retired fellow runner of his acquaintance made a habit of shooting 10 rounds a day at a measured 1,000 yards each day for recreation. He alternated between two Sharps, one .40-90-420 and the other .45-120-550. After shooting 350 groups, sworn evidence, perhaps with a demijohn in one hand and Bible in the other, indicated that not one group was larger than 26 inches while the majority averaged about 20 inches.

The buffalo runner needed a heavy rifle of large caliber to kill the animals swiftly at long range as well as handle the high rate of sustained fire needed to fell enough buffalo to make the time spent economical. He employed it with crossed rest sticks, the forerunner of the bipod. The popular rest was nothing more than two stout staves about 40 inches long joined together about four inches from one end. The rifle was placed in the short apex while the longer ends, which had been previously sharpened, were planted into the ground. From this rest the hunter could assume the sitting position and begin his harvest.

Sitting, while shooting from rest sticks, was the preferred position for several reasons. First, and probably most importantly of all, it allowed an alert hunter to keep his eye on his surroundings and have early warning of approaching hostiles. The rifle, perched a yard or so above the ground, was very steady and made less noise and dust, as would be the case with the prone position. The greater distance between the rifle and the ground lessened the rifle's report, reverberation, and vibration through the ground while allowing the breeze to carry away the powder smoke. The buffalo were less likely to be spooked and this allowed the hunter to get within 250 or 300 yards of a herd and to stay there while he killed the day's quota.

Perhaps the most fêted long-range shot by a buffalo runner was that of Billy Dixon at Adobe Walls in June of 1874. Dixon was staying north of Amarillo, near the site of the abandoned Bent Brothers trading post known locally as Adobe Walls, with some two dozen hunters and teamsters.

Before dawn approximately 400 to 600 Comanche, Kiowa, Arapahoe, and Cheyenne warriors, surrounded and attacked them. The surprised hunters dropped what they were doing and, grabbing up their rifles, made for the saloon. The experienced buffalo runners set up shop and methodically shot into the charging masses just as calmly as they would a herd of milling buffalo. By noon the mass charges had ceased in the face of the accurate fire and the attackers took to individual action, crawling in close under the cover of the tall grass.

For almost two days the Indians kept the hunters besieged. When the Comanche Chief Quanah Parker was wounded, they abandoned the battle. The survivors of the siege were forced to remain for several more days as their horses had all been killed or run off. From time to time small bands of Indians would appear to silently scan the battle site from a safe distance.

Dixon spotted just such a group on a bluff nearly a mile away. Picking up his 50 caliber Sharps, he checked the conditions, ran up his sights, steadied the rifle, and squeezed off a shot. The smoke had cleared by the time the heavy bullet and sound reached the mounted Indians, pitching one of them from his horse. His startled companions scattered but returned to recover their fallen comrade. Later a government survey team, who happened to be in the area, measured the distance at 1,538 yards. The feat would become known as "The Shot of The Century". Given the conditions, rifle, ammunition, and distance, it might also be appropriate to call it the luckiest shot of the century. The modest Dixon accepted the praise but insisted he was just firing at the group and was just lucky to get a hit.

Noted firearms writer Mic McPherson enlisted the aid of Bill Falin, chief ballistician at Accurate Arms and, in 1996, they attempted to duplicate the fabled shot. Noting the 1,538 yards is 0.87 miles they prepared a Sharps rifle and powder charge that was a close to authentic as possible. For a target they constructed a like size silhouette of an Indian astride a horse. After zeroing the rifle for the distance they commenced a series of record shots using a single aiming point. The mean radius of the shots was such that if the target had been the center of a group of mounted men it is a certainty that someone would have felt the sting of a heavy bullet after its 5 second flight through the hazy and dust laden atmosphere. Almost a century and a quarter separated the real shot from the reenactment but both were impressive examples of long-range marksmanship.

Around the same time that the Indians were dragging off their surprised comrade and Billy Dixon was swabbing out his barrel, long range shooting was a hot topic of conversation accompanying the post dinner brandy and cigars at various gentlemen's clubs in the New York City area.

General George Wingate and some of his associates were concerned about the poor level of marksmanship evidenced by the recruits to the Union Army during the late Civil War. In an attempt to bolster national defense and encourage marksmanship they formed the National Rifle Association Of America on November 21, 1871. They were able to enlist the aid of the New York State Legislature and on June 21, 1872 the newly constructed range, just 20 miles from New York City at Creedmoor on Long Island, was opened with a major match pitting teams from the National Guards of various states and the regular army. Events in Great Britain would soon thrust the new facility into the international spotlight.

For some years eight man rifle teams from England, Scotland, and Ireland had vied for the Elcho Shield. The contest required the teams to fire at ranges of 800, 900, 1,000 and 1,100 yards. When, in 1873, the Irish won the match for the first time they were so enthused that they issued a challenge to the United States to engage in a world championship. Not knowing of the existence of the NRA, the Irish directed the challenge to The Amateur Rifle Club of the United States. The president of the Amateur Rifle Club happened to be General Wingate who picked up the gauntlet for the NRA. Considering that the club had barely five-dozen members and no experience at ranges beyond 500 yards it was a bold reply. The match was fired on September 26, 1874 at Creedmoor. It would be more than a contest between nations; it would also be one of competing technologies. The American team fired breechloading cartridge rifles made by Sharps and Remington while the British Empire preferred Rigby or Metford muzzleloaders. The Remington rolling block rifle became known as the "Long Range

Creedmoor Rifle." It was designed, and its manufacture supervised by noted marksman L.L. Hepburn. The rifles were chambered in .44 with 90 grains of black powder pushing a massive paper patched 550-grain lead bullet.

The rear sights, copied from the English, were of a vernier tang style that mounted just behind the receiver, or near the heel of the butt stock, depending if the competitor was shooting either the prone or supine position. The front sights were of the wind gauge style. In original form they were dovetail blocks that were lightly tapped with a tool for windage adjustment, later a more accurate and easier to use horizontal vernier was employed for left or right changes. The rifles of both sides used heavy loads of black powder that required them to be wiped clean after each shot, a necessity with paper-patched bullets.

The competitors took the line to shoot 45 record shots apiece at cast steel targets with a four point square bullseye. Each man would discharge 15 shots at each of 800, 900, and 1,000 yards. There were no sighters. The match was tight all the way to the finish with just three points separating the victorious Americans from the Irish.

In a splendid example of sportsmanship, Major Arthur Blennerhasset Leech presented an ornate Victorian standing cup to the host team who placed it in national competition the next year as the Leech Cup. It has always been a long range trophy except for 1951 and 1952 when it was awarded to the highest scorer using the service rifle in the 600 yard Marine Corps Cup Match. The Leech Cup is the oldest trophy presented in shooting by the NRA. After the 1913 National Matches the Leech Cup went missing and was not found until 1927. The NRA responded by requiring that all trophies would be held at NRA headquarters and keeper awards would be given to the match winners.

The Irish again challenged the Americans in 1875 and invited them to compete at Dollymount, Ireland. The visiting team repeated its performance of the previous year, only opening the margin of victory to 39 points. The Americans then traveled to Wimbledon, the British range just outside of London, to compete for the prestigious Elcho Shield. It turned out that the rules excluded the American team and caused some hard feelings. To assuage the visitors the British National Rifle Association prevailed upon Queen Victoria's daughter, the Princess Louise, to present a large three-footed silver tankard to the Americans for competition amongst themselves.

The first winner of the massive trophy, now known as the Wimbledon Cup, was Major Henry Fulton. Fulton himself was honored with a trophy when, in 1987, International Shooting Hall of Fame member and Palma Alumnus Arthur C. Jackson presented a trophy to be awarded to the high scoring individual in the International Palma Team Competition in Fulton's memory. The Wimbledon Cup returned to the United States with the team and was placed in competition by Fulton. It has become the premier long-range prize for marksman in the United States, as it has never been contested over any distance other than 1,000 yards.

"The Great Centennial Rifle Match" was fired at Creedmoor on the 13th and 14th of September 1876 as part of the celebration of the 100th anniversary of the independence of the United States. The fledgling National Rifle Association of America hosted eight man teams from Australia, Canada, Scotland, and Ireland for the first meeting of what would become the longest continuously running international rifle match in history. The target was a six by ten foot frame of canvas that had a 36 inch black five ring, or bull's eye, and a 54 inch four ring printed upon it. The remainder of the inner six by six foot section, outside of the rings, was worth three points. A two-foot wide panel ran down each side and was valued at two points. The teams fired twice across the 45 shot course in two days and when the billows of black powder smoke had cleared, the home team had won the first Palma Match.

The Palma Matches quickly became the preeminent long-range international shooting event. However, it would be a misnomer to refer to these early events as prone matches as most of the shooters fired from the popular back or 'Texas' position. Lying supine, with their feet pointing towards the target, the shooters would rest the rifles upon their legs or feet and blast away. The long barreled rifles and the tall vernier sights of the time favored this seemingly ungainly, but strong, position making it a less formidable task to shoot than it looks. The 32 to 34 inch long barrels and sights mounted close to the butt gave shooters an incredibly long sight radius.

The Palma has evolved into "The World Long Range Shooting Championships, Individual and Palma Team Matches". It has gone through many changes since 1876 and has developed its own set of rules and requirements in regard to target, rifle, and cartridge. The United States has, overall, experienced great success in this special match that is held at three to five year intervals. Teams consist of 16 firing members and two alternates along with a support group of a team captain, adjutant, five coaches and a non-firing armorer, with total team size not to exceed 26 members. The current rules allow for the use of a manually operated rifle using .308 Winchester or 7.62mm NATO ammunition loaded with the Sierra 155 grain Palma bullet or its equivalent. The rifle must mount metallic sights and not weigh more than 6.5 kilograms. It is interesting to note that the rules state that the use of a sling is not mandatory.

The match is fired at 800, 900, and 1,000 yards or 700, 800, and 900 meters depending on the range available to the host nation—the distances being almost identical—and at the National Rifle Association of America's Long Range Target. The Palma is a match of great distinction, so much so that nations, or rifle associations, that are celebrating special events or anniversaries apply to host the match to add extra glamour to the occasion.

The advent of smokeless powder did not spell the end to long range black powder shooting. It is very much alive today. The NRA conducts a series of black powder competitions with the Castle Trophy awarded to the winner of the Creedmoor Match. This trophy, which first came to the United States in 1873, and was awarded to Colonel John Bodine as the 1874 International Champion at Creedmoor, is now awarded to the competitor who bests all comers over a 30 shot match, ten shots each at 800, 900, and 1,000 yards. The rifle must be a single shot black powder cartridge arm with period sights and be shot from the supported prone position. The trophy was originally a gift of Lord Elcho, the patron of the Elcho Shield, to the 25th Lanarkshire Volunteers to commemorate their victory over England and Ireland in a match in 1871. The trophy went missing sometime after 1879 and eventually found its way back to the NRA, by purchase, in 1985. For those that say that mysterious things come in threes, the loss of three major long range trophies, the Palma, Leech, and Castle, certainly fits into this category.

United States Army Lieutenant Colonel C. J. Shaffer, who served as the Director of Civilian Marksmanship, Executive Officer of The National Matches and later as a member of the NRA competitions staff, donated a highly engraved German schüetzen rifle as a trophy to be awarded to the high scorer in a match demanding the use of a single shot black powder cartridge arm with period sights. To win the Shaffer Trophy one must shoot twice across a course of fire that requires ten shots standing at 200 yards, ten shots sitting with crossed sticks at 300 yards, and a final stage of ten shots prone at 600 yards with crossed sticks.

While high power held the competitor's and public interest at the end of the 19th century, and into beginning of the 20th, 22 caliber rimfire smallbore was beginning to make some inroads into outdoor shooting and would add another meaning to the lexicon of long range. At this time the use of .22 rifles was looked upon as primarily an indoor sport for distances up to 25 yards. During World War I, Army Captain Edward C. Crossman saw that the smallbore rifle was the perfect tool to teach recruits the fundamentals of marksmanship at much less cost and without the need of extensive outdoor range facilities. During planning for the 1919 National Matches "Ned" Crossman suggested that it was time to schedule some smallbore competition to run in conjunction with the service rifle shooting.

The National Rifle Association thought it a good idea and wasted no time appointing Crossman to set up just such a program. Time was short, the NRA gave Crossman the go ahead in June and the matches were scheduled for August, so Crossman enlisted the aid of some of his friends. Having never organized a smallbore tournament of this scale, Crossman relied upon

a British officer, Captain E.J.D. Newitt, who had experience organizing the "miniature" rifle matches at Bisley, England. W. H. Richard of Winchester, Captain Grosvenor L. Wotkyns of the US Army, and Frank Kahrs of Remington Arms Company were also pressed into service preparing the tournament. The program included a slow fire 200-yard stage fired on a reduced military 1,000 yard bull's-eye with a 7.2 inch five ring surrounding a 4-inch V ring. Unfortunately torrential rains washed out the 200-yard firing line and the match was cancelled.

While the traditional ranges for outdoor smallbore prone are 50 and 100 yards, during the years between World Wars there were two long-range smallbore courses of fire that were quite popular. The first was the Palma-fashioned after its high power brother-that allowed two sighters before 15 record shots at each of 150, 175, and 200 yards. The second match was known as the "Swiss Match". The target was a 1/5th reduction of the standard six foot by ten foot 1,000 yard 'C' target, designated the 'C5' for smallbore matches. The black bull's-eye was a 7.2 inch five ring with a four-inch V ring. After the allowed two sighters, the shooter could continue firing for record as long as the shots stayed inside the five ring. Any shot straying out of the black meant an instant end.

These long-range any sight smallbore matches were most popular in the Middle Atlantic States. Popular venues were Sea Girt, New Jersey; Camp Ritchie, Maryland; and Peekskill, New York. From time to time a 300-yard match was held in conjunction with the more common Palma and 200 yard courses of fire. The standard military "A" target, with its ten inch black five ring, was used in this ultra long range smallbore match.

Limited to just two sighting shots a wise long-range smallbore competitor would have taken the time to obtain a good 100 yard zero for both elevation and windage with quality match ammunition. From this point it was simply a matter of clicking up the Winchester 5A, or its successor the Lyman 5A telescopic sight, a matter of 20 minutes from 100 to 200 yards and 21 minutes more for 300 yards, assuming the bases were 7.2 inches on center. In the mid 1930s, when Lyman, Unertl, and Fecker introduced scopes with larger diameter objective bells and higher magnification, shooters had to go to taller bases to keep the scope clear of the barrel as the externally adjusted scopes were elevated.

At a time when the quality of ammunition and rifles was such that perfect scores at 100 yards were worth space in shooting publications, some of the runs of consecutive fives and Vs at 200 yards are phenomenal. Famed belly shooter Thurman Randle, of Texas, and his Winchester 52 rifle "Bacon Getter", established a national record in 1933 of 196 bulls that would stand for seven years.

During the summer of 1940 the grandly titled "Smallbore All Range Championship" was held at Poughkeepsie, New York. This anysight event called for ten record shots at 50, 100, 150, 175, and 200 yards with sighting shots allowed only at 50 yards. Military style pit service was provided at 150 yards and beyond to insure that the shooters might see shot location. The final match of the day was the Swiss Match. A young Art Jackson lay down at 4 PM with half of a box of Western Super Match ammunition to try his luck. Four and a half hours after he started, the setting sun made it difficult to see the cross hair reticule of his scope and, finally out of ammunition, light, and feeling in his left arm, he was forced to stop with an unofficial count of 325 bulls. The scorekeeper's official tally marks showed one less and his scorecard declared he had fired a new record of 324 consecutive fives with 238 Vs. The feat stands as a monument to both the endurance of the shooter and the generosity of the bystanders who donated some six boxes of Super Match ammunition to keep him going when his scanty supply gave out.

The Second World War all but shut down competitive shooting for the first half of the 1940s. The war had both a positive and negative effect upon long range shooting. When the standards for the award of the Distinguished Rifleman Badge were reviewed after the war, the 1,000-yard stage was dropped. As a result, for almost two decades shooting at distances beyond 600 yards were pretty much restricted to the National Matches. It would not be until the Palma resurgence in 1966 that attention would be focused on long range shooting other than the Leech and the Wimbledon matches shot each year at Camp Perry.

On the other hand, troop ships had disgorged hoards of the returning veterans with marksmanship skills that they wished to continue to hone on rifle range and in the hills. With them also came an unknown number of souvenir rifles of all makes and descriptions, as well as a desire to see just how well they might shoot. In formal competition the numbers of people participating in NRA events soared.

However, there were those who were not interested in National Match Course shooting. What they sought was one hole accuracy based upon experimentation with powder, ball, and rifle. As early as 1881 William Wellington Greener had written about a special class of target rifle that he described as " a sort of scientific toy" with which the end is absolute accuracy by use of any artificial aid that an active mind can conjure. Today we know such a firearm as a bench rest rifle. Starting with informal activities by the Puget Sound Snipers Congress in 1944, on the west coast, and some matches in Machias, New York and Lisbon, Connecticut on the Atlantic side these varmint hunters and accuracy fanatics soon met at the Pine Tree Rifle Club in Johnstown, New York on Labor Day weekend of 1947. By the end of the weekend the assembled men had elected officers and the National Bench Rest Shooters Association was born. Harvey Donaldson, Townsend Whelen, Sam Clark, Ray Biehler, Al Marciante, Warren Page, and Lucian Cary were some of the legendary firearms experimenters who laid the foundation for the development of bench rest competition as it is known today.

Center fire bench rest competition is usually shot at 100 and 200-yard distances, with an occasional 300 yard match added if the range construction permits. In this game the group size, not placement, is the criteria for success. The bench rest community has been responsible for many of the developments that have improved the overall accuracy of target rifles used in both NRA and international competition. As far as long-range bench rest is concerned the ultimate came about in 1967 when William Theis, George Reeder, and David Troxell put together the first 1,000-yard benchrest match across the lands of the Lynn and Waltz farms in the Williamsport area of Pennsylvania. The first match, held on October 1,

1967 was won by James Barger who wielded a 7mm Remington 40X and banged out a 16 inch group.

Within a year "The Original Pennsylvania 1000 Yard Bench Rest Club" was incorporated and had obtained a 99-year lease to land from shooter Gene Plants. Construction followed and pits and a concrete pad were soon in place to be followed, eventually, by ten covered firing points and a clubhouse. The club runs a series of matches each year from May to November with a hundred or more shooters attending each shoot.

Much of firearm development has been a by-product of military necessity. The relative short distances and massed troops of World War One brought about the formalized training of soldiers to insure competent marksmen to use specially manufactured or modified rifles for sniping. As a rule the distances were somewhat short, some 100 to 300 yards, but from time to time there was a need for a hard-hitting rifle at longer ranges. The British used what was known as "African Rifles", large bore high shock power firearms that would otherwise be used to take down elephants, rhinos, and hippos.

The Germans developed the bolt-action 13mm Mauser anti-tank rifle while the United States called upon John Browning and Winchester to devise a firearm to meet the challenge. What would become the classic heavy machine gun of the 20th century-and perhaps beyond, the .50 Browning Machine Gun was ready to be tested but developed too late for employment in France. During the years between wars the .50 BMG would undergo further development and develop into the classic familiar M2. The M2 was employed, on a very limited basis, in a sniper role during the Second World War. The Perfex Corporation of Milwaukee, Wisconsin manufactured the 3.25X M1 telescopic sight for use on the BMG and, in good conditions, the gun and sight combination were accurate to over 2,000 yards in single fire mode.

The long-range capabilities of the .50BMG cartridge would begin to be fully exploited during the Korean War by two innovative and inventive soldiers, Frank Conway and Bill Brophy. Conway, who won back-to-back Wimbledon Cup victories in 1955 and 1956, lead the way in 50-caliber employment. As early as

1946 he was championing the BMG long range concept. He adopted a German PzB39 anti-tank rifle to the big fifty and demonstrated during the course of its development its effectiveness at 1,400 yards, with 2,800 yard shots being feasible.

The war in Korea eventually reached a stale-mate that was reminiscent of the trenches of World War One, setting the stage for a rebirth of sniper activity. Brophy, a Distinguished Rifleman and Ordnance officer, found that the state of the sniper program within the Army in Korea was poor. The equipment, mainly M1Ds and M1903A4s, were in poor repair, the infantrymen assigned them were not trained, and the supply and maintenance system was incapable of providing adequate support. Brophy reached into his own pocket and purchased a Winchester Model 70 and a 10X telescopic sight. Within short order he made effective use of the combination and believers of the Army snipers. However, there were many targets of opportunity that were far outside of the range of the 30-caliber Winchester's 1,000-yard capability.

While rummaging around a cache of captured enemy equipment Brophy came across a Soviet 14.5mm PTRD1941 anti tank rifle. Building on Conway's pioneering work he had it fitted with a BMG 50 caliber aircraft barrel and attached a skeleton stock, cheekpiece, and bipod. A Unertl 20X telescopic sight was mounted upon it and this particularly homely looking collection of welded pipe and spare parts was soon making distances between 1,000 and 2,000 yards most uncomfortable for the enemy. Brophy would go on to even greater fame in a second career in firearms when, after retirement, he served as Marlin Firearms Company's Senior Technical Manager, author of seminal books on the L.C. Smith Shotgun, .30-40 Krag, 1903 Springfield, and the Springfield Armory, and was a competitor with the Palma Team.

Within the shooting community there exists a less formal, but no more intense group of competitors, who are very much cut from the same bolt of cloth as the benchrest shooter-the varmint hunter. Not as formally organized, but no less fanatical about accuracy, these long-range hunters often deal in distances that certainly would be considered long range. Varmint hunting may best be described as a cross between bench rest and hunting. The major differences being that he distances are longer than bench rest's traditional 200 yards and the targets are smaller than the average deer hunter's quarry.

Varmint shooters consider distances in excess of 850 yards to be ultra-long range. To be successful they quite often are involved in customizing rifles, ammunition, and optics. Armed with a truck loaded with gear that might include a bench rest table, sand bags, a mechanical rest, range finder, and an array of long-range optical gear the varmint shooter seeks out rockchuck and prairie dog colonies. After scouting out an area the truck is unloaded, quite often in the dark hours before dawn to take advantage of the most favorable shooting conditions of the day, the quiet time just after dawn. After setting up shop the shooter and spotter spend some time observing and becoming familiar with the target area and the calm conditions at day break.

May 31, 2000 dawned as a perfect morning on a mesa near Pueblo, Colorado as Kreg Slack and his spotter Nadine Parry peered out at a prairie dog town some distance away. The light was coming up, the air was clear, it was still too cool for mirage to build, and there was not a breath of wind. Slack was very familiar with the area as he and his regular shooting companion, Bruce Artus, had been working up an Dillon/McMillan stocked Obermeyer barreled Winchester Model 70 action in .308 Ackley Improved for some long range shooting at the site. He was shooting at a 16-inch metal gong that the pair has earlier set as a target. As Kreg peered through the Leupold scope, modified to 40X by Premier Reticules, he noticed a prairie dog lounging in the sun near the gong. Taking up the slack on the two-ounce Jewell trigger he broke the shot.

Pushed by 85 grains of IMR 7828, a 338-caliber 300-grain Sierra bullet was in the air at a muzzle velocity of 2,750 feet per second and quickly struck near the unsuspecting varmint. Making a quick adjustment Slack fired another round that kicked up another column of dust just a foot or so from the now curious, but not alarmed, animal. While his target looked about to investigate the source of the strange dust spouts Slack made a quick adjustment to the scope knobs, squinted through the scope, and fired a third shot.

Much like General Sedgewick, the fearless dog was taken unawares by a long-range shooter. The distance was ultra long range not just by varmint shooter standards, but also by anyone's reckoning. A laser range finder measured the distance at an astounding 3,125 yards! The shot, at 1.78 miles, is the world's longest successful, recorded, and verified aimed rifle shot to date.

The history of long range shooting in the United States is fast approaching 400 years. Since European explorers and colonists first brought gunpowder to these shores the definition of long range has grown along with the nation. While the United States may have reached the extent of its physical boundaries the imagination, ingenuity, and success of those living there who seek to hit a target at further and further distances has not.

Chapter 3

1000 Yard Military Sniping

by Norm & Rocky Chandler

One thousand yard sniping is magical. Historians describe thousand yard shots using scoped muzzle loading rifles during our Civil War. Buffalo hunters pinned by hostile tribesmen were alleged to have nailed their attackers at one thousand. During the Vietnam Conflict such shots were made by both Marine and Army snipers, and a few dramatic 1000 yarders were punched out during Desert Storm—where ranges tended to be lengthy indeed.

All of that said, we must also recognize that shots at 1000 are extremely rare, hits are statistically insignificant, and kills are absolutely minuscule. Those facts change nothing. 1000 yard sniping can be possible, so we have to train for it.

Much of the mystique surrounding effective 1000 yard shooting has been encouraged by fiction writers. When the co-author of this section was researching *Tim Murphy, Rifleman*, his study of the Revolutionary War Freeman's Farm battlefield indicated that Murphy was most likely to have shot British General Simon Fraser from about 300 yards—and that shot in those times would have been an exceptional feat. But, in this day of every deer hunter accepting 600 yard kills as common, the author doubled all ranges in the Murphy novel lest readers feel Tim was just a run-of-the-mine shooter. You can do that in fiction writing.

In one of his novels, the best-selling author Stephen Hunter featured a planned 1200 yard head shot using a once-fired .30 caliber bullet held by a sabot in an oversize barrel—to pre-serve incriminating rifling marks on the bullet. Imaginative fiction.

An author of a Vietnam War memoir spoke casually of "Having just made an 1800 yard kill." Holy Cow! A lot of dreamy stuff gets written, and those dazzling fictional performances can affect our awareness of how purely tough long range shooting is in the real world.

Take the Civil War 1000 yard shooting that is so regularly tossed about. As War Between the States buffs we have tried to pin down actual instances, yet even the justly famed Confederate sniping from Devil's Den to Little Round Top at Gettysburg did not reach 600 yards. A North Carolina private Devereux reported that on April 4, 1865 at Amelia, Virginia, a trooper using a Whitworth rifle killed a mounted federal officer at 1000 yards. Well, maybe, but a single witness who was unlikely to be an outstanding range estimator? Maybe not!

Because a soldier dropped without an enemy seen nearby should not foster an assumption of effective 1000 yard shooting, and although it may seem heretical, we have been unable to be one hundred percent convinced of any successful 1000 yard rifle shooting during the entire Civil War. It seems that long hits—or suspected hits—are reflexively reported as 1000 yarders. Isn't it intriguing that remarkable hits are so often at the titillating 1000 yards but only rarely at, say, 900 or 1025?

In other volumes, we have written about Marines who hit at 1000 and more yards.

Gunnery Sgt. Carlos Hathcock, USMC is the most famous name associated with that kind of shooting. Carlos, who was a Wimbledon champion, did that, and his shots were often properly verified (see *White Feather*, available from *Precision Shooting*,) but it is necessary to discuss such kill confirmations for a few paragraphs.

Until the Vietnam Conflict, military shooters did not (at least publicly or officially) record the number and ranges of kills. If there was confirming of kills, the confirmations were informal and more of a general interest than a statistical one.

Serious studies of sniping as a tactic during earlier wars tend to report effectiveness on the enemy rather than the personalization of body counts and ranges. Except for the Soviet Union's W.W.II sniping propaganda that listed huge kill numbers and sometimes extreme ranges, studies that do include distances do not list one thousand yarders. Sniper kills from World War I to the present have been mostly at much shorter ranges—typically two hundred to five hundred yard hits with a significant percentage as close as law enforcement's 100 yard shooting.

Sniper kill recording changed dramatically with the advent of Vietnam. Public information types adopted fighter pilot counting of planes downed and bomber missions flown and applied the practice to individual snipers who caught their attention. Body count reports to higher headquarters listed confirmed kills by individual (and named) snipers. Ranking officers began decorating snipers, and their accomplishments were touted in various publications. Long range hits sound more important than those closer, and 1000 yard kills were trumpeted.

When questioned closely, most combat snipers do not handily recall ranges and totals. In some cases, snipers legitimately did not care how many or how far. Others preferred not to discuss details. Many could provide only wild estimates that even they tended to discount. Memory is an unsure vehicle, and in the past, most ranges have been estimates and, as mentioned before, humans tend to stretch both distances and numbers.

The longest known kill from the notable Hill 55 during the Vietnam War was made by Marine Cpl. Steve Suttles who nailed an enemy at 1250 yards (see *Death From Afar V*, pages 104, 105). The enemy soldier was skulking about near the butts of the Marines' known distance range and Suttles had fired there often enough to handle the dramatic shot. That, believe us, is rare.

In Suttles's case, the pajama-clad enemy fell across a log and remained in view. Later, Marines were able to go outside and verify the kill. That is a solid confirmation, but consider most such shots—down goes the enemy and he is seen no more, but no one can check the body. Was the enemy hit or did he wisely duck and slither away? One thousand yards is so far that no one could be sure unless he was on a spotting scope and watched the target's physical destruction, as Marine Staff Sgt. Bobby Sherril describes in *White Feather*.

Our point is that, unless independently verified, reports of 1000 yards kills should be accepted with reservations. We should treat such claims with the healthy skepticism we would reports of shooting deer at unreasonable ranges. We, after all, can be certain of two things. First, because a target disappears at the shot does not mean that it was hit. Second, even trained snipers can stretch ranges by poor estimation and by wishful reporting.

We are belaboring all of this because 1000 yard sniping involves a lot more than estimating the range, getting steady, and letting the shot go. Consider some of the following, most of which is extracted from the *Death From Afar, Marine Corps Sniping* series of books. We can do that because we own the copyrights!

A bullet rotating in flight pulls to the right (in our rifles). We call that sideward drift Magnus Effect. Do not ho-hum this seemingly small detail. At one thousand yards the Magnus moves your bullet almost two feet.

Have you thought about air temperature? A one degree change in ambient temperature will move your bullet's impact up or down about an inch at one thousand. If you zeroed in the morning when it was cool, in the afternoon the temperature may have risen fifteen degrees, and at one thousand yards your bullet will be striking almost a foot from your morning zero.

Apply the above to desert warfare where early morning through afternoon temperatures can vary as much as sixty degrees. The thousand yard sniper had better be able to fit the data into his planning or his target might not even notice his shooting.

Barometric pressure? Who cares? We all should. Of course a sniper may encounter significant barometer changes at the same altitude as weather moves in or out, but physically moving to a different elevation is usually the great culprit. A one hundred foot climb above or below your zero point will move your bullet almost an inch at one thousand yards, and five or six hundred foot hills are not unusual—perhaps hardly noticeable—but a six hundred foot change in shooting elevation will move a bullet more than five inches. A thousand foot climb or descent will change bullet impact about nine inches, and that ain't hay.

Mirage is an interesting if difficult to explain phenomenon. Basically, mirage is distortion caused by heated air rising from the ground or even a hot rifle barrel. A shooter often sees mirage as a boiling effect in the air or as shimmering and waving like running water. Think *refraction*. Refraction is the condition that makes an oar stuck into water appear to have a crook in it. Air refraction does the same thing and can make a target appear where it is not. Do we remember to remember that at one thousand yards a slight breeze working with mirage can make a target appear a couple of feet from its actual position?

Shooting up or down hill is recognized as requiring holding lower than expected. How low becomes the question. In close, a marksman need not worry much about normal slopes either up or down, but at one thousand yards, a 30 degree slope will move a bullet's strike about eighty-two inches. Imagine, more than six feet! Now that has significance.

Yaw? Never heard of it? A rotating bullet leaves a barrel point high and retains that attitude in the air all the way to the target. In other words, a bullet does not fly like a spear or javelin which drops its nose as it descends. Air pressure is greater on the bottom of the spinning bullet as it descends causing a gyroscopic wobble that increases as the bullet slows down. That is why a .30 caliber bullet's actions, after dropping below the speed of sound at about nine hundred yards, become important. *Imagine a spinning top.* The bullet's nose wobbles as a top does. Common yaw can move a bullet one minute-of-angle at one hundred yards. That comes to ten inches at one thousand yards.

Rifle cant. In the field it is easy to assume a position that is not exactly straight up and down. A rifle can cant without a shooter detecting it. A cant of five degrees provides a practical example. Such a cant will move a bullet about an inch at one hundred yards. At one thousand yards the same cant will move a bullet ten unplanned inches. The remarkable D. I. Boyd, who shot all of the famed courses for most of his life, was so skilled at using cant that he could slant his rifle at most ranges and bring a slightly out of center shot dead on. For the rest of us, cant is to be avoided.

We can seem exotic in mentioning the Coriolis effect, but it exists and moves rifle bullets. Coriolis involves the rotation of the earth, and artillerymen have to include it in their computations. To simplify, if you zero your rifle pointing one way and then shoot at one thousand yards in the opposite direction, our planet's rotation can pull your bullet an inch off point of aim.

Sniping moving targets at one thousand yards will usually be fruitless. At that range a running man must be led by 17 feet. A trotting man by more than eight feet, and a walking man by more than four feet. That is if the targets are moving directly across. Any other angles have different leads that a marksman would have to instantly calculate—and hope that the target maintained speed and direction while the bullet was en route. Correctly estimating all of that on a target that appears as far away as the planet Mars is less than likely.

We might now evaluate the probability of a claimed 1800 yard shot in light drizzle with a 7.62 NATO round from a 700 Remington equipped with a Redfield 3X to 9X variable power hunting scope (see *Dear Mom*, page 163). The maximum effective range of the 7.62 is 1100 yards. The bullet will fly much further, but as it drops below the speed of sound at about 900 yards, hits beyond that distance become increasingly dicey. Still, intended kills have been made out to 1250 and beyond, so . . . ?

We are hard put to locate solid trajectories and striking powers for .30 calibers beyond 1000 yards, no one lists them, and as far as we can determine, no one tries to shoot them. But we can generalize.

At 1800 yards a bullet en route to a target can rise more than forty feet above the line of sight.

On arrival, its velocity will be below 400 feet per second. The bullet will be dropping as much as it is moving forward, and its retained energy will be so small that it is unlikely to pierce the one inch board which is considered a lethal wound. We might say that it is not a good idea to shoot at people 1800 yards away because you might "piss 'em off." You will certainly not do much more than that.

At 1800 yards, our barely detectable five mile per hour cross wind will move the horrendously slowed bullet more than 110 inches off target. Yep, that is more than 9 feet off the aiming point. We will add that over 1800 yards a wind can change direction and speed. How does one calculate that and other variables? (No wind flags in the field, remember.)

We will not even venture into the effects of a drizzle on such long shooting—even if a shooter could see through it. All we are trying to demonstrate is that if one made such a shot with a .308 Winchester it should be listed among the greatest wonders of the world. And, we will leave it at that.

Captain Jim Reifinger, of the Jacksonville, NC police Department, who, during the Vietnam fighting was a Special Ops Marine, conducts diverse and very superior sniper courses. Usually Reifinger asks his students two questions. The first is: "How many of you can shoot minute-of-angle with your rifle?" Most hands go up, but when firing gets under way, less than a third of the students are likely to meet the minute-of-angle (a one inch group at one hundred yards) standard.

That percentage will, of course, greatly improve during the course of instruction, but the figures demonstrate how hard it is for allegedly competent marksmen to shoot minute-of-angle at even one hundred yards—much less at the magic one thousand.

If the combat sniper is to hit a human-size figure at one thousand yards, his rifle must be exactly zeroed (despite its field abuse), and it must shoot within the ten inch circle provided by minute-of-angle. The sniper must be one hundred percent perfect in his range estimation, his mirage evaluations, his elevation and windage adjustments, his hold, his trigger release, and his follow through—tasks far better accomplished on the mowed comfort of a known distance range than in the field, under pressure, probably wearied to the bone, and perhaps scared nearly mindless.

An interesting fact is that most alleged sniper rifles cannot hold on at one thousand yards, and that is Captain Reifinger's second question.

"How many of your rifles can be zeroed for one thousand yards?" Most believe in their equipment. They sport well known brands touted in many articles. Of course they can zero for long ranges—they think.

Well, they can't. Almost no ordinary rifle can zero beyond six or seven hundred yards, and only an extremely few so-called "sniper rifles" can hold dead on at one thousand and have their bullets reach the target.

Even more shocking is the fact that some of our issued military sniper rifles fail to have enough elevation in them when actually used in the field. That sad discovery is sometimes due to variations in the bridge or receiver ring diameters in Remington actions. Over the decades, receiver measurements have changed perhaps due to machine-tooling wear or differing abilities in machine operators. In our sniper rifle business we have detected seven common variations in diameters that we have to correct by milling either the receivers or the scope bases. If those variations are not religiously corrected, shooters may discover that their vaunted sniper rifles die at about six to eight hundred yards.

Another and more common reason for range deficiency is that ordinary scope mounts do not have a built-in twenty degree tilt so that nearly all of the elevation clicks in the scope mechanism are available. Most rifle, mount, rings, and scope combinations zero at 100 yards with just about all elevation and windage adjustments centered. That always means very limited long range capability. During the Vietnam era, scope mounts were often shimmed at the rear to allow shooting approaching 1000 yards. Windage adjustments matter little, but for long shooting, a rifle must have all of the elevation adjustments it can squeeze out.

Now, if we were shooting something better than a 7.62 NATO round, exacting elevation adjustments would not be as critical because our trajectories could be cut in half, and the flatter a bullet runs to its target the less devastating a range mis-estimate will be. It is also noteworthy that the flatter a trajectory, the less elevation adjustment necessary in a scope and the less likely that a sniper will be shooting with his scope reticle screwed to its maximum—a condition never considered best. It is unfortunate that we are wedded to the 7.62 NATO, but turning to a superior round does not seem to be in the offing.

The NATO round was adopted (over vigorous protest by some other countries and some of our own test boards) as the standard for all of NATO back in the 1950s. The round is simply a shortened 30/06. In bean counter evaluating, the shorter round saved a significant percentage of shipping space. Wonderful, we guess, but the 7.62 NATO also lost about two hundred feet per second muzzle velocity to the venerable 30/06. For infantry combat, the velocity loss was not significant, but when applying the infantry round to long range sniping, the effect is devastating.

There are many bullets (not cartridges—simply bullets) that are far more efficient than the 7.62 (.308) in the NATO weight—which we will consider to be 168 grains. In *Death From Afar II*, pages 165 and 166, we compared the popular 7mm bullet to the 168 grain .308 bullet to demonstrate what could be accomplished by a change of caliber. Those figures are worth reviewing.

A muzzle velocity of 3000 feet per second was chosen for our calculations because there is something mystical about pushing any bullet that fast. At 3000 fps (using a .30 caliber bullet weight of about 168 grains) trajectories flatten, impacts soar, recoil remains light and a "magnum length" case is not required—which means that your cartridge will feed through a normal sized action.

Unfortunately, because of limited case volume, it is extremely difficult to make a 168 grain bullet move at 3000 fps from a NATO (.308 Winchester) case. 2600 fps is more like it. That is a huge deficiency that prevents the NATO round from being loaded hotter and in these examples made more efficient. We ignore that fact to demonstrate the superior qualities of a 7mm over a .308.

Additionally, for the rest of this discussion we will refer to the 7.62 NATO as a .308 or a .308 Winchester (which it is) to simplify the wording.

Optimum Distance of a 168 grain bullet's flight: 7mm= 4700 yards. .308= 3946 yards. *Advantage 7mm.*

Ballistic Coefficients: 7mm= 630, .308= 505. *Advantage 7mm.*

Sectional Density: 7mm=.290, .308=.253. *Advantage 7mm.*

Point Blank Range—meaning a maximum range at which a bullet will not rise more than five inches above the line of sight. 7mm= 370 yards, .308= 360 yards. Advantage 7mm.

Trajectories in Inches—if you were zeroed at 400 yards but had to fire at 1000 yards? A 7mm will have 197 inches of bullet drop, as compared to a .308's 305 inches of drop. *Huge advantage 7mm.*

At 168 grains, for 1000 yard shooting, a 7mm is clearly the better bullet.

If we chose to stay with a .308 bullet, a 300 Winchester Magnum or a 300 Weatherby might seem better choices because their larger cases—using more powder—could push heavier bullets flatter which in turn would improve all of the comparisons shown above.

Unfortunately, those rounds are cursed with very short barrel life because they are over-bore. While we have had .308 *Chandler* Sniper rifles retain accuracy for more than 10,000 rounds, and all exceed 5000 rounds, a typical 300 Win. Mag. will begin to fail at 1200 rounds. You cannot have that limited barrel life in a rifle which will be regularly fired for training and marksmanship proficiency.

In the early 1950s, Philip Sharpe, at that time a most renowned ballistic expert, addressed the problem of long range, flat trajectory, using a normal-sized case that would work through a 30/06 length action by producing his 7/61 Sharpe and Hart. Sharpe's round was—more or less—a 300 H&H case shortened and necked down to 7mm. Sharpe was able to push a 175 grain 7mm bullet at 2960 feet per second using only 60 grains of powder (versus a 300 Win Mag's 71 grains). It should be added, that in the early days, reloaders had difficulty matching Sharpe's velocity claims, but with our modern powders (particularly VihtaVuori Oy powders) we can exceed those early efforts with reasonable chamber pressures. We have liked the round and many *Chandler* snipers are built on it. As expected, the rifles excel at longer ranges and barrel life is about the same as the .308s.

More recently, superior long range .308 cartridges are appearing. As most of those cartridge developments are for hunting, there can be difficulty in obtaining cartridges loaded with sniper quality bullets. We refer in part to the 300 Ultra which shows great promise, but the "hot" cartridge at this time among experimenters is the 6.5 x .284, and its adoption would be a monumental step forward because its bullet flies as flat-as-a-flounder and may prove superior to the remarkable 7mm.

When babbling about more powerful, therefore flatter shooting rounds, we have to consider details other than barrel life and flat trajectory. There is, for instance, sound signature. If the military utilizes a sniper rifle with a distinctive report, an enemy will quickly identify it. Thereafter, when that sound is heard, the general area of the shot is likely to be saturated with mortar and/or artillery fire. Combat experienced snipers often comment on that feature of their shooting—no matter from what range they were sniping.

During the Vietnam War, the Marines on Hill 55 responded to suspected sniper fire with a .50 caliber machine gun, and anyone who has been on the receiving end of that weapon will vouch for the resulting discomfort. The less distinctive the sniper's shot, the better off he will be. That places limitations on hand cannons that might otherwise seem suitable.

These authors list among the unsuitable for normal sniping calibers like the .50 BMG and the .338 Lapua. As specialty guns, they have their places but not for regular sniping. Conversely, no one could tell a 7/61 Sharpe and Hart's report from a .308, and neither shakes tree limbs, raises dust clouds, or abuses the shooter. The British have just contracted for 200 Accuracy International rifles in .338 Lapua Magnum. We hope that purchase is for very special operations.

The above comments are actually wasted—except for interest among we gun people—because military snipers shoot what they are given, and handloading or utilizing special weapons are rarely viable options. Our military snipers shoot factory match ammunition in .308 Winchester, and that is that!

In the United States military forces all snipers are trained to shoot at one thousand yards. U.S. Army doctrine lists 800 meters as a limit, but in practice—in the field—their snipers go to 1000. All United States military snipers are armed with bolt action Remingtons chambered for the .308 Winchester cartridge. The Marine Corps uses the aging Unertl 10X scope on their M40A1 rifles, but the US Army snipers who once had 10X scopes are now being better equipped with Leupold variable power telescopic sights.

We say "better equipped" because it must be remembered that military snipers work at all ranges, and in close, the field of vision offered by a fixed 10X is too small—think of the hedgerows of Normandy in WWII or most urban sniping then and now.

It is generally conceded that a shooter needs at least a twenty foot field of view at one hundred yards and a 10X typically provides only a ten or twelve foot circle. Beyond that twenty foot minimum, most snipers will realize that a thirty foot field gives them significantly more effective shooting, and thirty feet is about what the new army scopes deliver. Readers interested in examining military sniper scope applications more intensely are encouraged to read *Death From Afar Volume III*, pages 88-92 and various issues of *Tactical Shooter* magazine.

Sniper school affords the opportunity to work up individual Rifle Data Books that become essential for effective long range sniping. These books that record rounds fired and rifle maintenance include scope settings a sniper finds correct for his rifle at various ranges including the long and imaginative shots. The Data Books are of utmost importance because snipers do not shoot often enough at extreme ranges to memorize and instantly remember adjustments for less-fired ranges. It is obvious that the further out one shoots, the less margin for error there is, and a range estimation error of fifty yards or a mis-setting of elevation of even less will at extreme ranges destroy any possibility of a hit.

At least as significant is the bitter fact that following formal sniper schooling snipers do not have the range time available to maintain or improve their sharpness at longest ranges. It can be recorded with some accuracy that a military sniper is fortunate if he is able to fire at 1000 yards four times a year. In most activities, we insist on at least three times a week application.

If there is logic to steady practice—whether weightlifting, running, or piano playing—how can we believe a sniper can retain long range proficiency with only occasional practice sessions? If we apply the old "Use it or lose it" axiom, only quarterly 1000 yard practice is pathetic.

Although at a shorter range, an example of self-imposed and effective law enforcement sniper practice can provide a handy comparison to the once-every-three-months shooting. In addition to regular training, Sergeant Tim Cameron, a dedicated SWAT Commander and sniper for the St. Mary's County, MD Sheriff's department, tries to fire one shot from his sniper rifle each working day. His target becomes a small ragged hole, and if a hit prints outside that group . . . Cameron is concerned.

Snipers can be widely deployed, and fitting their highly specialized training on the few available ranges can be unpopular with everyone involved—except the snipers—and even they find it difficult to "go to the range" with the best regularity. That means that when they do shoot long, they truly need their Data Books to get them on the target with the essential first shot no matter what the distances.

It would seem obvious that snipers should also be competition shooters, the idea being that the more they shoot the better—but it is rarely so. In fact, the lack of snipers on military marksmanship teams stands out. In general, they are simply not out there. Why is that?

To many, the appeal of military sniping is as much to scouting as it is shooting. Men who are woodsy turn to sniping. The skills of silent approach, unseen observation, small team actions, deadly, and single shot accuracy on important targets are primary appeals. Snipers tend to be warriors who prefer to work alone or with only one other. Lining up and punching holes in bulls eye after bulls eye on specific commands within exacting time limits is not the same and tends to appeal to a different assembly. Shooting groups or punching repeated "X" ring hits has minuscule application to sniping, and few snipers choose the KD game.

Could snipers profit from competitive shooting? Of course, but few will participate, and that will not change even in the distant future. If snipers were required to compete on conventional courses of fire, it is these authors' opinion that most would quit and turn to other activities. We authors and rifle makers hunger to see how our best snipers would do against the best KD shooters, but the comparison is only curiosity. The games are different.

In an aside, as sniper rifle manufacturers and former competition shooters (Norman Chandler is Double Distinguished), we not only understand the value of competitive marksmanship, but we wish that those who use our rifles would enter the matches. We not only wish to see our rifles in action, but having military snipers shooting competitively will further dispel arcane beliefs that snipers are somehow suspect and probably practice some sort of below-the-belt, unfair war—or something.

We have been emphasizing that 1000 yard sniping and 1000 known distance shooting are vastly different. On the KD ranges there are helpful range flags, and KD shooting means what it says, the ranges are known.

For the sniper, range estimating is a major and essential skill always practiced. Positions on raised berms are also not part of sniping, and we believe that the KD shooter who so consistently punches bulls eyes would not do as well firing at self-determined ranges, around trees, or through barely opened lanes within brush and grass.

On the other hand, the pressures of competition—struggling to win—could be valuable to a sniper. Tensions in war are debilitating, and anything strengthening or exercising emotional control should be valued.

A major difference between sniping and other thousand yard shooting is the emphasis a sniper places on his first, cold-bore shot. He gets no zeroing rounds, and if he misses, his target is certainly gone. Perfect range estimating is essential for successful long range sniping because of that first-shot, perfect-hit requirement.

We can happily conclude, however, that the immediate future will see simplification of range estimating. Knowing exact ranges out to one thousand yards will become a simple task of applying a laser binocular/range finder to your eyes, reading the to-target distance and adjusting your scope accordingly.

Laser range finders are already issued to some shooters and quite usable models are readily available on the open market for very reasonable prices. Military snipers are now often found with personally purchased range finders tucked into a convenient pocket.

It has become ludicrous for the military to assign a sniper rifle without an accompanying laser range finder. We suppose that the arguments for not supplying range finders to combat snipers lie in the hackneyed justification that "We are waiting for a next generation that will be smaller, more efficient, and affordable." Our military is often waiting for those conditions, and because of the policy, we just as often enter the next war with the last war's weaponry.

It is sad to accept that since World War II we have been teaching range estimation by judging 100 yard football field lengths out to five fields—or five hundred yards. Thereafter, one is supposed to simply double the five-field length to estimate further distances. Fortunately, our snipers have the very fine Mil-dot scope reticle, which in knowledgeable hands can estimate as close as twenty-five yards at one thousand yard range. The Mil-dot has made for some dramatic long distance shooting, but we should be far beyond that device and into the exact measurement possible with high tech equipment.

As this section is written, Bushnell offers a 6X monocular laser range finder that is workable, reasonably durable, and fairly accurate to one thousand yards. Because of its availability at a reasonable price, that is the model many active duty snipers purchase and carry.

For those who can afford the ultimate instrument, we have long recommended the rather heavy Leica Vector 1500 range finder that is said to be accurate to 2000 yards. Our own use of the 7X instrument at 1000 yards has proven the Leica remarkable. A best example is to focus on a target at that extreme range, read 1000 yards on the internal display, then take a single step either forward or backward and observe the indicated range change by one yard at each movement. That is real accuracy, and that exactitude removes most of the problems of knowing at what range you intend to shoot.

We recall one of Gunny Hathcock's favorite stories of a memorable shot that applies to range finding at great distance. We share a clear memory of returning from the Richmond, Virginia

gun show to Virginia Beach with Carlos in the front passenger's seat. Paraphrasing his words as we remember them, Carlos said:

"I was lying well into a cane field observing across a wide canal/stream. A Hamburger (Hathcock almost always referred to enemy soldiers as Hamburgers) came out on the far bank, set up a folding chair, removed his shirt to enjoy the sun, and began to study some papers. Other armed people bustled about him, so I figured he was an officer.

"The range was so far that I could not be sure of my hold, but that distance might also allow me to try some sort of ranging shot without the rifle's report spooking the sunbather. I picked out a big lily pad-looking plant in a backwater well off to one side but at about the same distance from my rifle. I fired once, and with the sun and reflection right, I saw the bullet strike the smooth water way short of the pad. One of the Hamburgers on the bank looked up, but nobody appeared excited. I held higher, and the second bullet struck just under the pad. That time one of the people looked toward the river bank on my side but did not appear greatly disturbed. After a moment, everybody else walked away, and my target was alone. I held on the top of the shirtless guy's head, and squeezed careful. I thought he might have slumped a little, but way out there you really can't see that well.

"While I was cranking my bolt one figure came back, took a look, and all hell broke loose. Hamburgers came running out of the brush. They grabbed the shirtless officer and dragged him out of sight. I got one shot into the crowd, but I saw no result. It isn't good to just shoot into a bunch, but everybody was moving, and you don't very often make hits on anything except still targets at one thousand or so yards.

"Three shots from the same position is dangerous, so, I just slid out of there."

Beyond entertainment, Gunny Hathcock's story prompts other comment. His closing mention of three shots being too many re-emphasizes the unimportance of snipers shooting five and ten shot groups. The sniper rifle need not be a one-holer for ten shots. It must, however, be deadly for a few—no matter what the piece has been dragged through. We could elaborate for chapters on how superior durability is attained in a sniper rifle, but military snipers shoot what their service proclaims is THE rifle, so gun making techniques belong in another section.

That Hathcock was out in enemy territory alone, selecting targets, and dropping those he chose demands amplification. Even during the Vietnam Conflict, few snipers had the privilege of taking off on their own or with their teammate. That War's practice of allowing scout snipers to roam is gone. The employment of snipers is now better understood, and snipers are assigned to units and given specific duties and areas of operation. Current doctrine does not allow for free roaming snipers, and there is no probability that policy will change.

The long shooting that we tend to write about has mostly occurred from prepared positions rather than discovered opportunities such as Carlos speaks of here. Hathcock's notable long range accomplishments often followed exacting ranging shots taken before enemy appeared, and routinely from positions within defensive perimeters used and reused until the master sniper learned how to hold for almost any spot before him.

That the enemy hearing Hathcock's shots failed to discover his position or to feel the distant sound was dangerous prompts other thoughts. Experienced snipers know that when firing from extreme ranges, enemy are most likely to search for them at much shorter distances. One thousand yards away is difficult to comprehend, and sniper hunting and counter-fire are most likely to be heaviest at two and three hundred yards—distances which ordinary men feel is long shooting.

Firing over water or past distant tree clumps can seriously confuse an enemy attempting to determine the source of shots. The rifle's report will seem to come from closer-in areas.

Most importantly, sniper detectability will depend on the number of shots he attempts. One shot is extremely difficult to locate. One of the authors used to demonstrate this fact to gathered troops by having a sniper fire one unexpected shot from only one hundred yards distance. When asked where the sniper was, the troops could only guess and point toward likely looking spots that were often in exactly the wrong direction.

A second shot listened for by alerted troops was a different matter with many soldiers pinpointing their enemy, and a third round invariably

betrayed a close-in sniper's position to nearly everyone.

One thousand yards adds detection complexity because the rifle report is soft and delayed, but if a sniper continues to shoot, experienced soldiers will judge the arrival of bullets against the sound of the shots and pretty well judge the distance. Then, the mortar rounds are apt to fall, and the flanking parties get into action. The wise sniper will be long gone before those disasters occur.

Readers will be interested to hear that a technology is in development that when used for counter-sniper fire can retrace a bullet's exact flight and point and fire an attached Vulcan machine gun on the point of origin within seconds. In these days of leaky national security, it can be expected that if we get it they will soon have it as well. Makes one-shot sniping even more important, doesn't it?

Hathcock spoke of being well within a field of cane, and that encourages discussion of how hard and how rare it is to find a 1000 yard field of view to shoot across and an enemy careless enough to expose himself to such an open expanse. Step beyond your own door, and unless you live in high mountains or in the desert you will not often find 1000 yard ranges. Lying in a typical field, a rifleman can see only about fifty yards. To see 1000 yards requires elevation and open lands. In Europe, except along roads, few areas provide such vast emptiness. In our Pacific war, we cannot recall any such enchanting vistas. The Korean conflict was partially fought in the winter when ridges were bare of foliage, and the Vietnam struggle afforded long viewing from various hills and fire bases we defended.

In attacking perimeters similar to those we have sometimes defended, it is probable that skilled enemy snipers could gain positions allowing deadly long shooting. But, we should have prepared defensive fires for artillery and unit mortars backed by air strikes laid on such potential firing points. Our enemies will do the same.

All of that means that against an enemy equally trained and equally equipped, even the long range sniper must fire seldom and move regularly. In Bosnia, where the British have employed .338 Lapua Magnums, and in other third world countries, we have not faced best-trained and equipped adversaries, but somewhere down the line, we will.

We have recently surveyed active duty snipers from two services ranging from the Marine Corps' Master Scout Sniper, Neil Morris, through current scout sniper instructors, down to recent graduates of service scout sniper schools.

We have asked them a series of very specific questions and have consolidated their answers into the following short paragraphs.

1: (To combat experienced snipers only) *Do you know of any successful 1000 or more yard shots by yourself or anyone else?*

Answer: Yes, but few, and some of those were admittedly pure luck.

2: *Were those kills or shots of any tactical value?*

Answer: Varied greatly, some no value detected, a few others certain that they shot someone important.

3: *Do you believe in 1000 range sniping and should it be taught?*

Answer: Unanimous, YES.

4: *Why, if it is so rare and results are unmeasurable?*

Answer: Long sniping is a tool, and we need every tool we can get. 1000 yard sniping is a powerful confidence builder. If you can hit at that range, the closer stuff becomes simple. Snipers always keep an enemy hunched over and nervous. And, you never can tell—remember the General Officer that Carlos Hathcock shot at a huge range? That kind of thing can happen again, and we have to be ready.

5: *What is the future of 1000 yard sniping in the United States military services?*

Answer: All snipers will continue to be trained at 1000 yards. Sniping will be increasingly recognized as an essential weapon, and therefore more often and more wisely employed. That will mean that more shooting at all ranges will occur—including 1000 yards.

As equipment improves, 1000 yard sniping will become more practical. Range finders, more powerful cartridges, and increasingly better trained snipers will reinforce better leadership and more

sniper-knowledgeable officers and NCOs. The result will be more and better use of snipers.

6: *Your greatest sniping fear, if you have one?*
Answers:

That in current infantry training basic marksmanship is being neglected, and that neglect will develop into lack of understanding and therefore distrust of sniping in general.

Too much emphasis on urban, short range sniping to the neglect of the longer ranges. This is deemed important because, despite the recognition of future battles often being in cities, all of those interviewed believe that sooner or later we will face China, and those battles will be in the open where effective long shooting will be essential.

These authors concur.

Having written all of the above, certain exceptions and unmentioned details must be touched upon.

1 - The primary note is that there exists an elite brotherhood of world class snipers who can and have shot effectively—in combat—well beyond 1000 yards using the .308 Winchester cartridge.

Here is an example.

During Desert Storm, an Iraqi vehicle halted at great distance was detected by a sniper team. *It was night under an almost full moon.* The team was able to determine the vehicle's exact range using a more primitive ranging device than we now have. Two men dismounted from the Iraqi vehicle and crouched to examine documents. Using a then experimental SIMRAD Image Intensifier mounted on a .308 rifle, the sniper fired one round collapsing one man. The other dragged his companion into the vehicle and drove away. The range was just under 1300 yards.

The Kigre Inc.'s KN 200 SIMRAD is usually considered effective out to 800 yards and the .308 Winchester to 1000 yards, but here is a confirmed *planned* hit at almost 1300.

A combination of conditions combined to make the shot possible. Bright moonlight contributed, a range finder helped, and the SIMRAD made seeing possible, but the sniper who made the shot had been practicing at such ranges, he knew his tools, and he has since been recognized as a premier Master Sniper in everybody's book.

There are a handful of exceptional sniper-shooters who can and have performed similar feats. For the rest of the pack, such shooting can only be dreamed about.

2 - We have not addressed scope reticles because this section is not about eqipment, but in offering our writing to various critics it has been suggested that we need to describe the reticles applicable to 1000 yard sniping.

There are only two "best" scope reticles for such shooting. In Europe, the sharp-tipped (pencil post) has a devoted following. In the United States the crosshair reigns supreme and unchallenged. Is either superior? We believe so, and these are our arguments.

As long ago as World War I (call it 1918) competition shooters noted that as visibility declined, a tapered post user was forced to "shove" more tip into his target because the fine point—so exacting for zeroing—became lost in the darkness. Using the thicker areas of the point results in holding and hitting high.

Hunters have forever bewailed the loss of fine-point accuracy when using pencil posts in early or failing light. Post lovers usually turned to flat top posts which worked nicely on rifle ranges but covered too much animal (or enemy) in field use—and the advantage of that fine-tipped exactness of the pencil post had disappeared.

At longer ranges, the problem of disappearing tip is magnified far beyond hunter difficulties or an ordinary rifleman's 300 to 500 yards. At 1000 yards, even minute aiming changes deliver dramatic differences.

In the 1970s, Quantico user-testing compared squads of Marine shooters armed with low-power scoped M16s. The intent was to compare real world accuracy of pencil post versus crosshair reticles. The technique was to have the squads fire courses with each weapon. In normal light, little difference was detected out to 600 yards. Thereafter, pencil posts began shooting high because the fine post point was lost. In twilight, the problem intensified. The crosshair shooters were unaffected.

While far from definitive, such testing demonstrates an inherent problem with pencil post reticles at longer ranges. Low light testing drove the fact home and few should argue for the pencil.

Crosshair reticles' only weakness lies in thickness of the hairs. A typical crosshair might cover one inch at 100 yards. If the crosshair is in a variable power scopes' first focal plane, it will thicken as magnification is increased. At extreme ranges, the hair can block an aiming point or an entire target. Nearly all variable power scopes now have second plane non-enlarging reticles, and usually, the hair covers less of a target as the range increases—therefore allowing ever finer holding.

3 - We have been told that we would be remiss in not mentioning what a 1000 yard sniper rifle should be. We will describe that rifle in broad terms, but a defense of our choice could require chapters, and detailing the exact rifle would demand many more.

So, these authors believe with all of their hearts and souls that only a rifle of basic turn-bolt Mauser design with a simple composite stock allowing for perfect stock weld and a free floating barrel with the action properly bedded carrying a variable power scope mounted as strongly and as low as can be managed in the flattest shooting most accurate round obtainable is 100 percent right. Any detail varying from these basics weakens the system.

4 - Finally, for entertainment as well as amazement, we list three informal shooting competitions that our snipers sometimes enjoy. In visualizing these shoots the reader must remember that when snipers go to the range they are unlikely to number more than a handful. Having only a few shooters allows many freedoms on the ranges that most known distance marksmen will rarely experience.

Game 1. The aspirin shoot at 100 yards. There are no zeroing or warm-up shots. Miss and you are out.

Game 2. At 600 yards the target is either the end of a Coke can or a three inch spotting disk. Same rules.

Game 3. The Coke can at 1000 yards. The can is tossed onto the berm behind the butts. Any rules—including having pit personnel call the hit or miss for the snipers on line.

Chapter 4

Live Varmint Shooting at 1,000 Yards and Beyond

by Steve Hanson

I believe ultra-long range varmint shooting is actually an extreme excrescence of varmint shooting in general. All the ultra long range varmint shooters that I know endorse (to the newcomer) a menu of normal range type varmint hunting first, to allow the shooter to get one's feet wet before taking the big plunge into the world of ultra long range shooting. I will assume that the reader knows something about long range shooting and is perhaps contemplating advancing his/her varmint shooting prowess out to around 1,000 yards and beyond.

Before discussing the idea of ultra long range varmint sniping, it would be perhaps best to devise a game plan. My game plan divides my chapter into six segments which follows.

- **Choosing Cartridges and Equipment**
- **Loads and Testing**
- **Personal Experiences—Shooting Ultra-Long Range**
- **Auxiliary Equipment and Optics**
- **Ballistic Tables**
- **Appendix**

Introduction

Perceptive shooters will immediately notice that live varmint shooting at extreme range is a bit different than shooting targets at 1,000 yards. For one, your quarry will be at an undisclosed range which you won't know exactly until you make a range reading with some type of rangefinder. And unlike paper targets, varmints have a bad habit of frolicking about and ducking down their burrows at the most inopportune times.

The nature and complexities of ultra-long range varmint shooting quantifies it as a specialty sport which is generally not suited for the typical or average varmint hunter shooting a typical varmint rifle. If you expect even a modicum of success in this sport, special equipment along with a lot of practice and even some good luck from time to time will help. The mystique and uniqueness of ultra-long range varmint shooting may lure you into its trap, so be sure you are ready for the ride and have the time and patience to practice and refine your shooting skills.

Destructive varmints, such as woodchucks and rockchucks, as well as prairie dogs, make for suitable 1,000 yard targets as well as any varmint. Chucks (meaning both woodchucks and rockchucks) are larger in size over the prairie dog which, of course, gives the shooter a larger target to hit. Many ranchers welcome the varmint hunter with open arms, because when these pests are controlled via the varmint rifle rather than poisoning it means less cost and hassle for the rancher. It is also nice to know that varmint thinning by shooting rather than poisoning is environmentally friendly.

Locating a suitable 1,000 yard (or thereabouts) varmint shooting area may not be exactly easy to find. I always search for an area that is devoid of humans and livestock for miles around. Safety is an issue that we shooters can't take for granted. Post warning signs around the circumference of your shooting area if you have any doubts about safety with people wondering about. In addition, I also inform the land owner what my plans are so he is aware of the extreme shooting range involved.

If you expect to be reasonably effective at this endeavor, you should take a look at what equipment the 1,000 yard bench shooters are using. The first thing you might have noticed is that this hobby is not exactly inexpensive. Expect to pay a reasonable sum for good equipment. Custom actions, match-grade stainless steel barrels, and high magnification scopes can help to make you competitive. The next part of the equation has more to do with your commitment to the sport, rather than equipment. Don't expect right away to shoot a record target or mow down dozens of chucks at about 1,000 yards without practice. Good shooting technique and extra practice is what often separates the gold from the silver and bronze. Before you start to spend your hard earned money on equipment ask yourself— do you have the time and inclination to practice your shooting skills at ultra-long range several times a year?

Lets say at this point you are strongly considering extending your live varmint shooting to around 1,000 yards and beyond. Perhaps you are already an active 1,000 yard benchrest competi-

tor. I mention this because so many 1,000 yard shooters that I know are practicing both competition and varmint shooting. Many ultra-long range shooters bring out their 1,000 yard competition rifles to the varmint fields and have a fair chance at hitting some very distant quarry. Ultra long range varmint shooting has its rewards and its drawbacks. Be forewarned, because if you much prefer to shoot a large quantity of varmints in a short time, you best go back to shooting prairie dogs at 300 yards, ultra long range varmint shooting is probably not your cup of tea. *As you start to shoot varmints at progressively longer ranges, you are also most likely to be <u>shooting less</u> <u>and spotting more</u> for something to shoot at.* My experience in ultra long range shooting has been of a slower and more methodological nature.

Choosing Cartridges and Equipment

The logical thing to consider first in this endeavor would be cartridge selection. Once you have selected a cartridge, you can move on to the configuration of your ultra-long range rifle.

At the light end of the spectrum we find a few extra-long range varmint shooters who find favor with a large powder capacity .224 caliber wildcat. Wildcat cartridges such as the .22/6mm Remington, or .224 Clark, or the .22/284 Winchester chambered in a custom rifle and setup to shoot 75 grain or 80 grain or heavier VLD (Very Low Drag) type of projectiles can provide surprisingly good long range results. I

The common prairie dog provides a challenging 1,000 yard target.

Chucks can be difficult to locate, once the range exceeds 1000 yards.

have yet to shoot a varmint at a bona fide 1,000 yards with a .22 caliber, but I have been informed that it has been accomplished more than a few times.

I have used my custom 22/6mm Remington (which has a 9" twist Pac-Nor barrel) loaded with 70 grain VLD bullets to take varmints out to 806 yards. While I have shot a few custom rifles chambered for the .224 Clark loaded with 80 grain projectiles out to around the 1/2 mile marker with better than expected results, I think most experienced shooters consider the .224 Clark and other large .22 caliber wildcats a little light for consistently effective varminting out to 1,000 yards or so. In my opinion, an increase in bullet weight is what is needed for more precise work out to around 1,000 yards.

I tend to think a varmint rifle chambered in one of the hotter 6mm cartridges would be more appropriate and have more potential over a hot .224 caliber wildcat. I have rifles chambered for the 6mm Remington, the 6mm Remington Ackley Improved, and the 6mm/284 Winchester. I tend to shoot my 6mm Remington at varmints out to about 700 yards, or so. My other two 6mm rifles are most often selected when my quarry is

ranged from around 700 to 800-900 yards.

By and large, I think most shooters would have better luck with larger calibers starting with the 6.5mm. The 6.5mm is blessed with many new aerodynamic bullets in the 130-155 grain weight range. The downrange momentum and energy from these projectiles make for an easier to spot impact point over the smaller caliber projectiles. I have custom rifles chambered for the 6.5mm/284 and the 6.5-06 Ackley Improved. Both of these rigs have 8" twist barrels to shoot the 140 -155 grain VLD bullets.

In recent years, I have been shooting my 7mm STW with the heavier VLD type of projec-

Bob Boyd displays his dual purpose 1,000 yard competition/varmint rifle. This custom rig weighs 80 pounds, and is chambered for the wildcat .330 Baer. It is one of the few 1,000 yard rifles you still see with a walnut stock. It has a Geske action, and a fluted 35" Lilja barrel, topped off with a Nightforce scope. Bob's load launches a 300 grain Sierra at 2800 fps.

The author's ultra-long range cartridges L to R: 6.5mm/06 Improved, 7mm STW, .338/416 Rigby Improved.

tiles for shooting at ranges over 1000 yards. With my 7mm STW I killed a chuck at 1542 yards, and this remains my best shot with a 7mm rifle. The .308 caliber has a very good selection of bullets, but I felt I needed more bullet weight for shots over 1400 yards, or so, and I moved up to the .338 caliber. My .338/416 Rigby Improved remains my ultimate machine for knocking off very distant chucks.

Questions and opinions

If a varmint hunter asked you to build a ultra-long range varmint rifle, with the intention of using it at ranges starting at 1000, and out to around 1500 yards; but the rifle might also see some action in Unlimited Class competition, at the 1000 yard matches. Can an effective dual purpose rig, as described, be built, or are there too many compromises involved?

Bruce H. Baer 1000 yard competitor and custom gunsmith

"Yes, a dual purpose rifle can be built, as I have built many. The customer has to understand to be competitive in the Unlimited class, rifle control on the sandbag is very important. As to that I recommend a rifle that weighs 50-70 pounds; with a stock diameter of 5" to 6" wide in the front for torque control."

Dan Lilja President of *Lilja Precision Rifle Barrels, Inc.*

"Yes a dual purpose rifle would work. Probably a 338/416 Rigby or a 338/378 Wby."

Bruce A. Thom President of *BAT Machine Co. Inc. :*

"No compromises would be needed. My first choice would be a .308 Baer or similar case. For shooting at a 3 to 4 x 6" target I feel accuracy is far more important than velocity."

In your opinion, are the top 1000 yard competition cartridges, also the best for ultra-long range varmint hunting? (1000 yards and over)

Bruce H. Baer 1000 yard competitor and custom gunsmith

"In most cases yes. When you have A: car-

tridges that are able to shoot tiny groups at 1000 yards with a very good remaining energy and velocity. There are many cartridges capable of shooting small groups at 1000 yards when the conditions are good but cannot handle wind changes like the bigger 30 cailbers. For the longer shots out to 1500 yards you need all the help you can get in both varmints and competition."

Bruce A Thom President of *BAT Machine Co. Inc. :*

"I don't think you could go wrong with the 30 calibers that do most of the winning. The 338 caliber is also gaining a following and should be a consideration."

Eric Williams Ph.D. is a research chemist and a former columnist for *Precision Shooting Magazine.* Eric has been involved in shooting .50 caliber rifles for some time and is also a member of the Fifty Caliber Shooters Association. For those who might someday be interested in shooting the fifty caliber I could think of no other person to help answer a few questions. For more information read Eric's chapter—Living In Half Inch Heaven—in *The 1992 Precision Shooting Annual.*

Gerry Geske holding his 45 pound custom rifle that features, of course, a Geske action. This rifle is chambered for the .338-378 Weatherby, and has a 36" inch Lilja barrel in a barrel block. It is an example of a typical rifle you see at many 1,000 yard matches. This type of rifle also works well for 1,000 -plus yard varmint shooting.

I asked **Eric Williams** the following questions:

If you had the inclination to use a .50 caliber on varmints, in what configuration would you build your rifle, as to the total rifle weight, type and brand of action, barrel contour and length, stock design, muzzle brake, etc.?

"I would not be inclined to build a fifty caliber solely for the purpose of varmint hunting. With regards to varmint hunting, the same performance (not considering terminal energy) can be obtained with the likes of a .30/378 Weatherby in a package that is much easier to tote and much cheaper to shoot. In general, my experience in hunting with fifties leaves me with the belief that they are a pain in the butt to hunt with. They are very difficult to get in and out of a vehicle because of their size and weight, and you can't carry them very far. Added to that, one has to have more concern regarding the impact of stray fifty caliber bullets.

This doesn't mean that I wouldn't hunt varmints with any fifties that I own; I have, indeed, done so. The fifties that I prefer to employ for varmint hunting are the ones which are the most accurate and the most comfortable to shoot. I'm basically talking about a fifty built specifically for competitive 1000 yard benchrest shooting. A typical gun in this category might be built on a McMillan bolt action and possess a barrel of 1.5-1.75 inch diameter and 30" to 35" in length. This rifle would likely weigh 50 lbs. (the weight limit for the FCSA heavy gun class). The stock would be either a McMillan or Six Enterprises fiberglass with built in runners. I would use a muzzle brake which exits from the sides rather than the type with ports around the whole circumference. When you're sending 250 grains of powder down the barrel, you can kick up a lot of dirt with a muzzle brake which directs gasses downward.

Also of importance, I would prefer to use frangible bullets (Hornady A-Max or custom lead core swaged). The solids, which tend to be the preferred bullets of the match shooters, have a greater ricochet potential and tend to wear barrels faster."

At what range would you start thinking about putting your .50 caliber varmint rifle into service, if your targets were very distant rockchucks and you had no viable means of getting closer to your target.?

"This is difficult to answer because the maximum effective range capability of the fifty caliber on quarry similar to rockchucks depends a lot on other factors. Of greatest significance is the atmospheric conditions and the ability to measure range. If you wanted a hit probability of greater than about 80% and you had windy conditions and no ranging device, I'd limit my shots to no more than 300 yards. On the other hand, I'd give an experienced shooter behind a finely tuned match rifle on a calm day with a laser-ranged target a greater than 50% probability of hitting a chuck at 1000 yards.

With high ballistic coefficient, fifty caliber bullets which have a transonic range of around 2500 yards, I'd be willing to take some pot-luck shots at ranges considerably farther than 1000 yards. I wouldn't have high expectations for those shots, but it sure would be fun."

Choosing your Rifle

After having made up your mind about a cartridge, you are ready to ponder the possibilities of your rifle. If you have chosen a factory cartridge, you might opt to also choose a factory rifle and tune it up. The quality of the trigger will most likely need some attention, unless you have chosen a top-end semi custom rifle. By and large, I find that most shooters who are extremely interested in shooting varmints at extreme range are willing and motivated to purchase a custom special purpose rifle assembled for the express purpose of sniping varmints out to around 1,000 yards. Frequently, a special purpose custom varmint rifle may also see use as a 1,000 yard competition rifle. Heavy custom rifles utilizing stout single shot bolt action designs seem to be the most popular.

As far as selecting a stock for your rifle, you have many choices. Heavy synthetics are currently in favor, however the newer aluminum stock is making a showing at 1,000 yard matches. The progression of high-tech stocks has been interesting. During the 70's the laminated stock was in vogue, then came the synthetic stock, now the aluminum stock is being experimented with. It remains to be seen if the aluminum stock will offer an real advantage and become the new standard.

The 1,000 yard varmint shooting enthusiast will most likely be shooting from a portable bench. The sturdy portable bench will give the shooter the necessary stable platform to perform his miracles from. Without a bench, a low bipod would be my second choice, assuming the particular rifle in use has a bipod stud attached. Most of my varmint rifles that I might consider for this type of shooting weigh over 20 pounds, and as such they perform much better when shot from a bench. A bench that rotates will solve the problems of shooting multiple varmints that are facing you at many different angles. Make sure your portable bench is solid and stable enough for the weight of rifle that you plan to be shooting. A 40 pound rifle may not rest well on a 20 pound bench!

I discovered a most noteworthy heavy duty rotating bench made by Varmint Masters LLC. This exceptional bench is called the BR Pivot and is the smoothest bench I have seen yet—it even works well with my 52 pound custom .338/416. The BR Pivot will soon be my newest shooting bench.

Let's say you've already decided on having

Duane Capehart shooting his dual purpose 1,000 yard competition/varmint rifle. This rig is chambered in .308 Baer, and features a BAT action attached to a 31" Krieger barrel. It is topped off with a Nightforce 12-42X scope. The aluminum stock is from Rick Piccarreta of RDP Rifles. The goal of the aluminum stock is to dampen barrel vibrations, which in theory, will produce more consistent long range accuracy.

your own very special custom rifle built—I strongly recommend that you first build it on "paper." Make a list of all your chosen parts that will make-up your custom rifle. When your list is complete, go over it several times while you conceptualize and determine if all the parts are truly compatible and complementary.

Dan Lilja President of *Lilja Precision Rifle Barrels, Inc.*
I asked Dan about the configuration of an extreme range varmint rifle:

"For long range rock chuck hunting I would look for a rifle that is chambered for a big cartridge, "over bore" for its bullet diameter. To take advantage of the newer high BC bullets it has to have a fast twist and extra length will help velocities. The whole rig should be big and heavy with the barrel as big in diameter as is practical to retain stiffness. These rifles are not meant to be carried any farther than from the pickup to the shooting bench. Rifle weights of 40-50 pounds or more are not unreasonable. When shooting at a small target that far away the ultimate in accuracy is a must. This accuracy must come from both the rifle and the bullet after it has left the barrel."

The Custom bolt actions:

Most often I find the serious ultra long range shooter will be shooting a non traditional varmint rifle and projectile. Custom rifles and wildcats tend to become the norm, rather than the exception. Extra heavy rifles (16 pounds and up) are also more common in conjunction with the larger calibers. The true dedicated ultra-long range aficionado will have some means to accurately range his distant varmints and will also utilize some type of a ballistic program to develop a bullet trajectory chart.

There are several reasons for going the full custom route when assembling your custom rifle. Some reasons are pretty straightforward, but some shooters also mention reasons a little more on the esoteric side.

Say you are going with an extra large varmint cartridge for ultra-long range shooting, with the likes of a wildcat based on the .378 Weatherby, or perhaps the .416 Rigby case. Now with the cartridge choice out of the way, you start to present your idea to a few accuracy-oriented rifle-smiths and are flabbergasted when they turn down your custom project and want nothing to do with your large wildcat—if your wish is to chamber it in any "ordinary" commercial factory bolt action.

The reason is simple, most gunsmiths would rather err on the side of caution, and build a rig that is over-engineered instead of something marginal. (What if you decide to test a "proof-load" or accidentally fire an "over-load" and nearly blow-apart your factory action and become injured in the process?) Most conservative and conscientious custom rifle-smiths would also look at bolt thrust numbers generated from a

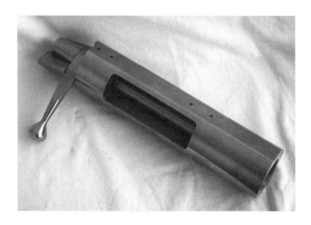

Bruce Thom's 10" BAT action.

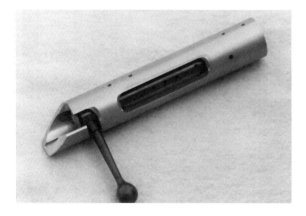

The Geske action above is a large action making it suitable for big wildcats. Photo courtesy of Gerry Geske.

big wildcat. Dan Lilja tells me a big case such as the .378 Weatherby, when loaded to a chamber pressure of 65,000 PSI, will generate a bolt thrust of some 12,760 pounds! A Remington 700 bolt would only offer bolt lug shear strength of about 37,480 pounds. While big custom actions designed for such cartridges as the Geske, and the large BAT actions have bolt lug shear strengths of 72,620 pounds and 69,770 pounds respectively. (This should help to keep you out of trouble and add peace of mind.)

Arcane reasons for going full custom could be, in part, for better re-sale potential. In fact sometimes a particular custom action may end-up costing about the same, or only a little more than a re-worked and blue-printed factory action. The reason for this is that you won't (or shouldn't) be spending money on a new custom action to bring it up to accuracy standards, i.e. squaring and truing etc. Some shooters also like to join an elite crowd and own something that suggests it's the best in its class. It has also been conveyed to me that some shooters favor custom actions by such a big margin that they compare it to a race driver building an exotic, custom high-bread racing machine complete with a state of the art engine, (the engine in this case would be comparable to a rifle barrel) only to compromise the project by using a basic army Jeep for the body! (in a rifle the army Jeep body would be comparable to the action) Then, again, there are shooters who prefer actions that are heavier and stiffer than normal. Another popular reason is that many times you simply have more choices to personalize your custom rig with options that are not available (or readily available) with factory actions. These options would include, (but not limited too), a titanium firing pin, (for faster primer ignition—i.e. lock time), and actions with bases and rings attached that have been machined at various angles for increased scope elevation. Or the shooter can completely change gears and opt for an action with a more ergonomically correct (for right-handed shooters) right-bolt with a left-port configuration.

I should point out that for my own piece of mind, while shooting custom rifles with right-bolts, and left-ports, I have always gone with a design that places the gas-vents on the opposite side from my face, so if I ever pierce a primer, or shoot a case that decides to come apart, it will vent on the opposing side where it will cause no bodily harm.

Chambering and Throating

Choosing a pre-planned bullet for your new rig can be tricky indeed. Sometimes it works, and sometimes your specific bullet won't shoot worth beans. You won't discover this possible dislike to a particular bullet until later, of course, when your custom rig is all finished and you start testing it. It would be best if you chose a range of bullets that are similar—that is in weight, length, style, and ballistic coefficient. This way, if one particular bullet refuses to shoot well you have others to fall back on in reserve. However, I am aware that sometimes only one bullet may be available in certain calibers with regard to a particular weight, and style, and therefore you may not have any other choices or back-up bullets. If this is the case, then you can only cross your fingers and pray that your one-bullet rifle will shoot well.

Does your rifle-smith have a reamer in stock for chambering your chosen cartridge? If he has a reamer,—does he know what the throat length is? Is the throat compatible with your chosen bullet? You may need to make up a "dummy"

cartridge (no primer or powder) to give to your rifle-smith with your bullet seated to the overall length that you deem best. Perhaps you need a slightly shorter overall length so your cartridges will fit into a magazine? If you are using a single shot action, or plan to load and shoot as a single shot, then you have the option to extend the bullet out a little further and gain addition powder space. Here again, use a little judgment. It would be best not to extend your throat out to the very maximum, because, as you shoot over the years your throat is going to erode and lengthen. If you left some extra neck-space, with regard to your "dummy" cartridge, then later you can compensate for this erosion to some degree and adjust your over-all-length (OAL) to again seat your bullet closer to the rifling.

While on the subject of chambering, you might also ask your rifle-smith if he can chamber you a set of loading dies at the same time he is chambering your rifle. The goal here, of course, is to achieve a perfect match between your

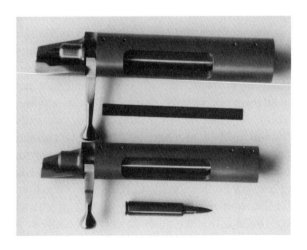

Hall Express actions: the "G" action on top with the original Express action, the "E" on the bottom. Author had a 7mm STW built around the "E" action. Photo courtesy of Allan Hall.

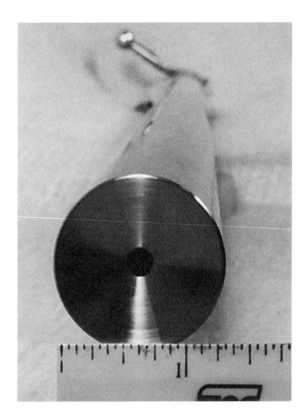

For enhanced long range accuracy, varmint shooters commonly opt for a heavier than normal, large diameter barrel.

chamber and dies with the expectations that you can make better and more accurate hand-loads.

Barrels

This would definitely not be the part to economize on! The barrel is *one* part of the custom rifle that can make the biggest difference in accuracy, and is said by many to be the *most important* part of any rifle. Personally, I wouldn't choose anything less than a match-grade barrel for any custom rifle that I would be thinking about.

Many choices need to be made when specifying a barrel for your custom rig. Among these are barrel material, twist rate, length, contour, exterior finish, to flute or not, throating, crown type, and whether or not you opt for cryogenic treatment at this point. With all this in mind... yes, It's understandable, (and even politically correct), if you start pulling out a little hair, ... it happens to the best of us at some point in our lives.

There are two basic types of custom match-grade or premium grade of barrels made today: the more common button rifled variety and those with cut-rifling. While there are strong proponents of each type ready to debate the merits of each process, I have never come across any categorical evidence that states one method is decidedly better, or more accurate. Personally, I have had good luck with both types of barrels, and cannot even state empirically as to which type is the best.

Stainless or Chrome-Moly barrels which do you usually recommend to your customers?

Bruce A Thom President of *BAT Machine Co. Inc. :*
"All I use are stainless steel barrels. This is mostly because customers request them. I believe they do last longer."

Doug Shilen of *Shilen Inc.:*
"The stainless barrels are a better value for the money over the chrome-moly barrels. Two primary reasons:
a) Less maintenance, because of the rust resistance.
b) Longer accuracy life, because of better resistance to throat erosion."

Chris Dichter President of *Pac-Nor Precision Rifle Barrels:*
"Stainless—has higher chromium content, throats last longer. * Special note: 416 gun quality stainless steel is less abrasion resistant than chrome-moly. Bad cleaning practices i.e. aluminum cleaning rods, not using bore guides, using stainless brushes in stainless steel barrels, can and do scratch good stainless barrels."

Darrell Holland of *Holland's Gunsmithing:*
"I feel that stainless steel will last approximately 25% longer than a chromemoly barrel. (Provided it is taken care of) The biggest problem with chromemoly being the corrosion wrecking the barrel before one shoots it out. The average shooter does not clean the rifle correctly or thoroughly. Moisture collects in the barrel and after a season or two we start to see pitting in the bore. This contributes to increased fouling and poor accuracy. I always try to use a good quality stainless barrel unless the customer is adamant about a chromemoly one. Most of the chromemoly barrels are made from 4140 or 4150 steel, the 4150 being the better of the two. Accuracy, well both barrels if made correctly will shoot extremely well. The stainless steel might have a slight edge due to it's better machine-ability."

Dan Lilja President of *Lilja Precision Rifle Barrels, Inc.:*
"I always suggest a stainless steel barrel if asked. Stainless barrels will last longer, being more resistant to erosion from powder. And with our barrels at least, we can get a little better internal finish when they're lapped. This results in a little bit less fouling and better accuracy. Normally the only people that buy a chromemoly barrel are those that have a nice wood stock and they want a conventional bluing job to go with it."

Barrel Fluting and Barrel Rigidity

Fluting a barrel can help to keep a barrel cooler due to more surface area, but the practical effect is subtle and is often overstated. The major attraction to barrel fluting is with its weight reduction benefits. Fluting a barrel lessens its weight without *appreciably* reducing its stiffness, *(the latest tests I've read, indicate that a very slight reduction in rigidity takes place when one flutes a barrel).* Say you started with a five pound, number seven contour barrel and fluted said barrel down to weigh 4.5 pounds; now you have a stiffer barrel over that of a 4.5 pound non-fluted number six contour barrel of the same length.

Barrel contour also has a correlation with barrel length as pertaining to barrel stiffness and rigidity. A rifle barrel increases in rigidity with the fourth power of its diameter and decreases with the third power of its length. This works out that a 2" inch diameter barrel is 16 times stiffer than a 1" inch diameter barrel of the same length. Using this formula we find that a 1" inch diameter 24" inch barrel is 49% stiffer than a 30" inch tube of same diameter; and if you wished to keep the rigidity of the 30" inch tube equal to the 24" inch barrel it would have a diameter of 1.25" inches.

Barrel Bedding Blocks

If you are thinking of building a very long range and very heavy varmint rifle, you might consider using a barrel block. Barrel blocks are usually larger in diameter than most actions and help support very heavy and long barrels without stressing the barrel thread shank or the action. With a barrel block setup the barrel is either epoxied into the block or a split block is used with the barrel clamped in. In any case, the block is pillar bedded to the stock and the action and remainder of the barrel are floating. The method by which a barrel block supports a barrel gives

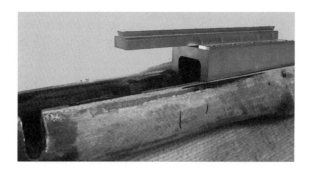

This large barrel bedding block also incorporates a scope mount rail.

the effect of increased barrel rigidity and therefore more accuracy potential. With a barrel block setup you gain rigidity without resorting to using a shorter barrel. You will find that many 1000 yard benchrest competitors have been shooting barrel blocked rifles for years with good success.

Loads and Testing

It seems like we varmint shooters are always testing some type of load and bullet. My personal goal of acceptable varmint accuracy at 100 yards is to perfect a load with an average 5 shot group size of under .50," and I much prefer an even smaller group average. However, shooting 100 yard groups with an ultra-long range rifle gives me little information about grouping potential at 1000 yards. Granted there are not that many 1000 yard rifle ranges around, but if you look around hard enough you may find a 600 yard range for you to work up loads and practice. It is important to test each rifle/cartridge combination at or near its dedicated range before heading out on a varmint safari.

Your final results are limited by the weakest link in your system. Your weakest link could originate from some part of your rifle or scope, or could have more to do with load consistency or simply from a lack of practice. Testing will hopefully show you any weak links and give you confidence in your ability to reach way out there and knock out those varmints. Many things need to fall into place before success usually happens. My longer range rifles will get checked and tuned at 500 or 600 yards.

I have even taken my extra-long and ultra-long range rifles way out in the "sticks" to practice. After setting up my portable bench and a few wind flags, I will place targets out to 700 or 800 yards and proceed to test group size, and of course, my predicted bullet impact and drop.

When testing groups at long range, pay special attention to vertical dispersion. Vertical dispersions due to variation in muzzle velocity will be exaggerated at extreme ranges. The cure is to strive for a minimum extreme spread in velocity. Sometimes a simple cure is to change primers and retest. Lacking a barrel vibration tuning device, about the only other cure is to adjust and tune your powder charges for the least vertical dispersion, while keeping an eye on standard deviation and extreme spread.

For over a decade I have been using computer ballistic programs from several different sources. When these programs came on the scene the shooter was able to program a trajectory chart that corresponded to his rifle and loads. This trajectory, or bullet drop chart, comes in especially handy for the long range shooter who also has access to an accurate range-finding device. However, I soon noticed that most ballistic programs gave slightly different numbers between brands, even with exactly the same information plugged into them. Then too, after testing at long range I discovered my actual bullet drop was sometimes off by a few inches (or more) when compared to the ballistic programs printout.

I developed a method to compensate for this deviance. Sight in at 100 yards very carefully and then precisely note your bullets impact at 100, 200, 300, and with longer range rifles 500 or 600 yards and if possible 1,000 yards. Return to the computer ballistic program and "fudge" the ballistic coefficient of your bullet slightly either up or down to match your actual bullet drop at the ranges tested. This way your ballistic trajectory chart will more precisely match your actual bullet drop throughout it's range. This relatively simple "real-world" adjustment should help your long range potential and allow you to hit your intended varmint a little sooner with less ammunition expended.

You may discover that your impact will be perfectly predicted by a ballistic program at one distance and off at another distance. The best way around this dilemma would be to use the correct ballistic information that best matches the range that you shoot most often, and then note your impact deviance at other ranges. You may also discover your "fudged" ballistic coefficients may work perfectly with one ballistic program, but may not work correctly with another ballistic program.

An alternate way (with the die hard experimenter in mind) would be to use two chronographs and figure your own personal ballistic coefficients. Keep in mind, for this to work accurately you need to keep very precise measurements between chronographs and also record the local barometric pressure, temperature and humidity, plus note the altitude. One shooter that I know who tried this method noted that he still needed to fudge his personal ballistic coefficient to match his computer program.

High ballistic coefficient bullets

Normal varmint bullets have a lower ballistic coefficient (B.C.) as compared to a true Very Low Drag (VLD) bullet and, as such, they are blown (actually deflected) off course easier. When you start to shoot varmints out to the ranges in this category, you need all the help you can get and the majority of normal varmint type bullets just don't quite make it. High B.C. projectiles are the most popular with this clan of shooters. Once you enter the realm of extra-long range shooting and push the range envelope of my category, you can almost automatically disregard bullet expansion as a factor, even if you are shooting a true extra-frangible varmint bullet, because most likely impact velocity will fall below the threshold of effective bullet expansion. Hits to the vital organs, (or very near to a vital

The author attempting to wrestle his 52 pound .338/416 to his pickup truck.

organ), of the varmint are required to anchor a very distant critter whether or not you are shooting a true varmint type bullet, a VLD projectile, or a match-grade target bullet. However, I have discovered a tendency for long VLD type bullets to sometimes tumble when they hit a critter, and this tumbling action is quite destructive and instantly lethal. Bullets that display good accuracy with a fairly high ballistic coefficient are the prime requisites for success here.

A fairly small increase in B.C. will flatten trajectory more and show less wind deflection, than merely an increase in velocity of 100 to 150 fps. A computer ballistic program is a good way to compare the down-range performance of various bullets at various velocities. If you've played with ballistic programs before, you probably already discovered that velocity has more effect on bullet trajectory, and ballistic coefficient has more effect with wind deflection.

One important point to remember about VLD bullets is that they almost always shoot best when either almost touching the lands, or just touching the lands, or firmly pressed into the lands. (You will have to experiment a little in this regard to find out.) If you are shooting a hot cartridge and loading VLD bullets, you must keep an extra careful eye on throat erosion, because before you realize it your throat can move forward .010" and accuracy can go sour fast! This also means it may not be wise to load upwards of 500 rounds at one sitting at the original overall length (OAL) of a cartridge that was measured and setup for a new barrel and throat. I try to remember to check the throat of a hot cartridge chamber every 150 rounds, or so, and adjust my bullet seating depth if necessary. Most normal bullets, (or non VLD), are more forgiving with their relationship to the rifling, and accuracy degrades slower.

Personal Experiences—Shooting Ultra-Long Range

My Ultimate Shot

Under the clear star-laden sky, the full moon was casting an eerie spotlight on us as the crickets unrelentingly sang their song. As we packed our supplies in my truck, it felt strange starting a varmint hunt so early, but then again this outing was not intended to be an ordinary hunt. We were preparing to do battle with the Western rockchuck again, but this was a very different type of hunt and these conditions were very different from your so-called normal long-range varmint shoot. You see, we were heading to a spot where, in order to connect, we had to shoot across a long Rocky Mountain canyon to hit these "hermit" chucks. The range was previously checked out, (courtesy of Barr & Stroud), at 1640 meters or 1794 yards! We left early in order to be at a pre-ordained spot before sunup. We learned that usually the best time for such ultra-long range shots is at first sun (before the wind and mirage get a foothold! This shoot at the crack of dawn theory works some of the time, but it's certainly not foolproof.

Perhaps I should regress to the day before to explain how this all started. My informal guide Alan Brown, a local native from around this remote Montana outpost, had previously tried to connect on these very same chucks from the same spot with his 35 pound custom target rifle chambered for the .300 Weatherby. Alas, Alan was defeated with his earlier attempts by the range, wind, mirage, loads, and who knows what else. However, after talking with Alan about our mutual interests in shooting, and his discovery that I possessed a very-long-range rifle, he escorted me to this remote spot to check out these far-out "hermit" chucks, as Alan called them. This particular colony of chucks were entrenched atop a small mountain and far across a canyon, and there appeared to be no other location from which to shoot these chucks. I had along my Barr & Stroud rangefinder and made several range

Author's .338/416 Rigby Improved on a portable bench and ready for action.

readings to these chucks. We refrained from shooting that afternoon because of the strong mirage and wind; it would have been totally fruitless. Later that day we made plans to try an early sunrise morning hunt.

Upon our early predawn arrival at our shooting post, this "back-forty" colony of rockchucks soon followed our prediction by slowly crawling out of their dens to warm themselves on the fresh sun-bathed rocks. Before they even poked their noses out that morning, we aimed plenty of high magnification glass towards their location, (no less than 2 pairs of spotting scopes and my 20X binoculars, plus the 14X Barr & Stroud range finder). My 52 pound custom .338/416 Rigby Improved set stable atop my portable bench, which was also aimed toward these fur-balls who were more than a mile in range from our location. My enthusiasm dropped a notch after locating these targeted "fuzzies" in my Nightforce scope and noting their extremely small apparent size, even with my scope cranked up to 42X magnification. I tried to mentally dispel this dash of premature disappointment and doubt of ever connecting, as I double checked the prevailing wind conditions with my Davis turbo meter—(a wind speed indicator.)

We were in luck. My wind meter confirmed the atmosphere as calm with gusts up to a mere 2-3 mph. Temperature was around 50°f with a light hazy sun. I figured it was about time to fire up my "cannon" and see what I could do at this distance. Twenty yards or so, to the right of two standing chucks was the spot (on a lighter than normal colored rock) I chose to check bullet impact and the accuracy of my ballistic computations. As I released the trigger, boom, my shot bellowed, and after nearly three seconds of bullet travel time we saw impact on yet a different rock, as my 300 grain bullet hit about four feet to the right and about one foot high. Gyroscopic (spin) drift came to mind for the probable cause of most of my bullet drift. But of course, who knows how much wind was pushing my bullet around during the long flight over the canyon. I was guessing that my normal accuracy dispersal would lend me to a normal group size at this range of about 1.5 to 2.5 feet! You see, I have never shot on paper at this range to actually check my group size, but in retrospect, it would

have been a good idea. For correction I "clicked" my scope for both elevation and drift as per my spotter impact. Usually I do not correct my scope (with clicks) for lateral compensation, however, in this situation I was shooting at basically one range with little apparent wind deviation involved, and I figured this technique, under the circumstances, would give me the best chance of making a hit.

After my initial shot, one of the chucks went subterranean, but the other became curious about my bullet impact and wandered over in that direction. I quickly loaded another round and found that chuck in my scope. Carefully I squeezed the trigger with my allowance for apparent drift and elevation that was observed from my test shot. My correction for aim ultimately found my 300 grain Sierra whizzing only inches over the targeted chucks head. As it turned out, that was about the closest near hit I had all morning. I fired ten well meaning shots (11 counting my test spotter shot at a rock) at this colony, and during this time the wind slowly increased its intensity. Then, concurrently with a temperature increase, some mirage started to become very apparent with its wavy optical effects, and my shooting was over for the day. I had some very close misses and actually did not feel too bad about my cannonade, even though I did not connect. I felt sort of bound by this type of shooting, and with so many near hits I felt compelled to try this again. However, I had only one more day to complete my mission before I had to pack up and head for my home barn.

Meanwhile, Alan had fired 9 rounds towards these chucks, but was again unsuccessful. Alan loaded his .300 Weatherby with Sierra's 220 grain MatchKing bullet, a wonderfully accurate bullet, but at the distance we were shooting it was somewhat difficult to see and precisely locate its impact. Perceived bullet impact was imprecise for at least six of his nine shots.

The next day started as a repeat of the day before, except for one factor, my wind speed indicator was acting dead. The highest reading we were able to observe was .5 mph! This was always a good sign for shooting—a dead calm! About the only negative thing, at the time, was that a swarm of hungry mosquitoes were out buzzing around near us and we were considered breakfast. Alan decided not to shoot his rifle that morning, instead he opted to help me out as a spotter and man the spotting scopes.

Once sunrise was upon us, it was time to peer through my Nightforce optics atop my wildcat .338 "cannon" again. My initial view through the scope yielded eight chucks, of which two were standing. I had always considered lateral group dispersion (with more factors effecting it) a more difficult correction, versus vertical elevation, especially at this range, so correspondingly I chose a big horizontal positioned chuck as my target. To make a rather long story short, I missed with my first seven shots, however, Alan thought I was close enough with one shot to clip some hair!

This was an encouraging factor for me and with my eighth shot I tried to concentrate extra hard on shot placement. The wind was not a big factor, as our posted wind flag laid virtually dead in the vertical mode. Mirage was light and workable, (it slowly crept in with a light vertical boil). For my eighth shot of the morning, I believed I had located my initial targeted chuck of the morning, (a chuck with a bigger, lighter colored head), so again I aligned him in my scope's view. After a bit of time lag during bullet flight, Alan and I both witnessed something fairly rare at this range—my targeted chuck being blown back by bullet impact! Yes, I actually connected at this extreme range!! It goes without saying we were ecstatic. It took awhile, but I did it with a total of "only" 19 shots during two mornings, under near

perfect shooting conditions. After I made this "mile-long" shot I almost expected old Rod Serling of *The Twilight Zone* to mystically appear before us and finalize the event with a bizarre narrative epilogue. I was floating on "cloud-nine" and felt naturally high.

We packed our gear in my truck and made an arduous end-around hike to the rockchuck colony, where I made my 1794 yard shot. There laid on a rock was a lifeless chuck, which confirmed my ultimate shot.

I do believe the 300 grain .338 caliber Sierra's helped considerably by allowing me and my spotter to see my bullet impact. They simply have more momentum at extreme range over most of the .30 caliber projectiles, and this factor enabled us to see my bullet impact splatter easier at extended range. Missed shots are a lot more common than hits, so the shooter must learn from this and correct for his missed shots. However, if you can't get a good "reading," or location mark from your bullet impact, (as when bullet weight and momentum are too low), then how are you going to correct and aim for the next shot?

Ultra-long range varmint shooting may, or may not, be your cup of tea, but you will never know until you try. I know of a few varmint shooters who were considered "all-purpose" type of shooters and hunted at many different ranges, but after becoming involved in this ultra-long range business they have practically given up with the short range stuff and now concentrate on their long shots exclusively.

Problems at ultra-long range

Shooting in the wind

At an early age, we all discovered that our planet Earth was "programmed" for both gravity and wind, but most of us probably didn't really think that much about it unless we became interested in the shooting sports. Most long range varmint hunters find that wind is by far more difficult to compensate for. Chronographs, computer ballistic programs, and rangefinders can help the varmint hunter tremendously as far as compensating for bullet drop. But coping with the wind is a whole new ball game. Wind is the varmint hunter's Achilles heel, because it can vary so much, so

A Leupold 12-40X60mm Variable power spotting scope helps the author locate distant varmints.

quickly and shift direction on a whim. Predicting its deflecting effect on a bullet at long range can sometimes seem hopeless. While most of my better long range kills have occurred under mild atmospheric conditions, I still get lucky, occasionally, with a great calculated windage shot. Still, I usually don't shy away from shooting in the wind (unless we're talking about gusts over 35-40 mph). Gusty winds may considerably shorten my effective range and my percentage of long-range hits will certainly take a nose-dive. But in order to keep in practice and continue to learn about what the wind does to my projectiles at long range, I must keep on shooting.

A 90° degree crosswind from the shooter's location actually has more effect and will cause more total deflection of a bullet, versus the same crosswind, say 500 yards downrange at the target, even though the bullet is traveling at a much lower velocity when it reaches the target. The experts say this is so because the lateral bullet deflection that originated from the shooters location has more time to deviate off course before it comes close to the intended target. The ballistic experts have lots of data to illustrate their predication, and it sounds more logical to me than the other sometimes spouted "theory" that an identical angle and force of wind at or near the target nudges the bullet off course more. Wind deflection, commonly called drift, is always a challenge for the varmint hunter. Tail winds can cause the bullet to shoot a tad higher and head winds can cause a bit more bullet drop than expected at long range.

Mirage

This can be a big problem for long range enthusiasts. Mirage is an optical distortion resulting from alternate layers of air pockets that vary in temperature. While peering through a high magnification rifle scope, have you ever seen a prairie rodent that appeared to be dancing a fast hula, or perhaps the twist? No it's not Dick Clark playing old records that causes these rodents to dance. It's old mother mirage up to her shimmering special effects. These optical effects can sometimes fool the most experienced shooter and can easily cause a *two to three inch refraction of the target at around 600 yards*. The net result of

mirage is that the shooter, when viewing his magnified target, will not see that crystal clear image. Instead, the target may be a dancing, wavy image, with little resemblance to the actual target; it may also appear to be floating in and out of focus. The longer the shooting range the more potential for mirage, and bringing with it probable stronger optical refraction effects. I have found that the best time to shoot is typically early in the morning, from sunrise to the first hour or two of daylight, before mirage usually starts to become noticeable. The next best time is usually later in the evening, about an hour or two before sunset, when the temperature has dropped and the wind has hopefully calmed down a tad or has dropped off completely.

The only positive thing about mirage is that it enables us to see the wind, and let us not forget, for it is wind that moves our bullet horizontally not mirage. Usually the best way to see mirage is to focus your spotting scope just shy of your intended target; this way the patterns of wavy air should become clearer. Vertical refraction is known as a "boil" and indicates a lack of wind.

In mild wind and mirage conditions you can sometimes get away with simply pursuing your spotter shots and basically ignore the wind and mirage. However, this happens infrequently, and if you pay attention to the mirage reading before and after your long range shots, you can learn how to get a "feel" for mirage and work with it. The trick is to work with both mirage and the prevailing (most prevalent) wind conditions. You should have at least one wind flag near your bench; in addition, I also use my wind meter along with reading mirage through my scope. Once you have some practice and can see what mirage does to your shots, (impact wise), you can start predicting your hits better.

Heat waves generated from a warm rifle barrel can also cause mirage, but this type of mirage can be controlled somewhat by the shooter. Long sun shades and mirage shades that screw into the front of a scope can help block barrel-heat induced mirage. Many benchrest shooters use a thin plastic strip about 3 or 4 inches wide. This strip is placed over the barrel and in front of the scope which deflects the warm air to the sides. These plastic strips are secured to a barrel by a hook & loop type of fastener.

Gyroscopic drift

As if we ultra-long range shooters don't already have enough to think about when shooting, besides wind deflection and mirage, we are also plagued by yet another potential problem—gyroscopic drift, or spin drift. Bullet drift due to gyroscopic action will start to become noticeable when shooting at ranges of over 1000 yards. The ultra-long range shooter should be cognizant of this effect. Gyroscopic drift is technically called a true drift, while many shooters call the effects of wind—wind drift; the experts tell me it is technically wind deflection. Here again the experts can expand on this topic with advanced mathematics; I would rather condense this topic with a little practical awareness. The next time you shoot extra-long range, think of your projectile as a flying gyroscope with a spin induced by (usually) a right hand twist barrel. *With a right twist barrel gyroscopic spin drift will nudge your projectile to the right and must be accounted for algebraically with that of the wind.* At ranges out to about 500 or 600 yards this effect has little importance. However, tests conducted by the U.S. Army infers that a bullet shot from a .30-06 will drift about 1 foot at 1000 yards. Ultra-long range shooters, who were gathered together at a 1000 yard match that I attended, were of the consensus that this effect varies considerably, depending on your cartridge, twist rate, velocity and ballistic coefficient, and who knows what else. At ranges out to 1500 yards, it may effect your projectile anywhere from about 2 feet to around 5 feet. One way to minimize this effect is to zero your cartridge at nearly (or 75% to 80% of) the longest distance that you ever expect to be shooting out to.

Another potential problem is rifle cant. Canting is tilting a rifle to the left or right as it is shot. When this happens the sights (or scope alignment) and bullet are not on the same vertical plane, and this causes the bullet to impact on one side of your intended target. As your shooting range increases, this effect becomes more apparent, and your bullet impact error may be several times the amount of cant. The ballistic experts tell me that a one degree cant error will give approximately a five inch horizontal impact error at 1000 yards when shooting a typical 30 caliber

magnum type cartridge. Therefore, most extreme range shooters use anti-cant bubble level devices mounted on their scopes.

6.5 mm and ultra-long range

For some time I have been sort of mesmerized with six point-five millimeter cartridges. It all started years ago while shooting at the rifle club, an acquaintance of mine was shooting a custom 6.5x55mm Swedish Mauser and doing very well with it, too. When I finally received an invitation to shoot this rig, I made the most of it and put all five shots into a tight cluster. I pulled out a nickel to check group size and my nickel covered all five holes (a nickel is about .840" in diameter). This shooting was with a fairly light sporter weight barrel! My fellow shooter also had a very good shooting custom .264 Winchester Magnum. This magnum weighed upwards of 24 pounds and utilized a sleeved Remington action which was attached to a 30 inch barrel. At the time I thought it was intolerably heavy and unwieldy. However, at the bench my friend was easily shooting five shot groups that averaged under half an inch. My friend worked up slowly, with caution, to his safe maximum load utilizing 140 grain Sierra MatchKing's and zipped them through his chronograph, that day, at an average velocity of 3330 fps. (An easy number to remember and one I noted in a ballistic journal.) One thing that impressed me about that .264 Magnum (and the shooter) was that my friend

Scoplevel's anti-cant bubble level device. Photo courtesy of Sinclair International.

could still shoot those good groups under rather windy conditions; while during all of this I was shooting my .22 caliber hot-shots and could not usually shoot my normal group size under those conditions. I recall my friend also claimed to have slain several rockchucks at over 1100 yards with his custom .264 Magnum. At that particular time in my varmint shooting career, I thought such statements were pure over-exaggeration and poppycock (now I know such things were indeed possible).

A few years later I became the owner of a new Winchester featherweight in 6.5x55mm. (Strange how my collection keeps growing by itself). I used this rifle a few times on rockchucks as a way to tune-up my shooting for deer hunting season. It was several years later, however, when the 6.5 mm really started to shine and became popular with the long-range crowd, that I actually thought seriously about having a custom 6.5-06 Improved built for extra-long range rockchuck sniping. Better late than never.

Left to Right: A 6.5mm-06 ready to fireform to the improved configuration, 6.5mm-06 Improved, and a 6.5mm/284 Winchester.

The 6.5mm (.264") caliber is now blessed with many fine match-grade bullets, most of which also possess a high ballistic coefficient. Ballistic coefficients run up to a high of around .630. We have Berger, and JLK, each producing a 140 grain VLD, and Norma producing 130 grain VLD match-grade projectiles. Lapua has a 139 grain version out. In addition, Bob Cauterucio is producing a custom 141 grain VLD HPBT in this caliber. Sierra offers several versions with their MatchKing line in 120, 140, 142, and 155 grain weights. Hornady also produces a match-grade 6.5mm bullet with their 140 grain A-MAX version. This great selection of projectiles is a real boon to long range shooters who favor this caliber.

Quick comparison of my ultra-long range cartridges

(700 yard zero, Altitude 4500 ft. 10 mph wind at 90° degrees)
Sight Height = 2.75"   JBM—On Target ballistics
800 yd: impact—**Velocity bullet trajectory wind deflection energy**

	(fps)	(in.)	(in.)	(ft.lbs.)
6.5/284.**	1982	-26.0"	31.7"	1221
6.5-06 Imp.	2136	-22.6"	28.9"	1418
7mm STW	2305	-19.9"	24.7"	1982
338/416 Imp.	2312	-20.4"	22.3"	3559

(6.5-06 Imp. with 140 gr. JLK VLD at 3140 fps muzzle vel., 7mm STW with 168 gr. JLK VLD at 3255 fps muzzle vel., 338/416 Rigby Imp. with 300 gr. Sierra BTHP at 3130 fps muzzle vel. ** a friend's 6.5mm/284 with 140 gr. JLK VLD at 2945 fps muzzle vel.)

The 6.5-06 Improved 40°

Thinking back to years ago . . . back to that day when I met my fellow long-range enthusiast at the rifle club shooting his custom .264 Winchester Magnum and his claimed long range antics prompted me to take another look at his cartridge. I had always planned on someday building a long-range custom rifle based around some 6.5mm cartridge, but I wasn't sure as to exactly which cartridge or wildcat to chamber and how much case capacity I really needed. My plan was always on the "back-burner" and took years before it actually came to fruition. At the time I was already shooting the 7mm STW and the 338-416 Rigby Improved at ultra-long range, so logically I wished for a bit more efficiency and a less capricious case. Wow, wasn't this a surprising change of pace—I reversed the usual trend of choosing something "bigger and better"?

I started to hear about the great accuracy and also read many good things about the 6.5-06 Improved 40°, and this became the cartridge that I was swaying towards. By chambering for the 6.5-06 Improved in a new custom rifle I could save my 7mm STW for my 1000 yard and longer shots and use my 6.5-06 Improved to fill the gap for my 800-1000 yard shots. Well, at least that was my reasoning for building one, along with a healthy dose of curiosity about what the 6.5-06 Improved could accomplish at long range.

I based my custom rifle around AMT's new, (at the time), single shot custom action in a right-bolt and left-port configuration. A Jewell trigger adjusted for a 10 ounce pull complemented the action. Bruce Thom was my rifle-smith for this project, and I had Bruce assemble it around a custom barrel block setup. This rifle features a heavy 27" inch BlackStar Accumax barrel with an 8" twist. Diameter at the muzzle is 1.01", at which point I also had Bruce install a muzzle brake of his own design. I specified a minimum neck of .297", which means I don't need to turn case necks and I still end-up with .003"to .0035" of neck clearance on a loaded round depending on the brand of brass and the brand of bullet.

McMillan's MBR Tooley style stock was chosen because of its comfortable bag-riding qualities and extra long fore-end. I had McMillan use their solid pour technique with added lead to bring the total stock weight to 15 pounds. The extra weight was added to "soak" up recoil and minimize muzzle jump. Scott Minugh painted the stock and gave it a subdued fern pattern that appears very complementary. A NightForce 8-32X56 graces the top and gives it sort of a menacing look. The scope mount is setup with a 1° degree forward tapered base to give the scope some added elevation. This setup effectively adds upward travel to the scope for extra-long range work.

My completed rig weighs in with scope at a

hefty 26 pounds. Perhaps a rifle this hefty was not really necessary, but I shouldn't complain because I'm capable of easily viewing bullet impact—even with the scope cranked up to 32X magnification. This type of bench rifle wouldn't be carried very far anyway, usually only from my truck to a portable bench, so the extra weight is really no burden, and it keeps the rifle extra stable on the bags.

Producing fire-formed fodder for my 6.5-06 Improved proved to be an easy task. I simply necked down 30-06 brass in a 6.5mm-06 trim die, then full length resized the brass. Next I trimmed all cases to the same overall length and, of course, to finish the job I needed to fireform my brass to the improved configuration. I "broke-in" the barrel with mild fire-forming loads using (necked-down) Lapua 30-06 brass and encountered no case problems, whatsoever. The improved version increases case capacity from 68.4 grains of water (to overflow) to 71.7 grains of water. In addition to the increased case capacity is the fact that my improved cases stretch and lengthen very little; which means I save time by not using my case trimmer. The BlackStar barrel seemed to "break-in" quite readily, showing the barest minimum of fouling, then after about 16 rounds were fired the barrel showed no fouling. After I had 100 rounds of brass fire-formed I started testing the good improved stuff.

Velocities with moly coated 140 grain projectiles varied from around 3040 fps to 3190 fps. Accuracy with most loads when tested at 100 yards varied from three tenths of an inch to just over the half inch mark. The load I settled on for my first varmint hunt consisted of a moly coated

Author's custom 6.5-06 Improved—in a left-port right-bolt configuration. Port side view. Notice size of barrel block in relation to size of the action.

Hornady 140 grain A-Max bullet combined with 55 grains of RL-19 powder and a Federal 210M primer. (*Caution! Work up loads slowly while watching for excess pressures. Keep in mind I was using moly-coated bullets and a long-throated wildcat chamber.*) This load zipped through my Oehler skyscreens at an average velocity of 3098 fps and printed groups in the low three's at 100 yards. When tested at 200 yards, this load printed groups that averaged .42". Most notably this load showed a low standard deviation of 8 fps and an extreme spread of only 15 fps.

My runner-up load consisted of JLK's moly coated 140 grain VLD and 56.6 grains of RL-22. This load gave an average velocity of 3140 fps and printed an average group size at 100 yards of .35" and at 200 yards my groups averaged .52"

My first test at 1,000 yards was not really encouraging. It was just after a 1,000 yard match was over and a few shooters were practicing that I came on the scene with my 6.5-06 Improved. I was not blessed with luck that day, as the wind was just starting to howl and a thunderstorm was just about to unleash when I started to shoot. I decided to shoot 5 shot groups instead of the usual ten. I placed four shots into about an eleven inch group, then my fifth shot went way out. (I was not paying enough attention to the lone wind flag!) Next it started to rain. Then it hailed, as the thunderstorm boomed in the background, and my next five shots went into about a 14 inch group as

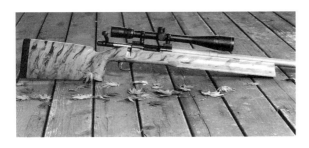

Author's new Darrell Holland-built Vee-Block rifle chambered for the wildcat 6.5/284 Winchester. This exquisite rig is built around a Remington 700 action and a Pac-Nor Super Match barrel, with a Jewell trigger and a McMillan MBR Tooley stock in desert tan camo. This 21 pound rig is topped off with a Bausch and Lomb Elite 4000 series 6-24X40mm scope.

I rushed my shots to the target before lightning struck around the shooting range!

I was curious as to how 6.5mm match grade projectiles would perform on live varmints when shot at the half-mile marker or even longer. About a month after my 1,000 yard test I had my chance to find out, during a vacation outing in Western Montana. Early one morning, while scanning an area known for rockchuck colonies, I spotted some rodent activity across a canyon. The rocky ridge was scanned, using a laser rangefinder which informed me that a group of chucks were out at 670 yards and another group at 842 yards. Wind was relatively mild with gusts up to around 7-8 mph and originating from about a true 45 degree angle. I made a lucky first shot kill at 670 yards, while shooting during a lull in the wind, but could not repeat this feat at 842 yards. After sending three 140 grain projectiles down range with hair-singeing misses, the chucks were temporarily spooked. However, after about a five minute wait one chuck decided the coast was clear and I had another chance. I used a bit of patience and waited until my wind flag, (which was placed about 20 yards in front of my bench), laid almost perfectly still. Then I slowly squeezed off a shot. It was a direct hit! Upon impact the chuck was blown backwards over another rock! A little later I was able to hit another chuck at the same distance.

Yes, my 6.5-06 Improved seems to work quite well as an extra-long/ultra-long range chuck cartridge with the Hornady match grade bullet. While it's true my test was just short of the half-mile post, I don't think my results would have been much different even if the range was extended another 100 yards or so. Actually, those chucks at 842 yards were very much within range of my 6mm/284, and I think I could have also dispatched them with the likes of my 6mm Improved. But my 6.5-06 Improved was my new "toy" at the time and needed to be initiated and tested. I did perceive a difference downrange, though, while shooting my 6.5-06 Improved with its "heavy" 140 grain projectile. The heavier 6.5mm bullet made it easier to see and view bullet impact over that of the lighter 6mm projectiles that I have been shooting. I am only speculating here, but I have reason to believe that if those chucks had been another 100 or 200 yards further downrange I think the heavier 6.5mm bullets would really shine with their superior momentum and ballistic coefficients and make them the clear-cut choice over any of the 6mm bullets and cartridges.

As far as my 6.5-06 Improved evolves, I think more testing will be in order, as there are many bullets that I mentioned which were not tested but look promising. Other powders that are also known to work well with this cartridge are RL-22, RL-25, N 165, AA 3100 and IMR 4831.

The 6.5/284 Winchester

The prolonged wait for Norma 6.5/284 brass is over and we varmint shooting wildcatters are lucky because Norma is also noted for producing exceptionally good quality brass. When Winchester introduced their new rebated .284 cartridge back in 1963, some speculate that almost immediately it was necked down to both .25 caliber and 6mm, thus creating the .25/284 and the 6mm/284. Another popular variation of the .284 Winchester case of more recent times has been the 6.5mm/284. Many 1,000 yard competitors and high power shooters have been shooting the 6.5mm version. This strong high-pressure case design was ahead of its time. Its first plus is that it is short and fat, (considering its powder capacity). Many benchrest shooters favor the short-fat design because it reminds them of the PPC case and its penchant for accuracy. Its second plus is that the case has little taper and a sharp 35° degree shoulder, which results in less case stretching. Actually, the way Winchester configured the case of the .284 you could call it a pseudo Ackley Improved design.

My newest extreme range varmint eliminator is a Darrell Holland built custom rifle chambered for the 6.5/284 Winchester. This rifle is based on Darrell's Golden Eagle series Vee-block design. This custom rig is built around a trued Remington 700 short action and features a 3 groove Pac-Nor Super Match barrel. This 8" twist barrel measures 26.5" in length with a muzzle diameter of 1.01" and also features Holland's varmint magnum muzzle brake. It is throated for the longer VLD type bullets. I chose the McMillan MBR Tooley type of stock, because this rifle is destined to be shot from a bench only. I had McMillan add lead to this stock during construction for extra recoil absorbing weight, as the rifle weighs 21 pounds with scope. Darrell adjusted the Jewell trigger for a 4 ounce pull. For optics, I attached an impressive Bausch and Lomb Elite 4000 series 6-24X 40mm scope.

I finally located some new Norma 6.5/284 brass and promptly started working up loads. I broke-in the barrel slowly, cleaning with Butch's Bore Shine while using my new Bore Tech cleaning rod. Load development started around RL-19, because that is the powder that works well in my 6.5mm-06 Improved. A moly-coated Hornady 140 grain A-Max was the initial projectile for testing. Forty nine grains of RL-19 gave me 2866 fps and fine accuracy. (*Caution! Work up loads slowly while watching for excess pressures. Keep in mind I was using moly-coated bullets and a long-throated wildcat chamber.*) Bench testing at 200 yards during a calm day at the range gave me groups that averaged .41". I am presently waiting for my order of Vihtavuori N-165 powder to help me "wring out" this cartridge along with it's bigger brother, the 6.5mm-06 Improved.

The 7mm STW as a varmint cartridge

While chanting some technical words, (like presto-change-o), I take an ordinary 8mm Remington Magnum case and neck it down to 7mm; and presto . . . I just made another 7mm STW case. This increasingly popular cartridge is the brainchild of gunscribe Layne Simpson. With Layne's help, the cartridge has become quite popular, but evidently Layne was not the first writer to neck the big 8mm down. By accident I spotted an article by Col. Charles Askins in the

The author's 7mm STW with a Nightforce 5.5-22X ranging reticle scope.

June 1985,—Vol. 133 no.6—, issue of *American Rifleman*. In his article titled "Wild for Wildcats," Askins describes his experience necking down the Remington 8mm Magnum case to 7mm. Askins referred to this cartridge as a .284/8mm Wildcat; he noted it was accurate, easy to work with, and consistent. Over the past few years, I have heard accounts from many riflemen who consider the 7mm STW as "The ultimate elk cartridge".

So why would I really consider this "elk" cartridge as a varmint round? Surely I am jesting? You might be thinking that launching 168 grain projectiles at nearly 3350 fps toward little 12-16 pound rodents, is just a wee-bit of overkill, right? Well . . . yes . . . and no.

To my way of thinking, it all depends on how far the targeted rodents are "out" from the end of your muzzle. Take my 23 pound 7mm STW and set it on a bench, now look through my 22X Nightforce scope at the little rockchucks, way out yonder . . . Yes, those chucks . . . the furry little dots, on the other side of the ravine, scurrying around on that rock pile over 1000 yards away. That poorly located ravine and the darn trees in front of us make it impossible for us to stalk any closer. It was for targets and conditions like this that I conjured upon the 7mm STW as a special purpose varmint cartridge.

Actually, some hunting camps, who specialize in ultra-long range varmint sniping, consider the 7mm STW as somewhat of a "light-weight"; these ultra-long-range gurus, who think shooting out to around 1000 yards is just a mere "starting point," and "utopia" doesn't really start until you have reached out to about 2000 yards. This crowd usually opts for big booming wildcats like the

Author shooting 700 -plus yard rockchucks with his 7mm STW.

.30-378, or .338-378 Weatherby Magnums. But lately, there seems to be a strong surge of interest in the .338-416 Rigby. And there are still others who consider the .50 BMG as the "ultimate" cartridge for mile-long shooting.

After shooting my custom 6mm/284 for a few years, I found it to be a superb performer on rockchucks out to about 850 yards or so. Yet I still yearned for something bigger. Something as flat shooting, that could send a streamlined projectile downrange with superlative wind bucking momentum, but with still more "punch" way out there. I wished for something that would really make the dirt fly upon impact. You understand that when I miss, which is more often than I care to, is when the heavier projectiles show an advantage with a bigger impact splatter. This extra impact energy tells the forlorn shooter (me) his shot placement was off and he better get in gear and correct for it. Yet, I did not wish to lose sight of my quarry because of recoil jump. The question then became, how large a caliber? And how much case capacity would be needed to best achieve my requirements?

Over the past few years I was getting good results from a customized 7mm Remington Magnum. This 7mm magnum, with it's 26" Shilen Select Match barrel, was easy to load, accurate, but a bit lighter then I cared for in a special purpose extra long-range rig. With the ultra long hunting ranges I was planning to expand upon, my loads with this belted 7mm would fall short. I have used this 7mm rifle out to around 650 yards, and it surely does kill rockchucks; but for busting chucks around this range I have other more suitable rifles. (Meaning my 6mm/284, my 6mm Remington, or my .22/6mm Remington. These rifles are all heavier and more stable when shot from my portable bench, and also exhibit less recoil and jump).

At the time, I was hoping someone would come up with a heavier VLD type projectile in 7mm. If I could only propel a VLD type of bullet down range fast enough, I should have the best of both. A few years back, I had previous experience with a friend's rifle chambered for the wildcat 7mm-300 Weatherby. In fact, I even made a connection on an unsuspecting rockchuck at over 1000 yards while using this rifle. The handloads for this wildcat were utilizing Nosler's 150 grain

Ballistic Tips. And even though the ballistic coefficient for this excellent bullet doesn't compare to a true VLD type bullet, we still put away a fair number of rockchucks on the far side of 700 yards.

Jimmy Knox, of JLK bullets, had been producing VLD type bullets for some time, and had just introduced their new line of 7mm VLD type projectiles. These VLD bullets were offered in both 168 grain and 180 grain weights. The 168 grain has a reported ballistic coefficient of .690, with the 180 grain projectile coming in at .710. This new 168 grain bullet was destined to be "my" bullet to shoot from my 7mm wonder rifle. I knew about the 7mm-300 Weatherby and a few other 7mm wildcats, but I was hearing more and more about the exploits of the 7mm STW. I talked to Dan Lilja next, and then made my decision to go with the 7mm STW as my new 1000 yard Varmint Zapper.

The next question that popped up in my mind was . . . how much recoil and muzzle jump could I endure, while not losing sight of my target through the scope? Or how heavy should my rifle be made? I knew in advance a muzzle brake would be needed for this rifle, and I proceeded to plug some numbers into my computer. I was trying to come up with some recoil figures I could relate to. I was comparing weight of rifle and projectile, with velocity, and powder charge, for my new STW to other rifles I have owned or shot. The computer churned for a minute, I scratched my head, and . . . well, more or less, guessed at a projected weight for my rifle. Twenty two pounds was the number, and yes, it seemed a little hefty for a varmint rifle, but a lightweight for a genuine 1000 yard target rifle. So in theory only, at this point, if I build my rifle to a total weight of around 22 pounds (or 23 pounds with scope) I should see bullet impact.

When it came time to start building the rifle, I elected to go with Alan Hall's excellent Express action. This action is designed for big cartridges, and it has enough stiffness to support long, heavy barrels. I called Dan Lilja and ordered a 30" Lilja barrel with a 9" twist rate, with a taper to .900" at the muzzle. The reason for the taper? So I could get a Standard size, "Varmint Snyper" muzzle brake from Answer Products to fit. I kept the barrel length at 30" so I would not need a barrel block system. (For barrels over 32" in length, a barrel block is highly recommended by most gunsmiths). I had this rig pillar-bedded in a McMillan benchrest type stock, with the standard 3" wide fore-end. This McMillan stock is a solid "pour" with lead added, for a total weight of 10 pounds. I needed the heavier stock to bring my total rifle weight up to my designed 22 pounds. Dan Lilja did the chambering and fitting, Steve Kostanich pillar bedded it, and Scott Minugh painted the stock. It has a Neil Jones modified, Remington trigger set at 1 pound. A Leupold 6.5-20X scope was sent off to Premier Reticles for a power boost to 8.5-26X with custom dots installed for holdover, and windage. I have also used my Nightforce 5.5-22X scope with a varmint ranging reticle (NP1-RR) on this rifle with excellent results.

When I started load development, I broke in the barrel with Sierra's 168 BTHP and discovered something about my lot of 8mm Magnum brass. If I did not seat the bullets out to touch the rifling I would risk a misfire. Case stretch was .005 to .007 on the first firing. Just recently, I tried WW 300 H&H magnum brass necked down and then fire-formed, and case stretch was about half as much. I plan to make up test loads with this brass and check both accuracy and velocity; it may prove to be better then the more common parent 8mm Magnum brass. After fire-forming I have been neck sizing all subsequent reloads, and case stretch has been minimal. My normal load of 74.5 grains of IMR 7828 powder, Federal 215 primer, 168 grain JLK VLD bullet, is good for 3346 fps; and some of my cases have been loaded eight times without any problems. At 200 yards the average group size is .42", and I am happy to report that I can see bullet impact even with my scope at 22X, if I grip the rifle fairly strongly, including the fore-end. But I also discovered I must use this shooting technique, rather then letting the rifle recoil freely, because if I don't, my group size will enlarge to about double my normal .42" average. Presently, with different powder and primer lots my velocity has dropped to 3255fps.

After I worked up my normal load with this rig, for the past six years, I have been saving this rifle for ultra-long range rockchuck shooting only. Normally, I don't uncase the thing unless the range is at least 700-800 yards. My first chuck I shot with this rig was taken more out of curiosity and was not meant to be the ultimate test at long range. My buddy Russ Foster spotted a good size rockchuck out around the 350 yard marker, and as such, it was a very easy shot. Later that day I tried using the STW on a few chucks at a Barr & Stroud ranged 760 yards, but the wind and mirage were too much for me, and I missed with three shots. Seems even with the best of equipment I am still dependent on old Mother Nature. But things got better; as the following day I picked off several out to 710 yards, and even my buddy, Russ, got into it and shot a few over 600 yards.

But my best outing with my STW happened in the Spring of 95, in Western Montana. Here Mother Nature was kind to me and gave us a perfect day for long-range shooting. By 8 AM. it was about 50 degrees, sunny, with the wind in almost a dead calm condition. My Davis Turbo meter was telling us the gusts were up to a mere 3 mph. I had my Nightforce 5.5-22X scope attached, and "zeroed" my rifle at approximately 400 yards. While shooting off my portable bench, at 400 yards, I punched two five-shot groups of 1-1/4" and 1-3/4". To say the least I was enthusiastic, as these groups gave me confidence that my rifle and loads were up to the task of shooting over the creek and into the next county. For that is where we located several colonies of rockchucks scurrying about, with the nearest colony at a ranged 680 meters away.

I spotted for my friend, Gene, as he found the range with his Remington 40-X chambered for the .25-06. However, the load Gene was using seemed to fall a bit "short" when shooting around 710 meters. I popped a few chucks with my 6mm/284 loaded with 85 grain Speer boatails. The longest chuck I hit and killed was ranged at 890 meters or 974 yards! Then I un-cased my STW and things started to get serious. I made several hits on these rockchucks, all the way out to 1220 meters, and considered the morning as my ultimate triumph in varmint hunting glory. I was about ready to put my STW away, and just spot for my friends, but while peering through my Leupold 12-40X-60mm spotting scope, I located some rockchuck movement in the upper corner of the scope. I cranked up the spotting scope to 40X and guessed the chucks were liter-

ally in the next "county" and out of range. We put the range finder on the colony and it came back with a reading of 1410 meters. Nobody in our little group cared to take a shot, so I was volunteered to try. I did a quick study with my ballistic charts and figured I needed to use my maximum hold-over dot and also crank in considerable elevation to my Nightforce scope. The chuck appeared as only a small furry spot in the scope, but amazingly, the first two shots were actually close to hitting this chuck. I waited about 5 minutes, then perhaps 20 yards from where the "shot at" chuck had dived for cover, a rockchuck appeared. Whether it was the same chuck, or not, may never be known, but it gave me another target. The next shot impacted just below the chuck, and he jumped over to another nearby rock. I touched off my final shot of the morning, and after the prolonged wait for bullet flight, I witnessed my longest hit to date! (back in 1995). We confirmed again with the rangefinder, it was 1410 meters! (when converted to yards it came to 1542.5) Next we confirmed it was an actual kill, by hiking 45 minutes to the body. It was a lucky shot for sure, but my 7mm STW and my Nightforce scope made it possible.

Update: This cartridge is, of course, now factory legitimate as Remington is producing both rifles and ammunition for the 7mm STW.

I made another test using WW 300 H&H Magnum brass. I necked down this brass using a Redding form and trim die #83544, and then I fireformed it to the 7mm STW configuration. When I filled these fireformed cases with water to overflow I discovered I gained two grains of water capacity. WW 300 H&H to 7mm STW = 101 grains of water. / RP 8mm Magnum to 7mm STW = 99 grains of water. While testing my moly coated JLK VLD bullets using 75.5 grains of IMR 7828, I was able to push these 168 grain bullets to 3328 fps with seemingly mild pressures. Accuracy averaged .44" at 200 yards for five shots.

Update: After approximately 1,100 rounds my STW barrel was showing its age and somewhat regrettably I sold the complete rifle. If I were to replace the rig I would most likely chamber it to some sort of .308 caliber wildcat. I would also design the rifle to be heavier for better control under recoil.

The 338/416 Rigby Improved 35°

For some strange reason I couldn't rest and let my 7mm STW remain my longest range varmint zapper. The 1,000 yard competitors were shooting .308 and .338 calibers with good success. Talking with Bruce Thom again, over at BAT Machine, I decided to go with his biggest action and build yet another ultra-long range rig.

I crunched some numbers on my computer about long range bullet impact regarding both momentum and energy. Since I already had a heavy 7mm varmint rifle, it seemed logical to skip the .308 caliber and jump over the to a heavy .338. To stay away from possible problems of expanding belts, I decided to focus my attention toward large un-belted cases to base my big .338 wildcat around. The old .416 Rigby case, when necked down and improved, had an enviable accuracy record as a special purpose ultra-long range varmint round and became my selected wildcat. Sierra's 300 grain .338 projectile has an amazing ballistic coefficient of .790 which helps to keep this bullet transonic all the way out to over 2000 yards!

When a bullet slows down enough at long range it may enter a transonic range, (velocities approaching the speed of sound). It is at this velocity range that a projectile is likely to become partially unstable and develop a bit of yaw and, therefore, be less accurate. Therefore, as far as the ultra-long range varmint shooter is concerned, one should avoid this range or select a bullet with a higher B.C.

For this rig I went all out and did not compromise. This rifle was designed with a single special purpose—to be used for ultra-long range shooting only. This meant it would have to be heavy, in fact very heavy, to soak up recoil and

Author's .338/416 Rigby Improved with muzzle brake.

dampen muzzle jump as much as possible. I took a cue from the 1000 yard competitors, as most of their rigs weigh from around 40 to over 90 pounds. Mine came to weigh in at 52 pounds with scope.

Bruce Thom's large action known as the ten inch BAT action is a no nonsense stiff and extremely well built receiver. BAT Machine is building on a very good reputation with the 1000 yard shooters. Mine is in a right-bolt and left-port configuration with a titanium firing pin for faster lock time.

This rifle is from the combined efforts of two skilled craftsmen, Dan Lilja and Bruce Thom. Dan Lilja, as some remember, used to build rifles as well as make barrels, but as his barrel production increased he stopped making custom rifles. My 338/416 was Dan's last custom rifle he produced, and I feel a little sad that others may never have the pleasure of experiencing his handiwork. Dan, of course, chambered one of his own 10" twist, 36" inch barrels 1.450" in diameter with no taper to the .338/416 Improved. The throat was setup to shoot Sierra's 300 grain Matchking BTHP. Dan built a large barrel block in which the barrel is epoxied into the block and the rest of the action is floating and does not touch the stock. This is a method of retaining barrel stiffness while using longer than normal barrels.

Dan also chambered a set of press mounted loading dies for this rifle. I simply ran 60 lubed Norma 416 Rigby cases through an intermediate neck-down die, then through a full length sizing die. I uniformed the primer pockets, then my cases made a short stint through my K&M neck turning tool. Next, I fireformed the brass to the improved configuration while breaking in the barrel, and before I knew it I had 60 cases made. After fireforming I trimmed all cases to the same length, then weighed them for uniformity. I kept my weighed cases segregated for potentially more accurate loads with hopefully less deviation.

Bruce Thom provided the finishing touches, as in pillar bedding the barrel block, and made a set of custom scope rings and blocks with a 1.5° degree angle. This way the barrel is angled upwards in relationship to the scope, for added elevation. The stock is a modified Lee Six unlimited benchrest. This stock was fortified with a steel reinforcing bar and extra lead to make it heavy, as it weighs 18 pounds! Bruce ordered a Jewell trigger, and I told him to adjust it for an 8 ounce pull. Bruce also installed the recoil pad, the stock runners and produced the custom muzzle brake. Scott Minugh was responsible for the paint, which has received many compliments over the years. A Nightforce 12-42X56 scope graces the receiver and provides exceptional long range clarity and precision. This scope also has 1/8" inch clicks which helps out immensely for a more precise zero at extra-long range.

The best and most efficient powders for this cartridge are the super-slow burners and are usually classified as .50 BMG powders. Even experienced hand-loaders usually don't know what I'm talking about when I mention one of the powders that I feed my .338/416 wildcat. Have you heard of 24N41 or WC-860, and what about WC-872? These powders are slow—so slow that in the next slower burning category of propellants we find charcoal briquettes.

The .338/416 Improved case is big, as it holds 133 grains of water to overflow. One hundred and nine grains (109) of Vihtavuori 24N41 topped off with a moly coated 300 grain Sierra MatchKing gives me an average muzzle velocity of 3130 fps. Extreme spread with this load is a mere 13 fps. One hundred and thirteen grains of WC-860 gives me 3166 fps. I use Federal 215 Magnum primers for reliable ignition.

One thing that took me sort of by surprise was the fact that most of my "normal" loading tools did not fit this huge case. You see, I needed to modify a RCBS shell holder (for the 416 Rigby) to fit a modified Lee Auto-Prime in order to prime

my cases. I also needed to find a loading block to fit the huge cases, and I ended up using a 20 gauge shotgun loading block. My neck turning tool also had to be slightly modified in order to work. Next, I needed a huge custom rifle case just to tote my beast around. I called the head honcho at Impact Case Company and he took my order for an oversize "black-powder" case.

Until my third year of ownership with this rifle, I had to settle for 904 yards as my longest rockchuck kill. Sometimes it's not easy trying to find a location to shoot far—as in over 1000 yards in distance. This brings up another topic in regard to actually needing an ultra-long range rifle, or just assembling one for the challenge? Only on occasion do I actually require a rig to shoot out past say 1000 yards or so,—as when I can't physically get closer. When I assembled my .338/416 Improved I sort of expected an ultra long range opportunity over 1000 yards to show up, which it didn't until the third year, when I made a kill at 1794 yards! I also made an impressive and surprising first shot hit on a rockchuck

Author ready to let loose with his .338/416 Rigby Improved.

The Davis Turbo Meter.

at 1115 yards under very calm conditions, but I considered this kill as serendipity and not likely to ever be repeated, so I won't go into any details.

Another type of competition that can keep the ultra-long range enthusiast's sharp are 1000 yard matches. The big .30 caliber cartridges currently dominate this game. Very heavy custom rifles and wildcats seem to rule the roost here. Long range shooters come from all parts of the country to compete and see if they can break the record for the smallest 10 shot group.

Auxiliary Equipment for the 1,000 Yard Varmint Shooter

Auxiliary equipment that I find useful seems to be growing every year, as we (the human race) advance into the space age. Most modern varmint hunters who welcome technology are not sheepish with their assembly of new gear to help aid in their quest.

That darned WIND again!

Wind speed indicators, or anemometers, are showing up with increased frequency in the varmint fields. These meters help determine the severity and angle of the wind, and therefore, the shooter has a better chance to compensate for bullet deflection. I remember back a few years ago when my wind meter was indicating gusts of 30 to 40 mph, my partner and I simply left our equipment in the truck and headed back to the restaurant for more coffee as we waited out the wind storm.

An anemometer is perhaps more fully utilized when the shooter is also equipped with a laptop or palmtop computer. A field computer with a ballistic program up-and-running can provide the shooter with updated information never before attainable. With such a setup the shooter can simply update to the current conditions with temperature, altitude, barometric pressure, wind speed and direction, and receive a more accurate up to the minute printout. The modern compact palmtop, laptop, or notebook computer is a technical marvel, and they are starting to show up in the longer range precision shooting camps.

Rangefinders

Laser rangefinders are also modern day marvels and have a place in most varmint hunters arsenals. I have used and tested several types of laser rangefinders over the past few years. It seems most optical companies are bringing out new laser rangefinders every year, or so. We now have in alphabetical order: Bushnell's Yardage Pro series, Laser Technology, Inc. has its Impulse 2K, Leica has the Geovid and the LRF 800, (a compact model), Nikon has the Laser 800, Sports Electronics has their SE Sports Laser Range Gun, Swarovski's markets the RF-1, Tasco has the LaserSite series, and Weaver is due to market their line of new laser rangefinders soon. Pentax is also coming out with a compact 1100 yard rangefinder. Swarovski has a laser ranging rifle scope that has been on the market for several years now. In addition, Nikon has just introduced their new Laser600 3-12X50 rifle scope. I also hear that Tasco and Weaver are working on rifle scopes with laser rangefinding capability.

A laser unit needs a certain amount of laser reflectivity back to it's pickup diode for it to work, and typically the natural surroundings of where varmints live are not conducive to high amounts of laser reflectivity for long range usage. If the unit is rated, for say, 800 yards by

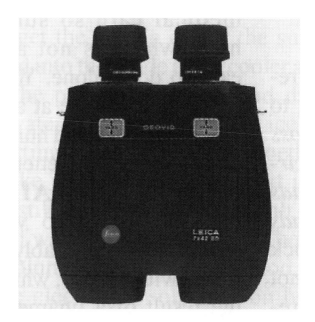

The Leica Geovid rangefinder, under good conditions, has given the author accurate readings out to 1300 yards.

the manufacturer, the varmint hunter should heed my little warning that the rating is based on ideal ambient and atmospheric conditions and high target reflectivity. So to play it safe, only count on 60% to 75% of the rated range under most field conditions. The exception to this, that I know about, is the Leica Geovid which can give accurate field readings out to over 1300 yards when placed on a tripod or other solid support when determining the range.

How does a laser rangefinder work? Here's a crash course for the working varmint shooter: A laser rangefinder sends out a beam or a pulse of light via its laser diode (invisible to the naked eye, except for superman) in the near-infrared range. This light travels downrange until it encounters an object, whereas it reflects back to the laser unit and is intercepted by a second diode. Total elapsed time of transmission to the target and reflection back to the unit is measured and computed by a microprocessor; then the distance is displayed in (or on) the rangefinder. The majority of rangefinders use "first-read" technology, that is, they receive the first signal back to the unit, which is the one that is displayed to the user. The Leica Geovid uses multiple pulses that are averaged by its microprocessor.

Laser beams also diverge with range somewhat like a shotgun pattern; this divergence is expressed in milliradians (or mil rads). At 1000 yards a one mil rad beam will cover one yard in diameter. The Geovid has a divergence of 1.5x0.3 mil rads, which means at 1000 yards its beam is 4.5 feet wide and 10.8" inches high (or tall). Most lower priced units have a wider beam divergence. The wider the beam the less accurate the readings. It can be difficult to get an accurate reading on a very distant varmint with a wide beam rangefinder because usually some part of

Optical coincident rangefinders: (a) Wild, (b) Barr & Stroud. Photo courtesy of Deutsche Optik.

the laser beam's divergence will be reading the ground, 100 yards or more in front of the targeted critter.

However good laser rangefinders have become, the ultra-long range shooter may wish to keep a good optical coincident rangefinder as a backup. In fact, I have seen a phalanx of rangefinding equipment in more than a few ultra-long range camps utilizing both laser technology along with the older optical rangefinders. Barr and Stroud, an English made unit, and Wild, a superb Swiss made instrument, are still around in used condition but are becoming scarcer to find. These finely crafted and designed older units work by triangulation and are quite accurate (generally within a few yards) out to over 2500 yards, but of course they are slower to use. These coincident units work by lining up an inverted image in the right eyepiece, while the range to the subject is displayed in the left eyepiece. The unit by Wild was produced from the 1940's to the 1960's and featured 11.25X magnification, while the readings are calibrated in meters. The Barr and Stroud units were made from the early 1940's to the early 1960's. Some Barr and Stroud units were calibrated in yards while others were calibrated in meters, and some had a minimum distance of 250 yards while other models started at 500 yards. A few of the later units featured coated optics and 14 X magnification. When the modern laser unit runs out of range or "zip," I have witnessed these older units on the scene that saved the day by providing the shooter with accurate range readings to his very distant chuck. However, it is best to use these units during low mirage conditions because they work optically and are also affected by mirage just like your rifle scope.

Computer Software

Most serious students of long range shooting already know the advantages of using an exterior ballistic program but few know about combination programs that feature both external and internal ballistics. I recently discovered some new software that ardent wildcatters should find especially interesting. I am talking about a program called QuickLOAD which is marketed by NECO. QuickLOAD is a fully functional external ballistics program combined with a ballistic predictor program. I have been playing with a demonstration version of QuickLOAD and I am favorably impressed. This program is quite extensive and unlike any other on the market. The hand-loader stipulates the many parameters of any real or designed chambering and gun, then receives ballistic predictions including chamber pressure. For those varmint shooters who are interested in improved or wildcat chamberings, QuickLOAD can provide valuable information.

Optics

Magnification

Magnification in a rifle scope has its price. Generally, the greater the magnification the larger and heavier the scope will be. Also, unfortunately the greater the magnification of a scope the less its light transmission which results in a darker appearing image. However, several companies have made optical advances and offer features to partially compensate for this gloomy fact. Larger objective lenses and larger tube diameters, combined with multiple-coated optics have increased light transmission to a point that when you crank up your magnification you don't notice the slight drop in light transmission as much as you did with many earlier model scopes. The very high magnification scopes have limits to their usefulness because of their tendency to magnify mirage. Under certain conditions mirage can render the higher magnifications almost useless. During high mirage conditions I generally find that 12X to 16X is about tops for any kind of target definition. The popular variable scope can be a godsend because it gives the shooter the option to change magnification according to the conditions and according to field of view requirements.

I try to choose a scope with enough magnification that, when the chosen scope is married to a rifle, the shooter is likely to receive the rifle's full range potential while blending the size of the scope to the size of the rifle. If I were to choose a scope for one of my extra-long range rifles I would choose a variable scope with enough magnification (a top end magnification of at least 20X to perhaps 42X) and brightness (multi-

coated optics) for shots out to around 900-1000 yards, or so.

Custom Reticles

Even with a very flat shooting cartridge, a varmint hunter is going to someday holdover his intended critter and try to lob a bullet into it. The question has always been how much do you hold over with a standard scope reticle. If you know the range to your intended varmint and how many clicks it takes to elevate your trajectory to the target, you have half the equation already figured out. Instead of all this scope adjusting to the target and possibly becoming confused, many

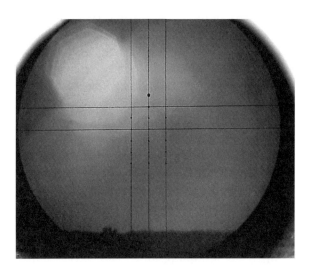

An actual view through one of the author's custom reticles.

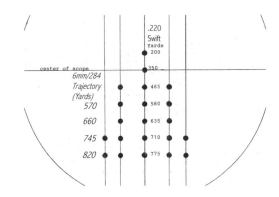

One of the author's custom designed reticles with 2 MOA hold-over dots.

shooters prefer to use a reticle with customized holdover dots. A useful arrangement is to design a scope reticle that uses a series of dots to your best advantage that is tailored to your shooting and your particular rifle and cartridge. An accurate rangefinder used in conjunction with a customized scope can yield some amazing results.

A popular custom arrangement, as an example, is a series of dots that are spaced 2 or perhaps 3 minutes of angle apart running down the vertical crosshair. Your top dot could be placed above the center crosshair for a zero at 100 or 200 yards, with the center crosshair to be dead on at say 300 yards, and the next lower dot at 400 yards or so. There are two methods of designing a custom reticle. Like the method we've discussed using a fixed pattern of spacing between dots, or you can conform your holdover dots to provide a bullet impact point at certain chosen distances. This method is a bit trickier and requires the use of an accurate ballistic program to determine the specific dot spacing. I always run a computer ballistic chart that coincides (checked by actual tests) with my rifle's load while programming the trajectory drop chart for both MOA and actual scope click values. By using this method I know how many clicks I have between my dots and can adjust my bullet impact for just the precise range to a varmint, when needed. A custom reticle is also useful for extending the upward click value of your scope simply by using your lowest dot and then click upwards from it.

Options for customizing a scope

When choosing or designing your own custom reticle it's likely you will have the choice of either a first focal place reticle or a second focal plane reticle. You may be asking what's the difference?

A second focal place reticle is by far the most common and allows the shooter to change magnification without any change in the size of his reticle. If you design your own reticle (via a second focal plane system) in a 6.5-20X variable scope with, say a holdover dot pattern that is spaced 2 MOA (minutes of angle) apart down the vertical crosshair and you change your magnifi-

cation from 20X to 10X, then you should know that you have also changed your 2 MOA spaced dots to 4 MOA spaced dots. With that magnification change you have changed the relationship of your precisely designed custom holdover dots, and your bullet impact will be different except for your center dot.

Years ago I had Premier Reticles make up a few Leupold scopes for me with their first focal plane modification. I had the reticles designed with 2.5 MOA spaced dots down the vertical crosshair for holdover. When I change the magnification from 20X to 10X the relationship of these holdover dots remains the same at 2.5 MOA, and my computed bullet impact at any magnification doesn't change,—but my reticle and my dots appear smaller in size. To some shooters, this variable sizing of the reticle (that works correspondingly with the magnification) is disconcerting, but to others it is an improvement over the ever changing dot spacing relationship

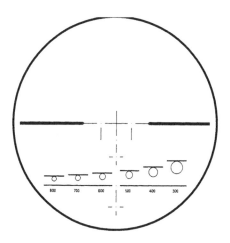

The Nightforce Ranging Reticle NP1-RR.

New. Vari-X III 8.5-25x50mm Long Range Target

This Leupold Vari-X III model has proven to be popular with many long-range varmint shooters.

of a second focal plane system. As long as I remember which scope and which dot system I am using, I do just fine.

Whichever system you use, it is a good idea to keep a master copy of your reticle design with the scopes serial number for future reference. You may end up designing different reticle patterns for future scopes, and if (or when) your memory fails as to what your holdover dots are spaced at, for which scope, you will have a sketch of your reticle to refresh you memory. I also place a miniature sketch of a scopes reticle inside the ocular flip-up scope cap for quick reference.

Scope Specifications

Things to consider when selecting a varmint scope would include the click value of its sight adjustments. Finer click values are more important to the extra-long range and ultra-long range shooter. Consider a scope with 1/4" inch clicks (at 100 yards); when adjusting said scope for a long range target; each click will move bullet impact 2" inches at 800 yards and 4" inches at 1600 yards. Now consider a scope with 1/8" inch

Mitchell Optic's model MO25 2-1/2" Objective Lens external adjustment scope. Photo courtesy of Mitchell Optics Inc.

The Nikon Monarch 6.5-20X44mm. Photo courtesy of Nikon, Inc.

clicks (at 100 yards); when adjusting said scope for such targets, each click will move bullet impact 1" inch at 800 yards and only 2" inches at 1600 yards. This is the reason 1/8" inch clicks are favored by the long range shooters. *It is always a good idea to verify on paper your scope's actual adjustment per click to see if it coincides with its specifications.* There is one possible downside to a scope with 1/8" inch click adjustments, as it may limit the scope's total adjustment range. This factor would, of course, be listed in the scopes specifications, and it may not be a limiting factor at all, with some brands of scopes.

When choosing a scope for a particular varmint rifle, it would be wise to gather together as many scope catalogs as possible and research all the pertinent factors of a contending scope. Make a list of all your contending scopes, while comparing such specifications as magnification, length, weight, eye relief, exit pupil, light transmission, twilight factor, field of view, click value, mounting length, adjustment range, type of reticle(s), target or standard type of adjustment turrets, type of external finish, and price. Once you have narrowed down your list you should personally compare optical quality for yourself, because this characteristic is usually overly subjective to accurately portray in words.

Conclusions

Nowadays, if I were to select a system of rifles for shooting at varmints out to around 1,000 yards and beyond I think I would make a few slightly different choices. I would plan my rifles under the shooting classes and rules of 1,000 yard competition. This way I could use my varmint rigs for both competition and varmint shooting.

I would build a total of four rifles under the Original Pennsylvania 1000 Yard Benchrest Club rules. One rifle for use in the Sporter classification (up to 11 pounds), one for Light classification (16.5 pounds and under), and two for Heavy classification (over 16.5 pounds).

My "Sporter" weight rifle would probably be a 6mm caliber, perhaps a fast twist version of the 6mm Improved or a 6mm Vais.

My "Light" weight rifle would be either a 6.5/284 Winchester or a 6.5-06 Improved. I would use an 8" twist barrel and throat the barrel for the longer VLD type of projectiles.

For a "Heavy" weight rifle I would actually have two rifles built, as one would serve in a backup role. Rifle number one would be chambered to a .308 caliber wildcat of some sort. Two wildcats come to my mind quickly, perhaps an improved version of a necked down 404 Jeffery, or a 300 Ultra Mag Improved. Heavy rifle number two would be my old faithful, the .338/416 Rigby Improved. Both of these rifles would weigh from 35 to about 50 pounds. I would use the best paper target grouping rifle for competition and both rifles for varminting. The .338/416 Rigby would get the most use for varminting at ranges over 1200 yards.

Shoot safely and remember, practice makes perfect,—or at least a trifle better shot.

(Caution: the loads mentioned here appeared safe in the mentioned firearms, but they may not be safe in other rifles. No representation as to their safety in your rifle is given by either the author or the publisher. Precision Shooting Inc. and the author(s) disclaim all possible liability for damages, including actual, incidental and consequential, resulting from reader usage of information or advice contained in this book. Use data and advice at your own risk and with caution.)

APPENDIX

BAER'S Gun Shop
19714 Swailes Rd. - P.O. BOX 228
Willow Hill, PA. 17271
(717) 349-4077
Fax: (717) 349-7647
Custom Long Range rifles built to your specification—Nightforce scopes

BAT Machine Co. Inc. (Bruce A. Thom)
11570 N. Bruss Rd.
Rathdrum, ID 83858
(208) 687-0341
Custom actions—BAT actions, Gunsmithing

Bear Basin Outfitters
WWW.BEARBASIN.COM
Orders only (800) 641-4470

Huge selection of premium optics, laser rangefinders

Berger Bullets, Ltd.
5342 West Camelback Rd.,
Suite 200
Glendale, AZ 85301
(602) 842-4001
Fax: (602) 934-9083
Match / VLD & varmint bullets

Burris Company,
P.O. Box 1747
331 E. 8th St.
Greeley, CO. 80631
(888) 228-7747
Fax: (970) 356-8702
Rifle scopes and optical gear

Bushnell Sports Optics Worldwide
9200 Cody,
Overland Park, KS 66214
(913) 752-3400
Fax: (913) 752-3550
Rifle scopes and optical gear

Deutsche Optik
P.O. Box 7518
San Diego CA 92167
(800) 225-9407
Military optical rangefinders, large selection of hard to find optics, binoculars, spotting scopes

Douglas Barrels, Inc.
5504 Big Tyler Rd.
Charleston, WV 25313-1398
(304) 776-1341
Fax: (304) 776-8560
Match grade barrels

Geske - Gerry
Box 517
Superior MT 59872
(406) 822-4917
Custom actions, 1000 yard actions

Grayback Wildcats
5306 Bryant Ave.
Klamath Falls, OR 97603
(541) 884-1072
Pre-formed wildcat brass (very large assortment)

Hammets VLD Bullets
P.O. Box 479
Rayville, LA 71269
(318) 728-2019
Match-grade VLD bullets

Hart Rifle Barrels, Inc.
P.O. Box 182
Lafayette, NY 13084
(315) 677-9841
Fax: (315) 677-9610
Match grade barrels

Holland's Gunsmithing, Inc.
P.O. Box 69
Powers OR 97466
(541) 439-5155
*Custom Gunsmithing, custom rifles,
chambering, muzzle brakes, recoil lugs*

H-S Precision, Inc.
1301 Turbine Drive
Rapid City, SD 57701
(605) 341-3006
Fax: (605) 342-8964
*Match grade cut-rifled barrels, custom rifles,
custom actions*

JLK Bullets
414 Turner Rd.
Dover, AR 72837
(501) 331-4194
Match/VLD bullets

Krieger Barrels, Inc.
N114 W18697 Clinton Dr.
Germantown, WI 53022
(414) 255-9593
Fax: (414) 255-9586
Match grade barrels

Laser Technology, Inc.
7070 S. Tucson Way
Englewood, CO 80112
1-800-280-6113
Laser rangefinder—the Impulse 2K

Leica Camera Inc.,
156 Ludlow Ave.

Northvale, NJ 07647
(800) 222-0118
Infrared laser rangefinder—Leica Geovid

Leupold & Stevens, Inc.
P.O. Box 688
Beaverton, OR 97075-0688
(503) 526-5195
Fax: (503) 526-1475
Rifle scopes and optical gear

Lightforce U.S.A.
19226 66th Ave. So.
Bldg. L-103
Kent, WA 98032
(425) 656-1577
Fax: (425) 656-1578
*Nightforce scopes and accessories, unequaled
candlepower spotlights*

Lilja Precision Rifle Barrels
P.O. Box 372
Plains, MT 59859
(406) 826-3084
Fax: (406) 826-3083
Email: lilja@montana.com
Match grade barrels

McBros - McMillan Bros Rifle Co., Inc.
P.O. Box 86549
Phoenix, AZ 85080
(602) 582-3713
Fax: (602) 582-3930
Custom rifle and actions—including .50 caliber

Mitchell Optics Inc.
2072 CR 1100 N
Sidney, IL 61877
(217) 688-2219
Fax: (217) 688-2505
Precision external adjustment rifle scopes

**NAIT—North American Integrated
Technologies**
P.O. Box 82049
San Diego, CA 92138
(619) 293-7111
Fax: (619) 293-7087
Laser rangefinder—the XLR

NECO
536-"C" Stone Road
Benicia, CA 94510
(707) 747-0897
Fax: (707) 747-0898
Moly coating kits/supplies, concentricity
indicator firelapping kits, computer ballistic
programs-QuickLOAD

Nikon, Inc.
1300 Walt Whitman Rd.
Melville, NY. 11747
(800)-Nikon US
Scopes, binoculars, laser rangefinders

Northwest 1000 Yard Benchrest Association
1,000 Yard Benchrest competition. Matches are
held in Missoula MT, Whitefish MT, and
Challis ID. In affiliation with the Original
Pennsylvania 1000 yard Benchrest Club.
(406) 756-0171, (406) 755-6388, or
(406) 892-3742

Nosler Inc.
P.O. Box 671
Bend OR 97709
(800) 285-3701
Fax: (541) 388-4667
Match/varmint bullets

Obermeyer Rifle Barrels
23122 60th St.
Bristol, WI 53104
(414) 843-3537
Fax: (414) 843-2129
Match grade barrels

JBM Ballistics
P.O. Box 3648
University Park, NM 88003
(505) 523-5191
Jbm@lascruces.com
Computer ballistic program

Pac-Nor Barreling
P.O. Box 6188
Brookings, OR 97415
(541) 469-7330
Fax: (541) 469-7331
Match grade barrels, chambering, huge
selection of wildcat cartridges

Pentax Corp.
35 Inverness Dr. E.
P.O. Box 6509
Englewood, CO. 80112
(303) 799-8000
Fax: (303) 790-1131
Scopes, binoculars, laser rangefinders

***Precision Shooting* Inc.**
222 McKee Street
Manchester, CT 06040
(860) 645-8776
Fax: (860) 643-8215
Publishes monthly magazines—Precision
Shooting & The Accurate Rifle, book publisher

Premier Reticles, LTD.
920 Breckinridge Lane,
Winchester, VA 22601
(540) 722-0601
Fax: (540) 722-3522
Custom scope reticles, Leupold scopes

QuickLOAD-ballistic software program—
see NECO

RDP Rifles
Rick Piccarreta
HCR 64, Box 33C
Huntington Mills, PA. 18622
(570) 864-0989
Custom rifles, Aluminum stocks

Rocky Mountain Rifle Works, LTD.
931 Stone Canyon Rd.
Longmont, CO 80503
(303) 823-6270
Cut-Rifled barrels—match grade

Schmidt & Bender Inc.
P.O. Box 134
Meriden, NH 03770
(800) 468-3450
(603) 469-3565
Fax: (603) 469-3450
Rifle scopes

Schneider Rifle Barrels, Inc.
12202 N. 62nd Place
Scottsdale, AZ 85254
(602) 948-2525   *Match grade barrels*

Scoplevel
977 E. Stanley Blvd. #365
Livermore, CA 94550
(510) 449-5052
Fax: (510) 373-0861
Rifle scope level device—to prevent canting

Shilen Rifles, Inc.
P.O. Box 1300
205 Metro Park Blvd
Ennis, TX 75119
(972) 875-5318
Fax: (972) 875-5402
Email: info@shilen.com
Match grade barrels, triggers, bullets

Sierra Bullets
1400 West Henry St.
Sedalia, MO 65301
1-800-223-8799 or 1-888-223-3006
Fax: (660) 827-4999
*Varmint & target bullets, handloading
manual/CD, computer ballistic program,
technical support*

Simmons Outdoor Corp.
201 Plantation Oak. Dr.
Thomasville GA. 31792
(912) 227-9053
Rifle scopes and optical gear

Sports Electronics
P.O. Box 696
Hinsdale, IL 60522-0696
(630) 920-1808
Fax: (630) 920-1819
Laser Rangefinder

Swarovski Optik
One Wholesale Way,
Cranston, RI. 02920-5540
(800) 426-3089
Rifle scopes and binoculars

Swift Instruments, Inc.
952 Dorchester Ave.
Boston, MA 02125
(617) 436-2960
Scopes & optics

Tasco
P.O. Box 520080
Miami, Florida 33152-0080
(305) 591-3670
Fax: (305) 592-5895
Scopes & optics—laser rangefinders 1

T.K. Lee Co.
1282 Branchwater Lane
Birmingham AL 35216
(205) 824-0250
Custom scope reticles

Varmint Hunters Association, Inc.
Box 759
Pierre, SD 57501
1-800-528-4868
*Publishes quarterly magazine—The VARMINT
HUNTER Magazine*

Varmint Masters LLC
P.O. Box 6724
Bend OR 97708
(541) 318-7306
Portable rotating shooting bench

Chapter 5

Ultra Long Range Shooting In Colorado (Parts 1-2-3)

by Steve Hugel

(Editor's introduction: We published Part I of this three part article in the July, 1998 issue of Tactical Shooter magazine. And stood a number of our readers on their collective ear. We published Part II in the September 2000 issue of Precision Shooting magazine. More hysteria in the streets followed.

These were two of the most popular articles that we ever published, and there was just no way that we were going to publish a book on 1,000 yard shooting, and not include them. So we asked our writer, Steve Hugel, to author a closing chapter (Which in a burst of creativity we labeled "Part III") to touch on any loose ends, and to incorporate answers to points where he'd had multiple inquiries. All three parts are herewith, and it is a fascinating read for anyone interested in long range shooting…and we do indeed mean just that…long range).

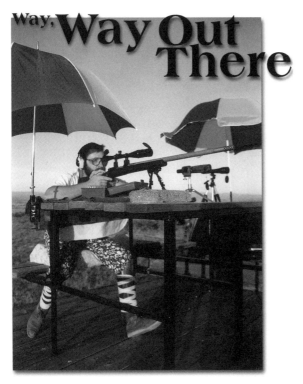

Part I

(Editor: Our Bill Shehane-authored article on long range (1000 yards plus) shooting in the very first issue of **Tactical Shooter** has drawn a remarkable request/demand for "more of this." Well, we've got another one for you. Enjoy!)

Bruce Artus from Bill's Gun Shop in Pueblo, Colorado shoots prairie dogs from his portable, homemade bench way, way out there. His Obermeyer barrelled Winchester 70 in .308 Ackley Improved is launching 220 grain Matchkings into the next millennium...And those singular leg gauntlets were not designed for leg protection during a night of dancing at Studio 54. Our shooter encounters maybe a half-dozen rattlesnakes a day out there in the prairie dog world. The gauntlets sort of level the playing field when meeting one of the scaley folks.

The distinctive sound the big Sierra made as it cut a path through the dense, early morning air will remain etched in my memory forever. I peered through the ocular of the spotting scope and heard the action of the Model 70 Winchester cycle, driving another cartridge home into the chamber of the big gun. Finally, after what seemed like an eternity, a puff of dirt and dust rose into the air downrange, scant inches from the prairie dog the bullet was meant for. As I began to relate the location of the bullet's impact relative to its intended target, I was suddenly interrupted by the report of the gun as it went off again sending another projectile on its way downrange. I glanced at my watch and then back

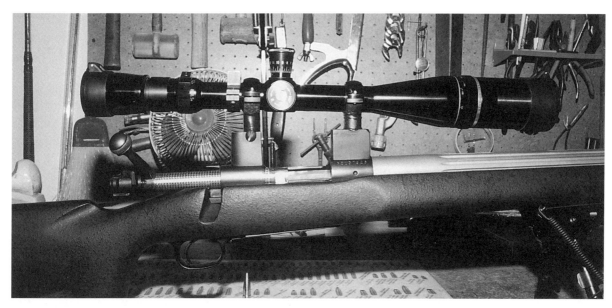

Bruce's Model 70 Winchester, Obermeyer barrel, Leupold-Premier 18-40X, specially designed bases, and altered Burris Posi-Align rings.

again to the spotting scope in an attempt to record the bullet's time of flight. The shooter cycled the action again, and then all was quiet as we both watched the prairie dog through our respective optics, anticipating a hit. Another puff of dust rose again in the mound just below the prairie dog, signifying the bullet's impact. I glanced at my watch and couldn't believe my eyes. Six seconds had elapsed from the beginning to the end of the projectile's journey at an unbelievable distance downrange.

A close-up of the action area of Bruce's gun.

The sun was just starting to peek over the horizon out on the prairie north of Pueblo, Colorado that day as several more Sierras were launched in an attempt to connect with a prairie dog at the longest of ranges. Bruce Artus, a gunsmith from Bill's Gun Shop here in Pueblo, and I were sitting 7 ft. off the ground on a specially designed shooting bench that was attached to a trailer he had towed into the pasture. I must confess, I was not used to getting up at 4:00 a.m. to go prairie dog shooting, but Bruce told me that at the ranges we were trying to shoot we only had a window of about thirty minutes or so

before the mirage would eliminate any possibility of even seeing our targets. I had brought along my Savage 112V 220 Swift but it was still sitting in its case, and would remain there for awhile. It would do me no good to even attempt to use it when the prairie dog town was so far away that I couldn't even see it without the aid of high-powered optics. Bruce's gun was resting on Harris's bench model bipod and looked a little strange with the barrel angled up as high as it was. It also took on an odd appearance due to the fact that the 24X Leupold was mounted in specially made rings and bases that were designed to angle the scope downward slightly relative to the axis of the bore. I guess this is what it takes when your target is over 2000 yards away.

Now then, if you've recovered yet from your jaw hitting the floor, I want to stress to you that this is not a misprint. You read it right. In fact, the prairie dogs Bruce was shooting at that day were precisely 2300 yards from our shooting position. I know that many of you out there are scoffing at this, and to tell you the truth, I was pretty skeptical myself when Bruce told me he had broken the 2000 yard mark on a prairie dog earlier this year. But since I knew both Bruce and Bill and had experienced their gunsmithing abilities firsthand, I knew that if anyone could do it, they could. I have been out with shooters, myself included, that indiscriminately pop away at dogs beyond 500 yards with their standard varmint rigs and waste 20 or 30 rounds before they finally luck one into their target, thus ending the melee. This was not the same. Bruce is a cool, calculating customer that understands trajectory and wind drift like few others, and leaves nothing within control up to chance. He already has the longest recorded shot on a rodent ever witnessed at 2067 yards, and is now trying to best his own record. He didn't get any that morning before the mirage washed us out, but using the methods he does, success is inevitable.

If you're still not scoffing, you might be asking yourself by now, what does it take to hit a target just slightly bigger than a Coke can beyond 2000 yards? First off it requires, as you may well imagine, a rifle chambered in a cartridge capable of chucking a very heavy, aerodynamic projectile through variable wind currents accurately (read: very accurately). Since Bruce works at a first-class gun shop here in Pueblo, he has access to the best gunsmithing supplies available. His choice of actions? Winchester's Model 70. As Bruce explained, it is a flat-bottomed action with an integral lug, leading to its time-proven strength and accuracy, which makes it an excellent choice for the task at hand.

Bruce feels that maintaining the integrity of the bullet is one of the secrets to success at long range; therefore, he chose to use one of Boots Obermeyer's fluted barrels at 28", as they have a reputation for treating bullets, shall we say, delicately? Boots' barrels incorporate an angulared odd numbered rifling that theoretically reduces trauma to the bullet. This design puts a land opposite a groove, which lessens bullet distortion relative to the more conventional land-opposite-a-land. This particular barrel is one that Boots unscrewed from one of his own rather well-used competition guns, for Bruce's use. Certainly, it's common enough knowledge now that fluting helps with the rigidity of the barrel, but there has been some question recently whether it actually

decreases cooling time as has been theorized. Basic physics states that a larger surface area dissipates heat faster than a smaller one. Simple logic and common sense would allow you to reach the same conclusion. Bruce has the whole package resting comfortably in one of H-S Precision's bench model stocks with an aluminum bedding block, using Devcon's Plastic Steel Putty.

When I first heard Bruce talking about shooting at 2000 yards and beyond, visions of large capacity 30 caliber cases, such as the .300 Mag., Kong, or some such relative of the 1000 yard fraternity, were dancing in my head. Believe it

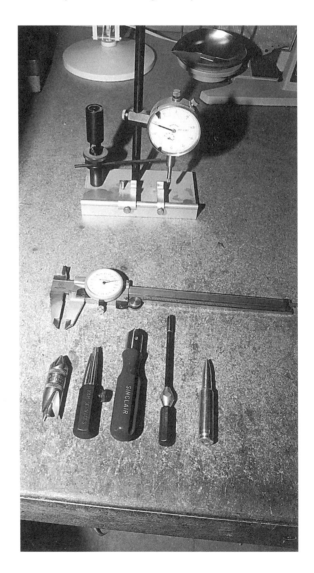

Some of the more familiar tools Bruce uses for brass preparation including RCBS's Casemaster Gauging tool in the background.

or not though, Bruce is doing his long range shooting with your basic garden variety .308 Winchester in Ackley's Improved configuration, standard SAAMI chambering, with a relatively large .342" neck. His choice was based upon availability, budget, and inherent accuracy of the parent case. As pertains choice of cases and preparation thereof, he uses Winchester brass. Flash holes are deburred with K+M's deburring tool, primer pockets uniformed with Sinclair's primer pocket uniformer, and necks are cleaned up and turned to a thickness of .0135" with Forster's neck turning attachment. An interesting tool that Bruce uses is K+M's tapered case mouth reamer. The idea here is to match the taper of the case mouth as close as possible to the angle of the bullet's boattail, such that it is seated in a manner that ensures no damage to the jacket. This is consistent with Bruce's bullet integrity theory. Certainly we would all agree that random scraping of the bullets as they are being seated into the case could cause problems later with external as well as internal ballistics. Any effect

on accuracy, however infinitesimal, can have a big effect on performance at these ranges. Brass is cleaned in Dillon's CV500 vibratory cleaner. Bruce uses Redding's Competition series die set, with a .332" titanium nitride bushing. Cartridges are assembled using Bonanza's Co-Ax press, and a Dillon 550B Progressive press. Charges are thrown with a Dillon powder measure, which

A close-up of the Leupold 6-24X converted to 18-40X by Premier Reticles.

Standard .308 Winchester next to Ackley's Improved counterpart.

The .308 Ackley Improved next to Sierra's 220 grain Matchking, and a recovered bullet on the far right.

according to Bruce renders exceptional accuracy with ball powders. Metered charges are verified with an Ohaus Model 304 scale. Cartridges are checked for concentricity using RCBS's Casemaster gauging tool.

What would you expect his choice of bullets to be? Sierra's 220 grain Matchking, certainly a proven projectile at long range. With a ballistic coefficient of .629 at the muzzle velocity that he is pushing it, it retains energy and velocity very well at long range. When questioned about his selection relative to the increased ballistic coefficient of Sierra's bigger 240 grain bullet, however, he looked me square in the eye, and responded in his typical matter of fact manner,

Bonanza's Co-Ax press with Redding's benchrest seater die installed.

"Why go up when I'm doing it with the 220?" Good point. A second later he chuckled and stated that the real reason was that the energy delivered to the 220 grain projectile is about maximum for the .308's case capacity. He explained that nothing would be gained in the field by using a heavier projectile. After considerable experimentation, 43.8 grains of H380 and Federal 210M Match primers produced the best groups, at a m.v. of 2400 f.p.s.

The heart of the entire system lies in the specially designed bases and rings Bruce has made for the gun. At these ranges he requires a system that will allow the scope to be tilted forward approximately 5 degrees from the bore. Consequently the scope must be raised somewhat to eliminate any interference the muzzle may have with the line of sight. Initially, I thought this was the poor man's method of avoiding a ranging reticle, but as Bruce enlightened me, these ultra-long ranges require considerably more than one scope's field of view for target acquisition. You'll have to excuse me for not taking into account the angle of the gun relative to the target. Unfortunately, there is a "slight" problem associated with this mounting system. Since the bases are offset, the rings are no longer in alignment. Normally this would make it impossible to mount the scope without completely redesigning the entire system. Actually, the solution was simple. Burris provided the answer in their Posi-align rings. Their .020" inserts allow for a point to point contact between scope and ring, eliminating the need to align the rings. It's not quite as easy as it seems though, as the body of the rings are still parallel with the action. This necessitates cutting the rings longitudinally so that the scope doesn't bind on the edges of the rings. Bruce freely admits that if it weren't for Burris' special design the alignment procedure would be considerably more difficult. They also present an added benefit of eliminating the lapping procedure for an entirely stress free system. I wonder if Burris, in their wildest dreams, had any idea what their design could be used for?

This arrangement now positions the scope's ocular too high off the gun to allow the use of standard bench technique in shooting. Bruce had to alter his technique to accommodate this unorthodox sighting system. By simply placing his hand on the cheekpiece of the stock he can raise his face high enough to be able to see effectively through the scope, and control recoil. The system, unusual as it may seem, does work though, as evidenced by his results. Bruce initially chose to use a Leupold 24X 1/8th" dot, but has since switched to a 6-24X with an 18-40X Premier (**TS** advertiser) conversion for increased resolving power with a fine-crosshair reticle.

Another question that you may be asking is how does one accurately measure 2000 yards in the first place? Actually, it's very easy if you have access to a Bushnell Yardage Pro 400 Laser Rangefinder. Bruce wrapped some aluminum foil around a large piece of cardboard and had a friend stand at a predetermined point in the prairie dog town holding the cardboard above his head. Bruce then walked off, taking readings with the rangefinder as he went. When he got to 500 yards he signaled to his friend to come up to him and they repeated the procedure six more times until they had accurately measured

3000 yards. This formed a basis from which any measurement can be taken from the initial point to any other spot in the dog town with a high degree of accuracy.

As important as the technical may be, everything goes out the window when Mother Nature is in an uncooperative mood. No other shooting discipline is affected as much by weather as extreme range shooting. Any irregularity encountered is magnified to a great extent way out there. Bruce explained that any inconsistency in wind velocity or misreading of mirage will send the bullet to a different impact point downrange. Wind flags are a necessity to keep track of downrange conditions as much as possible. The ground must also be very dry, such that the resultant dust cloud after the shot can be utilized to determine bullet impact.

Bruce likes to be in position and ready to go early in the morning when the first sign of activity is detected in the prairie dog town. From that point until mirage distorts the target beyond the

A view of Dillon's 550B Progressive press.

shooter's ability to see clearly, time is very limited, sometimes as little as thirty minutes. At that point the shooting is over for the day and you might as well pack it up and call it quits. Bruce explained that as mirage builds, it can act like a fog bank, coming and going unpredictably. He says that the combination of mirage and variable wind currents govern the outcome of the shooting more than any other factor.

His method of shooting is rather interesting. He uses Harris' excellent bench style bipod, which allows him to adjust the forend to be perfectly level with the aid of D.H.B. Products' anti-cant device. Once his target is located, he watches the wind flags until he feels confident that elevation and windage are adjusted in accordance with the conditions. At that point he begins shooting, observing point of impact each time, making a quick adjustment, then shooting again as soon as possible, in an attempt to send the bullet downrange as close as possible to the same conditions as the shot before. Six seconds may not seem very significant to those not associated with long range shooting, but it doesn't take Mother Nature long to change conditions to suit her fancy. The slightest change in wind velocity will blow the bullet off course several feet at 2000 yards.

When the shooting was over for the day we went downrange to see if we could find any of the bullets, as Bruce says they will skip along the ground 40 or more yards and can frequently be found intact, hardly any worse for wear. Walking around on hot days out here can be somewhat hazardous, as Bruce explained that rattlesnakes abound in prairie dog country. They love prairie dog mounds and often hole up in them to escape the midday heat. Bruce was well protected with a pair of homemade rattlesnake chaps he put together himself with thick pliable plastic taped round his shins. Normally I'm not much concerned with them but when Bruce told me he will sometimes run across five or six in the course of a day's shoot, I must admit it kept me thinking.

The impact craters in the dogs' mound that he was shooting at were unmistakable and proof positive of Bruce's ability to shoot accurately at these ranges. He has already begun altering the scope rings for even more range, and believe it or not, he even has the prairie dogs picked out he will be shooting at when he attempts to break the 2500 yard mark.

For those of you still scoffing, there's no question that a good degree of luck must be worked into the equation, especially when working so closely with, and at the mercy of, Mother Nature. But we all would certainly have to agree that even attempting this with less than the best of equipment would be an exercise in futility.

Shooting with Bruce that day was truly a humbling experience. You can bet I'll certainly never look at a successful 500 yard shot from the same perspective again. Doing what he does is so far removed from standard varminting that it almost seems like a different agenda altogether. I guess it just goes to show you though, the sky can literally be the limit when you really put your mind to something.

Steve Hugel
Pueblo, Colorado

Bruce Artus (left), and Kreg Slack (right) sit atop their portable shooting bench trying to connect on a 16" steel gong at a phenomenal 3,120 yards, with Bruce's .308 Ackley Improved, and Kreg's .264 Win. Mag.

Part II

Have you ever asked yourself the question, how far is too far? Do you ever look out there at that little speck of a prairie dog standing way too far out there on the horizon and wonder what if…, and then, just for the heck of it, take a whack at him? I know I have many times while using my standard varmint rifle/cartridge/scope combinations. But practically speaking, categorizing in 50-200 yard increments for the .223 and larger varmint cartridges, it usually goes something like this—out to 200 yards is a gimme, at around 250 —maybe 300 yards, let's call it reasonably confident, 300- around 350 how about "yeah-maybe", 350-400+/- would probably be referred to as "well-maybe", and beyond that is all just a big question mark, at least in my book. For some, specialized rigs will increase the confidence level to sometimes a considerable margin, depending of

Bruce Artus (right), and Kreg Slack (left) sit atop their portable shooting bench trying to connect on a 16" steel gong at a phenomenal 3,120 yards, with Bruce's .308 Ackley Improved, and Kreg's .264 Win. Mag.

course on degree of specialization even as far out as 800+/- yards. But beyond that it becomes a sort of no-man's land, only rarely investigated.

Right at the top of the list of investigators though has got to be Bruce Artus from Pueblo, CO. Bruce has the longest witnessed shot on a live animal ever recorded, at 2,632 yards, but is not done yet as his new setup has allowed him to set his sights (literally) to 3,000 yards and beyond. The first word that no doubt pops into your mind is baloney, or some such phrase that may not be quite as eloquent, yet effectively establishes the same point. No way Jose, you say? Well to put it simply and conventionally—WAY! Passion for some may be collecting stamps, for others racing fast cars, others still may be collecting Pokemon cards, and yet others may be attempting to hit a rodent-sized target with an airborne projectile as far way as is humanly possible.

Although the fraternity of Long-Range Rodent Shooters Extraordinaire is in its infancy, according to Bill Sturtevant, owner of Bill's Gun Shop here in Pueblo, there appears to be an underground movement among some accuracy-minded individuals to investigate this, as yet, uncharted territory. When I wrote the first article on Bruce's long-range shooting *(Tactical Shooter—July '98)* there was more controversy surrounding this endeavor than I had ever seen associated with any other shooting sport, even though I clarified the necessity for luck in the whole equation. In an attempt to quell some of the controversy this issue requires some much-needed attention.

As we all know, just about every endeavor requires a degree of luck to be completely successful—none more so than in the shooting/hunting sports. Bruce and his partner, fellow long-ranger Kreg Slack, also of Pueblo, have become a little leery of prying eyes these days, as the harassment they have received from fellow shooters has been rather unexpected. What a travesty it is when someone that could be a source of information to others has to be stifled by narrow-minded opinions. I for one, and others I'm sure, would like to know more about what is being attempted here. What validates Bruce and Kreg's endeavor is not so much what they are doing, but the fact that they are approaching it in a deliberately calculated manner. When something like this happens, where an interest may exist, we have a responsibility, as the vehicle for shooters everywhere, to help them answer the questions of how, and why, that inevitably arise. These guys that go beyond what seems to be the limits of practicality to investigate what is assumed to be impractical or maybe even impossible, to some are the dreamers, the innovators if you will, some of whom may eventually come to set the standard in the industry. Names like Ackley, Donaldson, Palmisano, and Milek immediately come to mind. In many of their pursuits they had to break away from mainstream thought to make their dreams a reality. In the end what it all boils down to is that precision shooting must be defined by the individual To some, satisfaction is in the attainment of it. Others are motivated by the pursuit of it. It may take them more than a little luck to accomplish their goal, but for

Kreg Slack's 30" Hart-barreled Model 70 .264 Win. Mag., and Bruce Artus' 30" Obermeyer-barreled Model 70 .308 Ackley Improved sit in front of 16" 3,120 yard steel gong.

Gong shot at 3,120 yards with Bruce's .308 A.I.

them the end justifies the means, whereas for the rest of us as observers it's just the opposite, in an attempt to gain information that may help us justify our own ends. Whatever the reason, on any given morning Bruce and Kreg can be found out on the prairie somewhere around Pueblo, sitting vigilant, watching the changing conditions for an opportunity to realize their goal. Anyone that is as motivated as they are will succeed, regardless of pessimistic opinions. The question is, will we be there to record the event, or are we going to be sitting in our armchairs with our feet up, criticizing?

Bruce is also getting some big name support from some of the heavy hitters in the business, namely Leupold scopes, Boots Obermeyer, and Dick Thomas of Premier Reticles. Boots has been supplying Bruce with a few of his precision barrels, and Leupold donated one of their 8.5-25X long range scopes, converted to 20-50X by Premier Reticles. These guys are all behind Bruce and Kreg 100%, and if that doesn't lend a bit of

credibility to their endeavor, I don't know what does.

That aside, let's get on with some more pertinent information. Bruce is still using the same equipment as before, with just a few minor changes. His Obermeyer-barreled .308 Ackley Improved is starting to show some throat erosion, which according to Bruce should be cured shortly with some new 28" 8.2 twist Obermeyer therapy, to be chambered in the same cartridge configuration. Kreg, on the other hand has been changing his equipment somewhat, to try different approaches. He started out with a .264 Win Mag., 30" Hart barrel, using the heavy 155 grain Sierra. Big and aerodynamic as this bullet is though, it isn't big enough for his purposes, as bullet impact was difficult to discern at these ranges. He just recently chambered one of Bo Clerke's 30" SS barrels to .338 Lapua in an effort to chuck as much weight as possible out there in the form of Sierra's 300 grain Matchking. His setup is based

Close-ups of elevated, tapered bases milled to fit Bruce's Win. Model 70.

around a Winchester 70 action, with a 2 oz. Jewell trigger, Dillon/McMillan collaboration tactical stock, Leupold 8.5-25X converted by Premier Reticles to 20-50X with a fine X-hair reticle. 85 grains of IMR7828 is giving him 2,750 f.p.s. muzzle velocity.

The big Lapua case dwarfs the .308 A.I., obviously giving more powder capacity, higher velocity, and consequently flatter trajectory.

Although high B.C. bullets are the real ticket to long-range success, increased velocity has an advantage in shortening time of flight. 6-10 seconds is a lot of time for a projectile to be hanging round airborne, leaving itself susceptible to changing atmospheric conditions. Flattening trajectory also helps in a way that may not be quite as readily apparent. Kreg says it eliminates the need for a duck and goose license, and it also

keeps you from interrupting shooting for low-flying 747's that may be trespassing in your air space.

Bruce and Kreg told me that the whole system pivots on optics—not just quality, but also resolving ability at high magnification. As Bruce explains, at 50X there is some residual mirage evident even during early morning hours so he tends to cut the magnification back some to around 40X. The fine crosshair reticle subtends about 1/8th M.O.A. which corresponds to about 4" at 3,000 yards, which just happens to be the same value for reticle movement for each click adjustment of the Leupold's windage and elevation knobs. Believe it or not, Bruce explains that at 2 miles the 40X Leupold-Premier conversion has the optical quality to resolve a T-post barb-wire strand against a contrasting background.

The heart of the whole system lies in the scope mounts. Obviously it would take more than a few fields of view to acquire the target at 50X with bullet drop approaching 900' at 3,000 yards. As described in the first article, tapered bases in conjunction with Burris's stress-free Posi-Align rings is the solution to this problem. As range increases, more taper (downward tilt) is needed,

necessitating higher bases to eliminate the barrel interfering with the field of view. Consequently what you have is something that looks more like a super-sniping Buck Rogers ray gun that ought to spit out laser beams instead of copper-jacketed projectiles. When switching from 2,000 to 3,000 yards Bruce needed to increase the angle of taper from 5 to 7.5 degrees for the .308 Ackley Improved, by relatively adjusting the height of each base, as well as increasing the total height of

Gong strike from Bruce's .308 A.I. at 3,120 yards showing 220 gr. Sierra jacket and core

Bruce's .308 A.I., and 3.120 yard gong strike.

both bases to allow for scope-muzzle clearance. The whole system is somewhat complicated, requiring different bases for various ranges, so Bruce, Kreg, and Bill put their heads together, and came up with a slick adjustable tapered base system that allows shooting at different ranges during the same shooting session, by simply adjusting base height with a turn of a screw. Bill intends to make these available to the public via the shop as soon as they work out all the bugs.

Several weeks ago as this is written, Bruce and Kreg encountered some unusually cooperative spring conditions, and after several sighter shots Bruce connected on a 16" steel gong he has been using for practice. Kreg was in the process of working out the bugs in his new .338 Lapua and consequently wasn't able to make a connection. After driving the mile and 3/4's to the gong, a perfectly mushroomed .308 copper jacket and core was found lying beneath it. As expected the bullet hit relatively perpendicular to the gong's surface since the jacket took on the appearance of a six-sided pinwheel, with all sides equally peeled to the bullet's base. With a gong strike behind them now, a freshly zeroed .338 Lapua, and late spring giving way to some more cooperative early summer conditions it was time to look for an unsuspecting victim.

The morning of May 31st, 2000 dawned clear and calm out on the prairie east of Pueblo. Kreg Slack and his significant other, Nadine Parry,

Gong strike pinwheeled jacket and core of .308" 220 gr. Sierra MK.

were sitting on Kreg's bench atop a low weathered mesa overlooking a shallow valley that rose up to a prairie dog town over 1 and 3/4 miles distant. Nadine was acting as spotter that day, as Bruce was at the shop working. As Kreg made some final adjustments to his equipment, the rising sun brought life to the prairie. Dozens of dogs scurried to and fro around the 16" gong Kreg was preparing to shoot at. Better conditions could not have been asked for that morning, with not even the slightest hint of a breeze to affect projectile flights. Nadine peered through a Premier-boosted Leupold scope set atop another varmint rifle, as Kreg chambered a cartridge in his .338 Lapua. The big, sleek 300 grain Sierra patiently awaited it's opportunity as Kreg settled into position for a shot. When all was right he took in a breath, held it, and began to apply just the slightest hint of pressure to the trigger. But just before it tripped, Kreg noticed a prairie dog adjacent to the gong sitting contentedly atop his mound. Sensing an opportunity, he instructed Nadine to turn her attention to the dog as it stood out boldly in the morning sun. A moment later the trigger tripped and the big Sierra was off and running. More than a few seconds later it struck downrange several feet from its intended target. The dog maintained his vigilance on top of the mound utterly oblivious to what had just occurred. A moment later, after the appropriate adjustments were made, another Sierra was launched downrange striking now only a foot or so from its intended target. As the prairie dog looked around inquisitively, trying to figure out what had just happened, Kreg made just the slightest of adjustments, and sent the third and final Sierra downrange. As the bullet descended towards earth the unfortunate fellow was struck amidships propelling him several feet into the air. He came to rest a few feet behind and to the side of his mound. The shot was measured with a laser rangefinder at 3,125 yards or 1.78 miles—the longest recorded rifle shot in history so far.

Wrapup, Part III

I can't quite recall the magazine the picture was in, so very many years ago, but for me I guess that's where it all began. The photo was part of an article written about varmint shooting, and the subject was a heavy-barreled rifle (the make of which also escapes me now) resting on sandbags, on the hood of a pickup. The gun was pointing away from the photographer toward a prairie dog town that dropped off to a valley, and rose again to a hillside maybe a thousand yards or so away. In the background were the rugged snow-capped peaks of what I assumed to be some isolated area of the Rocky Mountains. It was an inspiring photo unto itself, but what struck me most about it was the riflescope. It was a sleek long-tubed Unertl Ultra-Varmint that easily ran half the length of the rifle, and was absolutely the most fascinating thing I'd ever laid eyes on outside of Playboy magazine. The stark contrast between the rugged western landscape and the optical precision of that huge target scope held a fascination for a young teenager from Baltimore that can't be described by the written word.

Up to that point the only association with hunting and shooting I'd ever experienced was through the stories my uncles would tell me about eastern whitetail deer hunting with the popular lever and pump-action rifles of the day. But as I was destined to find out later, long range varmint shooting was different, actually worlds apart from that. That photograph triggered a fervent interest in varmint shooting and hunting for me that remains unsatisfied to this day.

Somehow this insatiable pursuit of varmint shooting landed me in Pueblo, a small town in Southern Colorado, three decades later. Through some local connections, I ended up one day in Bill's Gun Shop, which is where I first met Bruce Artus. Bruce was Bill's head gunsmith, and before I met him I really thought I was a long range varmint shooter. After all, out to around 500-yards or so, I was about as good as the next guy with the standard custom and factory varmint shooting equipment of the era. But the first time I went out prairie dog shooting with Bruce my whole concept of long range was blown right out of the water. 500-yards was a mere pittance compared to what he was attempting. 2000-yards?? It literally defied the imagination. And when I saw the specialized equipment he was using, I thought I was going to have to put my eyeballs back in my head, and like a cornucopia, the questions flowed forth. Six-second flight time? Oddball scope mounts? Why, wherefore, and how? This endeavor was so far removed from the average target and varmint shooting I had read about and been exposed to over the years I knew others out there would want to know what was going on also. Hence, the first two articles in **TS** and **PS**.

But there is one thing I'd like to get straight right from the get-go here. I have never professed to know anything about this very long range stuff (beyond my self-appointed limit of 500-yards). In fact I'm really not much of a target shooter either. My first love is the practical application of accurate guns, and reloading thereof, as pertains to standard varminting, and wildcat varmint cartridges. When it comes to this kind of shooting I am simply an interested observer with pen in hand. Most of the information garnered has come to me second-hand through Bruce and fellow long ranger Kreg Slack (who currently holds the world's record for the longest rifle shot ever recorded at 3125-yards), but in addition to 30 years experience striving for accuracy in the guns I shoot I have also had a little bit of additional help along the way.

Several years ago one of *Precision Shooting's* Annual Editions had a nice long chapter on long range written by Dan Lilja. It was well presented, and quite fascinating, I thought. There were also a handful of other articles, mostly by Dan in previous issues of **PS** describing his techniques of long range shooting. Recently, another **PS** publication was presented to us—Steve Hanson's book, "A Varmint Hunter's Odyssey". It is a long-awaited treatise of varmint shooting that contains a wealth of knowledge on very long range that should be considered the "bible" for serious varmint shooters everywhere. Any self-respecting varminteer that doesn't have a copy of this one in his shooting library is doing himself/herself a disservice, without question. These sources of information, and others helped give me a sort of theoretical background in my quest to understand the idiosyncrasies of this very long range game. But observing Bruce and Kreg on the firing line showed this basic trainee what it was like to hold a Doctorate degree in Long Range.

Recently, I asked the two what led them to embrace such an unusual endeavor? As Bruce explains, he began shooting at a very young age with archery equipment. Even then he was fascinated with shooting his bow at "long range". Some of the archery aficionados out there may remember when the first mechanical bows came out—the Jennings Model I compound being one of them. They were a conglomeration of pulleys and cables that turned the traditional world of archery onto its ear. With one of these in his hands, Bruce won the Arizona NFAA (National Field Archery Association) state championships three years running. They shot competitively out to 80 yards (a respectable distance for the "stick and string") and was really the beginning of "long range" for him. Bruce's interests eventually turned to Smith and Wesson, and Ruger .44 handguns, and then for some years later to various TC Contender configurations and calibers. Feeling a bit handicapped with insufficient scope magnification, and range limitations of the

Contenders in the varminting fields though, he eventually turned to long guns. Attempting shots further out led Bruce to customizing Remington and Winchester products, and eventually to changes in equipment (specifically cartridges and projectiles), up to his present battery or varmint guns devoted strictly to prairie dog shooting (.223 Ackley Improved, 6mm A. I., .25-06 A. I. And .308 A. I.). When asked why the switch from archery to guns, he told me although he still appreciated the challenge of archery, he just simply likes riflery and the challenge of connecting at the longest ranges possible, something archery doesn't provide.

Kreg explains that his interest in very long range began while he was an apprentice at Bill's Gun Shop, under Bruce's tutelage. Bruce's contagious exuberance for all things far and away sparked an interest in Kreg. Under Bruce's guidance Kreg built several varmint bench guns for prairie dogs, but his first attempt at a very long range rig was a flop. Based on the .300 Ultra Mag case necked to 6.5mm, 96 gr. IMR 7828 behind Sierra's 155 gr. MK was just a bit too much for the relatively small bore even with the

Bruce's reloading room, with several of the guns in his varmint battery.

32" Hart barrel, and the grossly overbore condition spelled inefficiency with a capital I. The 6.5mm has always been a favorite among thousand yard competitors due to the long, high B. C. bullets produced for it over the years, so Kreg decided to step down to a more conservative case design, while maintaining the same bore diameter in the .264 magnum chambering . 65 grains of the same powder was about right for the big 155, but he ran into another brick wall trying to observe bullet impact at 3000 yards. The 155, as efficient as it may be for its diameter, with a B. C. of .570 just didn't have the mass to kick up enough dirt and dust to be seen that far away, so it was back again to the drawing board. Since Bruce was doing well with his .308, and Sierra's 220 gr. MK, he thought why not go big also. Hence the .338 Lapua (technically the .338

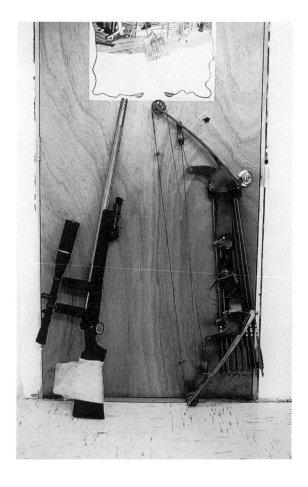

Two technological wonders—Bruce's .308 A. I., and one of the first compound bows to be mass-produced—the Jennings Model I.

Lapua Magnum) coupled with Sierra's huge 300 gr. MK.

Kreg's success with the rig is now history and he's quite pleased with the setup. He believes it to be a very efficient combination for volume shooting at these ranges, and also believes it will take him beyond 2 miles on a prairie dog. He already has a gong strike at 3600 yards with it, and has the prairie dog picked out, ready, and waiting in the wings. Bruce admits to being slightly outclassed by Kreg's flatter trajectory/big bullet approach, but he believes he won't be far behind, and actually enjoys the competitive spirit.

Looking at it from a practical standpoint, the .338 Lapua obviously has an advantage over the other two cartridges that can't be denied. After all, you're propelling a larger, more aerodynamic projectile at high velocity to extreme distance. The laws of physics dictate that an object that possesses large mass when placed in motion tends to be less reactive to outside forces than an object of less mass, and with a 10 second flight time, there are a lot of external forces working on that mass as it travels toward its target. Recently Bill Sturevant ran a ballistics chart for me to compare the 3 cartridges, bullets, and velocities at 3125 yards, using a trigonometric calculation on his home computer. As expected, the .338 Laupa/300 gr. Sierra at 2750 f.p.s. (B.C. of .768) came in first, with a bullet drop of 720 ft., a 360-ft. midrange rise above line of sight, and 7-second time of flight. The .264 mag. /155 gr. Sierra at 3050 f.p.s. (B.C. of .570) came in second with 748-ft. drop, 374-ft. midrange trajectory, and 8-second flight time. Bruce's .308 A.I./220 gr. Sierra at 2400 f.p.s. (B.C. of .629) gave 883 ft. of drop, 441 ft. at midrange, and 11-12 second flight time. With these figures it's not difficult to visualize the advantages of the high ballistic coefficient bullet at high velocity at long range.

But Bruce has couple of aces up his sleeve. First off he's just received a new .308" Obermeyer barrel. Boots' reputation for putting out the highest quality barrels has been well known for years in the shooting industry. Also, Bruce feels that although quality equipment is essential, nothing out there can replace experience—something Bruce happens to have a monopoly on, at the ranges we're speaking of. He believes that one of the most important qualities a long range shooter must possess is the ability to adapt shooting techniques to changing conditions, like observing slight changes in mirage and wind deflection, and knowing how to compensate for them. This would be akin to the professional baseball pitcher who instinctively knows where and when to release the ball when throwing a curve, a slider, or a knuckleball. Another important quality than can't be overlooked is good communication skills between shooter and spotter. These are the key ingredients that will make or break a long range shooter, and something only experience can teach.

Bruce feels that the various ballistic programs he's used in the past beyond 2000 yards are only good enough to get him in the ballpark. From there it's a matter of shooting and adjusting elevation until he's close, then taking the amount of elevation adjustment and converting it to the quantity of additional base height he needs. Sometimes all that is required is to cut a few hundredths off the front base to gain the required elevation for longer range. Other times a whole new set of bases is required to eliminate interference of the muzzle with the optics. Hopefully Bills' new adjustable base system will eliminate multiple bases for various ranges.

I also asked Bruce and Kreg if they're doing anything different relative to standard benchrest loading techniques. Bruce said he is doing only one thing different than what was published in the first article (**TS** – July '98). When turning necks on his Forster neck turning attachment, he found occasional variations in the thickness along the neck's length. He has resolved this problem by rotating the case 180 degrees, and recutting the neck as he withdraws the cutter, which he says, ensures a more consistent thickness, with no high spots.

There are really only 5 requirements to play this game, according to them. Big bullets, big cases, accurate guns, quality high-magnification optics, and most importantly, the motivation to excel. Bruce and Kreg stressed to me that you don't need 50 lb. guns to be dealt in. Simply fulfilling the aforementioned requirements will give you the edge you will need to expect a degree of success at very long range. Obviously there is a relationship between refinement of techniques and success, but not nearly as much as one might think. As a "famous" editor once told me, these guy are in "terra incognita" (unknown territory), and as there is no previous literature on what they're doing, they're learning the rules of the game as they go.

Of course the inevitable question is – where to from here? More range? More broken records? Bigger guns/ cartridges/scopes? When I posed this question recently, Kreg said he's going to continue on in range, and consequently, would like to see more magnification in the currently available optics. When he told me this I could see him 10 years from now developing a laser beam rifle or bases so high you have to stand on a ladder to see through the scope. Bruce says that although he's going to continue attempting to break his and Kreg's long range records, his time will be spent building accurate rifles at his shop. He wants to get more active in the competitive shooting scene, possibly helping to improve the local range enough to bring organized bench competitors to the area. Bruce feels there's a storm brewing on the horizon for prairie dog shooting and hunting in the western states. The emotional minority have already eliminated the Top Dog World Championships Prairie Dog Shooting Competition that was held in Nucla, CO every year because it "just isn't right", compromising a huge source of revenue for the local economies. He's not sure how many more years he'll be building varmint guns for the public, but varmint shooting, and gun building is his passion, so he'll stick to it as long as he can. For now though, there's always another prairie dog town over the next hill, and as long as there is a horizon in sight, Bruce, Kreg and others like them with a healthy imagination, motivation and resources, will be there reaching out farther and farther, always wondering, as we will, is there an end to it all?

Chapter 6

Recipes For Success — The Ingredients For A Great Long Range Rifle

by Ian Cheeseman

There is something immensely satisfying about lying down 1,000 yards away from a target and hitting the 10 ring (20 inches in diameter in high power long range competition) with regularity. All the problems inherent in good marksmanship multiply exponentially as you move back from the 600 yard line to 800, 900 and then 1,000 yards. Position, breathing, and technique must all be excellent, and when you add in light, temperature, and most of all wind, the variables can make shooting a great shot difficult, and shooting 20 of them a worthy and taxing challenge.

This chapter deals with the philosophy and execution of choosing and building a 1,000 yard rifle. I interviewed three excellent gunsmiths at length, spoke to others I respect, and I also own and regularly shoot several 1,000 yard rifles. All my shooting at the long distances is done on targets, which leads me to two caveats about 1,000 yard shooting in general and this article in particular. I feel strongly about this subject and do not apologize for my opinions:

One thousand yard, or longer, shooting is only valid in two circumstances and they are: at formal or informal, non-living, targets or in overt or covert military situations.

Hunting game or varmints involves a pact between the hunter and the quarry where the hunter tries his or her hardest to ensure a clean kill. Nobody, and I mean nobody, can come close to ensuring a clean kill on any mammal at 1,000 yards with a rifle.

As much better qualified writers than I will be covering military 1,000 yard shooting, this chapter will cover the art and science of building target rifles that will shoot significantly less than a minute of angle (moa) at the magic distance represented by ten football fields. For those shooters who do not live and breath this activity and who think that insistence on this kind of accuracy is obsessive, consider the 2000 National Long Range championships held at Camp Perry in Ohio. The winner of both the Leech Cup (iron sights) and Wimbledon Trophy (any sights) was 19-year-old Michelle Gallagher. To complete this feat she shot 200-15X in the Leech and 200-15X in the Wimbledon. The format of these two matches involves a shoot-off between the high scorers on each of the five

Michelle Gallagher at Bisley, July 2000.

relays. Michelle shot 100-7X in the Leech shoot-off and 100-6X in the Wimbledon shoot-off so that over two days she had shot a 600-43X. Looked at another way that means 71.7% of all her shots fell inside a 10 inch circle, and she was shooting from position, with a sling, not from a bench. Her group in the Wimbledon shoot-off is reported to have been 6¹/₂ inches tall by 4¹/₂ wide!

The point of all this is to illustrate that to win at the highest levels of long-range shooting requires an excellent shooter with a very carefully built rifle. The long-range gunsmiths I interviewed are 1992 and 1999 Palma team member Larry Racine (LR), long range shooter, precision engineer and Palma team armorer Alan Warner (AW), and Nevada-based long range shooter and gifted engineer McLane Tilton (MT). The other shooters and gunsmiths I talked to will be named as we go along.

Barrels

Q)   *What is the most important component involved in building a 1,000 yard rifle?*

LR)   For me it's the shooter, without a doubt. A long-range rifle must be shot well to show what it can do. In the end there is no special trick to building a rifle that will shoot well at this distance, but it will only shoot well if it is in good hands. After that, it is probably the barrel. Choosing a good barrel is essential. I have had a lot of good Krieger barrels but most of the good makers do a good job; Dan Lilja, Boots Obermeyer, Shilen, all of the custom makers turn out good barrels. I do prefer cut rifling because throats seem to last a bit longer, which is important when barrel life is as short as it is on some of the really hot calibers, but button rifled barrels, like Dan Lilja's, do look good. One thing I like about Krieger and Lilja barrels is that both John and Dan angle the side of the rifling and this seems to distort bullets less which must improve the bullet performance.

MT)   The barrel is definitely the heart of a long range rifle, and there are excellent makers out there. I use Border, Krieger, Obermeyer, Tru-Flite, McClellan, Gaillard, Shilen and Schneider barrels and they all shoot well. For a Palma rifle it is important to have a tight barrel. A .298" x .3065" to .3075" setup is now normal both here and in the other Palma nations. For standard .30 calibers such as the .300 Winchester Magnum, .300"x.308" is the accepted way to go.

AW)   I use Jack Krieger's barrels almost exclusively. I have always had good experiences with them and they are available. I use as many as 90 barrels a year in building or re-barreling rifles and I have only ever sent one of Jack's barrels back.

Q)   *What about seating depth and barrel life in long range rifles?*

LR)   You have to seat normal ogive bullets either well into the lands or have them not touching. I shoot all long range bullets off the lands except some of the VLDs which will not work unless they are seated into the lands. As for barrel life—a .300 Win. Mag. can be shot out in 1,300 rounds and some of the 6mm cartridges get less than that. Palma rifles (7.62NATO/.308 Winchester) can go to 3,000 with a Krieger barrel. I set mine back at least half an inch at 2,000 to 2,500 rounds.

The subject of throat length, particularly in rifles built for Palma competition using the compulsory 155 grain bullet, is interesting and somewhat vexatious. Accepted wisdom in the USA is that a short throat is essential, but here we shoot good or excellent ammunition almost exclusively. Norman Clark, one of the most respected gunsmiths in the United Kingdom (UK), explained that he and his UK-based peers prefer a longer throat in the 35 to 80 thousandths range as this gives less concentric ammunition a better chance to straighten out and enter the rifling more concentrically. Watching the results in the 1999 World championships in South Africa and the 2000 World championships in the UK would lend credence to this thesis. David Tubb, the eight-time national high power champion, gun designer and gun builder is quoted in Glenn Zediker's book (*Highpower Rifle*) as having success with VLD bullets seated well off the lands in his across-the-course rifles.

Calibers

Q) *There seem to be fashions in caliber selection, often driven by what the top competitors are shooting in any given year. Do you see an ideal caliber evolving?*

MT) Rather than any particular caliber, it is a question of bullet weight, bullet performance, ballistic coefficient and recoil. Currently the 6.5-284 is very popular and there is a good choice of bullets and weights in the 6.5 range from Sierra, Lapua and the custom manufacturers such as Berger, and Cauterucio and others. The 6.5-06 Improved (based on the ever popular 30-06 case) is another choice that people are shooting long range. The 30 caliber cartridges are also popular with the perennial 300 Win. Mag and 30-338 giving good results with Sierra bullets in the 190 grain to 240 grain range, offering great performance and enough accuracy to win the Leech or the Wimbledon.

LR) I also see a lot of 6.5-based long range rifles being requested as well as Palma rifles, which have become very popular in the past couple of years. The main factors are velocity and the ability to stay supersonic all the way to the target. In a Palma rifle with the 155 grain Sierra bullet that means that it must leave the barrel going 2,950 feet per second or it will be transonic at 1,000 yards or less. I don't get asked

to build magnums any more, they are completely out now. Whatever you do, the velocity deviation has to be as close to zero as possible – vertical dispersal at 600 yards that will stay in the 10 ring will show eight-ring to eight-ring variations at 1,000 yards. The 6.5 calibers I have built recently have included 6.5-284, 6.5-06 and 6.5 Remington Magnum, which will cycle through a short action and has ballistics similar to both those cartridges.

AW) All the demand I see is for Palma rifles and long range guns in 6.5—mainly 6.5-284 but also the 6.5 Remington Mag. which I build without the belt on the case. In fact, the beltless 6.5 Rem Mag is a better cartridge in my opinion than the 6.5-284, it's a better shape. Apart from those I do the occasional project—I am building a 6.5 Lazzeroni which has a really short, fat case, but the brass is supposed to be expensive and as you know, you need a lot of brass if you are going to shoot many matches.

In past years cartridges like the 7mm Remington Magnum have gained popularity, and people are shooting cartridges such as the Remington 6BR and .243 Winchester which drive the Sierra and Berger heavy 6mm bullets at enough speed to make them competitive at 1,000 yards, particularly in the new "F" class optical competitions which have proved very popular.

Author's note: I have included some examples of BCs listed by bullet makers for their products.

Some examples of Ballistic Coefficients

Manufacturer	Caliber	Weight (gr)	BC
Sierra	6mm	107 MK	.527
Berger	6mm	105 VLD	.565
Lapua	6.5mm	123 Scenar	.547
Norma	6.5mm	130 VLD	.545
Lapua	6.5mm	139 Scenar	.615
Sierra	6.5mm	142 MK	.595
Sierra	7mm	168 MK	.488
Sierra	.30 Cal.	155 MK Palma MK	.450
Sierra	.30 Cal.	190 MK	.533
Berger	.30Cal.	190 VLD	.583
Sierra	.30 Cal.	220 MK	.629

Note: All BCs are taken from the Sierra Infinity software package on CD-ROM

Some are obtained by calculation and some by scientific observation, but all are based on criteria that may not be reproducible outside the laboratory or test environment. I have shot all the bullets in the table, some of them very extensively, in real world competition at distances from 600 yards to 1,000 yards. In my experience Sierra's claimed BCs are most often reflected in competition, while those from Berger, Lapua and Norma are more difficult to match under non-laboratory conditions. One interesting observation is that the bullet with the lowest BC in this chart—the Sierra 155gr Palma Match King, is probably the most widely used long range bullet in competition around the world.

Actions

Q)   *There are more styles and types of actions, both custom made and mass produced, available today than in recent memory. Is there an ideal action, and if so which of today's available actions comes closest to that ideal?*

MT)   I don't think that there is one perfect action, in fact any strong, well made action will shoot if it is trued and absolutely square. Having said that, I personally think that the three lug style is better because it is easier to get equal balance on three lugs than on a four lug and it gives a better distribution of force than a two lug action. Having said that, the South Africans won the Palma Trophy (the Team World Championship) in 1999 with most of them shooting Musgrave two lug actions that were designed many years ago. Three lugs also require less opening force than four lugs. Currently people are having a lot of success with RPA Quadlock four lug actions, and I am a big fan of the Barnard action which I am importing from New Zealand.

AW)   I have been shooting a round RPA2000 four lug action for the past three years and I am very pleased with it. The best

value for money at the moment is probably the new RPA Quadlite single shot action which is doing very well. I have built three or four of them. The Stolle and Nesika Bay benchrest actions are well made and geometrically precise. I am also building rifles on the Barnard action and that is a good choice too. Mainly what you want in a long range gun is a short stiff action that is made to exacting tolerances.

LR)   I like a short stiff action, the shorter the better, firing short fat cartridges—a recipe with which the benchrest shooters have seen a lot of success. I have built excellent long range rifles on Savage, Winchester, Remington solid bottom 40X, Remington XP100s, RPAs, just about any stiff action that can be trued. (It should be noted that Larry shoots a Savage solid bottom, short action that was one of only a few made in the 1960s, and shoots it well enough to get on two Palma teams in the 1990s). I also like benchrest actions such as the Stolle and Hall products which are stiff and very well made. The main thing is to get the spring out and to be able to bed the action well into the stock so that it is properly supported.

The shooters on the successful United States Under 25 and Under 21 teams that took part in the Millennium World Championships shot a broad range of actions including Stolle, RPA, Remington, Winchester, Paramount and the new TUBB 2000 action. All the rifles held excellent elevation and there did not seem to be very much to choose between any of them for match accuracy. More important was the construction and maintenance of the rifle and the capabilities of the shooter. In the end, if the shooter has confidence in the rifle and the gunsmith that built it, he or she will shoot it well.

Stocks and Bedding

Q)   *Bedding an action seems to be the one*

area where gunsmiths really diverge. Is there a best engineering solution or can different methods all be successful?

LR) For long range single shot actions, there should be no bedding under the barrel, it must be free floated. I use Bisonite and add extra steel which is very tough and rock hard. It is important that the action screws do not add tension on the bedding, there should be no pressure at all—and then when you torque the screws down, I am a believer in the short end of an Allen wrench being all the torque you need. I frequently use Bisonite to make pillars. They are as good as steel but Bisonite can be hard to work with. I am not a big believer in bedding blocks, although they do help to stiffen stocks. When I use a bedding block I also use a thin layer of bedding compound to ensure an exact fit. I am looking at the PUG aluminum stock and the Choate varmint stock and they are promising. The aluminum stocks that are popular overseas do need a little bedding compound to make them shoot at their best. McMillan prone stocks are a good choice but they can be a bit heavy for a Palma rifle so you need to choose the hardware carefully.

MT) I am not sure that pillar bedding will provide enough support in a long range rifle. If you use a good bedding block and a skim of bedding compound for a round action, that will usually do an excellent job. I am using bedding blocks on the Barnard actions very successfully. The stock shape and design is very important if you are going to shoot long range well and within that, the grip should be compatible with the trigger pull to ensure that you get a clean break on the shot. My favorite styles are the Anschutz classic prone stocks, the 1411 and 1413 styles. I am not sure that an excellent across the course stock, such as the David

Tubb style, is a good way to go in a prone-only rifle which is dedicated to a single position. From an engineering and design point of view some of the new aluminum stocks look very good, but we need to see whether the action clamp style or the standard stock screw type are better.

AW) As far as bedding goes I am strictly a believer in epoxy and pillars. This system gives excellent results, is stable and it works. It works in fiberglass, laminated and wood stocks. I am not really convinced about aluminum stocks yet but some people are shooting them well. Before you choose a stock you should try as many types as you can, The shooting community is pretty good about letting you strap into a gun to try it and that is the best way to see what works. Style and looks are less important than fit.

Steve Gluck is a gunsmith who works in New York State and is a former Porsche and Rolls Royce engineer as well as a sought after cabinet maker. His wood stocks are works of art that he builds from scratch. Knowledgeable shooters beat a path to his door when they have stock problems.

SG) You can usually tell how well an action is bedded by attaching a dial indicator to the tip of the stock with the indicator on the barrel and then releasing the tension on the pillars and seeing if the barrel moves. Any significant movement, more than two or three thousandths, means the bedding is suspect. Zero movement also means problems because that shows that something is binding. I do not like to see recoil logs that are 100% bearing on all sides. Really the only surface that matters is the back of the lug because that is where all the pressure goes. I relieve the lug on the front, sides and bottom so that when you put the action in and out of the bedding you don't shave minute pieces off and have problems with seating the lug or the bottom of the action. I use Bisonite because it is strong and seems to be impervious to cleaning fluid and gun oil. Pillars need to be of stainless or chrome-moly steel and have sufficient clearance so that the bolts do not rub on the pillars. Wood stocks look great and feel right but stocks for long range guns should be fiberglass or laminated wood, because it removes one more variable in what is a complex package.

At the Millennium World championships one of the U21 team was having real problems with his Palma rifle not shooting on call and shooting big groups. Mid Tompkins—the captain of every Palma team since the mid-1980s, and an excellent gun builder in his own right (he built the gun that Michelle Gallagher shot with devastating results in the Leech and Wimbledon this year) took twenty minutes with just an Allen wrench and screwdriver to relieve the bedding which made the gun shoot like a house on fire. Bedding really matters in a long range rifle.

Some of the best stocks are being made in Canada and are keenly priced because of the dollar differences between the two countries. For a long range non-Palma, rifle the McMillan prone stock is an excellent choice but it is quite heavy, a benefit except in international matches where there is a very conservative weight restriction of 6.5 kilos or approximately 14 pounds, 2 ounces. There are excellent custom stock makers including Lone Wolf, who have stocked some of my guns.

Sights

The sights on a long range rifle come in two distinct types: iron sights which are really very fine adjustable and repeatable micrometers; and telescopic sights which can be either fixed or variable power. As most shooters only possess one long range rifle and the scope is mounted and dismounted for each any sight match, the mount must return to zero every time. With iron sights, a front sight that is adjustable for height is a real advantage as this allows the shooter to maintain his head position with minimal changes to the rear sight height.

1000 Yard Highest Scores At The National Matches

DATE	LEECH Iron sights	WIMBLEDON Any sights
1993	200-10x	200-15x
1994	200-10x	Match cancelled (Weather)
1995	199-12x	200-14x
1996	199-7x	200-13x
1997	199-9x	200-11x
1998	200-12x	200-11x
1999	200-11x	200-11x
2000	200-15x	200-15x
Average	**199.625 – 10.75x**	**200.00 – 12.86**

Note: Scores taken from the National Matches High Power Rifle Awards bulletins 1993 – 1999 and preliminary scores from the NRA Stats office, 2000.

To the shooter who does not shoot at 1,000 yards it may seem obvious that a scope will give markedly superior results at long ranges. As the table below shows, this is not the case. I have tabulated the highest scores with irons and scope sights at 1,000 yards at the Nationals since 1993 (all the figures I had on hand). In those eight years the average score in the any sight (read scope) matches was only 0.375 better than the iron sight matches or less than 1/5th of one percent. In the last three years the iron sight scores are actually better by one X. The scores shown are not necessarily the winning scores but are the highest shot on the day on any relay.

Q)   *What is the best sight set up for long range shooting, both iron sights and scopes, and what power and style of scope do you recommend. (Note: Alan Warner was not asked about iron sights because he manufactures them.)*

LR)   I like the look of the RPA rear sight, (*Author's note: which can be specified with either US direction knobs or with English direction knobs which turn the same way as a service rifle.*) But the best sight is the Warner that is specified by the Palma team. There are various ladder front sights and the RPA is popular. For a scope the bridge mount is the way to go, although a Unertl with solid mounts also works well. Any good scope will work, but it must be a good scope—it doesn't have to be too powerful, 10 or 16 power is more than enough.

MT)   For irons I like a ladder front sight

with an adjustable aperture, the RPA works well and keeps the sights as close as possible to the center of the bore. Either a Warner or RPA Trakker rear sight with an adjustable iris is an excellent choice and a magnifying rear diopter can be a big help. For scopes, a solid mount with Weaver or Piccatiny rail that extends three inches over the barrel and properly made rings such as Badger Ordnance or Burris Z rings are essential. You need 3¹/₂" of eye relief, with about ¹/₄ of tolerance to get your head position right. The objective lens does not need to be too large, 40mm to 42mm is about right. Again you want the center line of the scope as close as possible to the bore to avoid canting errors. Any quality scope will do a good job, and you don't need huge magnification, 16 power is about the upper limit. Burris is making some excellent scopes now.

AW) I recommend a ladder front sight for use with irons, it keeps your head position constant. With scopes it is a compromise between weight, quality and magnification. Too much magnification makes it hard to hold a sight picture and shows a lot of mirage. Too much weight on the gun, with a big scope and solid mount, means that you start to tire towards the end of perhaps 30 rounds at Camp Perry.

Alan's comments on sights are shorter than the others because he makes probably the best rear sight in the world. It is mandatory for the Palma team, and chosen by many of the best shooters in the world. If imitation is the sincerest form of flattery, then Alan is being flattered by PNW Sights who are making an impressive sight that looks very similar to the Warner but is beefier and which lacks some of the features of the Warner. In particular, the method of zeroing the dials is more complex and awkward. However, if money is critical, then the PNW or RPA will make an excellent substitute for the Warner, which can be hard to come by despite the price tag that reflects their quality.

I use Leupold scopes almost exclusively in competition, I have others by Pentax, Nikon and Zeiss but I return to the Leupolds because they work for me. My favorite reticle is a plain cross hair, but reticle choice is a personal thing and you should look through as many as possible before deciding.

Conclusion

What makes a winning 1,000 yard rifle? According to the experts I have spoken with it takes a good barrel, probably from one of the leading custom makers like Jack Krieger; in a caliber and cartridge that offers a high BC with good velocity, such as the 6.5-284; a well made, solid bottom action like a Barnard, RPA or Nesika Bay, that is robust and geometrically accurate in all dimensions; an excellent stock in fiberglass or laminated wood, that fits the shooter and which has a bedding job of the same quality, either directly in epoxy or using a bedding block; and good, repeatable sights from Warner or RPA if you are using irons; or one of the good scope manufacturers such as Burris or Leupold.

Finally, it must be engineered by someone who understands long range shooting and its specific requirements. In the hands of a good shooter you will have a winning combination on the range or an awesome 1,000 yard plinker. All for a cost of about $3,000 to $3,500, not bad for a gun that can shoot 6 inch groups at 1,000 yards, from position.....if you do your part.

Larry Racine
(603) 357-0055

Alan Warner
(603) 352-9521

McLane Tilton
(775) 588-9071

Steve Gluck
(914) 897-4238

Chapter 7

1000 Yard Benchrest

The Dawn Of A New Era

by Jacob Gottfredson

The Dawning of A New Era ... the firing line at Hawks Ridge Gun Club, NC. Photo courtesy of Bill Shehane.

The Birth and Objectives of Benchrest Shooting

Objectives of the National Bench Rest Shooters Association, Inc.:

1. *The development and encouragement of extreme accuracy in rifles, ammunition, equipment and shooting methods.*
2. *The achievement of extreme precision in rifles, ammunition, equipment, and shooting methods by shooting "groups".*

Although there are five objectives statements on the first page of the *Official Rule Book and By-Laws of the NBRSA*, those above are the most pertinent to the discussion at hand. And ... while the rule book of the NBRSA just happened to be handy, the goals are similar for all the benchrest organizations. The format has changed slightly over the years to accommodate new benchrest variants such as hunter, rimfire, and other scoring classes, but the philosophical intent has not changed.

Some reflection on the statements above may supply part of the answer to the question of why benchrest has remained a rather Spartan organization in the face of such huge involvement and participation in other shooting sports. Shotgunning, high power, silhouette, black powder, big game hunting, varminting, et. al. are populated by a great deal more enthusiasts than is benchrest.

"Pedantic", "purist", "academic", "accuracy for accuracy's sake" are terms that often come to mind to the rifleman who is turned off by the pursuit of benchrest. The vast majority of riflemen, to include competitors, are just not interested in accuracy to such a degree. And there is certainly a pragmatic logic to their disdain of such efforts. Even snipers are tolerant of, or satisfied with, minute of angle results ... and who should be more pragmatic. Certainly big game hunters are not worried about any better and, more often than not, are happy with 1.5 MOA.

Few are driven by the desire to take accuracy to such an extreme. Yet, fortunately, the pursuit seems to burn in the heart of a few, generation after generation. Ironically(?) ... the slow but sure adaptation of the accuracy improvements made by the benchrest clan are incorporated by the manufacturers of both assembly and custom rifles and by the general shooting population. The adaptation of benchrest accuracy techniques finds its way into the reloading sector as well.

And while benchrest might have had what is traditionally thought of as its fledgling beginnings at the shorter ranges of 100, 200, and sometimes 300 yards, the desire burns strong among some to make the rather considerable leap to the magic number 1000.

The "Original 1000 Yard Benchrest Club of Pennsylvania" holds a certain heroic claim to those fledgling beginnings of formal 1000 yard benchrest competition. It is interesting to note that the origin of benchrest, and of the shorter ranges, had its start not far from those of 1000 yard benchrest. In the past decade (the 1990's) the IBS and NBRSA benchrest associations have followed suit with the efforts of a few hearty and selfless souls ... Skip Talbot, Randy Dierks, Ken Johnson, Bill Shehane, Jim Brummerstedt being but a few of the major contributors to the new growth of 1000 yard benchrest shooting.

Could the progenitors of the sport of benchrest such as Harvey Donaldson, Warren Page, Al Marciante, Colonel Townsend Whelen, and others have guessed where it all would lead? Winning groups and aggregates in their day would be at the bottom of the pack in today's competition. Could they have guessed that on occasion the groups at 1000 yards would approach some of their best efforts at 200 yards?

Once started, the pursuit of benchrest grew quickly to a relatively large group of accuracy lovers, and by 1955, only 7 years after its beginnings, 163 shooters were on hand for the Johnstown match. Dave Brennan detailed the

Circa 1948-1949, at the range where it all started, at Johnstown, NY. Let's hope that it does not rain, because the host club has not yet finished the overhead cover at the time of this match?

equipment at that match in his May, 1985 *Precision Shooting* article. The grand aggregate winner, Sam Clark Jr. of Waterville, Maine, posted a .4098" grand aggregate. Not bad, seeing as how this match was held some 45 years ago. The ten round group at 200 yards went to Chet Benjamin, of Eldred, Pa. with a group of 1.382". The stats of the match ran from calibers of .222 to 6MM with barrels from Hart, Douglas, Apex, Pride, Johnson Automatics, and Gregorie. Actions were Remington 722, Mauser and FN, Winchester 70, Weber, Schultz & Larsen, Forster, Springfield, Enfield, and Sako. Bullets were from B&A, home-made, RCBS dies, custom, Sierra, Speer, and Sisk. Scopes used were Lyman, Unertl, and Fecker with powers from 20 to 30. And, of course, all stocks were fashioned from wood. Many of these suppliers have gone by the wayside over the years, but many still fight the battle to supply us with top quality equipment.

When asked why some climb Mount Everest, or dive headlong off tall bridges, the answer is quite often a simple, "because it's there." The same might apply to the pursuit of 1000 yard accuracy. Small arms, though effective at ranges to 300 yards in the hands of a decent hunter of the day, were not often thought of as extreme long-range target punching tools. But in 1968, or thereabout, some adventurous souls decided to do just that ... "because it was there". The Original Pennsylvania 1000 Yard Benchrest Club, Inc. of Williamsport, PA. was born.

1000 Yard Benchrest ... The Dawn of a New Era

Farmers and rural folks from the east have taken a dislike to a furry little creature they call a ground hog. Glen Newick, a Yankee by birth and author of *The Ultimate In Rifle Accuracy*, and I traveled back to Ohio early in this millennium year to attend the Super Shoot. Glen watched with some concentration and pointed excitedly whenever one of these small vegetarians appeared. The population of these ground digging rodents grew as we padded our way east. Although what he was pointing out seemed to me (a Westerner) to be a Rockchuck, or what some might call a Woodchuck, I will leave the naming to whoever's doing the shooting of them. And shoot them they do.

The act of shooting ground hogs began, to some degree, as an effort to control these crop-destroying pests. Consequently, the East became a Mecca for accuracy minded varmint hunters. And, in fact, it was from these beginnings that traditional benchrest events got their names: Light and Heavy Varmint. And it was with such rifles and components as described above at the 1955 match that these varmint hunters tried their skills against the furry marmot.

Two friends of mine, Gerald Perry of Perry-Systems (Perry's ballistics software) and Phil Sauer of benchrest fame, can talk for hours of their ground hog hunting adventures of 30 or 40 years ago in that area. And even today the pages of *Precision Shooting* are oft times glossed with stories of the long range attack on this animal, one of the Harts of precision shooting supplies giving in to such literary offerings. Walt Berger of Berger Bullets and George Kelbly of Stolle actions got their starts in the same way, and not far from the Pennsylvania border. The list goes on.

The logical course to follow for the more adventurous souls was to reach farther and farther afield with their tiny missiles. And they did so for years prior to formalizing the sport. It was just such a group of fellows that put the formal touch to 1000 Yard Benchrest.

Precision gunsmithing has been a tradition and a hotbed of accuracy rifles for decades in the Pennsylvania area. Alex Hoyer of Williamsport was one among this auspicious group, many of whom were wildcatters, and the father of the 6.5 x 300 Weatherby wildcat. Another gunsmith, Howard Wolfe of Mifflinburg, developed the 7MM-300 Weatherby as early as the 1960's. He is also responsible for the 30-378 Wolfe, a close relative to a cartridge that is re-establishing a bit of current acclaim.

From this, it is clear that 1000 yard shooters were learning early what velocity and ballistic coefficient could gain them at these long ranges … or rather the benefits of reducing time of flight to the target. Such over bore cartridges became the rule. It is rather ironic that in many courts the tide is changing. Yet, in the heavy gun competition even larger capacity cartridges often take the day. The formation of a .50 Caliber Benchrest Association took place not too many years prior to this writing.

The goal of the Original Pennsylvania 1000 Yard Benchrest Club is to put 10 rounds in the smallest group, but also to do so with the highest score. The Original Pennsylvania 1000 Yard Benchrest Club's course of fire is one of elimination. Competitors at each match are first arranged in individual relays. Each relay fires together for

June 13, 1993—first relay at the Williamsport, PA range.

both group and score. Two winners emerge from each of these relays, one with the smallest group and one with the highest score. After all individual matches have been fired, there are two shoot-offs to determine the champions of the day. The first is among the group winners, and the shooter with the smallest group in this shoot-off is the group winner for the day. The second shoot-off is among the high scorers from the individual relays, and the shooter with the highest score is the score winner of the day. The recently formed IBS 1000 Yard Association follows much the same format.

What you have just read came almost verbatim from Sierra's 1978 reloading manual. The manual does not list the author ... from whom a bit more plagiarism seems necessary. For those of you who know something about current 1000 yard benchrest performance it should be of interest to know something about the groups, cartridges, and loads of a time gone by.

Some records listed from 1968 through 1974 were:

8.500 inches by Paul Kempfer of Wellsburg, NY .... April 1968
8.468 by Lee Hocker of Camp Hill, PA .... August 1969
7.687 by Mary Louise DeVito of Williamsport, PA .... October 1970
6.125 by Kenneth Keefer Jr of New Columbia, PA .... September 1974

Sierra, of course, makes reference to their

MatchKing Hollow Point bullets in listing some of the cartridges and loads popular during the time. The Sierra MatchKing is still one of the major bullets used today in 1000 yard benchrest competition as well as many other center fire competitive shooting sports.

While there are more powders available today, especially of the slower, high energy variety, it is interesting to note that in 22 years not much has changed of the particular specifications given in Table 1 for the popular cartridges of 1978. Cartridges today are often of similar size and performance. Sierra bullets, and others, are generally in the same weight categories, and velocities hover around the same level, though the envelope may have been pushed slightly higher.

The time-honored 300 Win Mags, 300 Weatherby Mags, 30-378's, and necked down Weatherby's still populate the line. New cartridges have found their niche as well. And new gunsmiths have emerged to carry on this exacting sport. One among those who have been with the game for a quarter century is Bruce Baer, now of considerable fame in the Original Pennsylvania 1000 Yard Benchrest tradition.

The records of the late 60 and 70's were shot on the National Match 200 yard target. This target has a solid black center bull of the high power variety that is 13 inches in diameter (9-, 10-, and X-rings). The 10-ring is 7 inches in diameter, while the X-ring is 3 inches. Each

Table 1

Cartridge	Bullet	Powder	Load	Approx Muz Vel
6.5x300 Weatherby	140 MatchKing	H-202	89 gr.	3400 fps
7mm Rem. Magnum	168 MatchKing	IMR-4350	61-62	3100
	168 MatchKing	H-4831	64-65	3100
7mm-300 Weatherby	168 MatchKing	H-570	85-86	3350
.300 Win Magnum	190 MatchKing	IMR4350	69	3075
	190 MatchKing	H-4831	72	3075
.308 Norma Magnum	190 MatchKing	IMR-4350	68	3050
	190 MatchKing	H-4831	71	3050
.30-378 Wolfe	190 MatchKing	H-570	100	3380
.30-378 Wolfe	200 MatchKing	H-570	100	3350
.30-378 Wolfe	220 MatchKing	H-570	100	3275

white ring adds 3 more inches to the radius, so that the outside 5-ring is 37 inches in diameter. The paper on which this is printed is 42 inches square.

When the NBRSA and IBS organized their 1000 Yard Benchrest Associations recently, the NBRSA changed the course of fire considerably. The basic premise centers around their dislike of elimination fire. It is rather disconcerting to travel hundreds of miles and find oneself out of the game after only one match. They also thought this did not test the shooters sufficiently to declare a winner. Bottom line: they didn't want to be eliminated; they wanted to shoot.

But times are changing … and rapidly. As little as five or six years ago, 1000 yards ranges were primarily a pipe dream for those who wished to challenge the distance. Now, since 1998 alone, the IBS organization has increased participation at their nationals from 168 in 1998 to 206 in 1999 and an expected 300 shooters in this millennium year. With nearly 600 guns to run through the event, courses of fire might not be a choice. Running matches like the NBRSA would require a 150 bench line.

The pipe dream of being able to compete in 1000 yard benchrest is becoming a reality. Thousand yard ranges are slowly proliferating throughout the country. North Carolina, Pennsylvania, the Virginias, Arizona, New

Mexico, Colorado, and other states are holding regular matches.

It is truly the dawn of a new era.

The NBRSA and IBS Courses of Fire

Since it is almost impossible to locate bullet holes at 1000 yards with any scope, NBRSA 1000 yard matches are shot blind. Consequently, all records shot to date were shot blind. By blind, I mean that the competitors cannot see where their shots are impacting on the paper. Each shot is made without knowing if any of them are even hitting the paper. This is rather disconcerting to the traditional benchrest shooter who is used to placing his remaining shots by being able to see where succeeding shots have impacted. Even so, the course of fire has been established to give a fair round to all shooters. Both score and group size are counted, and six targets are shot in both classes.

A significant departure of 1000 yard benchrest from traditional benchrest is the (almost) lack of wind flags and mirage boards. While a traditional 100/200 yard field will be filled with literally hundreds of flags, the 1000 yard course will have from none to only a few. Many courses offering 1000 yard ranges may have large, highly elevated flags dedicated to high power shooters, but these are almost useless to the benchrest shooter who requires quicker response from a flag that is closer to the eye. On the other hand, one will see several hand held wind gauges near the bench of 1000 yard shooters. Mirage must be taken off the frame of the target, since it is difficult to post mirage boards on a 1000 yard range.

The light class is restricted to rifles weighing 17 pounds or less. The heavy class has no weight restrictions, and one might see some huge, rather spacey rifles on the line at most matches.

Five rounds are fired in the light class while ten rounds are launched down range in the heavy class.

Competitors are given 6 minutes to sight in and as many shots can be taken as possible during that time, depending on the pit crew's ability to plug a large orange disk in the new hole, patch the previous hole, and raise the target again. Shooters are also given a 3-minute sight-in period prior to shooting each new target.

Half the shooters are assigned to the pit to

A typical turnout at the Hawks Ridge Gun Club in Ferguson, North Carolina—site of the 1999 North Carolina IBS 1000 Yard Benchrest Championships. The club ran 374 guns through their paces in two days. Photo courtesy of Bill Shehane.)

pull targets; the other half shoot the first half of the light gun during the morning. When 3 targets have been shot, the shooters switch to the heavy rifle and complete 3 more targets. Then the shooters switch places with the pit crew, who duplicate the course fired while the morning's shooters spend the afternoon in the pits. One inequity may arise here. If the wind and mirage are much stronger in the afternoon, the morning shooters have the advantage. However, on day two this is switched for the remaining 3 targets in each class with the hope that conditions will balance out.

If the competitor is not hitting the target during the sight-in, the pit crew often finds it difficult to communicate this to the shooter in order to direct his or her fire. If the shooter is on paper, a good pit crew member can pull the target, mark it, and lift it again, giving the shoot-

The modern 1000 yard benchrest target with blue bull and 4" white center. The 1000 yard rifle laying peacefully atop the target belongs to stock maker, Bill Shehane. Chambered for the Shehane 6.5-284 cartridge and bedded in an ST-1000L stock, it carries Nightforce's newest: the NXS 5.5 – 22x56mm scope. This rifle was featured on the cover of the June 2000 issue of Precision Shooting magazine. Photo courtesy of Bill Shehane.

er a quick second shot. This is very helpful to the shooter who is trying desperately to shoot all wind conditions in an attempt to determine their push and propensity to group.

Missing the target is not hard to do when the wind doesn't cooperate. A ten mph wind pushes the bullet a long way off course at a 1000 yards, as you know. For example, the 190 grain bullet shot from my Sendero 300 Win Mag during the 1999, 1000 Yard National Championships was moving 76 inches laterally in a 10 mph wind but only 38 inches in a 5mph wind. One's guess of what the lateral movement of the bullet was at that range could easily be off 34 to 40 inches. With the total width of the paper target being only 42 inches, an entire miss was very possible.

The targets used for NBRSA Benchrest at 1000 yards are 42 inches square. The black bull is 13 inches in diameter and contains both the 9 and 10 rings. Rings progress outwardly to the number 5 ring in three inch increments. The black bull has a 4 inch white aiming square in its center, inside of which is a 3 inch X ring. This is the same National Match 200 yard target shot by the Original Pennsylvania Club several years ago, but with the addition of the 4 inch white aiming square. The other associations are using this target as well, although some of them changed to a blue bullseye in 1999.

IBS shooters have started using clay pigeons to spot sighter shots. Individuals are positioned behind the shooter with a set of "Big Eyes" (two spotting scopes tied together) to spot hits in the dirt until the shooter hits near the pigeon. The shooter then takes a couple of shots on the sighter target. This greatly speeds up the match. The North Carolina group does not use pits. They have found that by shooting pigeons and then targets without pits, but with a non shooting crew down range, they can run many more shooters through during the day. An additional plus about this system is that shooters who would normally be assigned to man the pits can now get a bit more socializing or rest as well as get on the road to home earlier.

Most matches, the National Championships being no exception, are held on the weekend. The shooters are required to arrive on Friday and register. The range is made available on Friday for sighting-in as well. It behooves the shooter to make the most of this. If the shooter comes from an area that is much different in temperature and altitude, it is possible that the point of impact will not be on the paper. If the shooter does not get on paper on Friday, the first match on Saturday is very stressful indeed. Also, one can be fooled by the first shot from a cold, clean barrel. For example, I had cleaned my rifle thoroughly on the Friday night before the match after getting on paper that day. To my surprise and dismay, my first sighter shot was at 6 O'clock, about 16 inches low. I clicked from my previous aiming point to the hole, and the round hit 16 inches high at 12 O'clock. It was not until the second day and the same thing happened that it occurred to me that the first shot out of a cold, clean barrel wanted to print low at that range. After that, vertical dispersion remained in the area of the bull.

Like any other benchrest match, shooter's strategy and habits vary. Most try to pick a predominate, familiar wind and shoot as fast as possible, hoping to get all shots down range during that same wind. Others pick at the target methodically, using their instinct and knowledge to hold a different aiming point for each shot.

The shooter is given 10 minutes to fire each 5 round string (which seems to the author to be a great deal more time than anyone needs). As you fire your group, you are wondering where the bullets are printing; you are wondering if you are hitting the target; you are wondering whether you are doing "good, bad, or ugly". You can't compensate on succeeding shots because you don't know where the preceding bullets are printing. If you choose a wind that you think will make the bullet fall into the bull, or if you hold off a distance that seems correct, you might shoot every round completely off the target and never know it. In fact, the shooter is not shown the targets until all shooting is completed for the day or maybe the weekend. When this is the case, there is little to learn because you cannot remember the wind or condition that caused an errant shot a day prior.

At this writing both the NBRSA and IBS 1000 yard organizations are less than five years old. World records are up for grabs, and they will continue to fall rapidly over the next few years. It is interesting to note some of the current NBRSA world records. Most were shot during the same match, and the majority were fired by the same individuals, some of whom are also heavily involved in the .50 Caliber Benchrest Association. Although the 1000 Yard Benchrest organization is just an upstart, some of the record holders are old hands at long range competitive shooting. But some are not. Roy Damron established 5 world records in his first year of 1000 yard competitive benchrest shooting with 2 custom built .300 Weatherby Magnums.

Larry Bartholome fired his 2.653" record shooting a 6BR. And although I dare say there was a bit of luck involved, Larry has been doing exceptionally and consistently well with his 6BR, shooting match after match around the country.

Looking at the groups and aggregates in Table 2 below, it is not difficult to see that equipment and components are becoming more and more refined, as are the skills of those shooting them. Skip Talbot and Jim Brooks shot aggregates of 30 to 90 shots that are smaller than the single groups fired in the 1960's and 70's.

Although groups and even aggregates are much less than minute of angle at such a long range, scores and x-ring hits seem to be lagging

Roy Damron (foreground) and Karl Hunstiger clean their rifles during the 1999, 1000 Yard NBRSA National Championships at the Whittington center just outside Raton, New Mexico. In the background you can see the site of the traditional 100/200 Yard National Championships that immediately followed the 1000 yard matches. Karl was the Heavy Class winner during the Nationals. Photo courtesy of Jim Brummerstedt.

behind. Here again, performance and world records will post significant gains over the next few years.

While the records above show the best of single performances, day to day performance is awe-inspiring as well. Take the Colorado Rifle

Table 2

1000 Yard NBRSA World Records As Of September 18, 1999			
Contests	**Light Gun**	**Heavy Gun**	**Heavy Gun—Light**
	17 Pounds	**Unlimited Weight**	**Gun 2 Gun Aggregate**
Single Groups			
Five Shot Group	Larry Bartholome		
	2.653 – 9/22/99		
Ten Shot Group		Karl Hunstiger	
		6.250 – 9/23/98	
Three Group Agg.			
Five Shot Groups	Skip Talbot		
15 shots	5.9167 – 9/18/99		
Ten Shot Groups		Jim Brooks	
30 shots		8.7083 – 9/23/98	
Two Gun Agg			Skip Talbot
45 shots			7.375 – 9/18/99
Six Group Agg.			
Five Shot Groups	Skip Talbot		
30 shots	7.3542 – 9/18/99		
Ten Shot Groups		Skip Talbot	
60 shots		9.0521 – 9/18/99	
Two Gun Agg.			Skip Talbot
90 shots			8.203 – 9/18/99
Highest Score			
Five Shot Score	Randy Dierks		
5 shots	50-1x 9/23/99		
Ten Shot Score		Gerald Duvall	
10 shots		97-1x 9/18/99	
Highest 3 Targets			
Five Shot Score	Roy Damron		
15 shots	145-5x 9/18/99		
Ten Shot Score		Michael Chapman	
30 shots		276-3x 9/18/99	
Highest 6 Targets			
Five Shot Score	Roy Damron		
30 Shots	281-6x 9/23/98		
Ten Shot Score		Randy Dierks	
60 shots		543-6x 9/18/99	
2 Gun, 6 Targets			
45 shots			Randy Dierks
			419-7x 9/18/99
2 Gun, 12 Targets			Randy Dierks
90 shots			820-9x 9/18/99

Club 1000 Yard year-end results for example. Jim Brummerstedt listed the results of the winner's average ten best groups and scores for the year 1999. I have shown the top 2 in each class in Table 3 below.

Solving The 1000 Yard Puzzle

Over the years benchrest has been won by a variety of cartridge configurations, bullets, powder, cases, primers, and rifles. Some of those wins had to do with nothing more than luck. But as you can see from above, luck is not the deciding factor in the long run.

Benchrest by its very definition takes care of some of the problems encountered by other disciplines. While some competitive rifle events require the shooter to hold the rifle still, say

Table 3

Light Class Group	
Jim Brooks 7.48
Bill Schrader ....…. 8.07

Heavy Class Group	
Jim Brooks 10.80
Jim Brummerstedt 12.67

Light Class Score	
Jim Brooks 455
Dave Wright 447

Heavy Class Score	
Jim Brummerstedt 885
Jim Brooks 872

Factory Class Group	
Dave Heintz ....….. 15.075
Jeff Lamer ....….… 18.29

Factory Class Score	
Dave Heintz 362
Jeff Lamer 361

within an arc of 1 minute or less, the rifle is held by the bench in our sport. Where some have to learn to control a 2 or 4 pound or heavier trigger, most benchrest rifles carry triggers with let off in the 1 to 2 ounce range. And while many high power shooters have to learn to control their breathing and heart rate, this is not necessary in benchrest.

What then is the challenge? It comes with trying to satisfy the objectives of the development of extreme accuracy and precision in rifles. Benchrest shooters are not interested in the techniques of shooting off hand, they are interested in developing the most accurate rifle and components for the off hand shooter to use (I might be going a bit far there). This greatly reduces the variables the bench shooter has to contend with. One simply sits by the rifle, almost as an onlooker. The conditions are read, the rifle is aimed, and the trigger is pulled. The rub comes in developing the best rifle and components to reign supreme, and proving that it is so.

Assuming that one has an accurate rifle, and 90 percent of the 1000 yard shooters that step to the line do, what are the deciding factors for performance excellence? Let's make the further assumption that skill is not an issue. Having

Match day at the Colorado Rifle Club. The club is very protective of their benches, note the boards and clamps used to prevent the front and rear rests from damaging them. The lovely lady in the foreground is Tonya Atherton (adjusting her scope with a 12 pound sledge?). If you look closely at and/or near the benches, you will see the shooter's wind gauges.

made some simplifying assumptions and having gotten the obvious issues out of the way, the final key becomes: what the bullet is doing once it leaves the barrel.

We know the range is full of bitter enemies: varying wind, mirage, dust devils, temperature variations, elevation changes. These are what we must overcome. The standard approach is to depend heavily on ballistic coefficient and velocity. We know that bullets of high ballistic coefficient handle the wind better at the longer ranges, and if increased velocity can be managed, we go for it. It is a general rule that higher ballistic coefficient comes with increase in bullet weight and decrease in drag. Oddly enough, the current darlings of the benchrest clan are the 6 and 6.5 x 284 case configurations. Why the

sudden turn away from the standard .30 and .338 calibers? Recoil? With the maximum weight of 17 pounds in the light class and the allowance of muzzle brakes, this hardly seems a valid argument. While this could be a factor in high power position shooting, it is certainly not essential in benchrest. Is it the reduction in cost and the ease of working with smaller cartridges … the majority being of better quality and consistent weight and thickness?

Regardless of the preponderance of fashion and fad, the key to success at 1000 yards is not necessarily time of flight or velocity, but ballistic coefficient. The drawback to this might not be recoil sensitivity to the shooter but to the rifle. Controlling the rifle under significant recoil

Table 4

Caliber	Bullet Weight	Velocity fps	Remaining Velocity at 1000 yards	BC	Wind Drift"	Time of Flight in Seconds
.338	300	2825	1763	.768	50.1	1.3464
.308	240	3000	1819	.711	50.5	1.2866
.308	220	3350	1939	.629	50.2	1.1805
.308	190	3900	2093	.533	50.5	1.0563
.308	175	4100	2138	.505	50.8	1.0206
.284	168	4250	2176	.488	50.8	.9948
.264	155	3650	2021	.570	50.6	1.1093
.264	140	3900	2089	.535	50.3	1.0549
.243	107	3950	2108	.527	50.4	1.0460
.224	80	5000	2339	.420	51	.8901

Table 5

Caliber	Grains	Velocity fps	Remaining Velocity at 1000 yards	BC	Wind Drift"	TOF seconds	~ Recoil of a 17 pound rifle
.338	300	2950	2297	.768	47	1.2837	30
.308	240	3100	1893	.711	48.1	1.2907	24
.308	220	3300	1903	.629	51.3	1.2005	23
.308	190	3400	1765	.533	61.1	1.2295	19
.308	175	3500	1757	.505	63.1	1.2155	16
.284	168	3350	1616	.488	70.5	1.2962	14
.264	155	3250	1750	.570	59.7	1.2620	12
.264	140	3400	1770	.535	60.8	1.2278	10
.243	107	3300	1620	.527	67.9	1.3232	6
.224	80	3350	1343	.420	93.6	1.4274	4

becomes a problem given the same weight and configuration.

Thousand-yard benchrest is narrowly defined by distance and approach. The distance is always the same, and bench technique is always essentially the same. I mean this in relation to the high power shooter who must deliver from the prone, sitting/kneeling, and standing positions. If the scope is mounted to keep the reticle reasonably centered, image is not a problem nor is constantly clicking the elevation dial ... one range, one position on the elevation dial. Whether the mid range trajectory to get to the target is high like the .308 Winchester that I shoot at 1000 yards in sniper competition or low like a 30-378, once you are on, you are on. Optical aberrations aside, the remaining variables are wind, mirage, and temperature changes. The bullet is going to be pushed either more or less by the wind, elevated by the heat of the day, or miss due to the aberrations cause by mirage.

To some degree, the longer a bullet remains airborne, the more it is affected by the wind. But the correlation is more closely related to ballistic coefficient than either time of flight or velocity. The following table illustrates this. Using Sierra MatchKing bullets, I have compared some of the most popular calibers against the .338, 300 grain bullet with a BC of .768 and a muzzle velocity of 2825 fps in Table 4. That velocity is possible with the 300 grain bullet, and it moves laterally exactly 50 inches in a 10 mph wind given standard conditions. The question I have asked is: what velocity is required to achieve this performance with the other popular calibers.

Several of these velocities are difficult or impossible to attain. Using a more realistic scenario, the results might look like those in Table 5 on the left.

Sierra's ballistic coefficient degradation with velocity deceleration was not used in Tables 4 and 5. Instead, highest ballistic coefficient was noted for comparison only. It is further assumed that one can drive the 300 grain bullet at 2950. Velocities attained above in 1978 were used for several of the other bullets.

There are several notables here. The reasonably attainable velocities for each bullet show a very similar time of flight, regardless of what that beginning muzzle velocity was. And, with the exception of the 300 and 80 grain bullets, they all have approximately the same remaining velocity at 1000 yards. With those exceptions, the velocities at the muzzle vary by 400 fps. Yet the velocity at 1000 yards varies by less than 300 fps. The notable exceptions are the 300 grain bullet which sustains its velocity, losing only 650 fps, while the 80 grain loses almost 2000. Loses in velocity are proportional to ballistic coefficient.

Note also that the increasingly popular 6 and 6.5 calibers produce recoil in the 5 to 10 foot pound range, far below the old standby 30 caliber bullets producing nearly twice that in a 17 pound rifle. The king of them all, the 300 grain Sierra MatchKing, pounds away at 30 foot pounds. But recoil in this table was generated for comparison's sake only. The competitors I see use muzzle brakes that reduce recoil at least 30 percent, helping to dampen the sting. Even so, there is considerably more upset of the rifle at 20 pounds than at 6. The consistent and competitive performance of Jim Brooks and Larry Bartholome with their 6MM's speaks highly for the little cartridges regardless of their less efficient wind bucking ability compared to the larger bullets in the .308 and .338 caliber class.

Atmospheric conditions are magnified considerably at 1000 yards over the traditional 100/200 yard benchrest event. These alone applaud the performance 1000 yard shooters attain, but they are not the only problems faced at this extreme range. Temperature change affects the bullet considerably at this range. During the 10 minute match, this is not often a problem, but the shooter will find himself adjusting the elevation dial if he or she expects to score well throughout the day. Apart from the disastrous affects of varying winds across the range, mirage plays a significant role, with the oft argued Magnus, Bernoulli's, Precession, and light changes playing minor roles. Yet these must be understood and used correctly if small groups and high scores are to be attained.

Mirage

Mirage is both an ally and an enemy.

Many 1000 yard benchrest shooters came from the ranks of the traditional 100/200 yard world. The preferred technique there is to shoot the predominant wind shown by several wind flags, which lends itself to shooting fast so long as the preferred and/or predominant wind is present. Mirage is seen at the target and is used as another wind indicator. Mirage often responds more quickly to a wind change than do mechanical flags, and benchrest shooters use it for that purpose as well.

At the 1000 yard mark, and with no wind flags present, the competitor must be content with feel and wind gauges at the muzzle . Because there are few wind flags during most 1000 yard matches, mirage becomes a very important indicator. On occasion, however, the mirage is so thick it presents a surreal apparition, and the target is a dark bullseye dancing amid a shimmering, liquid-amber background. Benchrest shooters do not often use mirage across the range with the aid of a spotting scope as an indication of intermediate winds, but prefer to use the shorter range technique of shooting when they feel the wind is right, and often this means shooting fast while it holds. Although, with 10 minutes to fire one's group, there seems ample time to learn and use such wind indicating techniques with a spotting scope.

Mirage produces an optical aberration caused by quickly changing density and heat as air rises from the earth. This is a differential process and can happen in both hot and cold weather. While an ally as a wind indicator, mirage can be an enemy if not used properly. Simply stated, mirage moves the target optically in the same direction as the wind flow at the position of focus. If mirage is seen through the scope to be moving from right to left on the target at 1000 yards, the target has moved optically from right to left as well. Thus it behooves one to shoot with the same aiming point in the same mirage flow. For example, suppose you aim center bull when the wind is not moving and mirage is not present, and you hit center bull. When you recover from the shot and look once again at the target to begin the second shot, you see that the mirage is now flowing from right to left. You once again hold center bull, but then realize that the wind will move the bullet exactly 5" (you should be so gifted). So you hold 5" right and expect the right to left wind to move your bullet 5" to the left for another center bull hit. Instead you hit 5" to the left of the bull. You are stunned. Aw well, you just misjudged the wind.

Not necessarily.

Remember that mirage has moved the target optically in the direction of the flow of the mirage (which is the direction of flow of the wind vector). It does not really matter what the wind is doing anywhere on the range for this to happen. It is an optical effect seen through the scope at the point of focus. When you aimed at center bull when the mirage was flowing, you were aiming at a target that did not exist. You were looking at an image of the target that was actually positioned to the right of what you saw. This effect is similar to the dispersion phenomenon seen when light passes from one medium to another of a different density. An easy way to illustrate this is to place a stick into water. The stick will appear to be bent where it moves from the air into the water. The image you see of the stick in the water is not the physical location of the stick. I used to shoot fish with my bow and arrow as a youngster. It was not until I began to realize where the fish was in relation to where I saw its image that I began to connect with a few of them. This same phenomenon is occurring when you look through your scope at changing mirage.

Thus, your 5" wind hold was correct, but you did not allow for the changing position of the target due to mirage. The new aiming point of 5" was correct for wind. But although you could not see it, your crosshair was actually in the center of the bull. The target, however, appeared 5" to the left. Since you were really aiming at the bull, you were not giving it any wind correction at all. In this hypothetical example, you should have used a hold that appeared to you to be 10" to the right of the bull. This same thing is happening in a boil, and it is one of the reasons that a boil produces so many vertical groups.

If one cannot get all shots off in the same mirage condition, one must learn to estimate the distance a target moves in changing mirage. There are a couple of methods to do this. One is with the use of a rail gun or one that is very steady in the bags. Be careful not to more it. Place the crosshair in the middle of the bull in a no mirage condition. Plot the position of the crosshair on the target as the mirage flows from left to right, right to left, and boils. You realize, of course, that the crosshair is centered in the bull physically, but the crosshair appears to be in different locations as the mirage changes. If you were to reposition the crosshair to where the bull appears to be, you would miss the bull by that amount plus the push of the wind in the same direction. Remember that the point of impact will be opposite those plotted of the point of aim. The second method is to use a friend. Have him position the crosshair centered in the bull on the rifle that is not touched and which is held steadily in position. As you shoot your rifle, aiming at center bull each time, the friend plots the position of the crosshair of his rifle. Your friend could just as well do this with a riflescope or a spotting scope with a crosshair only, so long as it is attached to something that will not move. Assuming the rifle you are shooting is not a return to battery job, you will have to reposition the rifle each time. Assuming also that you aim and shoot at center bull each time, the friend will show you where you should have aimed to have a center bull hold due to mirage. Your group size will be proportional to the difference between where you saw the bull and where it actually was. There are days when the mirage is so detrimental to image quality that you can barely see the center of the bull. At times the bull seems to jump and dance in a circle. When this happens, continue to move the crosshair to one extreme position of the bull's movement. You will find a position of the crosshair where the bull will just touch the horizontal and vertical crosshairs as it makes its rounds. Try to duplicate this for each shot.

This phenomenon does not necessarily occur in a linear relationship to increasing range. In other words, a 1" movement at 100 yards will be a 10" movement at 1000 yards. The riflescope does not know the difference between 100 and 1000 yards except through focus, depth of field, and field of view. The scope does not, however, increase its aberrant affect because the distance has increased. As long as the flow and density of the mirage remain the same, the aberrant movement is the same. Remember also that a 1" movement of the rifle at 100 yards is the same as a 10" movement of the rifle at 1000 yards. The target image gets smaller as the distance is increased and the error gets larger as a consequence. At 1000 yards, your view through the scope is subjected to a 1000 percent increase in atmosphere as opposed to looking at the same target positioned only 100 yards away. This tends to degrade the image. Cranking up the power of the scope in order to see the target better reduces light, adds extra haze to the image, and increases further the degrading affect of mirage on image quality.

The affect of mirage on image quality is reduced as power is reduced. However, just because the image appears clearer, and the mirage appears much reduced, the amount that the target is being optically displaced by mirage does not vary. In fact, it is sometimes the case that the eye cannot see the mirage, but since it is there, the image is still being displaced optically. This sometimes accounts for the flyers you cannot otherwise explain.

Many manuals give rules of thumb to relate the speed of the wind by the configuration of the mirage. While this is true in general, it has exceptions like anything else. Most of the articles written on the subject say that the mirage wave goes flat and disappears around 12 to 14 mph. I have seen mirage at speeds considerably greater than that, and I have seen mirage disappear at speeds less than that. I have seen mirage on very cold days. One has to learn what is happening on the range on that day. On some days, watching

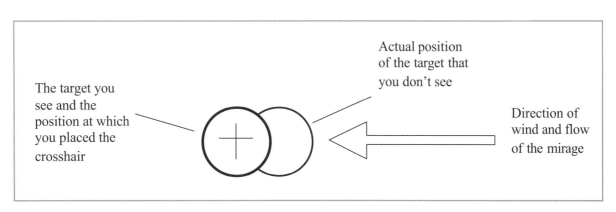

mirage only and paying no attention at all to the flags works very well. On other days, mirage does not help at all. Berms, trees, and other obstacles cause vertices on the range or changes in wind direction and/or differential wind directions. The wind at the muzzle may be blowing right to left and continue that way for several yards, then suddenly switch to left to right. The flags fly in opposite directions. The mirage at the target might match the direction of wind flow at the muzzle or it may not.

Shooters should learn to watch both flags and mirage, relying on neither alone.

Light

Fortunately, not every condition, aberration, or shooting situation applies to benchrest shooters. The benchrest shooter has a finite time in which to shoot his group, hoping that the score is acceptable as well. Seven minutes are allowed in 100/200 yard 5 shot matches. Ten minutes are allowed for 1000 yard strings. Some affects are not significantly important in those small time frames.

There are, however, two problems confronting the benchrest shooter involving light, both of which are magnified at 1000 yards. One of them is of little importance during the 10 minute time frame. The first is the angle of the sun to the objective lens, and the second has to do primarily with cloud cover.

The angle of the sun to the objective lens has an affect on image, creating a slight aberration of sorts. It is difficult to quantify the amount, but since it happens slowly throughout the day, it is not important to the group. It might be important to score. Placing the rifle in a rest on a solid bench that will not move will allow you to see this affect. Of course the day must be mirage free. Place the crosshair in the center of the mothball and log the movement of the crosshair as the sun changes positions throughout the day. You will note that the crosshair moves away from the mothball vertically, working its way down and then up again as the day progresses. This will not affect group size during a 10 minute event; however, it might appreciably affect score from match to match. This is often disconcerting to the fellow who sights in his rifle in the morning, and

then wonders why the group's impact position has changed the following afternoon.

The second phenomenon can affect the outcome of the individual, 10 minute group. Alternating lighter and darker periods will be present when the sky is dotted with clouds. This change can happen several times during the 10 minute time period. The rule of thumb here is, "light up, bullet up; light down, bullet down". Translated this means that if one starts a group when a cloud covers the sun, the bullet will print higher if you hold the same point of aim and fire when the cloud passes, leaving you in bright sunlight. Likewise, if you start your group during bright sunlight and then, using the same point of aim, fire when a cloud covers the sun the bullet will print low.

While this affect is difficult to quantify, it is worth noting the effects for oneself and practicing it a bit. When you are about to shoot a match, seconds before the range master is to give the commence fire, note the cloud cover overhead. If the entire sky is covered with unbroken clouds, not to worry. Likewise, if you see that it is clear with no clouds in the sky, not to worry. However, if you note that there are alternating clouds and bright clear areas, try to get all shots off in one or the other. Remember also that if you shot target one in bright sunlight, and are now faced with target two in cloud cover, your score may suffer if you do not compensate for the light differential.

Precession , Magnus, Bernoulli's, Coning, Yaw of Repose ... ?

Much discussion has centered on these phenomena during the 1990's in *Precision Shooting* magazine. For many years I understood this to be Bernoulli's affect. This, it seems, is not the correct term, nor does Bernoulli's effect explain the physics of what is going on. Magnus is another phenomenon that has been suggested as the culprit. In any case, and no matter what the name or the physics, experienced shooters know what is going on physically ... they see it often enough on the target.

This phenomenon does not always happen, does not always follow the rules, but under certain circumstances it is very visible, readable, and can be accounted for to allow the shooter to produce smaller groups and higher scores. To explain the result, let me use a scenario similar to the one I used above.

Assume that you hold center bull in a no wind condition, pull the trigger, and the bullet hits at point of aim in the center of the bull. Now the wind begins blowing from right to left. If the winds are laminar across the field, your next bullet will be pushed to the left of the bull if you continue to hold center bull. But … it will also move up. At 100 yards this will only be a half a bullet or so depending on the strength of the wind and how well the phenomenon is working in those conditions. Now suppose that on the third shot the wind switches and comes from the left. If you again hold center bull, the bullet will hit to the right of the bull … but it will also hit low. You will now see a group that is known as a weather report, but whose axis is tilted slightly up on the left and down on the right.

The correct way to shoot this condition is to hold into the wind and either up or down an amount dictated by the strength of the wind. The group should have been shot like this: when the wind blew from right to left on the second shot, hold into the wind the correct amount, but also hold down. When the wind blew in from left to right on the third shot, hold into the wind the correct amount, but also hold up. Correctly done, the group should be one hole (yeah, right!). If the shooter does not hold up and down, depending on the wind direction, but he or she does hold into the wind correctly for push, the group will be stacked vertically in the bull.

Stated another, simpler way, a right to left wind pushes the bullet to the left and high while a left to right wind pushes the bullet right and down in a right hand twist barrel. One should note this and practice it. However, each range (and day) is different, and it behooves the shooter to know early how much the effect is worth.

Wind Vectors

What was stated in the previous section has some import here as well. However, the main point is somewhat different. This important issue gave rise to the military's wind wheel, a very useful tool. It involves some simple trigonometry. Any wind blowing perpendicular to the flight of the bullet will exert maximum push against the bullet, moving it off its path in the direction of the wind. If the wind sustains the same velocity but moves to some angle to the perpendicular of the flight of the bullet, the push exerted will be a only a fraction of the maximum push and is expressed by a trigonometric equation. If the wind is coming out of the same hemisphere, the push against the bullet is the same whether it is coming from behind the shooter or from in front of the shooter, that is, whether a tail wind or a head wind.

However, this has another complicating factor to consider and another rule of thumb: wind from behind, bullet up; wind from in front, bullet down. Let's state that in scenario form. Suppose you shoot in a no wind condition with a center bull hold and the bullet prints center bull. On the second shot, the wind is coming from behind you toward the target (a tail wind). You once again hold center bull. The bullet will print high. On the third shot, the wind switches and is now coming toward you from the target (a head wind). If you once again hold center bull, the bullet will print low.

This effect is not trivial. For example, *Sierra's 50th Anniversary Reloading Manual* states that the .264, 140 grain MatchKing bullet will rise 3.82" in a 15 mph tail wind and fall 3.82" in a 15 mph head wind at 1000 yards. At 100 yards this would translate to less than .382 inches (.764" overall)… but would be enough to give you last place honors. Given this effect alone, your group at 1000 yards would have been 7.14".

Are you ready for the real life complication? Here goes. As the wind turns from the perpendicular, the push becomes less, and you do not need to hold into the wind as much. That much makes sense. However, depending on whether the vector is from the right or the left, the bullet will move vertically up or down respectively due to Precession, and it will also move vertically due to whether the wind vector came toward you or away. Confused?

Lets try some more examples. Suppose you hold center bull in a no wind condition and print center bull. On the second shot, the wind blows 10mph from right to left. You hold into the wind and slightly low. The bullet travels to the left and slightly up and into the previous hole. All is well. The wind remains 10mph, but it moves to a point off your right shoulder. That is, the wind now blows from 4 O'clock to 10 O'clock. You hold into the wind, but only 20 percent of a full perpendicular wind. You know that the bullet will move slightly high due to Precession. You also know that it will move slightly high because it is a tail wind. So you hold a bit lower still to overcome both effects. To confuse the issue even further, the first shot might have been taken when a cloud covered the sun, and now in bright light you will have to aim even lower still to overcome that effect as well.

On the third shot, the wind switches, blowing toward you from 2 O'clock to 8 O'clock. Again, you hold into the wind only 20 percent of a 10mph wind. Now you must again hold low for Precession but high for the frontal wind. It's a wash. This same strategy would be reversed for winds in the opposite hemisphere.

While these affects are minimal at 100 yards, they are manifestly greater for 1000 yards. Shooters who continue to win at the 100 and 200 yard distances take this into account subconsciously because of the thousands of rounds they shoot each year. Also, they ensure that they have exceptional equipment that stabilizes the bullet very early in its flight.

One thousand yard shooters must learn to master these affects to reduce group size over the long run. While such effects are minimal at the shorter ranges, they eat everyone's lunch at extreme ranges.

Unfortunately, this is not the end of the problems the long range shooter encounters. And, although I would like to cover every facet of this fascinating subject, there is not sufficient space available in one chapter.

Rapid, Large Temperature Changes

Temperature change, again, does not affect the benchrest shooter as much as it does other disciplines, but it does presents its problems. The short time period in which a group is shot helps overcome this a bit also. If the temperature is going up or down during the day at a normal rate, the group will not be affected, but score may. The temperature might be 50 degrees in the morning and 90 degrees in the afternoon. This 40 degree temperature change will change the point of impact of the bullet. Since the temperature change during a 10 minute match will (under normal circumstances) change only a fraction of a degree, it does not impact group size. However, if several minutes or hours pass between matches and the temperature change is significant, a center bull hold that was impacting center bull will no longer impact center bull. Without sighter shots, the shooter must have some idea of what this point of impact shift will be. Another problem arises from temperature change: The pressure, velocity, and harmonics that you tuned for so carefully at 70 degrees might produce much larger groups at 95 degrees.

Cartridges left in the sun versus the shade have an effect on pressure and point of impact as well.

More difficult to control are the rapid, large temperature changes that infrequently occur. I have seen situations where a cold, north wind was moving in so rapidly that the temperature dropped 30 degrees in 15 minutes. This resulted in an impact change of 5 inches at 200 yards. While we know that pressures and velocities change with changing temperatures, several other effects are taking place as well. One of them is the sudden, differential stresses induced by dissimilar materials. Case in point: a steel receiver upon which is mounted aluminum bases, rings, and scope. Not only does the degree of elongation differ between steel and aluminum, the rate at which they elongate is different as well. These differential stresses working in tandem often result in significant changes in point of impact. The movement of 5 inches vertically at 200 yards would have resulted in a movement of 25 inches at 1000 yards!

This phenomenon can be duplicated by heating up either the receiver alone, the scope and rings alone, or both when the rifle is held solidly in its rest. If you heat the scope, the crosshair will tend to move down from the bull. If you watch its position as it cools, you will see it move back into the bull. If you heat the receiver only, you will see the crosshair move up out of the bull, and then settle back into it as the receiver cools. Heating the scope, mounts, and receiver simultaneously will produce the effect you are most likely to see during a match. While this affect differs from rifle to rifle, it seems to be quite prominent in the current configuration of benchrest rifles. I will leave it to your experimentation to determine if and how much this occurs in your rifle.

The old Posa mounts or the new Talbot Quick Detachable mounts may help overcome this affect. The Posa mounts held the scope in an axial position with a spring that surrounded the scope body. The Talbot mount accomplishes the same thing, but the spring has been placed in the rear base. When heating or cooling attempts to induce stress between the scope and the receiver, the stress is taken up by the spring instead of by the scope and the receiver. I have tested this, though not thoroughly enough. I am convinced it works from a logical point of view. Brief tests indicated that it is correct from an empirical standpoint as well.

Velocity Spread and Standard Deviation

It has often amazed and confused me that the 100 yard groups from my benchrest rifle do not always produce the smallest group from the ammo that gives me the smallest velocity spread and standard deviation. I consistently go to the matches with the load that gives me the smallest groups and aggregates instead of the load that gives me the smallest velocity spread and standard deviation. This is a case of poor decision making on my part in 100/200 yard benchrest, but it is deadly for matches shot at 1000 yards.

On the other hand, I had recently been trying my best to develop a competitive load for a new barrel with no success. I resorted to chronographing the load, watching velocity spread and standard deviation. I could not seem to drop the standard deviation into the single digit range, nor the velocity spread below 20 no matter what the powder load was nor the seating depth. The groups were consistently poor, averaging .250". I was depressed, convinced that I had just mounted another mediocre barrel.

I remembered that I had tossed a bottle of N-133 in the back of the truck and went to fetch it.

I loaded 29 grains behind a Fowler 66 grain bullet in the 1 in 14 twist barreled 6 PPC and shot a group. Amazing! After 10 groups, the standard deviation was holding in the single digits, and the velocity spread was significantly less than previously. The groups were pounding consistent one's. A change in powder had turned the barrel around. This seldom happens. A great barrel will almost always shoot competitively with any appropriate powder, and will almost always tell you that is going to be the case after just a few rounds. That barrel placed 11th at the Super Shoot against 330 competitors, and shot a couple of groups in the zeros at other prominent matches.

At 1000 yards standard deviation and velocity spread are of even greater importance. Developing a load with a velocity spread of 25 fps, but that appears to shoot competitive groups at 100 yards during testing is sure to disappoint you at the longer distance. Another scenario seems appropriate. Let's assume I have a load that is grouping well in my .300 Win Mag during testing at 100 yards. But the velocity spread is 25 fps at standard conditions. If I have the same spread during a 1000 yard match, the corresponding group is likely to be at least 6" even if the conditions are perfect. A velocity spread of 60 fps would produce a group of at least 14", both groups a result of velocity spread alone. I could accept 6" groups with a velocity spread of 25 fps if that were the only thing I had to contend with, but it is not. Thus standard deviation and velocity spread have a very significant impact on long range shooting.

This is affected either for the better or for worse by ballistic coefficient. In the scenario above I used the 190 grain Sierra MatchKing with a ballistic coefficient of .533 at 2940 fps average, but as high as 2965 fps and then 3000 fps. If I switch to a 300 grain Sierra MatchKing with the same velocities and velocity spreads, the result is better. A 25fps velocity spread would produce a group of 5", and a velocity spread of 60fps would produce a group of 11" from velocity spread alone in perfect conditions. Some improvement has been made by bullet weight and configuration alone, but not much.

And The Work Goes On

As in any scientific endeavor, completeness

of understanding and explanation tend to elude us. The absolute physics of a bullet's flight haunts the ballistician for a number of reasons. To wit: There is no end to the number of configurations manufacturers produce from year to year; trying to tie down pressures, velocities, and barrel response the shooter might impose on his rifle is like playing the lotto; capturing the various motions that a bullet undergoes during its flight is like chasing a ghost.

The oft times quoted Sierra is responsible for much of the work that has been done on the sportsman's behalf. But even they recognize that there is still work to be done. The ballistics team of William T. McDonald and Ted Almgren, who several years ago gave considerable help to our understanding of a bullet's flight, thus improving our effort for precision fire, are being joined by Kevin Thomas of Sierra in a series of experiments in an effort to refine that understanding for us.

They recognize that more refined data, explanation, and mathematical modeling is needed for several of the phenomena that take place during a bullet's flight. Such phenomena as the effects of the vertical components of wind, the important 6-degree-of-freedom effects in bullet trajectories, "yaw of repose", the coning affect of slender, sharp-pointed bullets, to name just a few, are in need of refinement and explanation.

They also recognize that the G1 drag function does not adequately represent the drag forces encountered for velocities of sporting bullets in the transonic and subsonic ranges.

While much of this effort lies in the realm of academia, there is no doubt that some of it is of singular importance to the precision shooter. Understanding and using a mathematical model that will tell us how high a tail wind will cause a bullet to print above the point of aim at 1000 yards is important. Understanding and using a mathematical model that will tell us the vertical deflection that results from a crosswind coupled with a right or left twist barrel is important to all precision shooters, particularly those who do so at long range.

Yet, while this data, these mathematical models, and these explanations are important to us, they are not substitutes for experience. Their importance lies in teaching concepts that precision shooters can use, the effects the shooter can

look for and become familiar with, and helping to dispel a good deal of the confusion we all have about these subjects.

In talking to Bill McDonald about this, he expressed his great appreciation for the use given his team by the U.S. Army and the Yuma Proving Ground (YPG) and to those individuals who give of their personal time to help the international law enforcement community. Each year the YPG grants the Association of Firearms and Toolmark Examiners (AFTE) two weekend days of testing at YPG. AFTE is an international association of law enforcement forensics professionals. Sierra supports the tests that the team recommends, providing guns and ammunition for the test program.

Trigger Induced Vibration

This problem is not as significant in heavy rifles used in 1000 yard benchrest competition. To rifles in the 10 pound class it can spoil competitive groups. To test this, place the rifle in the rests on a solid bench. Place the crosshair in the center of the mothball. Being careful not to touch the rifle, squeeze the trigger until the firing pin falls. Of course, I mean to do this without ammunition. Try this first with an empty chamber a couple of times. Then try the same exercise with a spent case that still has the fired primer in place. If the rifle jumps, vibrates, or moves from the point of aim, you need to work this out. There may be several sources of this problem.

Practice, Mental Management, and the Concept of Primary Influence

While most of the phenomena and concepts talked about above were shown with the help of ballistics software, and are therefore mathematical and, at times, bordering on the theoretical, they are all present to some degree in reality. And they can be confusing. Understanding how to deal with them, overcome them, compensate for them, and become one with them, takes plain old practice and hard work to be successful. We all know that. We don't necessarily know how best to do that however.

Tony Boyer has been on top of the traditional 100/200 yard benchrest game for more than a decade. Over the long haul, no one can beat him.

He has racked up more than double the Hall of Fame points of his nearest rival. Is he so talented that no one can touch him no matter the amount of practice they put in? It may be so. On the other hand, he has recently stated that he shot every day for the first 10 years but has slowed to a couple times a week for his current and second 10 years. It is rumored among his competitors that he shoots as many as 30,000 rounds per year, and often goes through a dozen or more barrels per year hunting for that elusive hummer barrel. I am glad he is on top of the game. I am glad he wins most of the time. For if he did not, I would give up under the newly acquired frustration that the world turns in the wrong direction.

No doubt that the good Mr. Boyer is talented. But the amount of time, effort, and practice he toils under is the deciding factor in his success. And this level of success necessarily blends mental management with practice and above average equipment.

In the past 20 years everyone has become aware of the basic tenants of mental management. Without it, Olympic and other top level competitors could not be successful in events that are contested by a large number of people. I dare say that if benchrest were to become an Olympic event, only Tony and a few others would survive, if we remain at our present level. Few benchrest shooters have a top-level mental management plan to challenge those who compete at such a prestigious level.

The concept of practice entails teaching the subconscious to do the work by repetition. When I first learned to type, each stroke came with great difficulty, hunting the keyboard for each key stroke. The same holds true for the first time golfer who must think through the individual actions necessary to produce the correct swing. Only when sufficient practice has been expended does the subconscious and muscle memory begin to take over, leaving the conscious mind free to concentrate on the desired result instead of the mechanics of the golf swing. So long as the conscious mind has to dwell on what one is doing instead of the result wanted, the competitor will remain a poor or mediocre performer. Shooters like Tony Boyer no longer have to think about technique, trigger control, wind, Bernoulli's, or the other myriad phenomena that will affect group size. Those have become a learned response in both the muscles and the subconscious. Top level shooters need only focus the conscious mind on what end result they desire.

Once sufficient practice has been accomplished, the benchrest shooter must also learn to control emotions, forget poor performance, and gain the frame of mind that continues to relate superior performance to thinking and believing, "That is like me."

Stress and pressure are self induced, and self defeating as well. They are mental in nature and must be controlled. Lanny Bassham, the great Olympic shooter, in his book on this subject, related an example that brings out this fact. If asked to walk a 4x4 board laying on the floor, we can manage to do it quite well and without falling. However, if the same board is suspended out the top window of a 20 story building, we would have great difficulty walking its length. The only real difference is mental. We see the result of falling off while suspended 200 feet in the air as being a high stakes game. This, in itself, greatly reduces our ability and performance to walk the same board. This lack of mental management will affect our ability to produce good groups when in competition or faced with something unfamiliar.

While this is a worthwhile and exhaustive subject, it is of secondary importance to this chapter, so I will not belabor the point any further.

Finally, one must understand the importance of primary influence. By this I mean one should put the most time and energy where it influences the outcome the most … the most bang for the buck, so to speak. You recognize that you have influence over some aspects of shooting well, and that you have little or no influence over others. Of the things over which you do have influence, some of are great importance, while some are of little importance. It behooves your performance to spend your time on those things over which you have the most influence. These, of course, have to be prioritized.

You have influence over how well you turn case necks. You also have influence over you how much you practice. Spending more time turning necks than practicing does not result in the best performance at match time. Both might be important, but practice is much more important than turning necks. Practice, on the other hand, is rather boring. And although turning necks is as well, it makes for better print. Ninety-nine of all articles written are about the mechanics of preparing accurate equipment. Only one percent is spent on practicing for success. The reason is that benchrest shooters are equipment, gadget, and equipment obsessed. We can talk about it for hours, an activity we find to be a lot more fun than spending time on the range practicing how to shoot in the wind … and less expensive too.

By contrast, most high power shooters are more technique oriented than equipment oriented. The art of holding the rifle steady, practicing breath, trigger, and sight control are absolutely essential to success. Give them a good rifle, and they will spend hours on the range practicing how to shoot it well from the kneeling, sitting, and standing positions. Give a great rifle to a benchrest shooter, and he will spend hours in his shop trying to make it shoot even better. But this is as it was intended, and as it should be … remember the objectives. Give him a few months, and the benchrest shooter will hand the high power shooter a more accurate rifle to practice with.

One might use phases to describe competitive benchrest shooting at long range. Preparation, Approach, and Termination Phases sound good. The Preparation Phase might include building an accurate rifle and tuning it to perfection. It will also include long hours of practice and making sure that you get to the match (it's difficult to win if you don't make it to the match … it's a bit less difficult if you do). The Approach Phase will include getting to the bench, setting up, laying out one's equipment just right. Also included will be one's approach to studying the wind, deciding which to use, setting flags, and making sure the rifle is mounted properly in the bags. The Termination Phase begins immediately after you pull the trigger.

You have no influence over the outcome during the Termination Phase. It is the end of the run. The bullet will do what the bullet will do. You simply wait from 1 to 1.6 seconds to see the outcome.

The success of the outcome, however, is influenced in proportion to how you handled what you could influence and what you had the highest influence over. You have greatest influence over the final outcome the earlier on in the process you are. That is, you have more influence on the outcome in the Preparation Phase than in the Approach Phase, and you have more influence in the Approach Phase than the Termination Phase.

Thus, the choice, selection, and preparation of equipment is of most importance to the benchrest shooter, and it is the first obstacle to overcome along the road to the match. It is also the factor over which you have considerable influence. The next is practice, the factor over which you should have the most influence. Turning necks, for example, is under your influence, but is of minor importance. Next in line of the things you can influence is your approach to the bench and the technique used there, and finally the Termination Phase. The reason your technique at the bench is secondary to preparation is that preparation controls your influence over bench technique. Skip Talbot, the great long range shooter, was not successful over his competitors when he beat them time after time and set world records because of his bench performance on any particular day. His greatest self-influence came from what he did to prepare to influence his bench technique on that day. This includes the many times he had sat at the bench prior to that day, the practice he put in to prepare for that day, and his attention to the equipment he selected and prepared … again, attention to those aspects of 1000 yard benchrest shooting over which he had the greatest influence.

1000 Yard Equipment

And now to the gist of it all.

Having committed myself to the statement that equipment is of primary importance in shooting 1000 yard benchrest successfully, I had better belly up to the bar. I could, at this point, lecture about what I think is the best equipment, but you would undoubtedly be better served by knowing what is currently being used and why.

Cartridges and Bullets

Following the popularity of bullets used for 1000 yard benchrest is somewhat like following a flat sine wave whose median line is the 30 caliber bullet. Fads are not only a characteristic of the fashionably dressed. Still, there are many who stray from the flock year after year, and, in fact, the 1000 yard benchrest clan is more adventurous than the traditional 100/200 yard benchrest competitor who clings en masse to the 6PPC. Referring once again to the objectives of benchrest, this is as it should be. Where one will frequently see 15 to 18 of the top 20 winners in a weekend of shooting using the 6PPC at the shorter ranges, it is not uncommon to see a great variety of cartridges and calibers present among the top 20 finishers at a 1000 yard benchrest match.

One will see calibers ranging from .224 to .416 at a 1000 yard match. Over the years there has been a preponderance of .30 calibers, but fads vacillate around the old standby. In this, the year 2000, the darlings of 1000 yard benchrest are gravitating to the 6 and 6.5mm calibers in cases that are relatively efficient for the newer, very low drag (VLD) bullets that have been gaining influence over the past 15 years. It would be no great revelation to see the 6.5 win out in the short run, but if the sine wave analogy is predictive, the swing back to the .30 caliber will endure.

Believing that velocity is an essential piece of the puzzle, past case capacities have tended to be overbore. And, indeed, many still are, but the 6.5 x 284 pushing a 142 Sierra MatchKing bullet has gained a considerable following at 1000 yards in the past couple of years, and, I am sure, will grace the benches for another 5 years while everyone tries to beat it. High power shooters have taken a liking to this cartridge as well. The problem has been the acquisition of cases, and shooters enamored with this configuration hang

Table 5A

Cartidge	Action	Scope	Barrel	Case	Powder	Bullet
.243 Win	RFD	Weaver	Hart	Lapua	IMR4350	Berger 105
240 Moray	Rem	Leupold	Shilen	Lapua	H4831	Sierra 107
6.5 Phantom	Lazz	Burris	Sndr	Lazz	H4350	Berger 140
6.5 x 284	Rem	Leupold	K&P	Win	V165	Sierra 142
30 Patriot	Nesika	Leupold	Sndr	Lazz	H4350	Sierra 190
300 Wby	Wby	Weaver	Apex	Wby	H1000	Sierra 200
300 Ultra	Rem	Leupold	K&P	Rem	H1000	Sierra 240

Table 6

Light Gun						
Cartridge	Action	Scope	Barrel	Stock	Powder	Bullet
.243 Ackley	Rem 700	Leupold	K&P	McMillan	RL-22	Berger
6.5/284	Rem 40X	Leupold	K&P	McMillan	RL-22	Goodling
6.5 Ackley	Rem 700	Leupold	Lilja	McMillan	RL-22	Sierra
.300 Win Mag	Rem 700	Leupold	Hart	McMillan	IMR4350	Sierra
.300 Ackley	Rem 700	Leupold	K&P	McMillan	RL-22	Berger
.30-378	Rem 700	Leupold	Lilja	Shehane	Varget	Sierra
300 Wby	Rem 700	Leupold	K&P	Shehane	H1000	Sierra
30 Hart	Rem 700	Leupold	Hart	McMillan	H1000	Berger

on to those they have with a fury. Many shooters are squeezing the neck even farther to hold a 6mm, 107 grain VLD bullet.

The 6BR and the old but true .243 either blown out to accept a bit more powder or untouched are gaining popularity. Much of the 6.5 and 6mm configurations attractiveness is symptomatic of a belief that took on god-like stature during the 70's, and which promulgated the almost religious use of the 6PPC at the 100 and 200 yard distances. That is, a shorter, fatter case is better. However, this relates to edge cutting accuracy, not necessarily long range needs.

While it might be true that the smaller cartridges are more accurate, easier to handle, and disturb the bags less, greater accuracy is only true when conditions are mild, the shooter gets lucky, or they are superb readers of conditions over each of 10 football fields laid end to end. This also assumes the match does not have any .30 caliber or .338 caliber shooters present who are also superb readers of conditions.

But the move away from .30 caliber is not complete. Many still rely on the 300 Win Mag, 300 Weatherby Mag, 308 Baer and many other .30 caliber configurations. Table 5A (see page 21) is extracted from the July 2000 issue of *NBRSA News*. It lists some of the equipment used in an April 2000 match at Sahuaro, Arizona. Some of the cartridges may surprise you.

Traveling across the country from the Southwest in Arizona to the Southeast in North Carolina and the IBS Association (as taken from the August issue of *Precision Shooting*), the partial equipment list in Table 6 (see page 21) does not vary considerably from those at Sahuaro.

As you can see, Sierra has waned only slightly over the years with Berger making some inroads along with a few self-made, custom bullets.

I have not listed all the equipment here, as they tend to duplicate. Some wildcats are unknown, and bullet weight was not listed. There was, however, a preponderance of K&P barrels, McMillan stocks, and Leupold scopes. McNeil, Tooley, and Baity took the gunsmithing honors. While Remington actions clearly took the receiver category, AMT, BAT, and Hall were in evidence as well. Glass ranged from Nightforce to B&L to Tasco to Weaver with Leupold leading the scope category. Krieger, Douglas, PAC-NOR,

and Bison were represented, but shooters showed the strongest inclination toward Lilja and K&P barrels. Groups were mostly won with those around 6" with some going a bit smaller and some a bit larger. The largest was 12.455" in the heavy gun with the smallest being 5.754". The light gun largest was 10.197" and 4.089" the smallest. Note that the average group was only a bit over .5 MOA at that range with 1 group close enough to .25 MOA you can taste it. This is extraordinary given the extreme range and the conditions the bullet faces between muzzle and target.

Traveling north to the land of the Original 1000 Yard Benchrest Club of Pennsylvania, the same range of cartridges are used. The .308 Baer, a creation of the venerable Bruce Baer, wildcatted from either 8mm Remington Magnum or Weatherby brass, has been a steady contender if not dominated the distance for a decade and a half.

Bill Shehane holds court with a few friends from Down Under. Shown from left to right standing: Alan Peake, Tony Alliason, and Stuart Elliot ... all visiting from Australia during the Hawks Ridge 1999 State Championships. Bill Shehane is seated in front of one of his beautiful 1000 yard heavy rifles sporting a Bill Shehane laminated wood stock which many shooters favor. Note the flat rails resting on the adjustable front bag, and the similar rails on the adjustable rear rest. Both rests are capable of elevation and windage adjustment. I would swear that is a 12-42x56mm Nightforce scope which both Bill and Bruce Baer favor. Photo courtesy of Bill Shehane (photographer unknown).

Stocks

In or about the year 1970, Jerry Rogers of Texas, a noteworthy competitor and innovator of the time, attended a match in Midland, TX. Not an unusual occurrence, except that his stock was rather unconventional. It was made of plastic and fiberglass. Unless I'm mistaken, he did very well with it. Although they knew nothing of Jerry Rogers, Lee Six and Chet Brown were experimenting with fiberglass stocks in the late 60's. Lee and Chet consequently fashioned such a stock for a rifle that was the experimental brainchild of Neal Knox and Dave Wolfe. These now famous fellows used it to tote a mother lode of silver and gold from the 1971 Nationals (I might be off a year).

Having started limited production in 1970, Chet Brown and Lee Six, both of California, took the success to heart and started more aggressive experimenting in Lee's garage. Without the rest of the world knowing it, the dawn of a new era in the configuration of rifles and rifle stocks was being born. A great deal of hard work and perseverance on their part gave the industry the fiberglass stock, changing the gun industry significantly and forever. The McMillans joined the effort a couple of years later, having the vision to realize where it all would lead. Small changes in those early designs have been made, particularly in shape,

Happy winners at a Hawks Ridge match in August 2000: Mike Harris, South Boston, Virginia for group and Blake Daniels, Taylorsville, North Carolina for score. Photo courtesy of Bill Shehane.)

manufacturing methods, meeting the demands of several disciplines, and the occasional addition of Kevlar, graphite, and aluminum bedding blocks, but the basic concept has changed little.

Throughout the past 20 years, it has been difficult to find a competitor on a traditional 100\200 benchrest line with a stock that was not produced using some variety of fiberglass. The hunting market has even seen the proliferation of plastic injection molding. Aluminum stocks have been tried from time to time, and some die hard worshipers of wood continue to poke their head into the melee.

Although the 1000 yard coterie still cling to the fiberglass stock in its myriad configurations, many believe that wood has its advantages on 1000 yard rifles, and a slow move to aluminum is making inroads as well. Bruce Baer, for example, believes that wood laminates are superior for damping vibration. Many 1000 yard shooters are turning to the wood laminate creations of Bill Shehane of D & B Supply Company of Cramerton, North Carolina. Bedding blocks are often used on the heavier rifles to support the massive steel barrels and actions. These are attached to the barrel, leaving the rest of the barrel and action to float freely, eliminating the need for the action to support the heavy barrel.

The 1000 yard community favors very heavy rifle stocks. Some of the first attempts by the manufacturers of fiberglass stocks to satisfy this requirement were made with the addition of lead shot combined with resin. It was not realized at once that this addition somehow changed the vibration characteristics of the stock dramatically and deleteriously.

Barrels

At this writing, Krieger, Hart, K&P, and Lilja seem to be dominating 1000 yard benchrest. Lengths of 32 to over 40 inches also seem to be the norm, with a few barrels going either less or more. With regard to all the 1000 yard organizations, .308 caliber still seems to dominate with bullet weights ranging from 175 to 240 grains. Twist rates most often used range from 9 to 12 depending on bullet weight. And … the heavier the bullet, the faster the twist needed.

1000 Yard Benchrest ... A Paradigm Shift

Just thinking about shooting at a target 1000 yards distant is intimidating to most of us. The object you are trying to hit, the X-ring, can't even be seen with the naked eye. And yet, the discipline continues to grow at an almost exponential rate. While it took traditional benchrest 30 years to grow from 168 shooters at the National Championships on the east coast to 250 shooters, it has taken but a tenth of the time to surpass that number at the 1000 yard line in the same area.

The fever has not only infected benchrest. Long range shooting is taking the art of riflery by force. Civilians who are enamored by the pragmatic nature and the flexibility required of the long range sniper are thriving on it. Hunters are extending their range with flatter shooting rifles, better optics, range finders, and an appreciation for a burgeoning technology that can extend the breadth of their previous limits. Varminters are pushing the envelope to the extraordinary. Manufacturers are meeting the call with a plethora of far reaching, momentum engorged, nervous system wrenching calibers that cause immediate neurogenic shock to both the target and the shooter.

To quote Bill Shehane: It is the "dawning of a new era" for benchrest shooting.

The author watched Jim Brummerstedt fire this rifle during the 1999 NBRSA 1000 Yard National Championships at the NRA Whittington Center. It was a joy to watch him shoot it, and although unfinished, I coveted this beauty the moment I saw it. The rifle is built around a Remington action holding a Lilja barrel chambered in 340 Improved. Several things of interest here: Unertl scopes and Posa mounts still find favor among long range shooters; the barrel block is often used in the heavy class; the large muzzle brake graced more than one rifle at the match; and the Hart rest appears to be fitted to its own platform. Photo courtesy of Jim Brummerstedt.

Chapter 8

1000 Yard Glass

by Jacob Gottfredson

The Hard Won Beginnings of Optics

Long range shooting is by no means new. In the grand scheme of things, however, that statement is relative. Man's ability to launch missiles comprises only a small portion of the time he has been around. Using glass to aim those missiles fills but a smaller portion still. Even today, many events prohibit the use of glass. Iron sights do indeed have their place, and traditionalists still cling to the use of them. Under the right conditions, the iron brigade can shoot shoulder to shoulder with the best optics equipped firearms around. Indeed, the last thing I want when facing a charging cape buffalo at twenty yards is a scope. I might even take that back, having used some of the close quarter battle red dot sights I have seen.

It was not until the last century that Carl Zeiss produced one of the first usable sporting optics. It took a good deal of time for the new fangled gadget to catch on. My father, an avid hunter and guide, never did switch, preferring iron sights until his death in the mid 1950's. The progress of using glass to enhance the capability of firearms remained slow. Optics were improving and making their way into the private sector throughout the Forties and Fifties before the military resigned themselves to the superiority of optical aiming devices for specialized use. Military snipers were equipped with low power, sadly inferior scopes by today's standards. Even then it was a hard won battle. By contrast, the military is currently using optical devises that approach "Star War" fantasy ... far beyond the simplicity of a quality image in which a crosshair with mil-dots has been added.

The science and manufacture of optics is not uncomplicated. The design mathematics, the precision machining and grinding tolerances, and the use of high tech components found in modern optics are quite remarkable. In today's world, the quality of the instruments being assembled by major manufacturers is better than ever before, and the variety of features is mind boggling.

Early representatives of the riflescope were a far cry from today's offerings. Each time light enters or leaves a piece of glass, about 5% is reflected back. Some optics have as many as 16 air-to-glass surfaces with light lost at every surface. In early models, less than half the light got through to the eye; the rest bounced around

Photo courtesy of Zeiss.

inside the instrument, making the image hazy and difficult to see.

The Road To Modern Sporting Optics

Large objective lenses helped compensate for lost light, but they resulted in heavier instruments. In 1935, Professor A. Smakula at the Zeiss plant in Germany invented a process for reducing the reflection from glass-to-air surfaces. This made it possible to increase the light transmission of binoculars, telescopes, and riflescopes by 80 percent. Then in the 1940's, it was discovered that coating the glass with magnesium fluoride would let more light through. The original coating technology consisted of a single layer, which reduced reflections to 1 - 1.5% per surface. More recently, advanced multi-layered coatings have reduced reflections to as little as .25% per surface. Today, in the best instruments, 95% of the light gets transmitted to the eye. Some newer processes are claiming 100%.

Coating lens surfaces with a vacuum-deposited antireflection layer of magnesium fluoride only one-fourth of a wavelength of light thick increases the light transmission through the surface. The greatest reductions are achieved with multiple layer "multi-coatings" of zirconium oxide, cryolite, zinc sulfide, and other such materials. If the coating is a little too thick or thin, the coatings won't work. However, as the coatings get better, the expense of the instrument goes up. This same coating technology has been transferred to today's riflescopes.

Coated means that one coat is applied to the air-to-glass lenses only. Multi-coated means that one or more surfaces are coated, generally one layer thick; while multi-layered coated means that more than one coat is applied to the lens' surface (but it may be just to the exterior surfaces of the ocular and objective lenses), or it may be that every lens' surface is multi-layer coated, depending on the instrument and the manufacturer.

These coatings give you brighter images because of their increased light transmission. They also yield sharper, less hazy, and higher contrast images because they reduce the amount of light scattered randomly within the instrument. Inexpensive optics usually have only their outer lens surfaces coated to give the impression of more quality than they actually possess. "Multi-layered coated" uses a combination of multicoatings and a single layer of magnesium fluoride coatings.

To check the quality of optical coatings, examine the color of the image of a fluorescent light reflected in them. Magnesium fluoride coatings of the correct thickness produce a purple/violet tint to the largest reflected image (the one on the outer lens surface), although the tint can range from pale blue to magenta, depending on the type of glass in the lens. Magnesium fluoride coatings that are too thin yield a pink reflection, while coatings that are too thick look green. The smaller reflections (from the internal surfaces of the lenses) are generally off-white and tinted a faint violet, amber, or green.

Multi-coatings are usually green in color, although the reflected image can be any of a number of tints, even red and amber, depending on the type of glass and the coating materials used.

Catalog Specifications

Binoculars, spotting scopes, and riflescopes are marked with a formula such as "8x30mm" or "10x50mm." The first number in the formula is the power, or how many times the image is enlarged. The second number in the formula is the diameter of the objective lens in millimeters. The bigger the objective, the more light can enter, and the greater the potential resolution of the image.

Low-light performance is largely dependent on the exit pupil. Exit pupils are the small, bright

Photo courtesy of Zeiss.

circles you see in the eyepiece when you hold the instrument away from your eyes and up to the light. The exit pupil diameter is calculated by dividing the diameter of the objective lens by the power. A 7x35mm binocular, riflescope, or spotting scope has an exit pupil diameter of 5 millimeters (35/7 = 5). This is not completely true for variable riflescopes. Variable riflescopes often incorporate an exit pupil restriction device that restricts further enlargement as the power is decreased. This is done to help control resolution degradation.

At noon the pupils of your eyes contract to 2 to 4mm and at night they may open to 7 mm. If the beam of light exiting the eyepiece is wider than the pupil of the eye, the excess doesn't get in; the eye can't see it. The extra light is wasted. During daylight hours things look just as bright through binoculars and scopes with 4mm exit pupils as through those with 7mm exit pupils. In fact, if they have better coatings, optics with 4mm exit pupils may be brighter. Thus, the larger exit pupil is an advantage in low light. A larger exit pupil coupled with long eye relief provides other advantages. They are often more comfortable to use, allow a complete image to be seen by eyeglass wearers, and they are far more forgiving when quick target acquisition is necessary.

As we age, the eye loses some of its ability to adapt to darkness. While a 20-year-old person's pupils might open to 7mm, at 50 years of age the pupils may open only to 5mm. Therefore, binoculars and scopes with large exit pupils may not help the older shooter. The best binoculars and scopes are bright as a result of their advanced multicoatings and top quality optics that provide brightness you can see all the time, even in daylight.

Lens size is partially responsible for the amount of light transferred to the eye. You can compare the light gathering ability of two instruments by squaring their objective lens diameters. A 50mm objective lens would yield: 50 squared = 2500, while a 35 mm lenses would be 35 squared = 1225. Also, resolution (the ability of an optical device to show the small details) is proportional to the size of the objective. That is, the bigger the lens, the smaller the detail one can see. But as you have seen, coatings and other factors enter into the ability of a binocular or scope to transmit light and resolve detail.

Another specification called "relative brightness" is calculated by squaring the exit pupil diameter. For example, all binoculars or scopes with a 4mm exit pupil diameter would yield: 4 squared = 16. Since relative brightness is a mathematical relationship, it doesn't take into account aperture differences between optics. 8x32mm and 20x80mm binoculars have identical 4mm exit pupils, but they are hardly identical low light performers due to the 635% larger light gathering area of a 20x80mm. Relative brightness is only useful when comparing the low light performance of optics of similar aperture ... and then only when your eye's pupil is as large as the exit pupil of the scope.

Twilight Factor

Twilight Factor provides an indication of the relative performance of sizes of optics in low light levels, and is dependent on both the objective diameter (how much light enters the binocular or scope) and the exit pupil (how much light passes from the binocular or scope to the eye). It is calculated from the formula "the square root of the <u>magnification times the objective</u> diameter" or $TF = \sqrt{magnification \ x \ objective \ diameter}$. For example, an 8x56mm scope has a twilight factor of 21.2, while an 8x30mm has a twilight factor of 15.5 and an 8x20mm a twilight factor of 12.6. The larger the twilight factor the better the relative low light performance of the binocular or scope.

Exit pupil, relative brightness, and relative light efficiency comparisons are interesting and often useful, but they are not the best judges of how well binoculars and scopes perform in low light. For example, the 8x32mm and 20x80mm mentioned above both have 4mm exit pupils, a relative brightness of 16, and a relative light efficiency of 24, but the 80mm binoculars are much better in low light due to the larger light gathering capacity and the higher twilight factor of 21.2.

The twilight factor is a more useful judge of a scope's low light performance than exit pupil, etc., as it takes into account both light gathering and magnification, both of which affect how much detail you can see ... and seeing detail is what binoculars, spotting scopes, and riflescopes is all about.

The larger the image, the easier it is for you to see details in that image. By the same token, with a smaller image, the brighter it gets, the easier it is for you to see the same details clearly. So, within reason, if magnification goes up, brightness can go down without seriously affecting resolution, and vice versa. That is, small bright images can show you as much detail as large dim images.

Twilight factor allows you to compare various combinations of aperture versus magnification to determine the one that best balances an increase in magnification against a decrease in brightness (or vice versa). The larger the twilight factor, the better a binocular is for low light observing. A twilight factor of 17 and above is best for twilight or early morning use.

But here again, the twilight factor is a mathematical relationship only. It does not take into account light transmission differences between binoculars and scopes, so small numerical differences in twilight factors may not be visible in real life.

Keep in mind that just because an inexpensive scope and a premium model have identical twilight factors, you cannot assume that their optical performance will be the same. Distortions, optical flaws, and poor coatings in the less expensive binocular or scope can severely compromise its sharpness, brightness, and clarity. And while these attributes are important at any distance, they become paramount at the longer ranges such as 1000 yards.

Overcoming Optical Aberrations

With the above generalizations of scopes in mind we can turn to the aberrations that the optical scientist must overcome. While it is possible to almost rid the optic of some aberrations, it is not possible to avoid all of them. Some solutions create other problems and even, at times, enhance others. The optical scientist's efforts are pointed toward doing the best job of compromising these problems as he or she can. It is interesting to note, however, that one company's idea of what is best suppressed or overcome is not always shared by the other companies. Also, scopes are often designed to address a particular problem. In our case, this is the image and integrity of the scope we wish to use for 1000

yard or long range shooting.

Most instruments within our area of interest are made up of, at least, an objective lens at one end (nearest the object), an eyepiece at the other end, and a set of erector prisms in the middle. Most erector prism configurations fall into either the Porro (off-set light path) or roof (in-line light path) type. While reflections in these glass elements and prisms and the tubes that house them are controlled by the use of coatings, coatings are also used to increase durability of the outer lens surfaces and provide correct color balance ... and more.

The following is a list of common lens aberrations:

1. Chromatic
2. Five aberrations of Seidel
    *   Spherical
    *   Coma, comatic aberration
    *   Astigmatism
    *   Curvature of field
    *   Distortions

To understand aberrations and how they affect optical quality, one has to have some understanding of light.

Barrel heat creates its own mirage in light winds, causing the image to blur and distort. A simple mirage shield fashioned from a target, or the one shown here manufactured by Hart, deflects barrel image mirage around the objective lens of the scope and effectively solves this problem.

Light

The dictionary defines light in several ways. The important one for our consideration goes something like this, "electromagnetic radiation to which the organs of sight react, ranging in wavelength from about 4000 to 7700 angstrom units and is propagated at a speed of about 186,300 miles per second, and including a similar form of radiant energy that does not affect the retina, as ultraviolet or infrared rays". As Canon explains, "The most visible region is 400nm (purple) to 700nm (red). Thus light can be thought of as a type of wave. A light wave can be regarded as an electromagnetic wave in which an electric field and magnetic field vibrate at right angles to each other in a plane perpendicular to the direction of propagation. The two elements of a light wave that can actually be detected by the human eye are the wavelength and amplitude. Differences in wavelength are sensed as differences in color (within the visible light range) and differences in amplitude are sensed as differences in brightness (light intensity). A third element, which cannot be detected by the human eye, is the direction of vibration within the plane perpendicular to the light wave's direction of propagation."

What can we extract from this information? Two important facts: 1. That light hitting the eye is energy, and the eye reacts to energy. So, more light, more energy, more reaction. 2. That light is a wave. The distance between the peaks of the wave is defined by the eye as color, while the height of the wave is defined by the eye as brightness.

Several phenomena become important in understanding and managing light waves. Refraction and dispersion are two of these. Refraction is a phenomenon whereby the propagation direction of a ray of light changes when the light passes from one medium such as a vacuum or air into a different medium such as glass or water, or vice versa. Dispersion is a phenomenon whereby the optical properties of a medium vary according to the wavelength of light passing through the medium. When light enters a lens or prism, the dispersion characteristics of the lens or prism cause the index of refraction to vary depending of the wavelength, thus dispersing the light.

I guess that I first became aware of refraction as a youngster when I put my arm or a stick into the water of a swimming pool. I noticed to my amazement that my arm seemed to bend. Later, when I began trying to shoot fish with arrows, I realized that the image of the fish was not where the actual fish was and began to adjust my aiming point to compensate. Dispersion simply suggests that those angles are not always the same, depending on the medium. Mirage is an example of this phenomena.

Lens Aberration

Since most lens systems (binoculars, scopes, cameras) are constructed solely of lens elements with spherical surfaces, light rays from a single subject point are not formed in the image as a perfect point. Also, the focal point position differs for different wavelengths of light. Plus there are many requirements related to changes in angle of view, especially with wide-angle, zoom, and telephoto lenses.

The general term used to describe the difference between an ideal image and the actual image affected by the above factors is "aberration". Thus, to design a high-performance lens, aberration must be extremely small, with the ultimate objective being to obtain an image as close as possible to the ideal image. Aberration can be broadly divided into two classifications: Chromatic aberrations, which occur due to differences in wavelength, and monochromatic aberrations, which occur even for a single wavelength.

Chromatic Aberration

When light is passed through a prism, a rainbow spectrum can be observed. This is due to the prism's index of refraction and rate of dispersion. Since it occurs at different wavelengths it is called chromatic. There are two types: "axial chromatic aberration", where the focal point position on the optical axis varies according to the wavelength, and "chromatic difference of magnification," where the image magnification in peripheral areas varies according to the wavelength. The first appears as color blur or flare, and the second appears as color fringing where edges show color along their borders. Chromatic aberration is corrected by combining different types of optical glass having different refraction and dispersion characteristics. Significant performance improvements can be achieved using man-made crystal such as fluorite or UD (ultra-low dispersion) glass. Achromatic lenses correct chromatic aberration for two wavelengths of light. Apochromatic lenses correct chromatic aberration for three wavelengths of light, often used in super-telephoto lenses.

Five Aberrations of Seidel

In 1856, a German named Seidel determined through analysis the existence of five lens aberrations that occur with monochromatic light.

1. Spherical Aberration

Spherical aberration causes parallel light rays passing through the edge of a lens to converge at a focal point closer to the lens than light rays passing through the center of the lens. This tends to be greater in large aperture lenses. Spherical aberration affects the entire image area from the center to the edges, and produces a soft, low contrast image that looks as if it were covered with a thin veil. Correction of spherical aberration in spherical lenses is very difficult, although commonly carried out by combining two lenses, one convex and one concave. There is a limit to the degree of correction possible using spherical lenses. With large aperture lenses, the only effective way to thoroughly compensate spherical aberration is to use an aspherical lens element.

2. Coma, Comatic Aberration

Coma, or comatic aberration, is a phenomenon visible in the periphery of an image produced by a lens which has been corrected for spherical aberration, and causes light rays entering the edge of the lens at an angle to converge in the form of a comet instead of the desired point, hence the name. The comet shape is oriented radially with the tail pointing either toward or away from the center of the image. The resulting blur near the edges of the image is called comatic flare. Coma,

which can occur even in lenses which correctly reproduce a point as a point on the optical axis, is caused by a difference in refraction between light rays from an off-axis point passing through the edge of the lens and the principal light ray from the same point passing through the lens center. Coma increases as the angle of the principal ray increases, and causes a decrease in contrast near the edges of the image. Coma can also cause blurred areas of an image to flare, resulting in an unpleasing effect. The elimination of both spherical aberration and coma for a subject at a certain distance is called aplanatism, and a lens corrected as such is called an aplanat.

3. Astigmatism

With a lens corrected for spherical and comatic aberration, a subject point on the optical axis will be correctly reproduced as a point in the image, but an off-axis subject point will not appear as a point in the image, but rather as an ellipse or line. This type of aberration is called astigmatism. It is possible to observe this phenomenon near the edges of the image by slightly shifting the lens focus to a position where the subject point is sharply imaged as a line oriented in a direction radiating from the image center, and again to another position where the subject point is sharply imaged as a line oriented in the concentric circle direction (the distance between these two focus positions is called the astigmatic difference). In other words, light rays in the meridional plane and light rays in the sagittal plane are not subjected to equal conditions, so the two light ray groups do not converge to a single point. When the lens is set to the optimum focus position for the meridional plane, the light rays in the sagittal plane are formed as a line in the concentric circle direction (this condition is called meridional focus). Likewise, when the lens is set to the optimum focus position for the sagittal plane, the light rays in the meridional plane are formed as a line in the radial direction (this condition is called sagittal focus).

4. Curvature of field

Curvature of field is a phenomenon which causes the image formation plane to become curved like the inside of a shallow bowl, preventing the lens from producing a flat image of a flat subject. When the center of the image is in focus, the periphery is out of focus, and when the periphery is in focus, the center is out of focus. The degree of curvature of field is largely affected by the method used for correcting astigmatism. Since the image plane falls between the sagittal and meridional image surfaces, good correction of astigmatism results in small curvature of field.

Lens designers reduce curvature of field as much as possible using various methods such as changing the shapes of the various single lens elements making up the lens system and changing the position of the aperture. In doing this, one necessary condition that must be satisfied to simultaneously correct astigmatism and curvature of field is Petzval's Condition (1843). Petzval's condition states that a lens element is good if a result of zero is obtained when the inverse of the product of the index of refraction and focal length of that lens element is added to the total number of lens elements making up the lens system. This sum is called Petzval's Sum.

5. Distortion

One of the requirements of an ideal lens is that "the image formed by the lens has the same shape as the subject." Distortion is a type of aberration that causes straight lines to become curved (distorted) in the image, thus preventing this ideal condition from being fulfilled. Distortion which stretches the shape in the diagonal direction is called pincushion distortion, and that which compresses the shape in the diagonal direction is called barrel distortion.

Distortion is small in lenses with constructions symmetrically configured on both sides of the aperture diaphragm, but is likely to occur in lenses having asymmetrical configurations. Zoom lenses tend to produce barrel distortion at wide-angle positions and pincushion distortion at telephoto positions (due to slight changes in distortion characteristics during zooming). With zoom lenses incorporating one or more aspherical lens elements, however, this distortion is well corrected due to the compensating effect of the aspherical lens.

Since this type of aberration is caused by refraction abnormalities of the principal light rays passing through the center of the lens, stopping down the lens cannot reduce its effect.

If you didn't completely understand all that you just read, don't fret .... neither does anyone else ... entirely. Our objective is to recognize the effects of each and how to test how well the manufacturer has minimized them.

Minimizing the Effects of Aberrations

Modern lenses are designed using large-scale computers to perform mind-boggling calculations and high-level simulations to minimize all types of aberration and achieve superior image formation performance. Even with this technology, however, it is impossible to completely remove all aberrations, meaning that all lenses on the market still have at least a small amount of aberration remaining. This aberration is called residual aberration. The type of residual aberration in a lens generally determines the lens' imaging characteristics such as its sharpness and blur effect. Because of this, modern lenses are often designed with consideration given to achieving a pleasing blur effect (image characteristics outside the image formation plane) by using computer simulation techniques to analyze lens performance at the design stage.

Prisms, Coating, and P-coating

Binoculars provide an excellent example for understanding the benefits of coatings to overcome aberration and other problems inherent in lens design. They offer the opportunity to introduce prisms in the discussion as well. Roof prism binoculars have become increasingly popular. They offer a slim, compact design that is often lighter, more durable, and easier to handle than Porro prism binoculars. However, the precision required of a roof prism is so much more demanding than that of the Porro prism to achieve the same level of performance that expense becomes an issue.

Optical systems must be composed of several lenses to overcome the effects of aberration. How these lens elements interact is of importance. So too with the prisms. The pupil halves produced by the prism roof edge effect the light waves differently and result in a reduction in image quality.

As the original inventor of coatings, Zeiss explains. The structure of the retina, the pupil diameter, and its own set of aberrations determine the resolution limit of the human eye. This resolution limit measures approximately one minute of arc. For this to happen, the pupil must be at least 2mm wide to reduce diffraction phenomena. The pupil widens to 6 to 8mm in twilight or at night. Resolution is not increased, however, because the eye switches from cone to rod vision, and aberration becomes more pronounced. It is for this reason that 2mm is the minimum diameter that a scope or binocular's exit pupil should be designed for.

The paragraph above is of utmost importance to long range shooters and to the glass they choose to get that job done effectively. I have underlined the last sentence because it is of singular importance to the use of glass for long range shooting and will be discussed more thoroughly in a moment.

Light waves must arrive simultaneously at the image point to achieve maximum brightness. Thus image quality of optical instruments depends on how well the designer handles the recombination of light rays passing through the lens, the diffraction of light waves at the edges of the apertures, and the out-of-phase arrival of light waves at the image point.

Prisms require at least two reflections for lateral reversal, and two further reflections for vertical reversal. The 90 degree angles of the roof prism must be accurate to within only a few arcseconds to prevent double images.

When light is totally reflected, the light waves vibrating in parallel to the plane of incidence are retarded in phase compared with the waves vibrating at right angles to the plane of incidence. The incident beam is divided into two halves by the roof prism. Both half-beams differ in the sequence in which they are deflected by the roof surfaces and also in their type of phase shift. Both half-beams are put together again by the eye during observation, resulting in almost total destructive interference in the geometrical image point. The light does not simply vanish,

however, but reappears at the side of the geometrical image point.

The resolving power of optics is different for horizontal and vertical structures. A test pattern shows this phenomenon clearly. When watching specific details, an experienced observer will shift the zone of dwindling contrast by accommodation. This means that he constantly endeavors to find a compromise suited to the object viewed. This causes fatigue during long periods of observation and his concentration on the object drops.

Optical designers/manufacturers apply multi-layer coatings to the roof surface of erector systems to prevent the phase shift of the two half beams. The coating procedure is very similar to that used for anti-reflection coatings. Because of their phase-correcting effect, these layers are call "P-coating" in short. the P-coating eliminates all the disadvantages inherent in roof prisms and caused by the wave nature of light. The resolution of details at right angles and parallel to the roof edge is identical.

"Ray effects" no longer exist when viewing bright point-shaped objects. The image immediately appears sharper and richer in contrast to the experienced observer, particularly when viewing high-contrast objects. Long periods of observation cause no fatigue as the user's eye does not need to accommodate to perceive individual structures in the object watched.

In short, explains Zeiss, P-coating corrects the wave-optical effects due to phase shift between the half-beams separated by the roof edge. This increases resolution, improves the contrast of fine details, and enables fatigue-free observation over long periods

Lens Performance Evaluation

Resolution

The resolution of a lens indicates the capacity of reproduction of a subject point of the lens. It is common to hear resolution expressed as a numerical value such as 50 lines or 100 lines per mm. This value indicates the number of lines per millimeter of the smallest black and white line pattern that can be clearly seen or recorded on film. The numerical value used for expressing resolving power is only an indication of the degree of resolution possible and does not indicate resolution clarity or contrast.

Contrast

Contrast is the degree of distinction between areas of different brightness levels, i.e., the difference in brightness between light and dark areas. For example, when the reproduction ratio between white and black is clear, contrast is said to be high, and when unclear, contrast is said to be low. In general, quality lenses producing high quality images have both high resolution and high contrast.

MTF (modulation transfer function)

Modulation transfer function is a lens performance evaluation method used to determine the contrast reproduction ratio, or sharpness of a lens.

Optical designers like to use the analogy of frequency response of audio equipment. The sound source is recorded through a microphone and then played back through speakers. Frequency response indicates the fidelity of the reproduced sound with respect to the source sound. If they are very close, the equipment is classified as "high fidelity". If we think of the optical system as "a system for transmitting optical signals", it is possible to find out how accurately optical signals are transmitted as long as the frequency response of the optical system can be measured. In an optical system, the equivalent of frequency is "spatial frequency," which indicates how many patterns, or cycles, of a certain sine density are present in 1 mm width.

While we would hope that optical systems would transmit the subject image perfectly to the eye, this is not the case, explains Canon. Since actual lenses contain residual aberration, actual contrast ratios are always less than 1:1. As the spatial frequency increases (i.e., as the black and white sine wave pattern becomes finer, or more dense) the contrast decreases until finally becoming gray with no distinction between black and white (no contrast, 1:0). To make the measurement, data from several points is used in order to determine the MTF characteristics of the overall image. MTF curves are frequently given for camera lenses (and it is hoped manufacturers would do so in future for other instruments), graphed with the horizontal axis corresponding to the distance from the image center along the image area diagonal, and the vertical axis corresponding to contrast. In these curves, the closer the 10-line/mm curve is to 1, the better the contrast and separation ability of the lens, and the closer the 30-line/mm curve is to 1, the better the resolving power and sharpness of the lens. Although a good balance between these characteristics is important, it can generally be assumed that a lens will provide excellent image quality if the 10-line/mm curve is greater than 0.8 and that satisfactory image quality can be obtained if the 10-line/mm curve is greater than 0.6.

Color Balance

Color reproduction fidelity compared to the original subject depends on the light source illuminating the subject, and the light transmission characteristics of the lens.

It is difficult to focus all colors simultaneously. The image may appear soft, and contrast decreased because the edges of colors bleed into other image points.

Peripheral Illumination

The brightness (image surface illuminance) at the edge of the image is called marginal illumination and is expressed as a percent of the amount of illumination at the image center. Peripheral illumination is affected by lens vignetting and the cosine 4 law and is inevitably lower than the center of the image. Poorly designed lens systems will not allow the observer to focus all colors at the same time.

Vignetting and Cosine 4 Law

Light rays entering the lens from the edges of the image area are partially blocked, causing light fall-off in the peripheral areas of the image. The cosine 4 law states that the light fall-off in peripheral areas of the image increases as the angle of view increases, even if the lens is completely free of vignetting. The peripheral image is formed by groups of light rays entering the lens at a certain angle with respect to the optical axis, and the amount of light fall-off is proportional to the cosine of the angle raised to the fourth power. As this is a law of physics, it cannot be avoided. However, with wide-angle lenses having a large angle of view, decreases in peripheral illumination can be prevented by increasing the lens' aperture efficiency (ratio of the area of the on-axis entrance pupil to the area of the off-axis entrance pupil).

Inexpensive, poor quality binoculars show this phenomenon clearly. Hold the binocular at arm's length and look at the small exit pupil in the eye piece lens. You will see a square, clear area. The circular exit pupil will be completed by gray areas at the edges. It will appear as though a clear, square peg was placed in a gray, round hole, and results in a 25 percent loss of light. This will not be evident in quality binoculars, the clear area appearing to be round, filling the entire circular area of the exit pupil.

Testing Image Quality

The rather laborious considerations above consumed a considerable amount of ink discussing the mechanics of optical design and manufacturing, putting some optical terms in our pockets, and setting the stage for the remainder of the chapter and our choice of long range optics. With these tools in hand, we should be able to determine the image quality of the instrument of interest. And we should be in a position to know why it has such quality, and know how to test for that quality.

While much of the foregoing discussion is particularly suited to binoculars, it is inherent to spotting scopes, riflescopes, and cameras as well. Suffice it to say, however, that the instrument used in the following discussion is the binocular, and the subject is about determining superior image quality. The differences encountered in spotting scopes and riflescopes, for the most part, are that of range and the special difficulty that presents.

It is difficult for the average shooter to test optics and make good choices on his or her own. Comparing brands is almost impossible outside the store setting, and even the store setting pres-

ents its own difficulties. The store setting is a far cry from the laboratory, and the conditions and often the sales person are stressful. I am using binoculars as a medium because it will give the reader the most simplistic basis for understanding the procedures used. For the most part, one need only enlarge the Zeiss pattern supplied to test the more simplistic image provided by the single tube of a spotting scope or riflescope versus the double barrels of a binocular.

Resolution

Again, resolution is the ability of the instrument to resolve fine detail. While an instrument might have good resolution, this in itself does not a superior instrument make. Several other factors need to be tested and are important to overall image quality as well.

When selecting an instrument specifically for low light conditions, there are three factors to consider in order of importance: image quality, exit pupil size, and light transmission (lens coatings). Without good image quality, you might just get a bright, grainy image where the details are still difficult to discern.

The following testing device and instructions are compliments of Zeiss.

Place the binoculars or scopes to be tested/compared on a firm support. The point here is that it is difficult to judge the resolving ability of a shaky instrument. Also, if you are comparing one binocular against another, stick to identical magnifications. This same procedure is used for spotting and riflescopes. However, for the high power optics used for long range viewing of detail, the distances given below must be increased.

What I am suggesting is that you copy the Zeiss Test Pattern (ZTP) below and take it with you when testing optics. A bit of tape will allow you to hang it in the store or across the street in the case of spotting and high power riflescopes.

Stand approximately 30 feet away (60 or more for spotting and riflescopes) and locate the test pattern (below) in the center of each binocular's field of view. Eyeglass wearers should leave their eyeglasses on. Focus the pattern as sharply as possible, remembering to focus the diopter as well. It is assumed that everyone knows how this is done.

Check to see that all lines, regardless of their direction, are clearly in focus for each binocular, spotting, or riflescope. Note the number of the smallest pattern for which the instrument will allow crisp resolution.

If the horizontal lines are sharply in focus, but the vertical lines are not, this is an indication that the lens has an aberration called **astigmatism**. If the blacks and whites tend to the gray, then it is a sign of **poor contrast**. Note that all binoculars will have a point at which either the horizontal lines are in focus and the vertical out, or vice versa. Quality optics will have a point at which all lines are very sharp. Riflescopes may present some difficulty in this regard. Parallax is the result of the focal point of either the first or second focal plane not falling at the same point as the reticle. When this is the case, the image is also slightly (sometimes greatly) out of focus. A parallax correction devise may be positioned on the objective lens or a dial might be incorporated in the elevation and windage manifold. In either case, the device allows the viewer to adjust the focal length to correspond with the reticle. This in turn enhances focus of the overall image. In some riflescopes this can be further enhanced by slightly moving the diopter adjustment. Caution

is advised as this might also change the point of impact of the bullet when sighting in.

Now move the binocular, spotting, or riflescope so that the test pattern is one third of the way out of the center field and repeat the exercise. Again move the optic so that the test pattern is at the very edge of the field of view, and repeat the exercise. If the test pattern cannot be focused, it is an indication of **curvature of field**. If the area is blurred, but it can be focused, it is an indication of slight **spherical aberration**. Even the best optics will display a certain amount of these aberrations. The question is, how much compromising are you willing to endure. The least amount of residual aberration will cost the most amount of money.

I use other tests for determining image quality as well. One of these is to compare the ability of the optic to resolve or read certain objects on a one dollar bill. Look at the side of the bill that has the pyramid with the eye at the top. Better 10x binoculars will allow you to see considerable detail at 30 feet. For example, some will allow you to read the small number printed below the "E" at the end of the word "ONE". A high quality 8x will allow you to read this same number at about 25 feet.

Steve Ingraham of Better View Desired magazine uses a variation of this that is particularly revealing. Note what you can read on the same side of a dollar bill with the naked eye at approximately 12 inches (leave corrective eyeglasses on), or where your eyes focus best. Then note the distance at which the binocular will allow you to read the same detail when the dollar is moved out some distance (usually between 15 and 22 feet ... for spotting scopes this is approximately 60 feet). You will note that not all binoculars of the same power will allow you to read the same amount of detail at the same distance. He gives comparative distances for several popular binoculars at which he could read such detail (he uses the shadow below the word "ONE" and states that you should be able to clearly discern the lines that make up the shadow).

I also have a place where I habitually park on the way home from work to evaluate optics. Several signs and other particularly useful objects and colors are approximately 300 to 400 yards away. This gives me some idea of the long range ability of the instrument as well as color balance and color bleeding.

Flatness of Field

This naturally goes with the topic above, but looks at the problem in a slightly different way. Focus on a flat image like a poster. Image degradation resulting from the inability to focus sharply on both the center and the edges together indicates excessive curvature of field. You may be able to focus in areas away from the center, but then the center focus goes out. This is very common, and not many binoculars, rifle, or spotting scopes are in focus at the center and nearer the edges at the same time. Since one does not often concentrate on images away from the center, this is not a particular problem. However, when you find a binocular, spotting scope, or riflescope that focuses both the center and a good distance away from the center or clear to the edges simultaneously, you will be very pleased with the overall image. Keep them.

Distortion

Distortion can be caused by unequal image magnification. Focus on a straight edge like a shelf, door jamb, telephone pole, or the edge of a building. Bowing or curving at the top or sides indicates poor correction. Two common types of distortion are **pincushion and barrel**. With pincushion distortion, straight lines tend to bow in toward the center as you get closer to the edge. The opposite is true of barrel distortion where the straight lines tend to bow away from the center the closer you get to the edge.

Rolling distortion is a phenomenon that is particularly distasteful in optics used for panning such as is often the case with binoculars or hunting scopes. To test this, the observer must move the optic horizontally from either left to right or right to left. Objects coming into view will appear to enlarge as they reach the center of the view and reduce in size as they move out of the view. This can be described by imagining yourself to be standing in front of a very large merry-go-round. A man riding the horse at the extreme left will appear small. As that person approaches the center of the wheel in relation to

your view, he will appear to enlarge because he is getting closer to you. Again, as he moves away from the center of the turning wheel and to the right, he will tend to decrease in size because he is moving farther away.

Optics that are corrected for rolling distortion will project the object as the same size as it moves horizontally through the image.

Lens Element Alignment

If the exit pupils are fuzzy or misshapen, or they are not located in the center of the eyepiece, the lens elements may be misaligned. This condition can cause a part of the image to be blocked out. This will result in a reduction of light transmission and viewing discomfort.

Optical Path or Barrel Alignment

This condition can be determined by two methods. First, focus until the image is sharp. Rest your eyes for a few seconds, then cover one of the lenses and focus on the subject again. Now drop your hand from the lens. If the image is in focus, then slips out of focus, the eyes are compensating. This can cause severe eyestrain, or even a headache.

A more popular method is described by Zeiss, "Of utmost importance for the user is the absolute parallelism of the optical axes of both tubes of the binoculars as otherwise he would see a double image. Even a very small misalignment would force the eyes into an unnatural, strained position, resulting in fatigue and possibly a headache. A fault in the alignment of both tubes can be roughly checked by looking through the binoculars at a horizontal or vertical line, and alternately opening and closing each eye. If the line moves or jumps, the two tubes are not properly aligned." This is easier if you support the binoculars solidly as on a tripod. Use a small piece of cardboard or similar material. While looking through the binocular, quickly slide the cardboard in front of one of the lenses. Do this a few times, then switch to the other lens. If the image changes or seems to jump up and down, the barrels or optical paths are out of alignment.

Color

In my tests I use a pattern that I devised where the primary colors are touching. This was accomplished using simple highlighter pens. This allows me to observe **bleeding** of one color into the other if it exists. The observer should see a distinct separation between primary colors with no bleeding, flaring, or distortion of color. I watch this pattern as the light fades, comparing the optic's ability to present the colors correctly as light is decreased. This is good indicator of an optic's ability in twilight conditions as color and color differentiation are two of the first things to degrade as light is diminished.

A one-inch or larger red shooting dot placed on a white background will reveal a scope's ability to control **flare**. If this is not well corrected, the dot will flare at the edges similar to the glare seen around a car's headlights when viewed through a foggy or inexpensive windshield.

Color shift and flare can also be observed from a black image on a white background such as seen on most targets by moving one's head up and down or side to side while viewing the target. This will reveal the sudden appearance of yellows or blues, depending on whether on the top, bottom, left, or right of the center. This should be held to a minimum in top quality optics and disappear entirely when the eye is aligned with the optical axis of the scope.

Is Bigger Better?

I have expelled a considerable amount of technobabble to this point, and I apologize for that. But my audience is comprised of those accuracy obsessed individuals who are keenly interested in every part and piece they use to place bullets more precisely, and I have made that assumption here. The specific context here is 1000 yard shooting, which for most optics is simply infinity. And, unless conditions are just right, that means trying to see effectively through a considerable amount of atmosphere. Haze, mirage, and particles in the air accumulate between the shooter and the target the farther the range envelope is pushed, particularly at the earth's surface.

We have learned above that light is a form of energy and energy is what excites the eye to detail and color. We have also learned that bigger lenses transmit more light and more energy. We have learned that larger objective lens size and power produce higher twilight factors, a mathematically derived number used to evaluate the ability to see detail in dim lighting conditions. All these factors seem to force the issue toward bigger being better. It ain't necessarily so.

There are some problems inherent in the equation that can't be entirely overcome by enlarging tube and objective lens size. The human eye is a culprit in this case. So is optical quality.

The human eye has both limitations and built in adapters that prevent it from taking full advantage of the mechanical and theoretical performance of today's optical technology. Although this is not true in all cases, it certainly is in the context of the scopes and binoculars we use for 1000 yard and other long range shooting.

Although the eye may very well be the most complicated and adaptable mechanism we know, it is not capable of taking advantage of all we can build for them to look through. The exit pupil of a variable riflescope, binocular, or spotting scope increases as the power is reduced. If the diameter of the exit pupil of the scope gets larger than the pupil size of the eye, the additional light through the exit pupil of the scope is wasted. But another phenomenon takes place as well. The pupil of the eye contracts as the light is increased. Thus, as the power of a scope is reduced and the exit pupil increases in size, the pupil of the eye contracts with the increase in light. The result is that during bright days, decreasing power does not necessarily offer any help. Nor does larger objective lenses. In this case bigger is not better and is sometimes detrimental. The opposite, that is, increasing power, does not necessarily help either.

Color fidelity and clarity are not appreciably increased by objective lens size during the day. These mainly depend on the quality of the lenses and their coatings. As natural light decreases, the pupil of the eye begins to dilate to allow more light to enter. The pupil of the eye will dilate to approximately 5 to 8mm. Looking through a scope works well in these circumstances as long as the exit pupil of the scope remains high. However, relatively speaking, detail comes with power, and as power is increased, the exit pupil of the scope decreases. The cones in the eye switch to rods in dim light and aberrations are increased.

The bottom line is that we have to look for a compromise when searching for 1000 yard glass. We have to deal with conditions in the atmosphere, changing light, and the ability required to see detail well enough to aim properly. If power is increased too much, mirage and other atmospheric conditions disturb and distort the image. Power increase also degrades image quality when the exit pupil approaches 2mm (as we learned above). This can be seen in the charts below. Spotting scopes that are often used for seeing bullet hole impact as well as the flow of mirage and trace begin at high powers. Most popular zoom models in the 80mm objective lens range start at 20 to 25 power with the high end around 60 power. Many 60mm objective lens scopes start around 15x with the high end being 45x. The charts show the problem dramatically. An 80mm scope starting at 20x has an exit pupil of 4mm. This is not bad, but not great either. As the power is increased, the limit of 2mm is

quickly attained around 40x. From 40x to 60x the image degrades significantly. This holds true for high power riflescopes as well. In 60mm scopes, the same thing happens at 30x. This is a problem with variable spotting scopes that begin at a high power. That is, the power is not low enough to allow an exit pupil that will take advantage of the human eye. Thus, high quality lenses that are fully coated and aberration free are required for best results. Resolution, clarity, and contrast must be superb. When high quality in these characteristics are combined, the power needn't be extreme for long range viewing.

Although I have charted every objective lens configuration, in an effort to not belabor you too much, I have included only four of the most popular in our context. In the smaller 40 and 50mm objective lens sizes, you will note a significant change in the slope of both twilight factor and exit pupil near the end of the line. If you look at the power settings at the bottom, you will find the answer for this. I plotted power setting in increments of only one power change until I reached 10x, at which time I changed to 5x. In the larger objective lens charts I did not do that, so the lines remain linear.

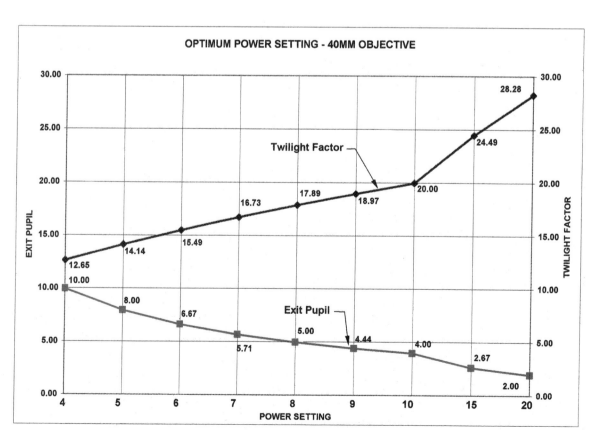

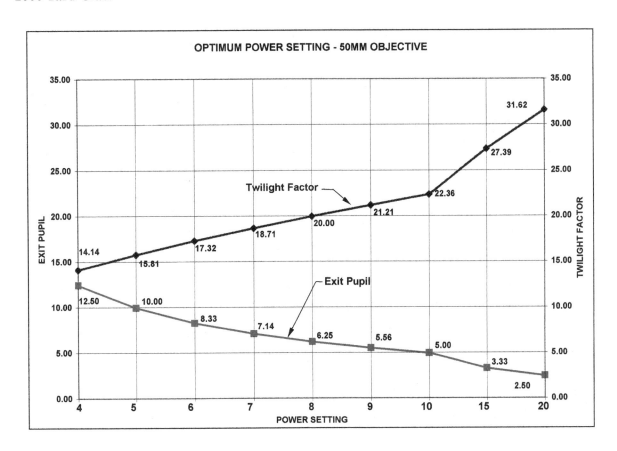

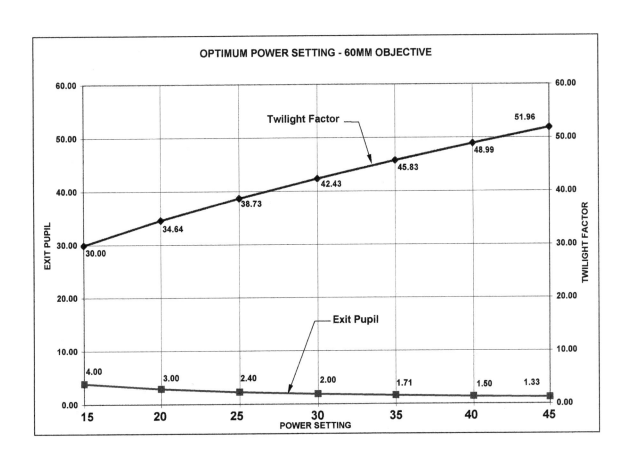

Using power setting versus exit pupil, I could have plotted several different results, but I chose twilight factor to show the significance of power versus objective lens size. The charts quickly point out where image degradation is likely to occur, or, conversely, what the greatest power setting is that will still produce satisfactory, all-around results given a particular objective lens size. This will occur at the power where exit pupil size nears 2mm. In the 40mm objective lens this would be between 15 and 20 power with a twilight factor (TF) well above 17. The 50mm objective lens would yield approximately the same satisfaction between 20 and 25x with a TF approaching 35; a 60mm objective lens would be between 25 and 30x with a TF of approximately 40; and an 80mm objective lens would be about 30 to 35 power with a TF of over 50.

Thus, increases of approximately 10mm in objective lens size result in approximately 5 power increases in satisfactory performance, with an accompanying increase in TF of 7 to 10.

I chose the 40 to 60mm objective lens sizes because they reflect most rifle scopes, while the 60 to 80mm objective lens sizes comprise the most popular spotting scopes.

Riflescopes have a similar problem, but not to such an extreme degree. For example, the Nightforce 12-42x56mm scope is one of the darlings of the 1000 yard benchrest folks as well as a lot of other long range enthusiasts. And well it should be. Nightforce's glass is top quality. At 12x the exit pupil is 56/12 = 4.7, or about the most the human eye can absorb. The Nightforce scope's image at that power sitting is excellent, offering clarity, resolution, contrast, and color fidelity that is unsurpassed in its class. At 42x, however, the exit pupil becomes 56/42 = 1.3, well below the cut off of 2mm. This image degradation can be clearly seen if you look at a distant object and begin increasing the power in the Nightforce scope. The 2mm limit in this scope is reached at 28x, and it is slightly beyond this point that one begins to see image degradation. The image becomes soft and hazy, resolution and contrast drop off, and clarity seems to become veiled as well. And, of course, atmospheric conditions are magnified at the higher powers. Image degradation will be even more pronounced in scopes that do not match up to Nightforce's superb image quality.

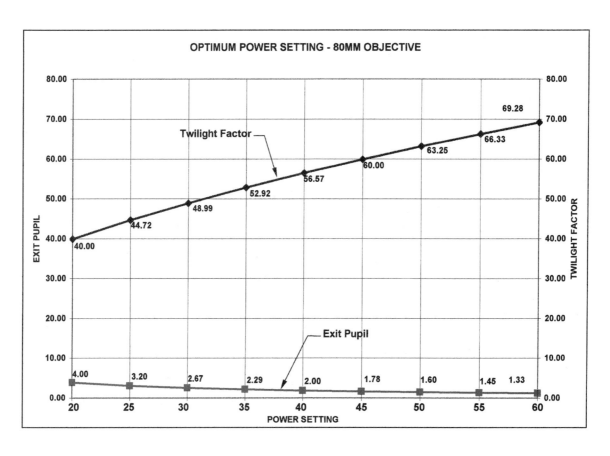

In the charts of exit pupil and power setting for 40 and 50mm objective lens riflescopes, we see that most power settings are satisfactory between 4 and 20 power. The 50mm objective scope has a slight edge in that it will retain the 2mm cutoff slightly above 20x while the 40mm objective lens reaches that point at 20mm. But the human eye has great difficulty in distinguishing light differences this small. In fact, it is difficult for the human eye to distinguish differences of 25%. If you test a 40mm against a 50mm scope in dim conditions, you will see very little difference between the two at the same power setting, and the time extension as darkness falls is so slight as to be insignificant. The real difference can be seen in superior glass and coatings, not in the numbers provided by objective lens size, relative brightness, or twilight factor.

Besides the obvious need for a riflescope to retain point of impact and click value and be able to take the punishing consequences of significant recoil, reticle subtension becomes important. A reticle that subtends the better portion of an inch at 100 yards will mask 10 inches of the target at 1000 yards, much too large for benchrest or varmint use. One that subtends just .05 inches at 100 yards will only cover a half-inch at 1000 yards.

The Ideal 1000 Yard Scope

What then makes up the ideal 1000 yard scope?

First and foremost, be it spotting scope or riflescope, is image quality. Image quality and single plane characteristics are, after all, the primary reason we put scopes to use at long range, otherwise we would all still be using iron sights. Superior glass, superior coatings, and lens design always accompany superior image quality. At 1000 yards this translates to acuity. And while it seems counter to good sense to put a $1,000 saddle on a $10 horse, the notion is growing in some quarters that one should put more money into the scope than into the rifle. I might agree with this concept for the average hunter, but it might be going a bit far for a 1000 yard bench shooter who puts 3 grand into his rifle. Still, it is faulty to scrimp on glass when so much has been put into the building of a truly precision rifle … and so much is at stake.

Second on the list of importance is mechanical integrity and function. The optic must focus and function reliably and repeatably. Reticles and elevation and windage turrets must be simple, understandable, and mechanically repeatable.

Scope mounts are important for two reasons. Many, if not most, 1000 yard rifles propel large bullets at significant velocities. In 17 pound rifles (light class) this can be as much as 30 foot pounds or more. Muzzle brakes are often harder on scopes and reticles than the original recoil produced without a brake. The scope mount should be rugged enough to take such punishment over the long haul. A sloped base is important as well. The crosshairs are subjected to considerable vertical movement to get to 1000 yards. A rear base that is 12 to 20 MOA higher than the front will put the crosshairs closer to the center of the image, providing less distortion and a clearer image.

Residual aberration should be minimal. Neutral color without flare or color shift is important.

From the preceding pages in this chapter, we have found that bigger is not necessarily better. A scope that is bright due to coatings versus a larger objective lens usually gives the best image. Thousand yard competition is shot outdoors during daylight hours. A high twilight factor and

Thomas Blahnik, long time Army sniper and now owner of Sniper's Paradise, at the 1000 yard line with the Nesika Bay light tactical rifle and Leupold's 3.5-10x40mm Vari-X III M3 BDC Tactical Scope, the design of which was called for by the Army.

great performance during dawn and dusk hours is not often required. Hazy, cloudy days presents the dimmest light you are likely to encounter. Therefore, an extra large objective lens is no panacea. It has to be accompanied by high quality glass and coatings.

The ideal power for resolution and contrast over the course of the day in today's riflescopes falls in the twenty's with 22 to 24 being ideal. Although you can see the object of interest better at 40 power, no scopes that I am familiar with can sustain superior resolution, contrast, and clarity at these high powers throughout the day. For these reasons variable scopes offer considerable flexibility to deal with changing atmospheric conditions at long range.

Unfortunately, compromises have to be made. Fifty-six millimeter objective lenses are about as large as we can comfortably handle on a rifle. Much larger objective lenses are available on spotting scopes, but come at prices that exceed the size of the tax, title, and license check I recently handed the salesman for my daughter's first car.

It is important to remember to not change power during the match. Equally important is to not change the ocular lens in order to focus the reticle during the match. Both operations should be accomplished prior to shooting for the day.

But if one feels the need to change either focus or power during the day, do it prior to shooting any single group. Changing the ocular, diopter adjustment ring on a scope whose reticle is in the first plane is not a problem, and often one can make minor adjustments to the diopter adjustment when power is changed to achieve critical focus. Most scopes used by Americans, however, have the reticle installed in the ocular or second focal plane and such adjustments often shift the point of impact … sometimes minutely, sometimes greatly.

Scopes manufactured at the time of this writing (I say that because scopes are changing and improving on a daily basis) that have the necessary optical and functional quality necessary to meet the demands of 1000 yard shooting are not found in great numbers, nor are they inexpensive.

Your choice of scope, reticle, mechanical function, and mounts may also be dictated by the type of 1000 yard or long range shooting you are doing. Many military and law enforcement personnel use straight 10x, 16x, or the 3.5-10x variable. Aiming at, seeing, and hitting a 12" x12" steel target at 1000 yards with a good 10x

A favorite of 1000 yard and long range shooters, the 6.5-20x50mm Long Range scope from Leupold is shown here aboard the author's Sendero, 300 Winchester Magnum. Features target turrets, side focus, and a 30mm body. The scope was mounted <u>without sloped bases</u> and the rifle zeroed at 100 yards. Only 27.5 minutes of elevation were required to bring the 190 grain, Federal Gold Metal Match bullet on at 1000 yards.

Vari-X III 3.5-10x40mm Long Range M1

Leupold's Mark 4 and the newer 3.5-10x40mm Vari-X III M1 are popular with Marine snipers. I have watched accomplished snipers fell 12"x12" steel consistently at 1000 yards with such scopes, prized for their versatility, rugged internals, and no nonsense reticle and turret designs.

scope is not difficult. During a recent sniper match, the majority of competitors used the 3.5-10x40mm Vari-X III with very good results. This can be accomplished without sloped bases

Nightforce's newest offerings, the NXS 3.5-15x50 and 56mm and the 5.5-22x56mm, feature an innovative reticle, illumination, side focus/parallax adjustment, 30mm tube, and superb image quality. Shown here aboard one of Nesika Bay's Light Tactical Rifles, the NXS has 110 minutes of adjustment, nearly 4 inches of eye relief, and many other innovative features.

provided the scope has a considerable range of elevation adjustment. I have used Leupold's 6.5-20x50mm scope on a 300 Win Mag Sendero with no slope in the bases that was zeroed at 100 yards. I turned 27.5 minutes of elevation to go to 1000 yards with no difficulty. A .308, on the other hand, might take as many as 40 minutes, and often the user discovers he is out of adjustment around 700 yards. This sort of flexibility is not often required, and the best results come when the range at which you will normally shoot has the reticle at or near the center of the main tube.

Leupold, IOR, Nightforce, Schmidt & Bender, and Kahles are among those with models that meet the criteria herein described for long-range, low-power riflescopes. Likewise, Leupold, Nightforce, and Bausch & Lomb produce acceptable scopes in the high-power, variable arena.

On days that are great for optical viewing, one can often see bullet holes in the white with the Nightforce 12-42x56mm scope. Their new NXS 3.5-15x50 and 56mm as well as their 5.5-22x56mm might very well be the best offerings the industry has for 2000. These scopes display resolution that is beyond what is theoretically possible.

This 8-32x50mm Burris Signature Series scope has a bright, clear image and fine crosshair. With only 25 minutes of adjustment, however, it has poor flexibility for long range shooting. Burris does have other models with more click adjustment suitable for 1000 yard shooting.

Swarovski is just one among many "High End" spotters that offer a quality image for long range viewing and spotting. Their zoom lens is said by some to be the finest on the market. Shown here on a Bogen Tripod is an 80mm APO model with a straight, variable lens and helical focusing.

If you read this during the year 2000, one of the scopes listed here may suit you admirably. At the rate technology is advancing, however, if you are reading this 3 or 4 years hence, they may all be at the bottom of the pack. But the physics and the criteria described in this chapter will not.

In the spotting scope category, I would list the top of the line models from Swarovski, Leica, Bausch & Lomb, Optolyth, and Nikon as contenders in spotting misses, clay pigeon hits, and maybe, on occasion, capable of seeing bullet holes at 1000 yards. If you can get your hands on one of the old Unertl Team Scopes with the higher power lenses, do it. Think long and hard about purchasing the expensive ED and APO models. Seldom do these features help you on the 1000 yard line looking at targets. Used in conjunction with a camera, the film might see the difference in color and fidelity, but it is doubtful that you will. If you have your heart set on a lower quality scope, you might find that ED does help the image. In the case of Nikon's 78mm or B&L's similar offering, they might only be available in the ED models.

Many 1000 yard shooters have taken to using "Big Eyes". That is: combining 2 spotting scopes on a fixture, allowing the viewer to use them like a binocular. This does not increase the quality of the image. But for those of you who simply cannot leave both eyes open while viewing through a monocular, you may find that you can view for much longer periods with such a set up. It will, however, behoove you to learn to keep both eyes open when using any optic. It does take some practice and use of the dominant eye, but after a short time it will come very naturally. The benefits are several. Holding one eye closed while viewing or shooting tenses and stresses muscles in the face. These become fatigued quickly. When they do, other muscles in the body become fatigued as well and shooting performance suffers. Peripheral vision is cut in half. If

Dennis Johnson sits behind his light gun on the 1000 yard line at Hawks Ridge Gun Club. The scope appears to be a Bausch and Lomb. Just above his turrets, a fellow is looking through a set of "Big Eyes" used to spot clay pigeons placed on the ground at 1000 yards and used for sighters. Two more sets stand on their tripods just beyond that. Photo Courtesy of Bill Shehane.

something is approaching from that side of the face, you will not see it. With some practice, the eye that looks through the scope can concentrate on the target, the reticle, and any other objects such as flags in the view. While the shooting eye is occupied thus, the other eye can concentrate on other important objects in front of you. Many benchrest shooters, for example, place the last couple of wind flags in the scope's view at the longer distances. The closer flags are arranged so that the non-shooting eye can watch them. In a sniper situation, closing the non-shooting eye may result in your not seeing something of life threatening consequences.

When a very steady rest is available, greater power gives the shooter confidence. The target's center appears to be so close that hitting it should be easy. Also, it allows the shooter to make minute adjustments in point of aim. If, on the other hand, the mirage is thick, reducing power gives the shooter confidence because if one can see more clearly, one can perform better. When a steady rest cannot be secured, increasing power has the opposite affect on confidence. High power magnifies one's view of a moving reticle. Reducing power leaves the shooter with the psychological feeling that they are shaking less and an increase in performance will follow.

From whatever well-spring your 1000 yard shooting comes, if it includes the use of optics, your performance as well as your enjoyment will be rewarded by superior instruments … those pieces of glass so arranged and manipulated that they meet the criteria described herein.

Chapter 9

Conventional Long-Range Competition

by Randolph Constantine

The *Conventional Long-Range Competition* of the title of this chapter refers to competitions held in the United States under the rules of the National Rifle Association of America (NRA). This type of shooting is also carried on under similar rules in England, Canada, and other countries. Because of this, I have included comments here and there about variations in the rules, equipment, and match formats used in other countries such as England and Canada in an effort to make this chapter as comprehensive as possible, insofar as my limited knowledge will permit.

A short, and fairly complete, description of what the word, *conventional*, means in this context is that the shooter lies on the ground in one of the conventional shooting positions, prone or supine, and shoots at bullseye targets at known distances while supporting the rifle with his body and a sling, but with no other support. The supine position is included because the "classical" back (or Creedmoor) position of the 19th century is permitted in the NRA rules although it is seldom seen in the United States.

There are very few restrictions on the rifles and cartridges used, at least in the United States; but there are a few. In that regard, things are a little different in other countries. In the United States, there are no rifle weight limits, nor are there minimum trigger pull weights as there may be in other countries. Rifle weight is limited mostly by the fact that the shooter has to be able to support and shoot the rifle without any aid

other than a sling — no bipods or sandbags are allowed — except for something called "F class", which is a Canadian development that is now shot in some matches in the USA. However, F-class has not yet been enshrined and formalized in the NRA rules.

Another thing that increases the challenge in "conventional" Long-range competition is that most shooting is done using iron sights; the exceptions to this are the "F" class and the few any-sight matches. This is something that most people think simply cannot be done with any chance of success, but that opinion is unfounded.

In the years since the 1950's, most people have become so wedded to their telescopic sights that they cannot conceive that a person could possibly hit something on a regular basis that he cannot see directly. The people who think this have probably never used a a rifle equipped with good match sights with an aperture (or "peep") in both the front and rear sight. With a little practice, most people will find that with such a sighting system, one can easily hold to within 1/2 MOA when the rifle is supported on sandbags. Since the 10 ring on the target used at 1000 yards in conventional competition is 2 MOA wide, it should be (and is) possible to shoot perfect scores on this target using iron sights. This author has not yet managed to do that, but I do regularly shoot scores in the 190's. The record at 1000 yards for 20 shots with iron sights (on a target with a 20-inch diameter 10 ring) is a perfect score of 200-16X, the 16X meaning that

16 of those shots were in or touching the 10-inch-diameter, tie-breaking X ring.

No matter how it is done, whether under strict rules in formal matches of some type, or just plinking at rocks or varmints 1000 yards away, Long-range shooting is always fun and a challenge. In the rest of this chapter, I shall lay out the details of what is involved in Conventional Long-range (CLR) competition, the standard rules (and variations), the target used, rifles, cartridges, sights, standard matches, etc. My hope is that this may tempt some readers to come out and give CLR competition a try, at least in F class, if not in the old-fashioned, standard way.

WHAT IS *LONG-RANGE* ANYWAY?

In the world of conventional competition under NRA rules, *Long*-range is a lot longer than many people think, especially to those who are casual shooters, or those whose only shooting on a target range consists of sighting in their deer rifles every autumn. While working as a helper to such nimrods during the Durango (Colorado) Gun Club's Sight-In Days, I have had the experience of being asked, "How far away are those targets, 300 yards?", when the targets in question were in fact only 108 yards (or 100 meters) from our permanently fixed benches. Most people do not overestimate the distance to our sight-in targets by that much, but many of them do think that the targets are a whole lot farther away than just a few yards more than 100 yards. Also, most of them are willing to state that they would not be likely to take a shot at a deer or elk at any distance farther than those targets, — something I think is a good thing, given how poorly I have seen so many of them shoot.

This experience led me to think that to most people, anything over 100 yards is "Long-range". To the readers of this book, it is probably obvious that 100 yards is nowhere near what you would want to call *Long*-range. Even so, many readers will likely think that NRA Highpower shooters are a little extreme. In conventional NRA Highpower competition, the four stages of the standard , or so-called "over-the-course" matches are shot at 200, 300, and 600 yards. The Standing and Sitting Rapidfire stages are shot at 200 yards on a target called the "SR" target, where "SR" stands for "short-range".

The Prone Rapidfire stage of the standard matches is shot at 300 yards on a slight modification of the SR target, which is called the SR-3 target. The size of the scoring rings is the same as those on the SR target, and the only thing that is changed is the size of the aiming black; the 8 ring is blacked in to make the aiming black of the SR-3 target (at 300 yards) appear to be about the same size as that of the SR target at 200 yards. In NRA Highpower, 300 yards is still considered to be *short*-range!

The Prone Slowfire stage of the standard matches is usually shot at a distance of 600 yards on a target that is designated as the MR-1 target; and, you guessed it, "MR" stands for "Mid-range"! In the NRA Highpower world, even a distance of 600 yards is not yet considered to be Long-range!

Long-range thus turns out to be anything <u>over</u> 600 yards, which, because of historical tradition and the necessity to have fixed firing lines, ends up meaning distances of 800, 900, and 1000 yards. For some reason, no formal target shooting is, or was, ever done at 700 yards in the USA, at least not to my knowledge. All conventional shooting at Long-range is done at a target called the "LR" target, which has a 10-inch diameter X ring and a 20-inch diameter 10 ring. The LR

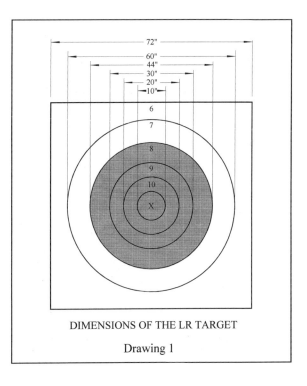

DIMENSIONS OF THE LR TARGET

Drawing 1

target is shown in Drawing 1 on which all of its pertinent dimensions are given. The entire target frame is 6-feet square, and a hit anywhere on it scores at least a 6. There is no such thing as a "visible miss" on the LR target.

A side comment concerning units of measurement. While most of the rest of the world has gone to the metric system, the United States has not done so even though England and Canada have. Most target shooting is done on ranges that were built long before there was any impetus to convert to metric, and the standard distances used (of inches, feet, yards, etc.) are long entrenched in tradition.

Since most rifle ranges in the USA have firing lines laid out in distances from the targets that are integral multiples of 100 yards (and in many cases those firing lines are elevated), it would be difficult and very expensive to rework these ranges to place the firing lines at distances from the targets that would be integral multiples of 100 meters. Also, conversion to metric distances would in many cases make it desirable to make a concomitant change in the dimensions of the scoring rings on the targets. For these reasons, Highpower rifle competition in the United States is likely to remain one of the last holdouts for the use of American units even if there is someday a move for the USA to go metric.

There has been no formal shooting in the United States at distances greater than 1000 yards, at least insofar as shooting under the NRA rules is concerned. The rules just do not address the possibility and so do not contain any provisions that would allow for such shooting to be sanctioned if there were any rifle ranges that could accommodate such distances. Unfortunately, there are very few ranges in the USA on which such shooting could be done.

I am aware that shooting is done in England on a regular basis at distances out to 1200 yards on the Stickledown range at Wimbledon, but I have never had the opportunity to shoot at such distances. Because such shooting at these extreme distances is done in England, a few ranges in the USA that do have the room are putting in a few firing points at 1100 and 1200 yards. It will be interesting to see if shooting at those extreme distances becomes a regular thing here in the USA.

RULES, MATCHES, AND RIFLES

As stated above, Conventional Long-range matches are shot under rules set down by the NRA. Talking about the rules of a game is often dull and boring, but, to a large extent, the rules of a game make that game what it is. In particular, in the world of CLR competition, the rules tell us, to some extent, what cartridges may be used and what restrictions, if any, are placed on the rifles that fire those cartridges. Because of this, I cannot describe the rifles, cartridges and matches without discussing some of the rules that define, and, in some cases, limit them.

There are basically three matches that are shot in CLR competition in the USA; they are: 1) any rifle with metallic sights at 1000 yards (usually 20 shots for record); 2) any rifle with any sights at 1000 yards (also usually 20 shots for record); and 3) the Palma match, which has a special format I'll describe shortly. All of these matches are shot on the LR target. Shooters usually call an any-rifle-with-any-sights match, an "any-any" match; likewise, an any-rifle-with-metallic-sights match is often called an "any-irons" match.

The two any-rifle matches shot each year as part of the National Championships are very important and bear the names of the trophies given for them. The any-rifle, iron sight match at 1000 yards is called the Leech Cup match because the trophy for that match is a large silver cup given to the Amateur Rifle Club of New York in 1874 by Major Arthur B. Leech of Ireland. That trophy was handed off to the NRA in 1901.

While the Leech Cup is the older trophy, the Wimbledon Cup is perhaps the most famous of all the trophies competed for in all the shooting sports in the United States. The Wimbledon Cup itself is a large silver tankard that was presented to the American team at the matches in England by Princess Louise in 1875. The Wimbledon Cup match is the 20-shot, any-rifle, any-sight match shot at 1000 yards each year at the National Championships. The winner of the Wimbledon Cup match is often referred to as the "Best rifle shot in America" even though that person may not have won the across-the-course championship. I know of no rifleman who would not like to have his name on one of these trophies.

The Palma match is the only one of the three

standard Long-range matches that includes some shooting at distances other than 1000 yards. Its history goes back to the Great Challenge match of 1874 that was held at the Creedmoor Range on Long Island, New York, between an Irish team and a US team. The Irish team had beaten all comers in the British Empire and issued a challenge to the US in 1873 in the hope that they might be seen as the undisputed world champions. The US was given a year to put together a team and determine a match format. The format that was ultimately selected was exactly the format currently used for the Palma match: 15 record shots at each of the distances: 800, 900, and 1000 yards for a total of 45 record shots for each team member. The Palma match is still shot in exactly that format. The Irish shot muzzle-loaders while the US team shot cartridge rifles. The US team won by a small margin, 934 to 931, and it was at that match that Major Leech presented the cup that now bears his name to the Amateur Rifle Club of New York.

I, and many others, think that the Palma match is the most challenging and rewarding of all the Highpower matches. The rewards are not tangible or fungible; they are only the personal satisfaction derived from getting better at meeting the challenges posed by this match.

This may not seem like very much variety, but I have not heard many people who shoot in these matches complain about being bored. If you are going to shoot Long-range as defined above, you have to do just that — shoot at distances greater than 600 yards — and usually from the prone position. There are only so many ways this can be done, and these three matches have proved to be more than sufficient in testing a shooter's skill.

Variations on the standard formats have not caught on. While it might be an interesting experiment to try shooting Standing, or even Sitting or Prone Rapidfire at 1000 yards, I don't think very many people would be interested in doing that on a regular basis. It is anybody's guess what the scores would be, but I don't think very many egos would be gratified at the results. Even so, it might be fun to try it.

RIFLE RESTRICTIONS

Before discussing the rifles and cartridges in detail, there are some general restrictions on the rifles that need to be mentioned. These restrictions also apply to rifles used for F-class shooting.

"ANY" RIFLES

First, let's look at the restrictions on the rifles used in the "any-rifle" matches since they are the simplest. Because there are some restrictions, the term "any rifle" is, in a strict sense, a misnomer; but the restrictions are actually very few and are mostly related to safety or legal concerns.

The major restriction is that the rifle may not shoot bullets larger in diameter than .35 caliber. Unfortunately, this bullet diameter is not defined any more precisely than what is stated here. Does it mean no bullets larger than 0.350" in diameter, or does it mean that a barrel of *bore* diameter 0.350" would be permissible, when such a bore would require bullets of 0.358' in diameter? The rules do not say, and I don't know the answer to these questions; but this is not likely to cause anybody much consternation because, as I'll explain shortly, there are very few people would be likely to want to shoot a rifle requiring such large bullets. Whatever the answers are, the rule definitely prohibits the use of the 50 BMG, or even the 45-70. The intent of the rule is to level the playing field and definitely to rule out cartridges such as the 50 BMG.

For those who might want to try cast bullets in one of the classic black powder cartridges at 1000 yards, whatever the bullet diameter, I say go ahead; I might even come out and join you. "Long-range Blackpowder Cartridge Rifle" shooting might become the next, "hot" competitive shooting game. It is just that you cannot do it under the current rules for Conventional Long-range competition. Sorry, but black powder and big bullets just aren't *conventional* anymore. However, Long-range Blackpowder competition just might have enough nostalgia appeal to catch on the way Cowboy shooting has. Who knows?

Back to the Highpower rules. Until a few years ago, there was a limit of 0.30 caliber for the bullet diameter for the "any-rifle" class of rifles, but that limit was recently increased to the current 0.35 caliber to allow people to use the 338 Lapua cartridge, which was being developed for use as a long-range sniper cartridge. The 338 Lapua is essentially the 416 Rigby case necked down to take 0.338" diameter bullets and had shown some promise as a cartridge for use in 1000-yard matches. However, bullet weight is high — initially it was 320 grains, now it is 300 grains — which, in any rifle that is light enough to be held up by a shooter, gives fierce recoil at the velocities that can be gotten from the voluminous Rigby case with that heavy a bullet — velocities may exceed 2800 fps from a 28 inch barrel.

For two rifles of the same weight, each weighing 18 pounds, the 300 grain (0.338 caliber) Sierra MatchKing at 2800 feet per second will increase the free recoil velocity of the rifle by 36.6% over that for a 300 Win. Mag. that is shooting a 190 grain bullet at 3000 fps; and the recoil energy will be increased by 86.6% (almost double!). This calculation assumes powder charges of 90 grains for the 338 Lapua and 70 grains for the 300 Win. Mag. The reason for this odd example is that most people think that the recoil produced by the 300 Win. Mag. with this load in an 18 pound rifle is about the upper limit of what most people can tolerate for Prone shooting.

On the target range, the 338 Lapua has been tried by only a few and without much success. When shot off a bipod or a rest, it may do well in its intended use, but it is just too much gun for our conventional target games.

Another thing that militates against the use of very heavy bullets at very high velocity is that the NRA rules prohibit the use of muzzle brakes. Muzzle brakes simply may not be used on any rifle in any sort of NRA Highpower competition, over-the-course or Long-range. This is another reason why very few people would be likely to shoot a 50 BMG even if bipods were allowed. The main reason for this restriction is simply to protect the shooters from the noise. Firing points on a Highpower range are only 6 feet wide, so a shooter's ears are likely to be no more than 8 feet away from the muzzle of an adjacent shooter's rifle. Under such circumstances, magnums are loud enough even when one is wearing both ear plugs and muff-type hearing protectors. The shooters do not need to be subjected to the additional noise of having the muzzle blast of any rifle directed back towards them by a muzzle brake, much less that from a 338 Lapua or a 50 BMG.

But that is it for meaningful restrictions. In sum, what "any rifle" means for conventional shooting is any rifle that does not have a muzzle brake, that does not fire a cartridge that launches bullets of diameter greater than 0.35 caliber, and that can be held and fired by the shooter in the conventional manner, supported only by his muscles and a sling.

Other than these few, there are no restrictions on rifle design, rifle weight, barrel length, or trigger pull-weight, at least in the United States. There are three further restrictions that are legalistic but that have very little real effect. They are: 1) You may not have a rifle capable of fully automatic fire; 2) Your rifle may not have a release trigger; and 3) you are not allowed to have a robotic sighting system that will fire the rifle automatically when the sight picture is perfect. I kid you not; that last one really is in the rules. Remember, you were warned.

Trigger pull-weight is something on which I feel I have to comment. Anyone who has ever tried any of the Benchrest games is probably convinced that a trigger with a pull-weight of 2 ounces or less is the way to go. Most experienced Highpower shooters will tell you, "Not so." There is one difference between Highpower and other disciplines such as Benchrest and Smallbore Prone that makes super-light triggers a chancy business, and that is that under the rules of Highpower (which govern CLR competition), a shooter may not fire any more sighting shots after he has begun firing his record shots — from then on, all shots count toward his score. So, if sometime after a shooter has gone for record, the rifle should happen to fire when the bolt is closed, sending the bullet into the dirt, or anywhere off the target, that shooter has just lost 10 points! Most Highpower shooters long ago decided that it is much better to have a heavier trigger than to lose points in this fashion. For this reason very few HP shooters use a trigger with a pull-weight that is less than 1 pound. A few may go down to about 8 ounces with a two-stage trigger, but almost none go lighter than that. It is not that it would be unsafe since the shooter is on a rifle range and would not be closing his bolt on a live round without the rifle's being pointed downrange. No, it is just too risky in terms of the possibility of losing 10 points at a whack should the rifle fire accidentally.

RESTRICTIONS ON PALMA RIFLES

Rifles for the Palma match are even more restricted, but then, nobody ever said that they were *any* rifle. The Palma match is also the only one of the three CLR matches in which the shooters are restricted to a single cartridge, and that is 308 Winchester cartridge. The rules are more specific and state that this must be the "unmodified" 308 Winchester cartridge. I interpret this to mean that the cartridge case (and the rifle's chamber) may not be "improved" by changing the body taper, shoulder angle, or case length. Other than this cartridge restriction and the fact that all proper Palma shooting is done with iron sights, Palma rifles are as unrestricted as *any* rifles, at least in the United States. It is these two restrictions, the cartridge and the requirement to use iron sights, that make the Palma match so challenging and so rewarding.

In Palma matches held in the United States, there is also no restriction on bullet weight or brand, but in the International Palma Championship match, which is held every three years or so, both the brand of the bullet to be used and its weight are specified. The only bullet allowed in the International Palma Championship is the Sierra 155 grain Palma bullet. Even so, in that match one does not get to use carefully crafted handloads; even if one is using the correct bullet. In order to make the playing field as level as possible, all shooters must use ammunition provided by the host country.

Again, things are usually different in other countries and occasionally in some matches in the US. Often, bullet weight is required to be 155 grains, but the manufacturer of the bullet may not be specified. Because of this, prospective competitors in Palma matches these days need to read the match program very carefully and comply with its requirements in order to avoid being disqualified on a technicality.

The rifle used for Palma matches is slightly more tightly defined than those used for other LR matches, but not by much. Aside from the (308 Win. only) cartridge restriction, the rifle must have metallic sights. Telescopic sights are not allowed in Palma matches except for F class. In the United States, there are no restrictions on rifle weight, nor is there a required minimum

trigger-pull weight; but in the countries of the United Kingdom, Palma matches are usually shot under the rules of the International Palma Match, which do state both a maximum weight for the rifle and a minimum trigger pull weight. Under those rules, rifle weight is required to be less than 6.0 or 6.5 kilograms (13.2 or 14.3 pounds), depending on the country; and must have a minimum trigger-pull weight that has recently been as high as 1.5 kilograms (3.3 pounds). These rules have been under review for some time and may change before this is published.

The rules for minimum trigger weights were originally put forth as a safety measure, ostensibly to prevent accidental discharges, but I think it was really more to level the playing field so that those shooting Service rifles would not be at too much of a disadvantage with respect to those shooting custom Match rifles. Under the current (US) NRA rules, the two Service rifles chambered for the 308 Win. are permitted for use as "Palma rifles", but their use is certainly not required.

Service rifles have a time-honored place in the history of the Palma match. In fact, in the International Palma matches held around 1900, the only rifle allowed was a country's Service rifle. An attempt by the US to bend the rules in 1903 resulted in one of the more interesting events in the history of the Palma match. In the 1903 International Palma Team match, the US team won using what were supposed to be Service rifles, the Krag-Jorgenson; but the match was declared void a year after the match was held when it was revealed that the rifles had not been equipped with barrels with the same rate of twist and number of grooves as the standard US Service barrels. The rifles had been equipped with special barrels made by Harry Pope. When the US recognized that it had violated the rules of that match, the trophy was returned to Great Britain, which had been the winner of the previous match and which had come second to the Americans in that 1903 match. The British felt that it would harm the sport of competitive rifle shooting to claim a win on the basis of the United States' *post facto* withdrawal and did not do so; they merely held the trophy until it could be presented to the winners of the next International Palma match, which was held in Canada in 1907.

Part of the reason for the current move to

review these restrictive International rules on rifle weight and trigger-pull weight is a recognition that most current Service rifles are not only <u>not</u> appropriate for use in Palma matches (since many are not chambered for the 308 Winchester cartridge), but also that in many countries, it is illegal for ordinary citizens to own their country's current Service rifles, usually because those rifles are fully automatic. In fact, in many countries there is a general anti-gun attitude that has given rise to laws that prohibit their citizens from owning any sort of rifle other than a single-shot. These considerations plus the fact that very few Service rifles would be competitive against a rifle built on a good single-shot action mean that, as far as Palma matches are concerned, the use of Service rifles is fast becoming a thing of the past.

The result of this evolution is that the term, "Palma rifle", is rather loosely defined — in fact, somewhat more loosely in the United States than in other countries. In the US, any rifle that is chambered for the (unmodified) 308 Winchester cartridge and has iron sights satisfies the rules and is a Palma rifle.

Until recently in the US, a Palma rifle had to be a "Match rifle", which meant that it had to have a magazine with a capacity of at least five rounds. Thankfully, that restriction is no longer in place since it put US shooters at a disadvantage to shooters from other countries who were using rifles with solid bottom actions. I say, thankfully, because there is little doubt that single-shot rifles with solid-bottom actions are inherently more accurate than rifles built on actions that have a cut-out in the bottom of the action for a magazine. As noted above, in some countries nowadays a Palma rifle *must* be a single-shot because of anti-gun regulations!

The stocks used on rifles for Long-range competition are generally similar, whether the rifle is intended for use in any-rifle matches or Palma matches. After all, the demands of Prone shooting are much the same whether one is shooting a 22 rimfire or a 30 caliber magnum. The pistol grip is relatively vertical to promote a good hand position relative to the trigger, and there is usually an adjustable cheekpiece to aid in supporting the head in an optimal position relative to the sights. A relatively recent development is the use of "ladder" front sights that are adjustable for elevation. Such a sight makes an adjustable cheekpiece almost unnecessary by allowing all coarse adjustments in elevation to be made with the front sight.

Photo 1 shows some of the author's Long-range rifles on which most of these features can be seen, except that none of the rifles pictured has a ladder front sight. Two Smallbore rifles are included in the picture just to show their similarities to the others.

As can also be seen in that photo, the rifles are equipped with a mix of iron sights and telescopic sights. Scopes are in the minority because, as stated earlier, more than half of all Conventional Long-range shooting is done with

Photo 1: Typical rifles for Long-range and Prone Shooting. From l. to r. (or top to bottom if you prefer): A Remington 40X in 30-338 set up for any-rifle, iron-sight matches; A 6.5-284 on an AMT action set up for any-rifle any-sight matches; A Palma rifle on a Winchester Model 70 Target action; A Winchester 52C the author uses for Smallbore Prone; and an Anschutz Model 1413 (without rear sight).

iron sights. That's it for the restrictions placed on the rifles by the rules.

BARRELS AND CARTRIDGES

One feature that might be noted in Photo 1 is that the barrels on all these rifles (except the smallbores) are somewhat longer than most people would consider normal. None of the Highpower rifles has a barrel shorter than 26 inches. The reason for this is simple: Shooters in Long-range matches want to launch their bullets at the highest velocity practicable while still getting good accuracy. Up to a point, assuming equal powder charges of the same powder, a long barrel will launch a given bullet at a higher velocity than will a shorter barrel.

High initial velocity is needed for two reasons, both of which are important: First and foremost, Long-range rifle competition is primarily a game of judging the wind. Most shooters could shoot a perfect score if they were shooting in a tunnel. It is the ability to determine what the effect of the wind will be on the bullet's flight and to correct for it that distinguishes the good shooters from the not-so-good.

Consider this example: Suppose you have two shooters of equal holding ability, and they each have rifles chambered for the same cartridge and are using ammunition loaded with the same make and weight of bullet and their rifles shoot this ammo with equal accuracy. If you have them shoot 100, 20-shot matches head-to-head at 1000 yards, you can expect that the shooter who is the better judge of the wind will win more than 80% of those matches. The only reason that the better wind reader may not win all of the matches is that luck is always something of a factor because nobody ever judges the wind perfectly over a long period of shooting at 1000 yards.

However, if the shooter who is not quite as good a wind reader has a load that starts his bullets out a couple of hundred feet per second faster than those of the better wind doper, he might close that gap and win a lot more of the matches simply because his (faster) bullets will be less affected by the wind. This could happen because a wind gust that neither of them saw coming might blow the slower bullet out into the 9 ring while the faster bullet might be blown out only enough to give a wide 10. A faster load with

the same bullet is said to shoot "inside" the slower load. For this reason, I do not know of any competitive shooters who would turn down something that would increase the muzzle velocity of their loads as long as there was no decrease in accuracy.

The second reason for wanting to have a high muzzle velocity is that for good accuracy on target the muzzle velocity must be sufficiently high that the bullet will still be going faster than the speed of sound when it reaches the target. Experience has shown that most modern match bullets become unstable when they "go through the sound barrier" while slowing down. This has been seen to have an especially bad effect on the accuracy of the 168-grain 30-caliber bullet at 1000 yards when fired out of an M14. Accuracy with this bullet out of this rifle is good enough that it is possible to shoot good scores with it in the 800- and 900-yard stages of the Palma match, but with standard loads, this bullet goes subsonic somewhere between 900 and 1000 yards. The results on the target at 1000 yards are usually ugly, with the bullets going through the target sideways (keyholing) and impacting all over the target, and occasionally missing the six-foot square target entirely.

It is not my purpose here to indict the M14 or the 168-grain 30-caliber bullet. It is just that this combination provides the most notorious example of this effect. The problem of bullets' going unstable when they undergo the transonic transition seems to be universal with modern, long, boat-tailed match bullets. For this reason, almost everyone who has ever shot in any Long-range matches agrees that one of the prime requisites of any load intended for use at long distances is that the bullet must still be going faster than the speed of sound when it reaches the target.

The speed of sound at sea level at what are called standard conditions (when the air temperature is 32°F) is 1087 feet per second (fps). At more normal temperatures (still at sea level), 70°F, the speed of sound rises to about 1128 feet per second. If you can tailor your loads so that the remaining velocity of your bullets will be 1170 fps or more at 1000 yards, you will never have to worry about this problem.

It is interesting, however, to note that transonic instability does not seem to be a problem with the relatively short, flat-based, blunt-nosed bullets used in the 40- and 45-caliber black-powder cartridges that were in use in Long-range matches in the late 19th century. The reasons for this are not completely understood, but probably have something to do with the fact that such bullets are so aerodynamically _inefficient_ that they spend less time in the critical transonic velocity region than do the more modern streamlined bullets.

It would be fun to pursue this question further, but it is outside our main area of interest here. No matter why it happens, the effect on accuracy of a bullet's going unstable when it slows down below the speed of sound is very real; and the only way to keep it from biting you and causing you to lose many points at 1000 yards is to make sure that your loads start out fast enough that the bullets will still be going supersonic when they go through the target. It also helps to use the best bullet you can get for the purpose, a topic addressed in the next section.

CARTRIDGES, BULLETS, AND BARRELS

The question of what cartridge to use in CLR matches has two answers depending on which matches you are interested in shooting.

For the Palma match, the answer is simple; for any-rifle matches, the answer is not quite as simple as it once was. Let's consider the Palma match first. We know there is only one cartridge allowed, the unmodified 308 Winchester (a.k.a. 7.62mm NATO) cartridge. An anomaly here is that some match directors allow people to shoot their M16's in a Palma match. While this is not explicitly forbidden by the rules, it certainly violates the spirit of the rule that defines a Palma rifle as one chambered for the 308. For Palma the 308 is it.

However, this cartridge restriction does not mean that you are restricted in your choice of which bullet you may use — at least in the United States. Back before the 155 grain Palma bullet was introduced, I and many others used 190-grain, 30-caliber match bullets made by Sierra and other manufacturers in Palma matches. Some shooters preferred even heavier bullets such as Sierra's 200- and 220-grain match bullets.

Not long after Sierra introduced the 155-grain Palma bullet, various small specialty bullet

makers such as Berger introduced a wide spectrum of bullet weights in 30 caliber including weights of 155, 175, 180, 185, and 190 grains, as well as some in even heavier weights. The Berger 175 and 185 grain VLD (Very Low Drag) bullets proved to be a solution to the M14's problem of bullets going subsonic between 900 and 1000 yards. Sierra also began producing 175 and 180 grain 30-caliber bullets which also worked well in M14's at distances out to 1000 yards. That problem was solved, but the question remained as to whether there was an optimum bullet weight to use in the Palma match.

For US shooters that question has not been answered; but for those who aspire to attain a berth on the United States Palma Team or who wish to shoot in Palma matches in other countries on their own, there is not much choice — the 155 grain Sierra Palma bullet is the bullet you have to learn to shoot.

The reason for this comes from the rules for the International Palma (team) Match which is now held every three to five years and which is designated as the "WORLD CHAMPIONSHIPS OF INTERNATIONAL LONG RANGE RIFLE SHOOTING". There had once been a rule for this match that required that the ammunition shot would be supplied by the host country and would fire a bullet having a weight of _no more_ than 155 grains. During the 1980's, this resulted in the use of bullets that weighed from 147 to 154 grains, which were often military bullets with full metal jackets and which were not up to the accuracy standards of the day. In 1992, the Palma Council, which is the governing body for this match, adopted the Sierra 155-grain Palma bullet as the official bullet for this match and also adopted the United States standard LR target as the target to be used for this match.

Prior to 1992, the target used was chosen by the host country, which in many countries other than the US often meant a 5-V target on which the 5 ring was sometimes as large as the 9 ring on our (10-X) LR target. The 155-grain Palma bullet is so much more accurate than the military bullets that had been used previously that the LR target with its smaller scoring rings was truly needed to discriminate between the winner and second place. Far too many people would have been shooting perfect scores.

When I say that the 155 grain Sierra Palma bullet is the bullet you have to learn to shoot, what I mean is that if you have any ambition to be a member of the United States' official International Palma Team you need to shoot this bullet to learn how it is affected by the wind. After all, this is the bullet that will be loaded in the ammunition supplied to the national teams at the International Palma Match and to the shooters in the individual matches that usually precede the team match. Since the rules for the International Palma match also specify a standard muzzle velocity of 2950 fps, one also needs to shoot that bullet loaded at that standard velocity level in order to become familiar with how it is affected by the wind at that velocity.

You will shoot much better scores with any rifle if you can look at a wind condition, whether indicated by the flags or the mirage, and know almost instinctively by dint of experience what correction you should put on the sights rather than having to look up the correction on a chart or do some computations in your head. If you practice with only one rifle and one load, you will learn the characteristics of that load. This principle also carries over to any-rifle matches.

The really serious Palma shooters use their Palma rifles with the standard Palma load with the 155 grain bullet in all Long-range matches, including the any-rifle, iron sight matches and the any-rifle, any-sight matches; and they shoot all of these matches with iron sights, even the any-rifle, any-sight matches, just as they would in Palma matches. This is one reason they are such good Palma shooters.

The look of Palma rifles has changed in the past few years. Only a few years ago, most Palma rifles had barrels that were 26 inches long. Perhaps a few had 28-inch barrels, but 26 inches was the norm. That changed with the advent of the 155 grain Palma bullet. The 155-grain bullet can be driven to velocities that would be unthinkable with a 190-grain bullet except from some sort of magnum, but its lighter weight causes it to shed velocity much faster than the heavier 190. For this reason, the 155-grain bullet has to start out at a higher velocity in order to ensure that it will still be supersonic at 1000 yards.

Everybody knew that a longer barrel gave a higher initial velocity than a shorter one, but the question was how much. As the cost of computers and related electronics steadily sank, most shooters found they could afford a chronograph. Suddenly, finding out what the actual muzzle velocity was of a particular load from barrels of different lengths became a matter of shooting a simple test rather than just playing a guessing game aided by loading manuals.

Some intrepid experimenters began trying longer and longer barrels, sure in their knowledge that they would get higher velocities from their old, standard loads, while hoping that accuracy would not degrade too much. Velocities did indeed go up and accuracy did not fall off, at least not enough to be of concern to someone for whom 0.5 MOA was a seldom-attained goal.

The point of diminishing returns did not seem to be reached until barrels got to about 34 inches in length(!), at which length the rifles began to be noticeably ungainly. At that 34-inch length, the 155-grain bullet pushed by a standard load of 44.8 grains of IMR 4895 came out of the barrel at almost 150 fps faster than it did from a 26-inch barrel, and that was deemed to be a significant and worthwhile increase. The only problem was that every inch of additional barrel length also added weight — weight that pushed the rifle weight up to and often over that 6.5 Kg limit for International matches. This was solved by the barrel makers by making slimmer barrel tapers and/or fluting the barrels.

Another thing that gave a little increase in muzzle velocity was a change in barrel twist. People decided that if they were never going to use a bullet any heavier than 155 grains, then they did not need the 1 turn in 10 inch or 1 turn in 11 inch twists they had always used. The conservative shooters went to a 1 in 13 inch twist, while the radicals went all the way to 1 in 15. They all shot the 155-grain bullet very well and the muzzle velocities often exceeded 3000 fps with standard loads.

The increased muzzle velocity produced a significant lessening of the wind's effect on the bullets; and as you can guess, scores went up. So that is where we are as this is written. Palma rifles are now specialized with longer, slimmer barrels that have slower rifling twists than rifles for shooting across the course, and they are reserved for Palma only.

CARTRIDGES AND BULLETS FOR ANY RIFLE

Things have changed so much in recent years in the realm of any-rifle shooting that it is mind-boggling, at least to anyone who knows something of the history of 1000-yard shooting. Let me recount a bit of that history so that the recent changes can be put in perspective.

The new era of 1000-yard shooting began in 1892 with the adoption of the Krag-Jorgenson rifle and its cartridge, which was then called the 30 US Government cartridge. Although the Krag cartridge was initially loaded with 40 grains of blackpowder (hence the modern name, "30-40 Krag"), the charge was shortly changed to smokeless powder. The Krag was used in many Long-range matches such as the International Palma matches; and as with all military rifles, it continued to be used for some time after the adoption of the 1903 Springfield, including in the Palma debacle of 1903 described earlier.

As soon as sufficient numbers of Springfields became available, the Krag quickly faded from the scene because its cartridge could not compete with the higher velocity and lesser wind sensitivity of the 30-06 cartridge. At the 1000-yard line, the Springfield and its 30-06 cartridge ruled the roost until 1935 when the Wimbledon Cup match (the 1000-yard, any-rifle, any sight match at Camp Perry) was won by Ben Comfort using a rifle chambered for the 300 H & H magnum.

In our more affluent times this event might have caused a large number of people to go out and buy a magnum for use in any-rifle matches at 1000 yards. Unfortunately, the country was at that time still in the midst of the Great Depression, and very few people had enough disposable income to be able to do that sort of thing. Certainly, there was some interest in trying different cartridges, but very few could afford it.

The US was just beginning to emerge from the grip of the Depression when the Japanese bombed Pearl Harbor and the country was plunged into war. And that put a stop to almost all civilian shooting activity. The National Matches at Camp Perry were shut down after 1940 in anticipation that the country might get involved in the war that was already raging in Europe, and the National Matches were not held again until 1951.

When the war ended in 1945, it took the country the better part of five years to get back to something resembling a peacetime economy, and it took a few more years after that before Remington and Winchester began putting out new cartridge designs such as the 222 Remington (in 1950) and the 458 Winchester Magnum (in 1956), the latter being followed shortly by the 264 and 338 Winchester Magnums in 1958.

The 1960's saw a spate of new cartridges introduced, including the 7-mm Remington Magnum in 1962 and the 300 Winchester Magnum in 1963, each of which would someday win the Wimbledon Cup match at Camp Perry.

Not long after the 338 Win. Mag. came out, wildcatting of it began, and someone, whose identity will probably remain forever lost, was the first to neck it down to produce the 30-338, which turned out to be one of the best 30-caliber cartridges ever produced for Long-range competition. P. O. Ackley, in his book *Handbook for Shooters and Reloaders, Volume 1*, says that it is identical to the 30 Belted Newton, which came out almost immediately after the 338 Win. Mag.

Although I do not have the data to prove it, the 30-338 quickly became so popular that it is my guess that there was at least one 30-338 shot in every Leech and Wimbledon Cup match from the early 1960's up through 2000. The main reason for this popularity was that it gave good accuracy while giving much better ballistics than the 300 H&H. When the 300 Win. Mag came on the scene in 1962, target shooters did not like its shorter neck and found that the 30-338 almost duplicated the ballistics of the 300 Win. Mag. with much less powder. Over the years, the 30-338 won its share of Leech and Wimbledon Cup victories, as did the 300 Win. Mag.

But what most Highpower shooters did not know back in that early postwar period was that they were being limited in their quest for Long-range accuracy by two things: barrels and bullets. Progress came quickly on both fronts, not from the major firearms manufacturers, but from specialty shops such as Douglas (for barrels) and Sierra (for bullets). Much of this progress was driven by demand from the Benchrest shooters to whom all shooters owe much.

There was, however, an unnoticed factor that (in the author's opinion) kept progress in Long-range shooting from being as fast as it might have been. This factor was unnoticed because it was as pervasive as the very air we breathe, something we do not often notice or think about. The progress we have seen in recent years has occurred because the two divisions of Highpower competition, across-the-course and Long-range, feed off each other. Progress in one usually leads to progress in the other. The factor that held back that progress for some time was the fact that almost all Highpower competition was done with rifles shooting 30 caliber bullets. There were several reasons for this, one of the most important being that all Highpower competition has its roots in the military training programs used for the Krag and Springfield rifles.

The United States had been a 30-caliber country since the adoption of the Krag in 1892. The 1903 Springfield and the M1 Garand both shot the 30-06 cartridge. The M1 had been the official Service rifle of the United States Armed Forces from 1936 until the M14 was adopted in 1957; and the M14 was still a 30-caliber rifle, albeit with a different cartridge. Also, most people were introduced to Highpower competition either by their training in the Armed Forces or through the programs of the Director of Civilian Marksmanship, which programs involved the shooting of (30 caliber) Service rifles.

Although production of the M14 was ordered to cease in 1964 by the Secretary of Defense, Robert S. MacNamara, no other rifle was officially adopted at that time. A large order (intended to be a one-time order) was placed with Colt at that time for M16's, but the M16 did not become an official, standard rifle until 1970. Even so, the M14 was still considered to be the standard rifle as late as 1983. Even as the M16 supplanted the M14, the US continued to be a 30-caliber country as far as most Highpower competition was concerned for one simple reason: the lack of match-grade bullets in any size other than 30 caliber. The M16 did not become a force in across-the-course competition until the late 1990's, for this same reason — lack of good bullets.

The first major change came in 1970 when Sierra introduced the 140-grain 6.5-mm match bullet when Paul Wright and Al Hoyer were experimenting with the 6.5-300 Weatherby-Wright-Hoyer cartridge for use in 1000-yard Bench rest matches. Also, in 1970, Sierra came

out with their 168-grain 7-mm bullet which was soon put to good use by Thomas Treinen, who used it in a 7-mm Remington Magnum to win the Wimbledon Cup match that year.

The 30 caliber continued to reign through the 1970's for both across-the-course and in most Long-range competition, but things began to change in 1980 when Remington began commercial production of rifles and ammunition for the 7-mm-08, a cartridge that had previously been only a wildcat.

In 1988, G. David Tubb won the National Championship (across-the-course) with a rifle chambered for the 7-mm-08, and he did that at least once more with a 7-mm-08 before winning the Championship in 1993 with a rifle chambered in 243 Winchester. Suddenly, the old 30-caliber idols came tumbling down. It seemed that if you had good bullets, the diameter did not matter!

The questions that arose in the minds of many were: Is there possibly a better caliber for across-the-course (or Long-range) shooting than 30; or, in fact, is there possibly a better cartridge than the standard ones in current use that could be used with some new diameter bullet? The answer to both it seems is: Yes, there are many.

From the late 1980's up to the present (2000), there was a flurry of activity by the bullet makers, both from the small, specialty houses and from the larger makers: Hornady, Sierra, and Speer. We began to see match-grade bullets of all different weights and designs for calibers that previously had been ignored such as the 6 mm (0.243") and the 6.5 mm (0.264"). From Sierra, we now have an 80-grain bullet for the 22 calibers that quickly became a standard for the 223's at 600 and even 1000 yards. And, at least one maker (JLK) is now offering a 90-grain bullet for the 22 caliber.

If we skip from the 1980's to the present what we find is that there are many bullets that would be very good for Long-range competition in almost any diameter from 22 caliber to 30. The only other thing that is required is a rifle/cartridge combination that will launch the bullet at a muzzle velocity high enough for the bullet to still be supersonic when it reaches the target. The result of all this is that just about any cartridge you can think of, short of the 22 Hornet, can now be considered to be a good 1000-yard cartridge, even the

223. After the barrel makers learned how to make really good barrels, the limiting factor was whether or not good bullets were available.

What makes a good bullet for 1000-yard shooting? Just a few things:
1) Uniform jacket wall thickness. This is required for good accuracy at any distance and is something all the bullet makers now have down to a science.
2) Good aerodynamic design. This usually means having a nose profile something like the VLD bullets designed by W. C. Davis, of which Sierra's 80-grain, 223 bullet and 107-grain, 6-mm bullet are examples.
3) Fairly heavy weight for the caliber. This last requisite is something that gives the bullet a high ballistic coefficient when combined with the good aerodynamic design. For Long-range shooting, what we are looking for is a bullet with a ballistic coefficient (BC) of 0.5 or greater, if possible. There are many such now on the market in almost any caliber except 22, where the Sierra 80-grain, 22-caliber bullet is listed a having a BC of 0.420 at velocities faster than 2200 fps.

Bullet weight must also be balanced by other factors. For all calibers, bullet weight and geometry determine the minimum required rifling twist rate; longer, heavier bullets require tighter twists. However, some shooters of my acquaintance have found that if you push certain bullets too fast out of barrels with tight twists, the bullets often "blow up" in mid-air and never reach the target. Bullet weight, powder-charge weight and muzzle velocity combine with rifle weight to determine how much recoil will be generated. Attempting to push very heavy bullets at high velocities can generate too much recoil for many shooters. In many cases some trade-offs have to be made.

With bullet availability no longer a problem, Long-range shooters began looking at case design. The Benchrest shooters have pretty well convinced everybody that short, fat cases that have very little taper and fairly sharp shoulders give better accuracy than the long, slim cases that have tapered bodies and long, sloping shoulders such as the 30-06, so LR shooters began looking at all sorts of cartridges they previously would not have been considered at all such as: the 22 BR; the 22-250; the 6-mm International, which is

sometimes known as the 6-mm-250; the 6-mm BR, the 6.5-284 and all sorts of other wildcats based on the 284 Winchester case. A collection of typical cartridges currently used in Long-range competition is shown in Photo 2.

The two jewels that have already been turned up are the 6-mm BR and the 6.5-284. The 6-mm BR has been used to win F class matches at 1000 yards in both the United States and Canada and to set a 5-shot, 1000-yard Benchrest record, which, however, did not last long; it was broken only two weeks after it was shot.

The 6.5-284 has been used to win both the Leech and Wimbledon Cup matches and the US Long-range Championship several times since 1995 and was used by Michelle Gallagher to win all of these in 2000. Yes, she won the Leech, the Wimbledon, and the US Long-range Championship all in the same year. She is one of the very few people who have won the Wimbledon Cup more than once, and one of an even smaller number who have won both the Leech Cup and the Wimbledon Cup in the same year,. That had been done only three times before when it was done by Charles D. Davis in 1968, K. K. V. Casey in 1908, and Frank Hyde in 1878.

At this time, the 6.5-284 is the cartridge of choice for any-rifle matches. If some experi-

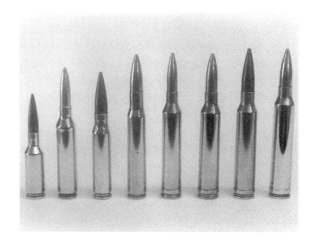

Photo 2: Cartridges for Long-Range Shooting From the left: the 6mm Norma BR, the 6.5-284, the 308 Winchester, the 30-06, the 264 Winchester Magnum; the 7mm Remington Magnum; the 30-338; and the 300 Winchester Magnum.

menter somewhere finds something that shoots better than the 6.5-284 at 1000-yards, he will have really done something; for the 6.5-284 is really that good.

And if someone does find a cartridge that is better than the 6.5-284, what will it look like? My answer is that it will probably look very much like the 6.5-284 unless some radically new interior ballistic principle is discovered. The case may be somewhat shorter and fatter and the shoulder angle may be even sharper than the 6.5-284's 35° shoulder angle. The shoulder might, however, not be straight, but instead might be curved like a Weatherby, or perhaps might be something we have never seen before.

For over 50 years, the 30-06 was thought to be the acme of cartridge design, and then the 308 swept it from the field, only to be replaced in much less time by the 223 in the "little black gun" for short and mid-range shooting. But we also once thought that nothing could beat the magnums at 1000 yards, yet the 6.5-284 has been doing that with boring regularity ever since it came on the scene. To someone who wants to begin any-rifle competition and who does not have a suitable rifle, my one suggestion would be: Get a 6.5-284.

There is a reason that the 6.5-284 and other cartridges of power less than that of the 30-caliber magnums win so often over the magnums. It has to do with how the rifle recoils. Now this is not a matter of how hard the rifle hits the shooter's shoulder and the effects that has on the shooter, physical or psychological; instead, it is a matter of how the rifle moves before the bullet gets out of the barrel.

I am well aware that there are those who think that recoil is mostly due to the "rocket effect" of the propellant gasses exiting the muzzle after the bullet has gone. That certainly does contribute to the recoil, but in almost all of the cases we have to be concerned with in CLR shooting, the rocket effect does not contribute as much to a rifle's recoil velocity as does the departing bullet. It's a matter of conservation of momentum.

For our purposes here, the momentum of an object can be thought of as simply the weight of the object times its velocity. If the gas pressure produced by the burning powder causes the

bullet to move down the barrel, then that gas pressure must also cause the rifle to move in the opposite direction in order for momentum to be conserved. Because the rifle weighs much more than the bullet, it does not move as fast as the bullet does. At any time during the bullet's course up the barrel, the momentum of the bullet and of the gas moving with it has to equal the momentum of the rifle and of the small amount of the gas that is moving back with the rifle. In real life this means that most rifles actually move about a tenth of an inch before the bullet gets out of the barrel.

Now all of that discussion in the previous paragraph about conservation of momentum relative to rifles assumes that the rifle is floating in space free of all restraint — something that in the world of Highpower rifle shooting is never true. Benchrest shooters may shoot what they call "free recoil", but it is never that way in Highpower. In Highpower, we have to hold onto the rifle; and when we do, we become part of the dynamical system involving the rifle, which means that the rifle will no longer recoil exactly the same way it would if it were floating free in space. While the rifle does not get to move quite as far when it is being held as it would when it is floating free, it does still move before the bullet gets out of the barrel. The problem with this is that if we hold the rifle the least bit differently from one shot to another, those shots, even if held and aimed perfectly, will not end up at the same place on the target. What's more, the difference in point of impact will almost be proportional to how far it is to the target, so that at 1000 yards that difference will be almost 10 times what it was at 100 yards.

This gives rise to a problem called, "magnum shots". I once bought a Remington 40X rifle that was factory-chambered for the 300 Win. Mag. This rifle gave me fits because I kept having shots go out the top or out the bottom at 1000 yards for reasons I could not explain. When I complained about this to one of the country's greatest Long-range shooters, I was told something to the effect that, "Oh, we call those magnum shots. They are why we quit using magnums and went to the 6.5-284." Another shooter told me that you really have to hold a magnum hard to control it. Later, when the 300 Mag. barrel was shot out, I replaced it with one chambered for the 30-338. With that chambering, the magnum shots still occurred, but much less often.

Why do magnum shots occur? Simply because of small variations in the way you hold the rifle from one shot to another, or small variations in sling tension, or having placed the rifle's butt at a slightly different place in your shoulder. In short, anything that will cause the rifle to recoil the slightest bit differently during that critical 1.5 milliseconds during which the bullet is accelerating down the bore and the rifle is moving that tiny fraction of an inch back into your shoulder. Rifles that shoot cartridges that produce less recoil are thus less affected by this phenomenon because the rifle's recoil momentum is less likely to overpower the way you are holding the rifle. This is a very important reason for why the 6.5-284 and other cartridges using lighter bullets have been beating the magnums on such a regular basis. If you are not using a magnum, you don't get "magnum" shots.

The upshot of all this is that people have come to a consensus that the best cartridges for conventional 1000-yard competition are probably not magnums and are probably not 30 caliber either. What is needed is a cartridge with a case that is short and fat, with little body taper, and a sharp shoulder, preferably with an angle of 30° or more.

For instance, the 284 Win. case necked up to 30 has almost exactly the same internal capacity as the 30-06, but the 30-284 would probably be a better cartridge for 1000-yard shooting than the original 30-06. The shorter, fatter case of the 30-284 and its sharper shoulder (35° for the 284 Win. as opposed to 17.5° shoulder of the 30-06) will promote more uniform burning of the powder and thus more uniform velocities. The only problem with this cartridge is that one would likely decide that for the best performance in the wind, it would be necessary to use 190- or 200-grain bullets, which would increase recoil to almost magnum levels. Because good 7-mm match bullets are now easy to obtain, the unmodified 284 Win. would be a much better choice than the 30-284; but the 6.5-284 would be an even better choice.

Well, if the 6.5-284 is such a good choice, why not the 6-mm-284, or even a 22-284?

The only problem with going down to calibers smaller than the 6.5 for the 284 case is that short barrel life becomes a concern. Large charges of powder relative to bore diameter will definitely increase muzzle velocity, but they also cause a lot of throat erosion, which shortens bore life. So it becomes a question of another trade-off. If barrel life is too short, you may not find an accurate load before the barrel is shot out. If your case does not have enough capacity, you may get long barrel life but insufficient muzzle velocity.

You have to balance case capacity with bore size and barrel life. For a given caliber, the bigger the case, the shorter the barrel life. If you want to drop down in caliber to 6-mm, the better way to go is to the 6-mm-250 or to the 6-mm BR. The 6-mm PPC may be the most accurate cartridge ever developed, but its case capacity is not quite large enough to give adequate velocity to the 107 grain bullet that most 6-mm shooters use.

This brings me back to bullets. In many cases LR shooters pick the heaviest bullet they can find for a particular caliber, but that is not always the best choice. Sometimes it is better to have a lighter bullet at a higher muzzle velocity. When the 155-grain Palma bullet first came on the scene back in 1991 we were astounded to see how flat its trajectory was compared to that of the 190-grain bullets most of us had been using. When you are scoring in a CLR match, you can often actually see the wake or "trace" of a bullet on its way to the target. The trajectory of the 155-grain Palma bullet at 2950 fps is remarkably flat compared to that of the 190-grain bullet at 2500 fps. And since the wind effect is essentially the same for both bullets, who needs the heavier bullet?

There are 240-grain bullets available for 30 caliber and 155 grain, 6.5-mm bullets. Few people that I know use them in CLR competition. Most shooters using 30-caliber rifles seldom use anything heavier than the 200-grain bullets with most choosing the 190-grain bullet. The 6.5-284 shooters seem to prefer the 140- or 142-grain bullets, and I have had very good results with my 6.5-284 with a 130-grain match bullet made by Norma. If the velocity is sufficient, accuracy and the wind-judging ability of the shooter become more important. Whatever bullet you choose, it should have a relatively high ballistic coefficient.

After a bullet is given a VLD design, a very high ballistic coefficient can be obtained only by increasing the bullet's weight, which often can be done only by increasing the length of the bullet — something that may require a tighter rifling twist. Increasing the bullet weight too much can reduce muzzle velocity so much that wind sensitivity is actually increased. The optimum is not likely to be found at either extreme of bullet weight.

The consensus is that the best cartridges for CLR competition are those that have a modern case design with sufficient case capacity to give a bullet of moderately heavy weight (for the caliber) a moderately high velocity with loads that are well under maximum. *Moderation* is the watch word. With these things in mind, a proper case and bullet can be found for just about any caliber that will do well in CLR matches.

WHAT HAPPENS DURING A MATCH

For the benefit of those readers who might like to try conventional Long-range competition, whether in the regular way or in F class, Palma or any-rifle, but who may have never fired in (or watched) a Highpower match of any kind, let me tell you a little about how the matches are conducted.

In a conventional Highpower match, the shooters are divided up (or "squadded") into relays. This is done so that the match can be shot in a reasonably efficient way. When one person is shooting on one of the firing points, there have to be at least two other people servicing that one firing point (and shooter). There has to be someone operating the target down in the target pits, and there has to be someone back on the firing line writing down the shooter's score for each shot since the shooter is not allowed to keep his own score. The actual shot values are determined in the pits, but the shooter's scorecard is kept on the firing line because the shooter has to sign his scorecard after he has finished shooting.

When a shooter fires a shot and it hits the target, the person(s) operating the target will hear the bullet hit the target; and if there is an impact area close enough behind the targets, will see the bullet kick up dirt in the impact area for that target. The target will be pulled down and the location of the shot will be marked by placing the spindle of a target spotter in the bullet hole.

In CLR competition, the shot spotter is a 5-inch diameter disc of cardboard that is white on one side and black on the other and has a plastic spindle in its center. If the shot hole is in the aiming black, the spotter is turned so the white side faces the shooter, while the black side is shown if the shot hit in the white part of the target. The value of the shot is indicated by placing a colored (usually orange) scoring disc in different positions around the margin of the target frame. After the shot has been scored and marked and the shot hole for any previous shot is covered with a paster, the target frame is then "run" back up for the shooter's next shot.

In any CLR competition, one does not get to shoot 5, 10, 15, or 20 shots before any shots are marked. Each shot is scored and marked individually, as soon as it is shot; and back on the firing line, the shooter's scorer writes down the value of the shot on the score card. If, as sometimes happens, the target puller has obviously marked the wrong value for a shot by putting the scoring disc in the wrong location, the shooter and the scorer may either agree on the correct value for the shot, or the shooter may ask a line official to have the target "redisked". A redisk takes a little time which the shooter may not want to waste if he is getting short on time, but may be worth it.

In most matches, shooters are squadded according to their classification. This means that the High Masters and some Masters are usually put on one relay, maybe some Masters and Experts on another, some Experts and Sharpshooters on another, and so on. The reason for this class structure is to arrange things so that most of the people in any one class are on the same relay and thus shoot in the same wind conditions. It often happens that the wind comes up and is awful on only one relay; or, on a windy day, there may be only one relay that gets relatively calm conditions. This squadding by class keeps such inequities to a minimum — at least within each class. If the only relay that gets relatively calm wind conditions is the one with the Sharpshooters and Marksmen on it, that will not be likely to affect who wins the match; but if there should happen to be a single High Master on that relay, it is obvious who is most likely to win the match.

The way things go for a relay that is about to shoot is like this: The relay is called to the line by the Chief Line Officer. They then have about one or two minutes to move their gear to the firing line. At most matches the shooters are allowed to move some of their equipment to the line (except for their rifles) before the official call-to-the-line. After that minute or two have elapsed, the shooters are given a three-minute preparation period during which they may adjust their equipment, dry-fire and prepare themselves mentally for their shooting. Firing during a prep period is a definite no-no. Any shot fired during a prep period will get a miss put on the shooter's score card for his first record shot. Anybody dumb enough to fire a second shot during a prep period will probably be disqualified and told to leave the range.

When the command to "Commence fire" is given, the shooters are given a time period that is approximately 1¹/₂ minutes times the number of record shots in that match or stage. During that time period, they must fire all of their sighters (or practice shots) and all their record shots. For example, the shooters are given 22 minutes for each stage of the Palma match (in which they fire 15 shots for record); while in an any-rifle match, in which the usual number of shots is 20, the shooters are given 30 minutes.

The newcomer to CLR matches (or any kind of conventional Highpower match) will find that the Chief Line Officers of these matches are very verbose compared to those running matches in other disciplines. Almost everything you need to know will be announced by the Chief Line Officer. For example, the command to commence fire at an any-rifle, any-sight match might sound something like this:

"This is the (name) match, 20 shots at 1000 yards with any rifle with any sights. You will have 30 minutes in which to fire an unlimited number of practice shots and 20 shots for record. On the line, with one round, load!... Is the line ready?... The line is ready.... Ready on the right; ready on the left; all ready on the firing line! You may commence fire."

Until recently, the targets were raised out of the pits some time in the middle of this command. Lately, the custom seems to be to hold the targets in the pits and change the last sentence of the command to, "Your time will begin and you may commence fire when your targets appear." The effect is the same in either case.

Also, that bit about, "...with one round, load!" In the Slowfire stages of any Highpower match, all firing is done, *single-load, single-fire*, and all CLR matches are Slowfire matches. This means that you may load only one round into your rifle at a time, and you must fire it before loading another round into the rifle. Everybody has to act as if their rifles are single-shots even if they are not.

Oh, I do need to tell you the difference between *sighting* shots and *practice* shots. Highpower rifle is, in the main, an individual sport. Except for the few team matches, coaching of any type is generally not allowed, but there is one exception to this. In the world of Long-range shooting, it is often necessary to help the shooter get some shots on the target somewhere. It is at these times when coaching is allowed in an individual match that the shots that would normally be called sighters are called *practice shots*. When practice shots (with coaching) are allowed, the scorer is allowed to tell the shooter things such as, "That one was over the target; come down 4 minutes."

Coaching of this sort is usually allowed in any of the individual any-rifle matches and in the first stage of the Palma match (at 800 yards), but not anywhere else. If a shooter shoots a miss with either a sighter or a record shot in a match or stage in which coaching is not allowed, he is on is own; nobody is allowed to tell him anything. In the 900- and 1000-yard stages of the Palma match, the shooter gets 2 *sighters* with no coaching allowed.

In a match in which unlimited practice shots are allowed, the shooter is required to tell his scorer that he is going to go for record before he shoots his first record shot; but once the shooter says his next shot will be for record; the coaching ends; and he is on his own. The scorer is no longer allowed to tell him that a shot was off the target to the left, or over the target, or that the wind has picked up, or anything other than the value and location of a shot.

Now and then, someone tries to put one over on the scorer by continuing to shoot "practice" shots with coaching until he shoots an X whereupon he will turn to his scorer and say, "That was my first shot for record." If the scorer knows anything about how the game is supposed to be played, that won't fly. The rule says you have to tell your scorer *before* you shoot that first record shot that it will be your first shot for record.

That is pretty much how it goes. You get called to the line. You bring your equipment up and get set up. You have a 3-minute prep period in which you can make final adjustments to your equipment, watch the wind, meditate or pray, dry-fire, or do whatever you think will help you shoot better when firing starts. In most Long-range matches, you are allowed to have coaching to help you "get on paper", except in the last two stages of a Palma match; but in any event, coaching is not allowed after you begin firing for record. Once you go for record, you shoot until you have fired all your record shots, or until you run out of time, whichever comes first. If you run out of time before firing all your shots, each unfired shot will be scored as a miss, something that will not contribute to your getting a high score. It is best to finish within the allotted time, which is more than adequate.

In fact, it is part of most shooters' strategy for coping with the wind to fire their shots as quickly as practicable in order to reduce the number of wind changes to which they will be subjected. It is well-known that many competitors in the game of 1000-yard Benchrest will fire their five (or 10) shots for group as fast as they can for just this reason. If the wind does not change significantly in the 30 seconds or less that it takes them to get off their shots, they will usually get a fairly small group. That sort of thing cannot be done in CLR competition because after each shot, the target is pulled down, and the shot is marked and scored. Even so, it is easy to shoot quickly enough to finish firing your 15 or 20 record shots long before the allotted time expires.

Consider the times involved: When you fire a shot, it will take the bullet somewhere between 1.4 and 1.8 seconds to get from the firing line to the target. It will then take the target puller(s) a second or two to recognize that the target has received a hit and pull it down. The process of locating the bullet hole, moving the shot spotter, pasting over the old bullet hole, moving the scoring disk and getting the target back up in the air can take anywhere from 4 to 18 seconds, longer if the bullet hole is hard to find or someone fumbles and drops a scoring disk or a shot spotter.

The average time for this is around 8 to 10 seconds, while anything more than 18 seconds is considered to be too slow according to the rules. When we put all this together, we see that from the time we fire a shot at 1000 yards, the target will be scored and marked and back up in the air ready to receive another shot in 12 to 14 seconds on the average and in 22 seconds at the outside. If you then get your next shot off within 10 seconds, you should be able to fire at a cadence of about one shot every 22 to 32 seconds. If, in a 1000-yard match in which you have unlimited practice and 20 record shots to fire, you fire 8 practice shots and your 20 record shots at a rate of one shot every 30 seconds, you will finish firing in 14 minutes; and you will not fall victim to any of the wind changes that occur in the last 16 minutes of your 30-minute firing period. When looked at this way, it is easy to see that shooting fast is a good idea.

In the United States, almost all CLR matches are shot in the format described above in that there is only one shooter on a firing point and that shooter is allowed to shoot as fast or as slowly as he desires. In the countries of the British Commonwealth CLR matches are seldom shot in this format. In those countries, there are instead usually two or three shooters assigned to a firing point and all of them shoot at the same target, obviously, not at the same time. The shooters shoot in rotation, with each shooter being required to get his shot off within a certain specified time (usually about 45 seconds) after the target has come up and it is his turn to shoot. Each shooter also has to act as scorer for one of the others.

It is possible under the American format for a shooter who is not a very good judge of the wind to shoot very high scores on days when the wind is not changing very fast merely by chasing the spotter, especially if he is getting fast target service. Shooting fast and chasing the spotter cannot be done under the British format because the shooter has to wait until one or two other shooters have shot and had their shots marked before he can shoot again. The British format thus places a much greater premium on a shooter's ability to read the wind.

If you finish firing before time expires, you may pick up your gear and move off the firing line, but you should do so quietly and in such a way as not to disturb those shooters on adjacent firing points who may still be shooting. Of course, you do this only after inserting your Open-bolt indicator and while observing all the usual safety rules. You are not required to remain in place at your firing point until the cease fire is given; that sort of thing is required only for children who are under instruction. That is pretty much it for what it is like to shoot in a CLR match, but there are a couple of other things you might like to know.

Usually, the squadding, pit assignments, and pit changes are scheduled so that each person shoots and then gets to serve as the scorer for the next shooter. The exception to this is that the match officials also try to arrange things so that people do not have to shoot immediately after their stint of working in the pits. Sometimes these two things conflict and some people end up shooting just after coming out of the pits. If there are four relays, it is unavoidable that someone has to shoot just after their time in the pits. When there are only three relays, a person who has just come out of the pits will usually score before shooting. Even though all Long-range shooting is done in the stable Prone position, you shoot better when your heart rate has a chance to get back to normal after the exercise of operating a target. If at all possible, the shooting order in most matches is arranged so as to give each shooter as good a chance as possible to shoot a good score.

This thing of practice shots and having to tell your scorer when you are about to shoot your first shot for record is pretty much limited to the United States. In most matches in the countries of the United Kingdom, the shooter gets only two *sighters*, but those sighters may be "convertible". This means simply that the sighters can be converted into record shots. The shooter shoots both his sighters and then, if he deems one or both of them to be good enough, he turns to his scorer and says, "I'll convert the last sighter", or, "I'll convert both sighters"; whereupon the scorer writes the value for the last sighter in the place for the first record shot, or the values for the two sighters in the places for the first two record shots. In this scheme you cannot convert the first sighter without also converting the second one as

well. This procedure was tried recently (in 1996) in Long-range matches in the US, but was abandoned after only one year. At present, sighters are not convertible in Long-range matches in the US.

SHOOTING A LONG-RANGE MATCH

The actual shooting of a Long-range match under NRA rules in the United States is pretty much just like shooting any other Prone match — you just lie there and shoot at your target. Conventional Long-range matches are not very interesting as a spectator sport, but for the shooters, the game is very challenging.

The challenge comes not so much from the relative size of the target as from the effects that are due to the distance to the target. The amount your bullets will be deflected by a constant crosswind is increased by much more than a simple proportion based on the distance to the target.

The scheme I use for determining the wind correction I put on my sights is based on a parameter I call the basic wind effect (or BWE), which is the amount a bullet will be deflected at a particular distance (measured in MOA) by a uniform crosswind of 1 mile per hour. To see the effect of the increased distance, consider the values of the BWE for the 155 grain Palma bullet at different distances when launched with a muzzle velocity of 2900 fps as given in the table below.

As you can see, the value of the BWE at 1000

Distance (yards)	100	200	500	1000
BWE (MOA/MPH)	0.07	0.14	0.40	1.02

BASIC WIND EFFECT OF 155 GR. PALMA
BULLET AT A MUZZLE VELOCITY OF 2900 FPS
TABLE 1

yards is much more than 10 times its value at 100 yards. The BWE is not a straight-line function of distance. It is also very important to realize that the BWE will have a different value at every distance, which will depend on both the muzzle velocity and the BC of the bullet.

The BWE is used to compute a sight correction by multiplying the value of the BWE by the estimated value of the wind speed in miles per hour to get a number I call the Basic Wind Correction (or BWC). The estimate of the wind speed can be gotten in several ways, but is usually estimated from the angle that the wind flags make with the flagpole. By the way, the use of electronic wind-speed measuring devices *on the firing line* is prohibited. You can use one back behind the firing line to get a correlation between the flag angles and the wind speed; you just are not allowed to use one while you are up there firing.

The Basic Wind Correction has to be scaled back by taking the wind angle into account to give the Actual Wind Correction. This is done by multiplying the BWC by a scaling factor that depends on the angle. All of the arithmetic is easy because most people use only five values of the scaling factor, three of which are: 0, 1/2, and 1. The other two values are 0.7 and 0.86. An easy way to use these numbers is to calculate a table of correction values based on the BWE of your load for different wind speeds and angles. These actual correction values are often put into the form of a rosette which is more useful than a columnar table. Such rosettes for military loads are often given in the front of Highpower score books.

At the risk of being accused of sneaking in an advertisement for my book, *Modern Highpower Competition*, I have to say that all of this material on judging the wind and determining wind corrections is laid out in detail in Chapter 18, "Shooting in the Conditions", of that book. Many other topics about Long-range competition that I have been able to touch on only lightly here are also covered in detail in Chapter 19, "Long-Range Competition", of that book. The necessity to cover so many disparate items in this one chapter perforce means that I cannot cover all of them here in the depth I might like.

The wind can do some very weird things in 1000 yards such as blow in different directions at different distances between the shooter and the target. When that happens, no simple calculation can tell you what to do; if possible, it is best to wait out such a condition. Coping with such problems is a matter of experience.

There are two basic strategies the beginning Long-range shooter should know about for coping with the wind. They are: chasing the spotter, and shooting on a condition. Their names almost completely describe what is meant by them.

Almost everybody knows about chasing the spotter. It is simply a matter of firing a shot (which has to hit the target), and then, once that shot is marked, putting the correction on the sight that would have caused that shot to go into the center of the target before firing the next shot. The process of putting on the sight correction needed to center the previous shot is repeated after each shot. This can be done by someone who does not have a clue as to what the flags and the mirage mean, and on a day when the conditions are not changing very fast can result in a high score.

Shooting on a condition is a matter of recognizing that a certain condition of wind speed and direction happens fairly often and then finding out what the sight setting has to be to put a shot in the center when that condition holds. The shooter then just waits and shoots only when "his" condition comes back. There are other strategies that also work, some of which are just variations on these two. However, these two strategies are basic and should be learned by every prospective Long-range shooter.

The great distances to the targets can have other effects. Haze or fog can make visibility a problem. It may be hard to see your target or even to read the number boards to find *your* target. It is very important to shoot only on your target because, once you have gone for record, a crossfire is a miss.

The last important effect of the extra distance I want to mention is the fact that small variations

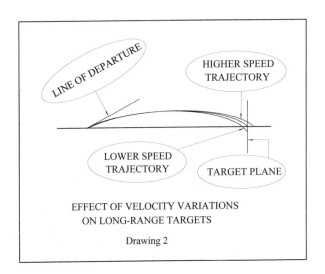

**EFFECT OF VELOCITY VARIATIONS
ON LONG-RANGE TARGETS**

Drawing 2

in muzzle velocity that would have little or no effect on your score even at 600 yards can cost you points at 1000 yards. This happens because at the long distances, the bullets are descending at a much steeper angle than the angle they started out at. This has the effect that small variations in velocity will produce vertical dispersions in point of impact on target much larger than anything you would see at shorter distances. Drawing 2 illustrates how this happens.

The author has done some studies on the exterior ballistics of the 155-grain Palma bullet, first with hand calculations on data taken from the ballistic tables in the back of the *Sierra Rifle Reloading Manual, 50th Anniversary Edition* and later with the computer program QuickTARGET™. Those studies have shown me that a variation of only 10 fps in muzzle velocity from 2900 fps can cause an elevation change in the point of impact at 1000 yards of more than 2 inches, and that a change of 50 fps will change the point of impact by more than 10 inches. That 50 fps change would cause a shot that would have gone through the center of the X ring to land out in the 9 ring! The change in point of impact is all vertical. What happens is that shots fired at the lower velocities will hit low, while those fired at a higher velocity will hit high.

From these studies, I concluded that one of the prime considerations one must give to ammunition that is going to be used for Long-range shooting is to make sure that velocity variations are kept to an absolute minimum. The best way to do this is <u>not</u> to rely on a powder measure to give you uniform charges, but rather to **weigh every charge**. Having a low standard deviation in velocity is very nice, but for Long-range shooting the categorical imperative is to have the lowest possible extreme spread in velocities. Making your ammunition as uniform as possible is what you have to do to ensure that.

SUMMING IT UP

Conventional Long-range competition is challenging and a lot of fun. To be successful at it requires a good rifle/ammunition combination as well as a good shooter. Obviously, a person can try any-rifle matches with just about any rifle, certainly the any-sight matches. The iron-sight requirement for the other matches may deter some from giving it a go; but more and more match directors are adding an F-class division to their matches, so things are opening up, even in Palma matches.

I would suggest that if a person wanted to get into Conventional Long-range competition with only one rifle, an easy way to do it would be to build up a Palma rifle in 308 and use it in the any-rifle matches as well. Most target-type metallic sights are easy to take on and off the rifle, so such a rifle with a Weaver-type rail on top of it allows you to easily mount a scope on it for use in any-rifle, any-sight matches. Such a combination does not give up very much to the magnums at 1000 yards. It is still up to the shooter to judge and correct for changes in the conditions.

Getting better at Long-range shooting of any type is largely a matter of experience. The way you learn the game is to just go out and do it. And the important thing to remember is that it is a *game*. I have shot beside National Champions and Palma Team members in conditions that were so bad that we both shot misses, and we just laughed about it even though we were trying hard to shoot as well as we could.

F-class has opened a door that previously did not exist. It has brought new competitors and some new cartridges onto the Long-range scene, and I think that is good. I just hope that even more people will come out and give conventional Long-range competition a try. Very few of the shooting sports are as challenging and as much fun.

Chapter 10

Replicating (?) Billy Dixon's Lengendary Long-Shot (Part I)

by M.L. McPherson

Synopsis: Billy Dixon's long-shot, which ended <u>The Battle of Adobe Walls</u>, although contentiously documented, is widely known and, undoubtedly, happened. Although we could argue the exact range and other circumstances surrounding Mr. Dixon's legendary shot, a recent study by Mr. Bill Falin (Chief Ballistician at Accurate Arms) and myself demonstrated one thing, at least, to our satisfaction: Given only the right shooting conditions and knowledge of the range involved, there is no doubt that Billy Dixon could have toppled a mounted rider at 7/8 mile, or beyond. This is especially likely if, as Mr. Dixon explicitly states in his memoirs, he had been shooting at a <u>group</u> of mounted horsemen. Use of *Accurate Arms' XMP-5744* smokeless powder made our study both feasible and productive. We do not believe this choice compromised the integrity of our results: For several reasons the best black powders available in the 1870s outclassed any type and brand of black powder (routinely) produced anywhere in the world today. Our choice of XMP-5744 merely allowed us to closely replicate the ballistic uniformity Billy Dixon rightly expected from the best loads of his day, while minimizing cleaning chores.

As dawn broke on the morning of June 27, 1874, a large band of Kiowa and Comanche warriors prepared to lay siege to a small settlement called Adobe Walls, Texas (several other tribes were involved to some extent). Sheltered at Adobe Walls on that eventful day were twenty-eight men and one woman. Most of these men were buffalo killers: Those who collected and sold buffalo skins to supply the lucrative European buffalo robe and domestic leather market. There were also a good number of horses and several dogs at Adobe Walls that memorable summer morn.

For several weeks prior to June 27, 1874, those then taking refuge at Adobe Walls had been trespassing on Kiowa and Comanche tribal lands in the pursuit of dwindling buffalo herds. Those men had long-since recognized the danger the growing numbers of mounted braves in the area represented; these market killers recognized that the congregating Indians were a bit perturbed with their trespassing and their activities upon tribal lands. Fearing retribution, the "White Eyes" had retreated to the shelter of Adobe Walls.

Who could blame the Indians for their hostility? To the Kiowa and Comanche—who were, after all, the rightful landowners—the activities of these trespassers' amounted to nothing more than a wasteful and senseless buffalo slaughter. Since buffalo were the primary means of livelihood for both Kiowa and Comanche, it is no wonder both tribes were a bit miffed.

Among the Indian leaders at that gathering was Comanche Chief Quanah Parker, who later in life enriched humanity by a very special gift; we will return to that point later. It is significant to note that Quanah was soon to become an early example of what we now call a "friendly-fire casualty"—in one of the subsequent battles he took a bullet in the back, almost certainly fired by one of his comrades! Quanah was not alone in personal bad luck, there were others. For example, after the battle had ended, Mr. Olds (whose wife was the only woman there) was scurrying down a ladder and managed an accidental discharge of his rifle—the bullet entered under his chin and exited from the top of where his skull had previously been.

Numbered among those at Adobe Walls that eventful morning were Bat Masterson and Billy Dixon. Long after the battle was over, those two men (and many others on both sides) orally recounted the subsequent events in some detail. Hollywood and many fiction writers have long-since corrupted the perception of what really went on at Adobe Walls—many have even gotten the name wrong, calling it Adobe Wells [sic]. However, thanks to Olive K. Dixon, Billy's persistent wife, we have a written account of the entire story of the Battle of Adobe Walls, as he dictated it to her. (For a fascinating read, I can highly recommend this book: Life of "Billy" Dixon by *Olive K. Dixon*, now under reprint by State House Press, Austin, Texas.)

Here Mr. Bill Falin lines up for another shot. Rifle is a custom C. Sharps, Model-1875. Chambering is 40-65 Falin—a cartridge easily made from 444 Marlin cases and which ballistically duplicates various original 40-65 black powder rounds. Load is 20 grains of Accurate Arms XMP-5744, Fed-215, home-cast 400 grain RCBS (40-400-CSA) semi-spitzer bullets over a NECO P-Wad. Note, we have fully elevated the screw-adjustable aperture sight. Also note that Mr. Falin's cheek is several inches above the stock's cheek piece!

In the early fall of 1874, shortly after the Battle of Adobe Walls, Billy Dixon joined the Army as a scout, guide, interpreter, etc. Late in 1874, the U.S. Congress and the President awarded Mr. Dixon the Medal of Honor: "For Heroism at the Battle of Buffalo Wallow." At that engagement, Mr. Dixon and several troopers fought off a hostile force of unknown but large size in a protracted battle. While the Medal of Honor might have been easier for an Indian Fighter to win, compared to a hero of the Vietnam War, Mr. Dixon's reception of this badge-of-courage still speaks volumes for his valor and, I believe, his character.

Billy Dixon later bought Adobe Walls, taking up residence there. He lived there the better part of his adult life. This speaks to two things: First, he certainly had ample opportunity to verify the actual range of his now-famous shot; second, obviously, proximity to the locale where such an unpleasant event had occurred failed to intimidate him.

Unlike his acquaintance, Bat Masterson, Billy Dixon was not a publicity seeker. Billy Dixon would not even have recorded his memoirs, had it not been for the persistence of his wife—who believed her husband's life story worthy of an accurate accounting—a gift to folks like you and me. Thanks to her prodding, late in life he began to record his memoirs. However, he died before completion of the manuscript

While it might not look it, air temperature was already climbing past 100ºF as we set up to begin shooting. Our biggest problem was keeping the very warm bodies from dehydrating! Crossed sticks hail from the buffalo-hide collector's era.

recounting his life's story—pneumonia after a short illness that he could not shake, in 1913. Mr. Dixon was born in 1850.

Billy Dixon's lifelong interests revolved around the rifle and what a competent man could do with one. He was an accomplished target shooter. Those who have seen the movie <u>Quigley Down Under</u> and have read Billy Dixon's memoirs cannot avoid the impression that, in some sense, Billy Dixon was the original Quigley. Mr. Dixon's chief vice was shooting at long-range targets. He did not take up buffalo hide collecting because he could make good money at it, he took up buffalo hide collecting because he could make money doing something he loved: shooting at long-range targets!

One other little anecdote: Mr. Dixon reports in his memoirs that early on in the battle at Adobe Walls he had climbed into a loft (to gain a better angle of fire and field of view?). He lined up to take a shot but he did not have a good purchase. When he dropped the hammer on his Big-Fifty Sharps (50-90), the resulting (not insignificant) recoil toppled him from the loft. He managed to save the rifle but in the process of landing he destroyed a table and scattered all manner of debris all over the room. As he tells it, that incident provided a bit of black humor in the midst of a grim situation. His recording of that inglorious event suggests to this author that Mr. Dixon was

not a man overly taken with himself.

Enough on that; my point here is to suggest that I believe we should take the written account in Mr. Dixon's memoirs very literally. If he says his long-shot happened a certain way, it very likely happened just that way. Forget Hollywood Hype and whatever other nonsense other folks might have written long after the fact. (Many of these prevaricators evidently cared less for the truth.)

Every pertinent fact cited here falls directly from Mr. Dixon's memoirs. However, I have added a few colorful details. I have taken those

Perspective-view looking over Mr. Falin's shoulder. Target is visible on the original 4"x6" photograph, where it shows as little more than a dark speck with a white line protruding. Here we have drawn an arrow pointing out the target location—target is slightly less than the length of the arrowhead in front of our arrow's tip. The larger dark spots are full-grown juniper trees. We had no trouble seeing this target through the excellent C. Sharps aperture sights. Doping the swirling wind was another matter!

Another perspective of the same shooting position. This picture shows the magnitude of elevation required to heave an essentially sub-sonic bullet across 1538 yards in 5.25 seconds. If this position looks uncomfortable, that visage is not coincidental.

from an oral account rendered in 1965 by Billy Dixon's great-great-great-nephew—family history (or tradition?).

To reiterate, in late June of 1874, owing to a gathering of Indians in the area, and fear of hostile action, most of those collecting hides for the buffalo trade in that part of the country gathered at the settlement of Adobe Walls, Texas. Indian reprisal was certainly not out of the question. Buffalo killers had been routinely violating treaty lands set aside solely for use of the Kiowa and Comanche. Worse than this trespassing was what the White Eyes were doing on those lands—dis-

robing slaughtered buffalo and leaving the carcasses to rot. One can well imagine the impact such an activity had on a people whose culture depended upon buffalo for its very existence.

An aside: Since, following the introduction of the horse, the tribes had themselves already significantly depreciated the buffalo herds long before the market hunters came to the game (a little known fact), conflict was inevitable. First, the horse, then the gun dramatically improved tribal hunting effectiveness. Tribal populations grew and hunting pressure had long-since increased dramatically. Even without the market

Close-up view of Mr. Falin as he prepares to fire his C. Sharps. Note that we have not yet fully elevated the tang-mounted aperture sight. I took this photograph before we got on target. Also note spirit-level located at front aperture sight. That feature is critically important when one is shooting at extreme distances. Chambering is 40-65 Falin—a cartridge easily made from 444 Marlin cases and which ballistically duplicates various original 40-65 black powder rounds. C. Sharps offers this chambering as a factory option.

Base elevation is 4700 feet, air is <u>extremely</u> dry and air temperature is 105°F. The 400 grain RCBS (40-400-CSA) semi-spitzer bullet, launched by 20 grains of XMP-5744 at 1200 fps, will take 5.25 seconds to reach the target. At 825 yards, it will raise 111 feet above the line of sight. It will impact with 478 foot pounds of energy. With a constant 5 mph crosswind, it would drift 10.3 feet. A crossing horse at a full run would travel just under 308 feet during the flight of the bullet. A man walking leisurely would cover 15 feet.

Telephoto shot showing top of rifle and sights (out of focus here) and distant target. Despite wind and our limited abilities, we had no trouble hitting this target, at least occasionally. Bushnell's Lytespeed 400 Laser Rangefinder was invaluable. By taking several intermediate ranges on the line to our target, we were able to establish 1538 yards to an accuracy of about 5 yards.

hunters and the U.S. Cavalry the massive buffalo herds were long-since doomed!

At about 2:00 a.m., on June 27, 1874, a thunderous cracking noise (like a rifle shot) awakened those sleeping in Hanrahan's Saloon (also his house). Those who rose in response to the noise believed the sound came from the ridge-pole of the building. They believed that the main cottonwood beam supporting the roof was in the process of failing. That would have dropped the heavy sod roof on their heads. Therefore, those folks were soon scurrying about the yard trying to find something with which to brace the structure's roof. They eventually went to Adobe Walls creek and cut a cottonwood pole, which was soon emplaced. Others set about removing the heavy sod from the roof. However, according to the oral account, a subsequent investigation revealed that the ridge pole was perfectly sound—Several then and many since have suggested that this could have been a case of Divine Intervention.

That was, no doubt, a rude awakening for those at Adobe Walls. However, it was nothing compared to the rude awakening seven-hundred Kiowa and Comanche warriors had planned for them. Quanah Parker and other Comanche and Kiowa leaders led this aggregation of warring braves. These warriors were the elite of a fighting group, whom experts in the U.S. cavalry routinely exalted as: "The finest light-cavalry ever assembled." Those War Chiefs devised a battle plan of pure simplicity and, considering the Little Bighorn-like odds, a plan bound to succeed. (Custer's infamous Last Stand was then still two years hence.)

Quanah and the others laid out their scheme: In the breaking light of dawn, "All the Indians in the world" would ride right down on top of the unfortunate inhabitants at Adobe Walls. (The Adobe Walls settlement then consisted of three main buildings, a water well and an insubstantial livestock corral.) The Indians' intention was to catch those at Adobe Walls in bed (many of the men were sleeping under the stars), before they had readied themselves for the rigors of the day. Thus awakened and facing overwhelming numerical odds, the White Eyes would have no chance.

Unfortunately for the braves, when the attack came, those at Adobe Walls had already been rudely awakened. So, when a vast and hostile mounted cavalry came storming over the distant horizon, the buffalo hide collectors were already wide awake; most were considering whether to get an early start or try to get back to sleep. To make matters worse for the Indians, by pure chance, Billy Dixon happened to be looking right at the warriors when they came into sight.

Given this edge, those at Adobe Walls were able to turn the tables. What the warriors had planned, a surprise attack, became, instead, a surprise counter-attack by their intended victims. Wide awake, and alerted in plenty of time to arm themselves, take cover and establish proper rifle-rests, the buffalo killers began to take a heavy toll

Mr. Falin points out one of thirteen hits we made while shooting at this target about 130 times (with the sights properly adjusted). At 4700 feet of elevation and shooting 7/8 of a mile, Mr. Falin's custom 400 grain RCBS (40-400-CSA) semi-spitzer 40-65 Falin bullet was carrying about 478 foot pounds of energy upon impact. All bullets that hit the target were point-on. Those hitting in the dirt around the target were also apparently traveling in stable flight. Such an impact would certainly have been lethal, given a proper hit. Mr. Dixon's heavy 50 caliber bullets would have delivered more energy—even when shooting through the much thicker air found closer to sea level. For example, consider a similarly shaped 625 grain 50 caliber bullet started at the same velocity fired at sea level. Such a bullet would deliver about 675 foot pounds of energy. Likely Mr. Dixon's bullets were heavier still.

on the onrushing riders. Bullets from several Sharps and other types of powerful long-range rifles began felling riders long before any of the Indians could return effective fire with their relatively feeble Henry-class repeaters, muzzle loaders, bows and assorted other weapons. It would be easy to suggest that with more than a dozen trained marksmen in attendance (skilled men equipped with long-range guns and plenty of superior ammunition) the affair was thoroughly one-sided. However, that was certainly not the case—odds matter, regardless of armament!

Most hide collecting groups consisted of four or more men, only one or two of whom killed buffalo. The others skinned and tended various other chores. It is almost certain that among twenty-eight men there were far fewer than a dozen highly skilled shooters (ammunition necessary to become proficient was very expensive). It is also unlikely there were as many as one-dozen long-range rifles at Adobe Walls (guns were very, very expensive). In any case, even twenty-odd single-shot rifles would provide precious little firepower to turn the tide of seven-hundred onrushing mounted horses!

When the battle was over, Billy Dixon, among others, stated his belief that it was a minor miracle that those sheltered at Adobe Walls suffered so few casualties: Adobe Walls counted

several wounded and three persons dead along with a total loss of livestock—only those dogs that high-tailed it at the onset of the festivities survived.

To add poignancy to this aspect, we will note the following anecdotes, taken both from Billy Dixon's memoirs and from oral history: At the battle's outset a dog had been sleeping under a wagon, where its master slept; that ill-fated mutt managed to reach cover before expiring from the effects of numerous bullet wounds. (Thirty-seven is the number quoted in the oral history!) In the initial battle, the two Shadler brothers, one of who owned the aforementioned dog, were soundly sleeping in a wagon in the yard. They never escaped the insufficient protection it offered. Billy Tyler, who had also been outside made it to the house but took a bullet through the lungs as he turned to close the door, he survived for about

Mr. Falin adjusting the rear sight, "A few more turns higher." We expended several dozen shots before getting elevation and basic windage correct. At 1538 yards, bullet rotation drift is substantial, perhaps about 50 feet right. We fired almost 200 shots this day. Not once did we have to stop our testing to clean the rifle. Likely, owing to the 105°F air temperatures and that we had no shade for the abused rifle or ammunition, we did experience minor bore leading. That did not seem to affect accuracy. Accurate's XMP-5744 is certainly a wonderful product for those who want to shoot black powder cartridges in black powder guns but without the black powder hassle. However, as noted in the text, we do not believe our ammunition was as consistent as that which Mr. Dixon was shooting at the real deal.

The majority of the approximately 130 shots fired with proper sight adjustment impacted within about a thirty foot radius of our cardboard warrior. Most of that scatter was horizontal. Were this target only one of a group of, say, fifteen similar targets, representing a small band of riders huddled for a conference, the majority of those 130 shots would have found some type of flesh!

thirty minutes. There was little safety at Adobe Walls that summer morning!

In the initial fiasco, the Indians took decimating losses in both horses and riders. Thereafter, albeit more cautiously, they continued attacking, organizing skirmishes throughout that day and the next, looking for a weakness or a safer means of attack—they evidently found none. On the third morning, with cool, calm and clear weather prevailing, a "group of about fifteen Indians" convened a war council on a bluff east of Adobe Walls Creek. According to Billy Dixon, the huddled riders were "not far from seven-eighths of a mile" from the settlement. We have to note that the distance was later surveyed. Mr. Dixon's stated range held up quite well. One number reported for that survey is 1538 yards (7/8 mile is 1540 yards)—no credible account claims a greater distance.

No doubt, these riders were strongly considering how to abandon the ill-fated attack with <u>dignity</u>—something of significance to any self-respecting warrior. However, at that moment, a pivotal sequence of events began to unfold. Events that changed those warriors' concerns about dignity and, no doubt changed Quanah Parker's path in life. Likely, this event ultimately contributed to Quanah's fundamental gift to civilization—the written Comanche language! (Had he been more successful at Adobe Walls it seems unlikely that he would have turned to scholarly pursuits.)

Knowing Billy Dixon was the best shootist there one of the other shooters pointed toward the group of riders and says, "Why don't you take a crack at them with your Big-Fifty, Billy?" Evidently Billy Dixon knew the range quite well. Perhaps he had previously used that very ridge for target practice, something that would not have been out of character for him. He certainly knew the proper sight setting for such a shot because he summarily adjusted his Sharp's rear sight and prepared to "give it a try."

Now, finally, we get to the meat of our story. Reiterating, Billy Dixon was a renowned rifle shot. Not only did he employ his marksmanship skills in making a living, but he also practiced the sport of long-range target shooting, in lieu of any other significant vices. Further, he had the best equipment then available and that, I must add,

was equipment that would rival some of our best today. Keep in mind that some of the long-range target records set in the 1870s & 1880s stood for generations, e.g., a 1000 yard group measuring 8.6" fired in 1886. Mr. Dixon was not handicapped by lack of equipment. In competent hands, given a good estimate of the range and calm conditions, Billy Dixon's 50-90 Sharps (a chambering introduced in 1872, or earlier) was a formidable long-range combination. We do not know details of his load. However, almost certainly he used a paper patched, pointed bullet that weighed well over one-ounce. Also he very likely handloaded, using the best powder then available and due care in all aspects of handloading.

After adjusting his long-range peep sight, Mr. Dixon took careful aim and no doubt made a few fine adjustments for any slight breeze, bullet rotation, alignment of the planets, that itch

We had plenty of other accouterments. Hearing protection, Bushnell's Lytespeed 400 laser range finder, a spotting scope and various 44 Magnum revolvers (to keep us entertained while the rifle cooled or as a gusty squall passed).

behind his neck, and any other effects he might have though significant. Then he touched the finely adjusted set trigger of the rifle to loose his (most likely) hand-cast and hand-loaded projectile. His admitted target was "the group of riders." He never made any claim suggesting he had been aiming at any one individual.

Assuming similarly shaped pointed bullets 1538 yard time-of-flight is practically identical —about 5.3 seconds. If his bullet was of the lighter Sharps fifty caliber type (approximately 500 grains) muzzle velocity would have been about 1350 fps. For the (more likely) heavier type (perhaps 700 grains) muzzle velocity would have been about 1100 fps. At 7/8 of a mile the lighter bullet would have delivered about 535 foot pounds of energy; the heavier bullet about 845 foot pounds of energy.

Meanwhile, if any among the Indians were watching, they would have noticed a cloud of smoke in the yard in front of the main house. It is easy to imagine their mirth at the thought of some foolish White Eyes wasting powder and lead. Then, an eternal 4.1 seconds later, if they were quiet, they would have heard the distant rumble of a Big-Fifty Sharps rifle.

About 1.2 seconds after that distant sound reached their ears the impossible happened! One of the assembled chiefs took a bullet. He then toppled from his horse—most undignified! Not surprisingly, the other assembled chiefs recognized that little incident as *bad medicine*; they therefore and forthwith terminated the Battle of Adobe Walls.

Billy Dixon believed he had killed the rider. Indian accounts claim the bullet hit the unlucky rider above the elbow, breaking his arm. Regardless, the bullet did the intended job.

What about Billy Dixon's equipment? What many modern shooters might not know is that black powder was, in that era, as highly developed as today's best smokeless powders. Produced in England, *Curtis & Harvey's Diamond Grade* was the world's best, likely because of a superior charcoal root stock and extended blending time. As folklore has it, their charcoal came from a certain type of willow tree that grew only in one locale. Further, *C&H* could afford to prolong the blending operation because they could get a premium price for the superior product thus

produced. Serious target shooters widely acclaimed *Kentucky Rifle* from a United States producer, *Hazards*, as the best alternative choice but, nonetheless, a second-best choice. Behind those two premier powders come an entire plethora of brands, manufactured in various places around the world.

Those lower-quality powders were less expensive and everyday shooters most often used those for everyday purposes. Considering Billy Dixon's interests, acknowledged skills, and accomplishments, we have to believe he used the best-of-the-best in powder, sights, bullet casting equipment and reloading equipment.

Powder limitations offer a comparative handicap to today's black powder shooters. We certainly do not mean to suggest today's products are not of a high quality; today's black powders are significantly superior to most of the powders that were available in the past century. However, today's black powders simply do not compare to the very best available to a young Billy Dixon, circa 1870. We should also note that this is partly a response to the dictates of supply and demand: If demand warranted, *GOEX* could afford to run the grinding wheels longer and thereby generate a more thoroughly mixed product composed of finer constituent particles.

I have included this photo only because it shows an interesting hit. Note the bullet balanced in the crotch of the elbow. Coincidentally, Billy Dixon's Comanche-Chief-toppling bullet was reported to have connected just above the elbow—breaking the arm. Here we came precious-close to duplicating that hit!

Such a blend would come closer to matching the performance of *Curtis & Harvey's (C&H)* legendary *Diamond Grade*.

Historical anecdotes, regarding barrel fouling and other powder characteristics, and long-range target data all support our contention that the best powders of days-gone-by were superior. Vertical stringing of representative long-range targets suggests that many of the best handloaders of that era achieved ballistic uniformity for any given shot-string representing low single-digit standard deviations. I dare say few combinations put together with modern black powder will <u>routinely</u> demonstrate that level of consistency—certainly, precious few smokeless loads do so well. Further, *Diamond Grade* was almost certainly cleaner-burning than any black powder now available. Nevertheless, this is not to suggest that current black powder cannot provide consistent results.

As an example, I recently tested the 45-70 using *Federal-150* primers, *GOEX FFg* and commercial-cast 405 grain bullets in fully prepped 186.0 grain +/- 0.5 grains R-P cases; the results were rather impressive and surprising. Standard deviation for a fifteen-shot string was 6.2 fps! In the past quarter of a century I have chronographed perhaps a thousand smokeless metallic cartridge loads of diverse types. Of those, I can recall exactly one that would routinely surpass this level of consistency, albeit slightly. Perhaps a dozen of my best smokeless loads come close to this yardstick—standard deviation less than one-half of one-percent of muzzle velocity. However, this was my very first try with FFg! Who knows, tinkering with neck tension, seating depth, lube choice, powder charge, charging technique, custom cast bullets, etc. might possibly afford an even more consistent combination.

The fact that the very best black powders of yesteryear surpassed those now available was self-serving in our study. We had no desire to shoot black powder! Since we are convinced that the ballistic uniformity of the load we were shooting is no better than what we could achieve with the best black powder handloads; and since we believe our best black powder loads would not be as good as Billy Dixon's loads were, we were satisfied that our use of a modern smokeless powder would not queer our results. Specifically, a demonstration that Mr. Falin's handloads with

cast bullets using *XMP-5744* had the intrinsic accuracy necessary to do the job, would satisfy us that Mr. Dixon's loads could have done the job. We must also note that neither Mr. Falin nor I would ever suggest we might be as good a shot as Mr. Dixon, perish the thought! (Further, we lacked a certain motivation Mr. Dixon had working for him.)

The test rifle was a custom 34" barreled *C. Sharps Arms*, New Model 1875 Target & Long Range. This rifle is chambered for a cartridge of Mr. Falin's invention—40-65 Falin. One can easily convert 444 Marlin cases for this application. This case design combines a long cylindrical neck section with a straight taper, which extends virtually to the solid case head. The straight neck is sufficiently long to support a *NECO P-Wad* and the entire shank of a 400 grain cast semi-spitzer.

For practical purposes, this cartridge ballistically duplicates any of the original 40-65 type chamberings. Capacity is essentially identical to the 40-65 Winchester. Excepting a slightly shorter length and a smaller rim, this cartridge is essentially interchangeable with the 40-70 Ballard. It should chamber and shoot in guns designed for that cartridge but is normally loaded

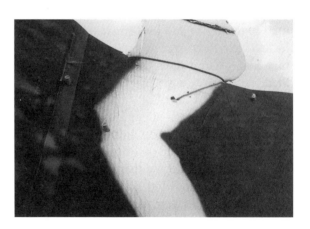

Close-up view showing three of our better hits. We have inserted recovered bullets in the holes. Note that all impacts were point-on. You might also note the extreme angle of impact. At this range, these bullets are dropping 1" for every 9" of forward travel! We used twine and nails to attach our cardboard target to a scrap-lumber framework.

with a somewhat larger bullet, 0.408" versus 0.403". This design is good enough that *C. Sharps* now offers it as an alternative factory chambering. Custom dies are available from *RCBS*. Cases are a one-step, full-length sizing die, conversion. (Necks are only about 0.021" smaller than the neck on the 444 parent-case.)

444 Marlin cases are readily available and feature relatively heavy construction. As an added bonus, *Remington* now offers a nickel-plated version (available through *Midway*). This plating is about 0.0005" thick on both inside and outside surfaces of the neck. Therefore, it reduces case neck-to-chamber clearance by about 0.002". Since standard chamber clearance is 0.004", use of these cases provides a bench-rest-like chamber fit!

Mr. Falin's load duplicates the pressure and velocity of black powder loads, although it does not quite match the uniformity of black powder loads. The charge is 20 grains of *Accurate Arms XMP-5744* ignited by *Federal's 215* primer (Large Rifle Magnum) for a muzzle velocity of about 1200 fps under the conditions we were shooting in (105°F with no shade). Standard deviation is about 15 fps. Tests in several similar chamberings suggest use of (milder) pistol primers would significantly improve ballistic uniformity. However, Mr. Falin had several-hundred of these *Fed-215* loads on hand and already had an idea of the external ballistics for that combination. Therefore, he stuck with his known load, rather than work up a new load and new ballistics data. I should also note that a slight reduction in velocity might also have improved accuracy since the bullets would not have been buffeted by transonic shock waves in the first moments after leaving the barrel.

We fired almost 200 shots that hot day. We did not have to clean the gun once owing to smokeless powder or metallic fouling, despite the fact that the gun got hand-blistering hot and stayed that way through most of the day (there was no shade).

Also significant, when loaded to an appropriate pressure level for typical cast bullets, *Accurate's XMP-5744* leaves only the thinnest powder residue in the bore. One does not observe unburned powder granules in the bore. The residue does not seem to build up beyond a mini-

mal level, regardless of how many shots one fires.

About *XMP-5744*: Serendipity is a wonderful thing. Using this powder, one can work up a <u>safe</u> black powder equivalent loading for almost any black powder rifle cartridge by pursuing the following procedure. For a starting powder charge, choose a loading density where the charge fills about 40% of the available powder space. To determine this, add *XMP-5744* to a dummy case until the powder level is about where the base of the chosen seated bullet would be. Pour the powder into the case using a standard funnel and do not settle the charge. To remove any inadvertent settling, place a finger over the case mouth and shake the charged case up and down vigorously several times. Verify the charge is still the same height in the case or remove powder, as necessary to achieve that goal.

Remove the powder and weigh it. Multiply the scale reading by 0.40. For example, the 45-70 case with a typical 405 grain cast bullet seated to 2.55" OAL would hold about 50.0 grains of *XMP-5744* (as-dumped) without any powder compression. Therefore, a correct starting charge would be about 20.0 grains (50 x 0.4).

Once you have established a starting point, load a test-batch with incremental charges. For a load that duplicates black powder performance, the maximum charge should not exceed about

This view shows the target and framework a bit better. The bracing board in front took an early ricochet. After cutting a trench in the hillside (about twenty feet below the target) that bullet hit this stake traveling sideways and with sufficient force to split it.

50% of usable case capacity. In our example, we might load groups of cartridges with charges at 20.0 grains, 22.0 grains, 24.0 grains, 24.5 grains and 25.0 grains.

Typically, when using *XMP-5744* at pressures and velocities lower than those generated by a typical black powder load (especially when using relatively light bullets), the shooter will note considerable unburned powder granules in the gun's bore. As he increases the charge, the amount of unburned powder will decrease. As he reaches the point where the charge duplicates typical black powder velocity and pressure (usually between 20,000 CUP and 28,000 CUP), he will note the absence of unburned powder in the bore. (Likely, when used with heavier bullets, in any given application, complete combustion will occur at a lower peak pressure.)

Significantly, such loads also generate sufficient pressure to properly obturate typical cast bullets. Therefore, as one approaches the correct (black powder duplicating) pressure level and velocity, three worthwhile things occur: The powder begins to burn very cleanly, bullets obturate properly (minimizing leading) and groups shrink! Rather nifty.

I should note that *Accurate Arms* does offer substantial loading data for many of the commoner and several more esoteric applications of *XMP-5744*, including smokeless era loads at higher pressure levels. However, if you happen to own a 40-70 Peabody chambered rifle in good repair you can work up a black powder equivalent smokeless load on your own. Just follow the aforementioned advice. However, when working with any gun of uncertain strength, never exceed about 45% usable case capacity, regardless of other indicators.

Mr. Falin's bullets weigh about 400 grains, as cast with his wheel-weight-like alloy. A surprising thing is the calculated and evident ballistic coefficient, near 0.405! See accompanying charts for a representation of the external ballistics of this load.

Owing to our inadequate compensation for bullet drift, it took us about 40 shots to get on-target. Mr. Falin had adjusted his rifle's sights to vertically zero this load at the desired range if we had been shooting at the NRA's Whittington Center at Raton, New Mexico—elevation about 6500 feet. However, we were shooting in the Grand Valley, west of Grand Junction, Colorado at an elevation of about 4700 feet. The difference in trajectory such a small base-elevation change can make when one is shooting across the better part of one mile might surprise the average shooter.

Also, in adjusting the sights to the longer range (having already established a zero at about 1100 yards for 6500 feet elevation) we failed to take into account the effects of bullet drift associated with such an extreme range. We should have thought of that. Owing to experience (shooting pistols at extended ranges), I knew his bullets would drift significantly to the right. However, it did not occur to me to mention the fact—we were very busy trying to get ourselves and all the equipment properly organized.

In any case, owing to these shortcomings, our first shots were falling low and far to the right. Unfortunately, the resulting impacts were occurring beyond an intervening low ridge, which obscured the resulting dust clouds—Murphy is alive and well. We did not figure out where those impacts were occurring until a lucky (low) hit on top of that ridge raised a significant cloud of dust within our view.

Once we had adjusted the sights to solve those problems, we started looking for mirage effects and otherwise trying to dope the wind. (Interestingly we were at or near the extremes of both the windage and elevation adjustments for that particular sight). Mr. Falin is very astute at observing mirage; I am not. On several occasions the wind settled down to a predictable pattern.

During one of those spells, I fired a string of seventeen shots. Bill called the wind and I did my best to fulfill his instructions, e.g., "Hold a bit high and about two horse-lengths to the left," I made four hits and two very near hits. Seven of the remaining eleven shots in that string were at the correct elevation and within about ten feet of the target. Had I been shooting at, say, fifteen mounted horsemen grouped on a ridge for a powwow almost certainly thirteen of those seventeen shots would have hit either a horse or a rider.

In all, we fired about 130 shots at the target after we got the gun properly zeroed. The majority of those shots were fired during bad wind conditions. Nevertheless, we made thirteen hits on the silhouette. We could not keep track of all our near-hits. Similarly, we could not keep track of where every shot went. We can say, however, that most of those shots would have placed a small group of riders in considerable danger.

Regarding caliber choice: Since Mr. Falin's bullets were arriving point-on, we do not believe use of 40 caliber bullets represented any significant handicap. Compared to the recoil generated by a 700 grain 50 caliber bullet at the same muzzle velocity, we feel these 400 grain 40 caliber bullets offered a useful advantage for our study. We hope to do a similar study next summer with otherwise similar rifles chambered in 40-65 Falin, 45-70 Springfield, 50-90 Sharps and using appropriate and similar bullets (same shape and sectional density: 400 grain, 505 grain, 625 grain). Next time I will locate a better range (less swirling-wind effect and easier access, I hope). We also hope to have a spotter along to call our shots *via* radio!

If the question is, "Could Billy Dixson have topped a hapless horseman from among a group of riders sitting at 7/8 of a mile," we believe the answer is, most assuredly, YES.

(*RCBS's* Designation for the 40-65 Winchester die set: Part #56483, 40-65 Shiloh Sharps - 0.408". The 40-65 Winchester will be in standard category C in the upcoming *RCBS* catalogue; 40-65 Winchester dies are also available from *Redding*. Designation for 40-65 Falin, discussed in this text, is 40-444. These dies (40-65 Falin) are currently available from *RCBS* by special order only and are labeled 40-65 Special. The bullet used in this study came from a custom *RCBS* mould #40-400-CSA, which is very similar to *RCBS*, Part #82086, Rifle Mould #40-400-BPS and Redding #740-F61. Both moulds cast bullets of typical alloys to about 0.4085" diameter and about 400 grains weight. (Use a 0.410" sizer die to lubricate bullets without disruptive sizing action.) *RCBS* Mould #40-400-BPS features a somewhat smaller meplat (the flat point at the front, pronounced *may-pla*) and a slightly higher ballistic coefficient but is otherwise similar to the bullet used in this study. The Redding mould seems to fall between these two, one of these three excellent moulds should cast bullets that work well in most rifles.

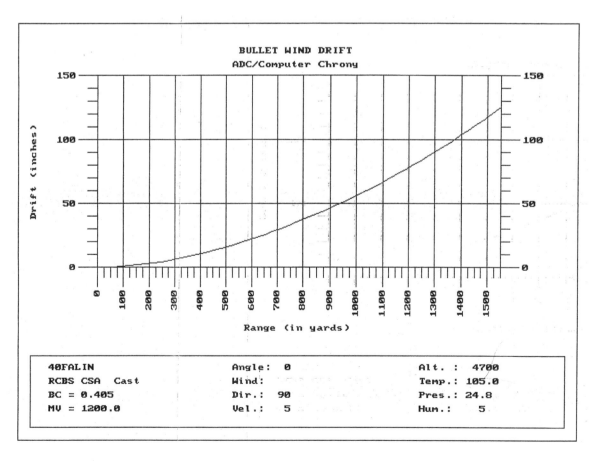

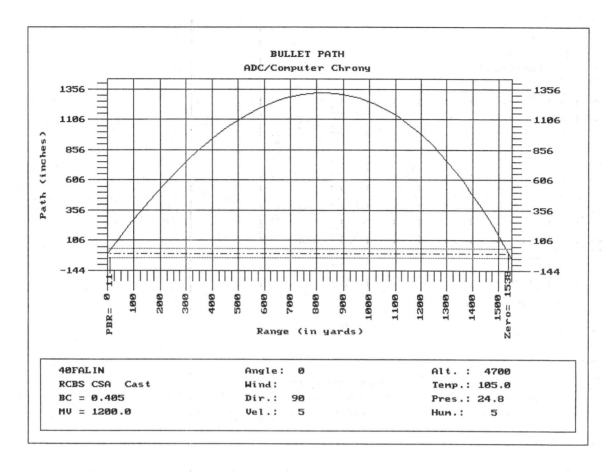

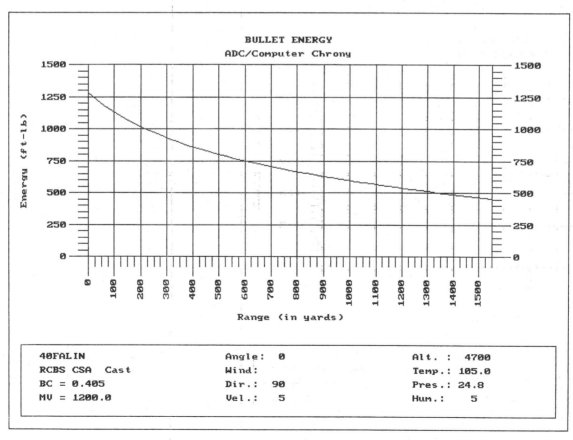

Billy Dixon Revisited:
or the Infamous Battle of Gut,
Gut & Butt (Part II)

by M.L. McPherson

Synopsis: Many shooters are fascinated with firing antique-style guns and loads at extremely long ranges. Perhaps the ultimate test is the Billy Dixon scenario—firing across 7/8 mile. Last summer three of us again reenacted that famous scene. Our test consisted of firing a 45-110 Sharps and a 50-90 Sharps at a target with an apparent height of about 7 feet and a width of about 14 feet—less than 100 square feet total area. As was noted the previous year, getting the sights adjusted to bring the impacts onto the proper hillside was our biggest problem....

Here Harvey takes aim. The light patch just in front of the arrow sketched on this photograph is the target. Note the extreme angle of the bore, compared to the line of sight. At the highest trajectory point, the bullet will be more than 110 feet above the line of sight.

A closer view of the target. This patched-together cardboard contraption is nailed to Mother Earth with 12-inch spikes. The system worked quite well. The various bullets arrived with sufficient momentum to penetrate into the shale bedrock below the 8 to 12 inches of adobe clay on this hillside. The shooting location was somewhat above the target, so the apparent target height was a bit greater than in this view. Referring to the Billy Dixon story, the noteworthy point is that you could not crowd very many mounted horses into a target area of this size.

For those unfamiliar with the Billy Dixon long-shot legend, a brief review is in order. At the heart of the great buffalo slaughter, a group of shooters found themselves congregated at a place called Adobe Walls. That assembly was no accident; rather, it was in response to shared fears that the locals might object in a meaningful way to the blatant trespass in which they were involved. As it turned out, their fears were well founded....

The Indians planned what should have been an effective attack. In the wee hours of dawn,

several hundred warriors rode toward Adobe Walls, intent on massacre. However, owing to an apparent miracle, the entire camp happened to be roused, out of bed and generally in a state of readiness. Moreover, in the dim light of the breaking morn, one of the whites just happened to be looking toward the direction of the attack. Therefore, instead of finding sleep weary men, still in bed and generally unready to fight, the attackers found a well-armed camp that was ready, willing and able to shoot back and to do it first....

Therefore, the intended surprise attack literally backfired. A deadly fire decimated the exposed attackers while the holed up attackees sustained relatively minimal damages. The battle lasted throughout that day, with the Indians trying one tactic after another, all to be defeated by the simple expedient of powerful and well-placed firepower emanating from more than a dozen buffalo rifles.

But that unexpected turn is not the reason this story resonates through history. The thing that makes this story unique is what happened in the early morning of the last day of the conflict; Billy Dixon made a phenomenal shot. The pertinent details were glorified by Bat Masterson (who was more vocal about the affair than Dixon) and verified in Billy Dixon's memoirs. Dixon was recognized as the best shot among those gathered at Adobe Walls and was, incidentally, a Medal of Honor recipient, for an unrelated episode. Paraphrasing the recounting, as if told by Masterson:

"A group of mounted Indians were assembled on a small bluff about 1500 yards away."
The actual distance was later surveyed at 1535 yards.
"They were apparently having a powwow."
Possibly they were discussing how to proceed with the thus-far unsuccessful attack or perhaps trying to figure out how to honorably call off the ill-fated affair.
"I says to Dixon, 'Billy, why don't you take a crack at them with your Big Fifty.'"
"Dixon found himself a solid rest and adjusting his rifle's sights, according to the range and conditions. He then squeezed off a shot. About five seconds later, one of the assembled riders tumbled from his horse. The group disbanded, forthwith."

Thus ended the battle of Adobe Walls, not with a heated volley but with a single, whimpering thud.

Two years ago, as reported in the pages of *Precision Shooting*, Bill Falin and I did a preliminary long-range study to see if we could duplicate that shot. We fired at a life-sized silhouette of a rider. We determined that given reasonably calm conditions and a tightly bunched group of riders, making a hit was not so outlandish an idea. In fact, we were emboldened to try an improved version of the study.

Originally, we had decided that a reasonable next step was to compare the 40, 45 and 50-caliber Sharps chamberings at the same long-range target, just to see if one particular caliber had any noticeable advantage. We accrued the assistance of Harvey Watt and Paul Armbruster of Atlanta, Georgia, and planned the big shoot for last summer. As it turned out, Bill was unable to join our little soirée (which fact figures in the subtitle...) so we could not include the 40-caliber in our test, but we didn't let that disappointment stop us.

We were all friends of Bill's; also Harvey and Paul were friends but I had never met them. This was certainly an interesting way to get acquainted, kind of similar to trial by firepower.

A different perspective and a view of the smoke generated by a blackpowder load. Note that the rifle has just fired. The buttstock has rotated down, as Harvey rocks back with the modest recoil. Despite the relatively heavy bullets used, these rifles are pleasant to shoot over the crossed sticks. Even from the bench, recoil is quite manageable.

This time we set up a less realistic, albeit more reasonable, target. After a bit of searching, we found a location where we could park the lead laden van at the shooting location and drive my old El Camino to the impact zone. There was also a convenient intervening hill and a very steep and sufficiently large hillside for the target. Our target was a simple construction of cardboard, nailed to the earth and with a black square near the center. From the shooting perspective, the apparent target dimensions were: 14 feet wide, 7 feet high with a 4 feet wide by 2 feet high bull's eye. Actual measured target area (corrected for perspective) was almost precisely 100 square feet. Range was measured at 1535 yards, give or take a few yards.

The intervening hill that was just to the left of the line of fire made an ideal location where a spotter could work safely. This hillside was only about 200 yards from the impact zone. Listening to the shots from that location was thrilling, I will return to that point. We established a radio contact routine to verify impact points, assess downrange wind conditions, etc.

The first day we finished setting up quite late. By then, we had a gusty wind to contend with. Worse, despite the wind, the gnats were arriving in hordes and seemingly from all points of the compass—I suspect that anyone in the surrounding four-state region must have noticed a significant gnat shortage that morning, owing to the pilgrimage those little pests made to our shooting site. It was all we could do to just get the target set up, paint a few spotter circles on the hillside at measured distances to both sides of the target, get the rifles zeroed for the various loads and fire a few shots for photographic purposes. By the time we finished, we were well bug bitten.

While we did all the "official" target shooting with smokeless loads, we did fire a few blackpowder rounds, just for nostalgia and comparative purposes. With a bit of sight adjustment, we had no trouble getting consistent hits on a similar-sized area adjacent to the target.

At the end of that day, we had to count and mark the target hits. This turned out to be rather difficult, but we got it done. This was necessary

Harvey Watt demonstrating the basic shooting pose. Contrary to appearances, properly used crossed-sticks provide an extraordinarily steady rest. Note the location of the rear peep aperture and the unusual head positioning its use requires. Also, note Harvey's fine hat, which looks period authentic but actually hails from a much more recent military unit.

Another blackpower shot, just for nostalgia. Here we were not actually shooting at the target but at a spot on the hillside beside it. We wanted to save the target for better conditions. Noting that the smoke is already blown well to the left of the line of fire should demonstrate that we had some rather heavy winds—sufficient to drift the bullet 50-feet leftward.

because we wanted to know how many hits we made each day. Moreover, since the idea was to try to do the "serious" shooting during calm conditions (just as Billy Dixon had), we intended to start shooting before sunrise the following day, when we hoped it would be calm. By marking the previous hits, we achieved a clean slate, so to speak.

The following morning we were set up and shooting before direct sunlight found us. As it worked out, Mother Nature cooperated; we had several hours of dead calm. Moreover, for whatever reason, there were very few bugs. We were thrilled to have such nearly perfect conditions; even the temperature was comfortable (I do not know how it could have been better).

Here Harvey Watt prepares to shoot while Paul Armbruster waits to spot the impact. In reality, there is no hurry at the spotting scope….
Since it takes the bullet more than 5 seconds to reach the target, the spotter can sit down after the shot is fired. If he hurried, there is no reason the shooter could not do his own spotting.

After adjusting out a considerable amount of windage, which had been required in the winds of the previous day, we were ready to begin. Using the adjacent test area we fired and made corrections. Very soon, we had the required vernier settings to put each rifle and each load on target.

Since I had done this before, and because I had done most of the shooting to get the rifles zeroed, I took up the spotter's location behind the intervening hill. Much as I love to shoot, for me, that proved to be a more enjoyable task, compared to pulling a trigger. Listening to the rumble of a big Sharps rifle firing ³/₄ mile away was a thrill. That was topped by the sound of the bullet arcing overhead. The crowning joy was the solid slap as the bullet impacted the adobe clay hillside 200 yards distant.

I was amazed at the volume of that impact. Despite the distance, it sounded like someone slapping a ripe watermelon inside a small room. It clearly resonated above our radio chatter.

In general outline, our radio and shooting routine went thusly:

Paul: "Harvey ready to fire the Big Fifty with the 710 bullet."
My reply: "OK, fire at poor old Will…."
Soon, the sound of the gun firing comes over the radio.
About three seconds later, an echoing **Kaboom,** *not particularly loud but clearly audible.*
About one-second later, the sound of the spinning bullet arcing overhead, **fuda, fuda, fuda, fuda, fuda.**
After about one more second, the sound of the bullet impact, **WHAP.**
My comment: "All right, you have a hit at 10 o'clock, about two feet from the bull's eye."

When the shot missed the paper, the observer at the shooting end (who was using a spotting scope) got a special thrill. More than five seconds after the shot was fired; he would see the dust geyser from the impact. Believe me, it takes a while to get used to waiting long enough to have a drink of water for a bullet to reach the target!

The second morning, after we got the guns rezeroed for the calm conditions, Paul and

Harvey took turns at the trigger. Of 42 shots fired, 5 found the bull's eye, 27 more hit the paper and 6 more went into a 2-foot high, six-foot wide area just above the paper at the upper left. While odd, I do not suppose that clustering was statistically significant. The remaining 4 shots were wild misses, which I attributed to bad bullets—at least two of those sounded wrong as they passed overhead. However, overall, if we had lowered the sights just three feet, we would have had 4 more hits (2 shots would have dropped off the bottom but 6 would have come onto the top). Our centering was also imprecise as none of the shots hit within 3 feet of the right edge of the paper. The impact rectangle of those that were on paper was just under 6 feet high and 11 feet wide.

Recounting the results: using open sights and firing over crossed-sticks at a 14 x 7 foot target at 1535 yards, we had a total of 32 hits out of 42 shots. To put this into perspective: the target was 10 x 5 MOA, 76% of the shots went into an 8 x 4 MOA rectangle.

At the time, I knew we were getting a lot of hits. Nevertheless, I was surprised when I counted the holes. While it was happening, I was thinking we were getting about 50% hits. I suppose that is a psychological thing—one tends to notice the errors, so to speak.

The bullets were home cast. Beyond eliminating those that were obviously flawed, those were not culled. We expected great things of the 570 grain, 45-caliber spitzer and the similarly efficient 710 grain, 50-caliber spitzer. However, the legendary 500 grain, 45-caliber round nose was the most accurate smokeless load we tested that day. They fired 15 rounds loaded with that bullet. Of those, 13 found the target—an astonishing 87%.

However, that does not prove the longer, more efficient, spitzers are inferior. In subsequent testing with those bullets, I was able to achieve significantly better accuracy by using a heavier charge of XMP5744. As it turned out, with the chosen seating depth, the same charge, 35.0 grains worked in all three combinations: 45-110-570, 50-90-610 and 50-90-710. This amounted to about a 5% increase over the loads used in our 7/8 mile test. Looks like we will just have to go back and do it again… I hate that, don't you know!

This side view shows the angle of the hillside. We chose this spot for many reasons; chiefly because it was readily accessible and about the steepest area we could work on to install the target and then mark any impacts.

Gut, Gut and Butt, our parting shot…. What more is there to say?

As a well-intentioned parting gesture, we fired a volley in honor of our absent friend (Bill Falin), whose fault our little adventure had been. I positioned the camera, set the self-timer and took my place alongside Paul and Harvey. As the tone of the timer changed, we prepared to fire in unison. The shutter snapped before we fired but it was still a good picture… except for one thing.

Yours truly failed to consider the sinister result of lining up on that side of the camera…. Because I am left-handed, I was facing away, providing an unintended backside view that wasn't all that photogenic. However, after reviewing the picture, it occurred to me that the front side view of this particular group is not all that much better! Anyway, that photograph did suggest a reasonable subtitle to this short piece.

Further load testing was completed during the Shootists Holiday last month at the Whittington Center, Raton, New Mexico. I and others took turns shooting at the white buffalo clanger target, which is a steel silhouette hanging in a small clearing on the juniper covered hillside at about 1100 yards.

With my new, heavier loads we were able to hit the buffalo with surprising consistency. Further, the 50-90 proved to be a far better choice. Not only did it make a higher percentage of hits but also the occasional miss was much easier to spot, owing to the larger dust geyser it created. This effect is hard to understand because the 570 grain, 45-110 bullet was arriving with more energy and momentum, compared to the 610 grain, 50-90 bullet. Nevertheless, the 50-90 did raise bigger splashes with both the 610 grain and even when shooting at dirt, frontal area matters.

The most amazing thing about shooting at the buffalo was the volume of the impact clang. Even with a gusty six o'clock wind it was obvious—

loud enough to be heard through the normal shooters' conversation by anyone who had removed his earplugs. Considering the volume at the shooting line, I had to wonder how it would have sounded to someone standing in that clearing, beside the target.

For the observers, the routine soon became: plug your ears with your fingers; chant, kill the buffalo; wait for the shot; pull your fingers out of your ears; then listen to the echoing of the shot as you silently count *one thousand one, one thousand two, … one thousand six*, then cheer in response to the impact clang.

Listening for and then hearing that impact was so much fun that I soon had trouble finding anyone who wanted to shoot… they all wanted to listen. Then we realized that, after firing the gun, the shooter had plenty of time to pull out a foam earplug.

In an extended morning of shooting and despite some rather serious winds, we managed to pepper that silhouette to the point that we

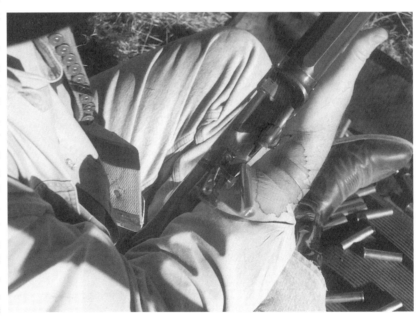

Here Harvey demonstrates the automatic case ejection feature of the Sharps rifle. By racking the finger-lever sharply forward, the case is flung clear of the gun. Conversely, opening the finger lever normally leaves the case in the chamber, an extension of the extractor provides for manually removing the case about 1/2-inch from the chamber, so the shooter can control it. For a hunter working 1000 miles from the nearest resupply depot, losing an expensive case in the tall grass was no small concern.

could no longer count the impact splashes on what had begun as a fresh coat of white paint. When the wind held reasonably steady, we had no problem making hits with either Sharps rifle. Just for a change, I tried a series of offhand shots. Fortunately, I had several witnesses because I managed to hit the buffalo two out of four tries with each of four rifles:

1) 30-06 Garand, firing handloads (which produced a barely audible clang);
2) 44-90 Meacham Highwall, 460-grain cast @ about 1350 fps using blackpowder (the sight on that rifle would not provide the required elevation, so I had to aim at a tree trunk above the target clearing);
3) 45-110 Shiloh Sharps, 570 grain cast @ about 1100 fps using XMP5744;
4) 50-90 Shiloh Sharps, 610 grain and 710 grain cast @ about 1100 fps using XMP5744.

Perhaps next year we can finally do a more formal study comparing the various calibers. For now, I am convinced the 50-90 has significant advantages for this type of pleasure shooting. Further, I believe that any of the original buffalo chamberings would be capable. All it takes is a good load (which includes a sufficiently heavy bullet), calm conditions, adequate rear sight height, a good zero and a reasonably competent shooter.

As noted in the original article, I believe Billy Dixon knew beforehand exactly what sight setting to use—the manner in which he discusses the matter suggests that he had already taken a few potshots at the bluff in question. He did have calm conditions and he did have good ammo. Importantly, he was most assuredly a fine Sharps-shooter. With all that in mind, I am more convinced than ever that if Billy Dixon had not drawn blood that long ago and fateful morn it would have been another miracle.

Regardless, firing a sub-sonic bullet across the better part of a mile has a special charm. My guess is that if you get a chance to play this game, you will not regret the experience. Meanwhile, please pass the ammunition....

Chapter 11

"Farky" Shooting
F-Class

by Larry Bartholome

Let me take a minute of your time and describe my *first* F-Class match relay…. It was a cool, misty morning in Mineral Wells, Texas. The humidity must have been about 150 percent. I don't think I could have gotten any wetter if it had actually rained. We started the match at 800 yards and I was on the first relay. At the command to fire, I settled the crosshairs of my new Weaver T-24 on the center of the X in the 10-inch X-ring and touched off the Anschutz trigger. Since I was shooting a 16-pound 6BR there was very little recoil. To my surprise, it appeared that I had fired a tracer into the target. I can still recall the bright silver wake of the bullet curving up and then down into the target. I watched it all the way into the X-ring. What a beginning to a great day! Every one of the sighters and 15-record shots gave the same display. In 36 years of shooting I had never seen the like.

What is F-Class?

F-Class is a fairly new shooting discipline, the newest of all the shooting sports in the United States. This type of shooting bridges the gap between long range Benchrest and USA High Power / Fullbore shooting. The game is played shoulder-to-shoulder with long-range prone Fullbore high-power competitors at quite a number of places around the world. Known as F-Class in Canada and the good old USA, it's called "free" class or "fun" class in others.

John Van Marter zero's his new G-250 in Capitan, NM before leaving for Canada.

F-Class, for those that haven't been reading their *Precision Shooting (PS)* magazine cover to cover (Doesn't everyone?) for the last year or so, is fired concurrently with the normal Palma® or Fullbore (as the Commonwealth countries call it) style match.

This game is spreading quickly around the world. In the Commonwealth countries F-Class is often shot at shorter ranges, such as 300 yards or 300 meters, while in the USA it is almost always shot at the Palma® distances of 800, 900, and 1,000 yards. Matches at 600 yards are also becoming popular.

At this point, perhaps I should explain the difference between Palma® and F-Class shooting as shot in the USA. A Palma® match, for those few sheltered shooting souls who don't know, is shot prone with a sling and iron sights in three 15-round stages (one stage each at 800, 900, and 1,000 yards). The highest possible score (HPS) is 450-45x. The Palma® rifle rule states that the *Palma® rifle* will be chambered for a .308 Winchester. A 155-grain bullet is recommended for most matches and *required* in a few championships. Not an easy game!

F-Class shooters, on the other hand, can use most any caliber (with a few restrictions at some ranges). They can use any type of sight, including a scope of any power from a bipod or front rest, and may use a rear bag. No muzzle brakes are allowed (in other words, "prone benchrest"). F-Class shooters shoot alongside Palma® competitors, but normally compete only against other F-Class shooters.

In the USA, the target used for both types of shooters is the National Rifle Association (NRA) long-range target, which has a black aiming mark of 44 inches. However, that includes the 8-, 9-, 10- and X-rings. The X-ring is 10 inches, the 10-ring is 20 inches and the 9-ring is 30 inches in diameter. The 8-ring is 44 inches. The 60-inch 7-ring is in the white, and if you hit the 6-foot square target frame at all, you score a 6.

Six feet sounds mighty big until you consider there is only 3 feet to play with, and a 5-miles per hour (mph) wind pick up or let off can move a .308 Winchester-match bullet well over 3-feet at 1,000 yards. So…you can hit an X and then completely miss in a heartbeat; it happens all the time.

Matches held at 600 yards use the NRA 600-yard target. This is a decimal target with a 6-inch X-ring, 12-inch 10-ring, 18-inch 9-ring, 24-inch 8-ring and 36-inch 7-ring. The 7- through X-rings comprises the bull, or black, area of the target. The 6- and 5-rings are in the white area of the six-foot square target frame. The 6-ring is 48 inches and the 5-ring is 60 inches. Even at 600 yards, the typical match bullet will move over a foot in a mere 5-mph wind.

Matches can be held at shorter distances using the standard NRA targets for those ranges or reduced targets to compensate for the reduced distances and the ability of F-Class rifles to shoot smaller groups than normal high-power rifles and iron sights.

The late George "Farky" Farquharson of Kamloops, British Columbia, Canada, was the man who originated the F-Class style of shooting. His bright, nay, brilliant, idea was to provide a means for those older shooters with poor eyesight or other infirmities to keep shooting past the time they would normally have to retire from competition. Farky reasoned that they would like to keep competing alongside the same people they shot against using iron sights. By starting an F-Class and allowing scope sights and rests, Farky allowed these people to continue enjoyable competition with their friends.

Of course, over time, others who were not old or infirm tried F-Class. Many came from the benchrest/varmint hunter ranks. They found F-Class a great way to enjoy long-range shooting. You don't have to get wrapped up in a hot and heavy shooting jacket, or hold an iron-sighted rifle still with just a sling for support. In F-Class the challenge is different, *but the urge to compete is still there*. Anyone who has ever had the desire to try long-range competition should give it a try.

F-Class is not currently a shooting discipline recognized by the NRA in the United States, but participation is becoming quite active here, mainly in the western states. I feel it will continue to grow because it is a sport that young and old alike can participate in on an equal footing. You don't have to have the eyes of an eagle to shoot F-Class. Your pot-belly will not prevent you from getting into position, even if you rock up and down a bit after you lay down! Your fast, heavy heartbeat will not disturb your sight picture as it does shooting prone with a sling. You will not run out of breath just as you get ready to break the shot, as often happens to the iron-sighted out-of-shape shooter. I, being probably, 25 percent overweight and in less-than-perfect physical shape, tend to be worn out when I finish a 15- or 20-shot string. Not so much from holding my breath as from the intense concentration required to watch the conditions, and shoot a good score in the 4 to 7 minutes it takes me to complete my string. (This is in the USA style "string shooting," not the Commonwealth pair or trio style.)

What prompted me to start shooting F-Class was the love of trying different shooting disciplines. I described my reasons for building a new rifle and trying F-Class in a *PS* magazine article published in the May 2000 issue. If you would like more information on F-Class when you finish this chapter, try my *PS* article and also the fine article by J.J. Conway in the March 2000 issue.

Rules

F-Class rules are very open compared to most shooting disciplines. There are no official USA rules. Naturally, all existing NRA range safety rules apply. Most clubs that hold matches follow the rules of the Rocky Mountain Palma Matches® (RMPM). This great match is put on each year, during the month of June in Raton, New Mexico. The RMPM rules state: "Any rifle, .33 caliber (cal.) or less, any sights, and/or rests are permitted (sand bags, bipods) prone or back position. No muzzle brakes allowed."

You can interpret this as you like. If you feel that a 90-pound Benchrest rifle is what you need, use it. But you'll have to get it up to the firing point and set up in the time the range officer allows you. Plus, and more importantly, you have to get your gear off the line as soon as possible to allow the next relay to put their gear in place. In addition, you have to have it all put away in time to go to the pits when it is your turn to pull targets. Storing your gear gets tough, if you shoot at a range like the Black Canyon Range in Phoenix, Arizona. There you are prohibited from parking your vehicle behind the firing line. It's not like carrying your gear 20-feet to the firing line. Folks, this is a modified high-power match, not a Benchrest match!

Having said this, I must emphasize that shooting F-Class does seem to be much more relaxing than high power. This may be due to the vision and holding problems that go away, to a large degree, when shooting F-Class. It's just a lot more fun!

The Dominion of Canada Rifle Association (DCRA), at the Connaught Range in Canada, has the following F-Class rules: "caliber less then 8mm; trigger weight of more than 1/2 kilo (1.1 pounds); rail guns and muzzle brakes are not allowed. Bipods and/or sandbags (fore and aft) are permitted. Any sights are acceptable". Essentially this is prone Benchrest. There are ammo restrictions to keep bullets inside the military reservation but most cartridges, including most belted magnums, are okay.

Sean Bartholome on the line at Mineral Wells, TX, in his first F-Class match, April, 1999. Rifle=my world record holder 6 BR.

Where is F-Class Shot?

F-Class is fast becoming popular in the USA, and most high-power clubs have either concurrent matches set up with their normal high-power or long-range matches or will allow shooters who want to try F-Class to shoot along with the iron-sight shooters.

In the Southwest, major matches are held in Mineral Wells and Waco, Texas, in Capitan and Raton, New Mexico, and Phoenix, Arizona. Of these, the Rocky Mountain Palma® Match©, held at the NRA Whittington Center in Raton, is the premiere United States match for both F-Class shooters and Palma® enthusiasts. Matches are also held in many other regions of the country. Lodi, Wisconsin, home of the Midwest Palma® Championships, is one such location. More F-Class shooters and matches are appearing every day. Contact your local clubs to shoot in or start an F-Class program.

Foreign Activity

Canada, the home of F-Class, holds a good number of matches for this style of shooting. The premiere match is the DCRA sponsored Canadian Fullbore Rifle Championships (CFRC). This championship is held at the Connaught Range near Ottawa, Ontario. In August of 2000 they hosted the 118th annual competition.

As I write this paragraph (July 18, 2000) **Great Britain** is holding its Bisley Millennium Championships at the Bisley Range in England. F-Class shooters are joining more than 1,500 Fullbore shooters.

Andrew Larkin, a well-known F-Class shooter from **Australia**, graciously replied to my query about this type of shooting in the *Land Down Under*. The following is a quote from Mr. Larkin:

"Distances shot in F-Class here have included everything from 300 yards to 1,200 yards. If we get the chance to shoot farther back, then we will!

There is a long-range match in a couple of weeks in Brisbane (1,000, 1,100, and 1,200 yards). I can send you some high-res digital photos afterward, if this is of interest.

For ranges out to 800 meters (900 yards), the targets used are either the standard Australian fullbore targets, or a specially designed Australian Championship F-Class target. Shooters prefer this championship target because it provides separation of scores that would otherwise result in a shootoff or a count back on the fullbore target, plus the aiming mark is far more friendly to scope shooters.

For ranges 1,000 yards and beyond, there is no defined target—usually, we use the fullbore target (800 yards), but occasionally a "sport" appears. For example, the Brisbane shoot in a couple of weeks will be using the USA Palma® target with a 10-inch white disk pasted in the middle X-ring to give a better scope aiming mark.

Currently, I would estimate that there are around 150 regular F-Class shooters here, with a couple of dozen that travel to attend prize shoots.

F-Class is well supported in Australia with prize shoots. It features in the State Championships ("Queens") for New South Wales (NSW), Queensland, North Queensland, Victoria, and South Australia. There is no national championship yet. F-Class is also included in the Australian Shooting Games, but this is not an "endorsed" event to my knowledge. There are heaps of prize shoots at the district and club levels around the country supporting F-Class. F-Class was also included in the Victorian Match Rifle championship last year (1,000 yards, 1,100 yards, and 1,200 yards).

The upcoming Brisbane shoot is a non-endorsed F-Class match running beside the Australian Match Rifle Championships".

When I contacted *Herr Ralf Rude*, a noted shooter and gunsmith in **Germany** and asked for his help concerning F-Class in his country, he sent me the following information that I will quote verbatim:

"Our one and only range is Diana-Range (D-Gallery) located at Military Training Area Sennelager. Nearest larger town is Paderborn. The range is under control of the British Army and it has 24 targets and firing positions that go up to 1000m.

Description of the range:
If you shoot in the first relay of the day you have to look into the sun. You can guess that the range is in a west to east direction. Not the very best layout for a range, but always better than none. Whether the direction of the range is a relic of the Cold War or was just dictated by the layout of the ranges one can only guess. The ground is flat with small ridges at the firing positions. Grass is kept short by military lawn mowers, so you may have to clean the ground before you put your gear down. Otherwise, you will add some greenish tint to your equipment. The range is not completely surrounded by a forest, so the wind has some channels to go through. One is from the targets to the 300m line and one from the 500m line to the 800m line. The third channel is more or less in range direction. So we have to shoot very often in a fishtail wind. The range has two safety areas, which are under surveillance by the "Range Control Office." Usually on the weekends we have the smaller area. It's a lot cheaper, the drawback is, that no magnum calibers are allowed and as a rule of thumb no cartridge larger than .308 Winchester. But we can shoot 6mm Norma BR or 6, 5x55. If we can afford to book the range during the week with the larger safety area, then cartridges up to .50 Browning are allowed, but the range fee is prohibitive. So this is very seldom done.

Long-range F-class type shooting in Germany is conducted by two federations, the German Branch of the European Rifle Association (ERA) and the Association of Military and Police Shooters (BDMP). While the ERA uses the original F-Class rules with the exception of trigger weight, it is unlimited, provided it is a safe trigger. The BDMP has other rules that allow muzzle brakes, but limit the rifle weight to max. 8.5 kg. The ERA uses the corresponding Bisley target at distances of 300, 500 and 600m. An additional white spot of half the diameter of the V-Bull is glued in the center of the target and is called an "X" as an additional help to sort out ties and as an aiming spot. The BDMP has different targets for distances of 300, 400 and 600m. From 700m to 1,000m the "Palma®" targets are used by both shooting organizations.

Redneck Rifle Team: Bill Wylde - standing: Left to Right—Larry Bartholome; J.J. Conway; John Van Marter; Dick Vesy. 4 out of 5 members have written for P.S.! Photo taken by Beverly.

About 40 F-Class shooters typically attend a match, but we always shoot F-Class, Target Rifle, Service Rifle and BPCR in the same match, separate classes of course. So sometimes the range is pretty crowded, but we are never overbooked and I think it will be some time before this will happen."

South Africa, is also active in F-Class shooting, unfortunately no data on their activity is available at publication time. There is enough shooting that Jan Rousseau in South Africa is writing an article for their NRA magazine.

The Challenge of Long-Range Shooting

There is something unique about long-range shooting that attracts people from all walks of life. I don't know what it is, but once people test the waters they keep coming back. I believe the challenge of trying to overcome the forces of nature in their attempt to move your bullet from the center of the bull's eye draws the shooters back. Of course, that very challenge turns away those that don't like to be defeated by nature and other better prepared shooters.

When you put that final ounce on the trigger and the firing pin flashes forward to set off the primer it starts a chain of events that culminates about a second-and-a-half later with the arrival of your bullet—you hope—at the center of the target. Most American long-range shooters have loaded that bullet in its case and know that feeling of accomplishment when it arrives in the right place. They've also felt let down when, because of a fluke of nature or something they failed do, that bullet is out of the 10-ring or is (horrors!) off the paper altogether.

When I look through my scope and see the mirage flowing across the field of view and lift my head to check what the wind flags are doing, I sometimes get the feeling, "What the heck am I doing here?" I know what I see is going to affect where my next shot goes, and that I am only going to be able to outguess the conditions most of the time. The rest of the time Mother Nature is going to win. But even when she beats the heck out of me, I still go back time and time again. Such is life on the firing line.

Speaking of being defeated by Mother Nature, I don't think there is a big match I go to that myself or someone else in my group of shooting buddies doesn't say, "Why in the heck do we do this?" or words to that effect! Another favorite is "Are we having fun yet?" Both of these sayings are usually uttered after a couple days of shooting in hot, wet weather.

What Do You Need to Shoot F-Class?

F-Class can be shot with almost any rifle that has the capability of firing bullets that are still supersonic at 1,000 yards.

Just because F-Class looks like Benchrest prone style doesn't mean you have to have a Benchrest rifle to win or do well. If you have a good shooting smoke pole of any type or caliber (.223 Remington [fast twist required] and above) that will not foul too much in 20 to 30 shots, you can make your presence known at any F-Class match in the world. I learned this when I tried 1,000-yard Benchrest and found I could be competitive with my 7 BR, .308 Palma® rifle and even my AR-15 space rifle. *It's not the rifle that counts; it is what you do with it!* F-Class takes away many of the physical limitations that keep some shooters out of the winner's circle.

However, if your wife is just begging you to build a new rifle, read the rest of this article and I will detail what goes into a winning F-Class rifle.

There are rifles that are *able* to shoot F-Class and then there are rifles that are *made* to shoot F-Class. In the next few pages I describe what you want in one of those *made to shoot* F-Class rifles.

What cartridge should I use?

F-Class is very lenient as far as what cartridge you use. Since we are only punching holes in paper, we don't need a large case or heavy bullets. F-Class has been successfully shot with many different cases. Consideration, of course, should be given to the wind drift of whatever cartridge you select. However, do not let wind drift be the deciding factor in your choice.

In my discussion of what cartridge to use, I base my thoughts on shooting at 800, 900, and 1,000 yards. Any cartridge that does well there will be fine at the shorter distances, even if there is a case of overkill.

In the USA a .338/416 Rigby, using 105 grains of powder and a 300-grain MatchKing (MK) bullet, would be legal. But I, for one, wouldn't like to shoot that bullet prone off the bags, a bipod, or a sling for the 55 shots needed sighters and record shots of a Palma® and then the 22-25 shots of an any-any match in one day as most USA long-range matches demand. For that matter, I would not like to shoot next to one either!

Come to think of it, I did shoot next to one of these during the 1999 National Benchrest Shooters Association (NBRSA) 1,000-yard Benchrest Championships at the NRA Whittington Range in Raton. Holy smokes, you really knew when it went off! This gentleman was launching those 300-grain pills with 105 grains of powder. The rifle had quite a muzzle brake (which was legal under NBRSA rules).

I, on the other hand, used 30 or so grains of Varget to send my 107-grain moly-coated Sierra 6mm needles toward the target. How did we do? Well, I set a new NBRSA world record of 2.653" for 5 shots in the light-rifle class. What happened to the .338 shooter? When I saw him at the International Benchrest Shooters (IBS) 1,000-yard championships in Remington, Virginia, a couple of months later, he said he was considering building a 6mm of some kind!

When someone asks me about my 6BR and how it compares to the bigger cases, I think back to that match in Raton. During that match I played a little mind game with the .338 shooter. I would pick up one of my little cases and walk over and pick up one of his huge ones. Then I'd look at both, shake my head, give him back his case and return to my bench.

Believe it or not, the .223 has been very successful in Canada. Shooters up in the frozen north are restricted to the .308 and .223 for most of their long-range competitions, so it was natural that the .308 and .223 would be used for F-Class.

The .308 Winchester is probably the most popular case in F-Class shooting. I am not saying that it is the best, just the most popular. The premiere F-class Championships, the DCRA Canada Championships, has been won with a .223, 6BR, 22-250, and .308 Winchester. The hotrod 6.5/284 is used by many as the "poor conditions" rifle.

What cartridge should *you* use for F-Class? Well, I wish I knew! The 6 Norma BR I have been using for the past year or so has worked very well for me, but I keep thinking that less wind drift would surely help on occasion. J.J. Conway, the grand old man of F-Class (By the way, don't let him hear you call him that!), normally takes two rifles with him to a match. He really likes his 6 Norma BR, but he has also been playing with a 6 Vais (6.5x55 necked down and improved). He shoots 54-55 grains of H-1000 with a 107-grain 6mm Sierra and gets 3,360 feet per second (fps). Believe me, he really has an advantage on me at 1,000 yards when the wind is varying! In the past J.J has done extremely well with a 22-250 and a 22 Vais. J.J., by the way, is 76 years young. In 1999, J.J. overheard a conversation between two Canadians looking at the scoreboard. When one asked, "Who is this J.J. Conway?" the other one answered, "Oh, he's some old geezer from Texas." J.J. should really learn to act his age! "Old Geezer" now adorns the back of his Redneck Rifle Team hat.

Bill Wylde, topnotch gunsmith, captain of the Redneck Rifle Team, and long-range rifleman from Indiana, says, "I've used the 22-250 for the past five years in Canada. It is a great cartridge, but results get a little sick at the "longs" when the 1,000-1,200 round point is reached."

Bill, who is also captain of the USA F-Class team at the Canadian Nationals, also said, " Good to hear that the 6BR is still rocking along at 2,000+ rounds. I'll guarantee you that 1,200 will kill a 22-250 for the longs. My little 6BR goes to the range on Sundays and still amazes me."

J.J. Conway & my wife Beverly.

The Canadian F-Class champion in 1994 was Major Colin Brown of Canada, using a .223/.308 combination. In 1995, Bill Wylde (USA), used a 22-250 for all the ranges to become the champion. In 1996, Dr. Jim Thompson from the Maple Leaf country won the match with a .223! In 1997, Bill Wylde was back with a 22-250 and a 6mm Remington (.244) combination. Raimund Weber, noted German long-range rifleman, won the DCRA Canadian F-Class Championship in 1998 using a 6BR. Bill Wylde came back again in 1999 to win for the third time. His choices were a 22-250 at short range and a 6.5-284 at long range.

In 1999, Bill won by one point over J.J. Conway! The match was decided after nine days of shooting in the last match of the last day when J.J. dropped a point.

The factors to consider when choosing a case and bullet for F-Class are numerous. The *most important* among these factors is that the bullet should arrive at the 1,000-yard target while it is supersonic. The speed of sound at sea level is, for ballistic purposes, usually given as 1,120 fps. This means you must use a fairly heavy bullet for that particular caliber. For the .22-caliber this would be at a bare minimum a 70-grain very low drag. It might have been even better at 75- to 80-grains. In the 6mm's, a 95- to 107-grain should be your choice. Shooters of 6.5 bullets normally try 139-142 projectiles. The 7mm's have not been that popular, but there is no reason a 7mm, 150- to 175-grain will not work well. In .30-caliber the normally used 175- to 240-grain bullets have all worked well. We must not, of course, leave out the world-famous Sierra 155-grain MatchKing Palma® bullet, or any of the other brands of 155s, such as the Lapua.

Whatever bullet you choose must be extremely accurate: 1,000 yards is a far piece. This means you will want to use match-quality slugs, even though they cost a bit more. A friendly piece of advice, if you want to be competitive don't scrimp on the bullets or other components!

The case should, if at all possible, be one available from a European maker (Lapua, RWS, Norma, etc.). I say this because you want a case as uniform in all respects as humanly possible. The neck and body thickness variations should be near zero. The case weight must be within a small spread of a few grains. If you use the normal

American cases from Winchester, Remington-Peters, Federal, etc., you will have to sort them and rework them to make them nearly as good as the European cases are out of the box. This can be a very time-intensive operation. This is not to say that great scores are impossible with USA cases, only that uniform cases increase your chances of an outstanding score.

You must do everything possible to make your ammunition as uniform as you can. This includes the bullets, cases, powder charges, and primers. I can't recall ever talking to a championship high-power long-range shooter who didn't believe in weighing his powder charges. He may use a Progressive loader and drop his charges for short range, but when it comes to long range, he'll weigh every time. If you have everything uniform, you will most likely have a small extreme-velocity spread. *This is what you are after at long range.* The various ballistic computer programs and loading manuals show a 2.1-inch average drop difference for a 10-fps difference in velocity. This can play hell with your group size and score at long range. I try to have an Extreme Spread (ES) of less than 25 fps, 10 fps if I can get it. Please note I am not talking standard deviation.

Please keep in mind the statement I am about to make: *"The smaller the group your rifle can shoot the less apparent wind drift that rifle has."* Let me put it this way. Let's say that I have a rifle that can shoot a 20-shot group of 0.0" at 1,000 yards (I wish!). You, on the other hand, have a smoke pole that can shoot a minute of angle or 10-inch group. We both fire a match in which the wind is switching from 11 to 1 o'clock and at a velocity that gives a wind drift of 10 inches left when coming from 1 o'clock and 10 inches right when coming from 11 o'clock. The conditions are such that we can't see the changes... there is no mirage, it has just finished raining and the cotton flags are soaking wet and aren't moving… you get the idea. If we both decide not to make any changes, *which might be the best thing to do in these conditions*, I can tell you what will happen. Every time the wind switches to 11 o'clock I get a scratch 10 at three o'clock and you may get, due to your potential group size, a scratch 10 at 3 or a scratch 9 at 3! When the wind next changes to come from one o'clock, I will get a scratch 10 at 9 and you may get a scratch 10 at 9 or a scratch 9 at 9. I think you get the idea by now. At the end of 20 shots, I have a 200 with x number of X's and you have a "one hundred and something!" I know that this is an extreme example, but the theory does apply.

What about barrels?

When talking F-Class barrels always remember one thing: *No muzzle brakes.* You can imagine what it would be like to be laying two to three feet from someone firing a 30-caliber Magnum prone with a muzzle brake just as you go to touch off your final shot on a clean string. Muzzle brakes are forbidden by the rules!

There are more topnotch barrel makers nowadays than you can shake a stick at. Most all of the barrels used by the better high-power and benchrest shooters are suitable for F-Class. Some makers that come to mind include Krieger, Hart, Shilen, K&P, Border, Douglas, Obermeyer, Lilja, Schneider, and PAC-NOR. Since there are no restrictions on the weight of an F-Class rifle, you can put almost any size barrel on it you want. I would keep rifle balance in mind, though, and the condition of your back since you will have to put this rifle on the ground and pick it back up. Your barrel will most likely be about 30 inches for maximum velocity. It will require a pretty fast twist for a given caliber to handle the long match bullets you will want to shoot (e.g., one in eight for .22, 6mm and perhaps 6.5mm; one in nine for 6.5; one in ten to one in twelve for .30 calibers).

Barrel life? Short or long?

Barrel life can be an even bigger headache for an F-Class shooter than for high-power riflemen. If you try to shoot in all the big F-Class matches around the country, and you use one of the barrel burner cartridges people are fond of, you are likely to have to change barrels before the summer is over! While I don't pretend to know how many rounds I will get out of my 6BR barrels, I will say that my BlackStar Accumax II currently has 2,400+ shots through it. It's showing minimal throat erosion and shoots like a house afire. Think of the situation I am currently facing. I am starting a new shooting season. I

plan to shoot the following major matches: the Alamo Palma® in April, the RMPM in June, the FireCracker Palma® in July, the DCRA (Canadian) National Championships in August, the Texas State Long-Range Championships in October and the Arizona State Palma® Championships in December. This adds up to about 2250 rounds. My current plan is to shoot the BlackStar through the RMPM and then screw my new Krieger barrel on for the rest of the year. If you shoot a barrel burner cartridge, you will have to re-barrel mid-year or use two rifles as J.J. Conway and Bill Wylde are prone to do.

What bullet should I use?

What type of bullets should we use for F-Class? Any kind you want, so long as they group on the target in little bitty bunches. Most shooters will use match hollow point boattail bullets. A few experimental souls are trying very low drag flatbase bullets even at 1,000 yards. These may work out fine, but I will wait for more evidence before I try them. I don't get to spend much time testing on the rifle range, so I can't afford to waste it checking out something that may not work for me. I try a bullet that I know has worked for someone else and work up a load for my rifle and go match shooting. The name of the game is competition!

What brands should you try? Sierra is always a hands down favorite. Berger, JLK, Hornady, Lapua, and Norma all make suitable match

J.J. Conway & his 6mm Vais 107gr. Sierra @ 3360 fps.

projectiles. Any bullet you select should have a high ballistic coefficient (BC) so it will retain maximum velocity at long range.

I don't mean to imply that bullet manufacturers are stating incorrect BCs for their bullets, but I feel you should not put too much faith in the published BCs of any bullet. For example, it has been my experience that if you have three 105 to 107-grain 6mm bullets, the actual wind drift for all three will be very close. A number of writers have commented on this in *PS* magazine articles. The most important factor to keep in mind is how well a given bullet shoots in *your* barrel! Shoot the one that you have confidence in. If you think one brand might blow up in your rifle due to thin jackets, don't shoot it. During the RMPM in June of 2000, one of the competitors who was having bullet blow ups pulled all his projectiles and substituted another brand and weight. Of course, he was way behind before he did this. The sad fact is that he was a fine shooter and could have won the whole championships, except for the mistake in bullet selection.

Bullet blow up!

The only thing that galls a competitive shooter more than putting an X on the wrong target is not having the bullet get to the target. A number of people I know have had bullets "blow up" on them between the rifle muzzle and the target. This happens, most often, to people who use large cases and push bullets above 3,200 fps in well-used barrels with worn throats. Ask Bill Wylde about this. In 1996 he lost the Canadian F-Class Championships because a bullet didn't show up on the target. He lost by one point! The 6BR avoids this by default—with a 6BR we can't get there from here! You just can't safely load enough power in the case to reach that velocity level.

Twists

Fast twists are required for long-range work. In a .223 Remington, a 1-in-9 inches *may* stabilize the 80 grainers. A 1-in-8 inches is a sure thing. With a 6mm I would stick with a 1-in-8 inches even though a 1-in-9 inches should be okay with a match-grade bullets.

In any long-range barrel make sure the twist will stabilize every bullet you plan on using under all shooting conditions. What works in the August heat at Raton may not do the job in February at sea level.

What actions are preferable?

Actions for F-Class have the same requirements that the Palma® or other long-range shooter has for his game. Among these are reliable ignition, stiffness, availability of good triggers, and a large bedding area.

Almost any of the custom actions will work quite well. Some of the ones that come to mind are BAT, Bruno, Hall, Nesika Bay, Stolle Panda, and Viper. Factory actions are more than usable; in fact, most F-Class rifles in use are based on factory actions or are factory-built with little or no modification. If you have a factory rifle that can handle a high BC bullet that will stay supersonic at 1,000 yards, don't hesitate to try F-Class.

What stocks are best?

I have seen wood, aluminum, plastic, and a combination of all three materials used for F-Class stocks. I have seen hunting, varmint, high-power and benchrest stocks on the line. They all work well. *As with most shooting games, the most important item is the nut behind the buttplate!* If you are going to build a new F-Class rifle for use on a front rest, I would recommend a 3-inch wide benchrest stock with an extended forend (similar to the McMillan Magnum Benchrest (MBR stock). A Bill Shehane Tracker stock from D & B Supply will work quite well also. These will give better balance with the long heavy barrels common in F-Class.

My own F-Class rifle was built with a number of goals in mind. I wanted it to meet the qualifications for the 16.5-pound Original Pennsylvania 1000 Yard Benchrest Club (OPBRC) rules with a 12-42x Nightforce scope. This would allow me to change scopes later if necessary, and I could shoot the rifle in any of the OPBRC, IBS, or NBRSA matches. I would also be allowed to compete with it in both the light- and heavy-benchrest gun classes. I knew this decision would be a big compromise, but it has turned out well. The finished rifle weight is 14.62 pounds, to which I added lead to the butt to bring it up to 15.97 pounds. This weight includes the Weaver T-24 scope. This rifle, in my opinion, is just the ticket for F-Class.

What trigger should I use?

F-Class is shot with all types and weights of triggers. In the USA there are no rules on the minimum trigger weight. However, many foreign countries do have weight restrictions. The DCRA (Canada) requires at least a 0.5-kg or 1.1-pound trigger pull.

Any *good* trigger will work well. A few American F-Class shooters use 2-ounce benchrest triggers, but I would recommend a little more weight. You don't want to lose 10 points because, in the heat of the moment, you brushed your trigger and had a round go off. If you are going to use a benchrest type trigger, the only one I recommend is a Jewell. A good two-stage trigger such as an Anschutz or Davies is ideal. The Davies, made by an Australian, Berry Davies, will fit most actions. They are available from Al Warner, famed iron sight maker, long-range shooter, gunsmith and president of Warner Tool Company.

Scopes, Rings and Bases

You will see a large variety of riflescopes in use by the people shooting F-Class. These scopes come in all powers and sizes. The most common seems to be around 24-25 power. A number of shooters use a variable power scope and many of those use the newer Leupold 30mm tube 8.5-25x scope, which has a large 56mm objective lens. This provides a bright, clear image in all conditions. Those that have the money (or must be seen with the very best) use the large and heavy Night Force 56mm variable scopes. These are considered the very best by most long-range Benchrest and F-Class shooters. What do I use? I have a new style Weaver 24x with a plain old crosshair. Unfortunately, I think this scope has been discontinued. The crosshair is three times as thick as the Leupold fine crosshair in their 24x and shows up much better in low light conditions.

I would recommend a power range of 12x-25x as the best all around. I favor the higher power myself. While I have seen a number of people who use more power than 25x, the mirage and small field of view become a handicap in many cases. I used 36x in a prone 1,000-yard match *one* time! This was in the desert southwest and I wouldn't want to do it again. Being somewhat slow in the head, I tried the same scope in a 1,000-yard BENCHREST match. There won't be a third time. The mirage is just too much. When all is said and done, just use what you have when you start this game. Most any target scope will work quite well.

It is, however, *very important* that the scope is mounted so that you can adjust the bullet impact onto the 1,000-yard target. With a number of scopes this is not easy due to the small adjustment range for windage and elevation. Most scopes will require that the bases be shimmed to reach 1,000 yards. The best option would be a tapered base with 20- to 30-minutes of adjustment built into it.

You can test your setup by shooting your rifle at 25 yards and adjusting the bullet impact to be 10 inches high. If you have this much adjustment you will be able to get on paper at 1,000 yards for elevation.

You should keep in mind that some matches may require you to shoot down to 300 yards, and out to 1,000 yards. You have to have a scope and mounting system that allows you to do that. Ideally you would set your bullet impact at 25 yards by shimming or adjusting the base with the

John Van Marter; Larry Bartholome; J.J. Conway.

scope adjusted in the center of its adjustment range. To do this, gently turn the scope knobs to one stop and the other while counting the minutes and then set the knob for the center of the adjustment range. This means that at 1,000 yards you will have maximum windage adjustment in the scope, and this is where you will need it the most. Keep in mind that at 1,000 yards a 5-mph wind can move a .308 Winchester match bullet three feet!

There *are* rings, and then *there are rings*. My action is a Stolle Panda, which has a built-in dovetail rail for Kelby style rings. I decided to use Jewell *live-center* rings to prevent the possibility of the scope tube bending when I shimmed the rings to give me the extra elevation I wanted for 1,000-yard shooting. Burris makes rings with the same basic principle and they have the added advantage of additional inserts, which are offset to allow you to gain the elevation you need.

Another thought to keep in mind is, given the large barrel and scope objective lens diameters; you must make sure your rings are high enough to give you clearance between the scope and the barrel.

Bipods and things!

In F-Class you are allowed to use a front rest and, if you like, you are also allowed a rear rest. The use of a rest or rests is up to you. When F-Class started in Canada and the USA, most shooters used a bipod attached to the forend rail on their prone target rifles. Bipods work quite well, and work even better when used in conjunction with a rear bag.

I prefer a benchrest type front rest and rear bag combo. The bipods don't seem to be repeatable shot to shot. There is just too much movement. J.J. Conway used a bipod for four years, until he tried my setup and switched.

There are many different brands of bipods and rests. Take your time picking one out. Go to a few matches and see what the better shooters are using before you lay down your hard-earned cash or put your life in hock for a piece of plastic.

Speaking of bipods, I just saw a very sturdy looking bipod on the Internet made by Australian F-Class shooter and gunsmith, Andrew Larkin. This one has a very impressive look, it's not

your run-of-the-mill bipod.

The bipod does have its advantages. Its lightweight and fast set up compared to my 11-pound front rest and 10-pound rear bag, has made me consider changing equipment. But I may just have to compromise and take the heavy sand out of my bags and replace it with normal weight sand. This should reduce my range load by a few pounds.

Reloading for F-Class

The most important loading technique you can use to improve your long-range score is to *weigh each and every powder charge*. I know it's possible to shoot good, perhaps even great, scores with powder-measured dumped charges, but in the long term you will be much better off using a good quality scale to weigh each and every charge.

Having said this, I must tell you about a friend of mine, Otto Homberg. He shot a 450-28x Palma course at the 2000 RMPM matches using dumped charges in his 6BR. However, I am certain he did this *despite* the dumped charges, not *because* of them! Otto has a very good rifle and knows how to point it. He usually shoots high scores no matter what he uses!

To load ammunition for F-Class you just need the normal reloading tools. You can, of course, go whole hog and load as the benchrest shooters do. This may or may not be overkill depending on how high up on the result list you would like to be.

One thing you should look into is the uniformity of your cases. As the benchrest shooters found out many years ago, the uniformity of the case walls and necks can greatly affect the grouping of your ammunition. I hate turning case necks, but I do it for F-Class. If you use Lapua or one of the other foreign brass makers, you may be able to bypass the tedium of this step in case prep.

You can apply as many of the benchrest case prep tricks as you care to take the time to perform on your brass. It may help your score. Me, I just use Lapua brass and turn the necks to fit the chamber. That's it!

I do one other thing in reloading my ammo. I check each bullet with an Ogive Checker. This is a little chamber-like device that attaches to a dial indicator. You slip the bullet into the chamber and it gives you a reading of the distance from the point where the ogive on the bullet touched the lands to the base of the boattail on the bullet. I haven't run any tests to prove that this makes a difference at 1,000 yards, but to my mind, if the distance from the base of the bullet to the point it contacts the lands in the barrel is different, then the bullet has a different shape. This cannot help the bullets go into one hole at long range. The BC must be different. I have found differences up to 0.035" in 500 bullets of the same lot.

Another thing to keep an eye on is primer seating. Be gentle; be consistent. Use a hand-type primer seater if possible.

Cost

One factor you shouldn't overlook in the equation is a smaller case costs less to feed. Smaller, lighter bullets cost less than big, heavy ones. Large cases use more powder than smaller ones (large powder charges also eat up barrels quicker). These factors equate to lower costs, which can lead to more shooting, which can contribute to higher scores. One other cost factor that many shooters, including myself (until recently) fail to consider in the equation is how much it costs in barrel life every time you pull the trigger. If a barrel cost $400, and will only give you 2,000 rounds of accurate life, it is costing you twenty cents *plus* the cost of the ammo each and every time you squeeze the trigger. Add this to the cost of reloading match ammo and the cost per trigger pull is about fifty cents.

Preparing For Your First F-Class Match

The first thing you should do before going to your first F-Class match is to get a copy of the match program and find out what ranges you will shoot and how many shots you will fire. I always figure I will need 60 rounds for a Palma® match and as many as 30 for a 20-shot 1,000-yard string. Make sure you take enough ammo. Don't scrimp on the sighters.

Once you know what distances you will fire, you need to get zeros for those ranges. If you don't have easy access to a local range with the needed distances, don't panic! Get yourself a computer ballistics program, measure the height of your scope centerline above the centerline of the bore, and find out the altitude of the range and likely temperature. You will also need to know the velocity of the bullets you are using. Using this data you can print out a come-up sheet.

Go to the local 100-yard range and put up a target at least three feet tall. Draw a plumbed vertical line from top to bottom. Put an aiming point near the bottom and zero for 100 yards. Next, mark horizontal lines on the target at the required height for 100 yards to hit at whatever ranges you will shoot at. For example: 300, 600, 800, 900, and 1,000 yards. Come up what you think are the required number of clicks on your scope to hit each line and zero for every distance and record the knob settings. The reason for the plumbed line is to keep you from tilting your rifle or to determine if the crosshair is crooked (canted). If you run out of adjustment before you reach the 1,000-yard line, you will have to shim your rear base or ring. (See the section on *Scopes, rings, and bases*)

You will find as you shoot the *actual* longer distances that your short-range windage zero will be off to the right and you will have to put on about a minute left wind at 1,000 yards and less as you come closer to the firing line. This is normal and is due to the right hand spin of the bullet causing a drift to the right.

Let me say here it is *very important* that you know your "**no wind zero.**" How else are you going to know what to do when the wind changes from the right to the left or just quits altogether? You need to know it for all ranges.

Shooting Your First F-Class String

Before the match starts, or rather before your relay starts, go up to the firing line and observe the weather conditions. Watch the way the wind is blowing and what it does to the flags and mirage. Take your scope up with you and watch all the indicators. Note how long the wind cycle is; that is, how long does it take the wind to pick up and then drop off? How long is the time between cycles? Pay attention to what the better shooters are saying about the wind. If you don't have a clue about what the wind is worth, ask one of the better shooters. Just don't ask him or her while they are in their prep time—when they are getting their head screwed on for the match. If you ask in a nice way, I am sure they will help you. Just don't be a pest! One day you'll be able to help someone else.

Move your equipment up to the line when it's time for your relay. I use a shooting mat to lay on, but most anything will work as a ground cloth. I put my mat down first and then place my front and rear rest down. I look down range and try to line up my front rest with my target. To do this, I will sometimes put my chin in the rear bag and then sight over the front rest and move it until it points at *my* target. Next, I place my rifle in the front rest and rear bag, and slide the rifle back and forth to settle it in the bags. It also helps to beat on the rear of the stock to settle the rear bag. I then look through the scope and move the rest until the rifle is aligned with the right target. I move the front rest adjustments to center the crosshairs on the center of the X-ring and again slide the rifle back and forth and hit the rear stock top to settle the bags in their new position. Make sure the rest and rifle are level and not canted to one side. Once I am happy with the rifle setup, I take off the scope caps and put them aside on the mat.

I move my shooting stool or range bag up to where I can reach it if I need anything during the string, and remove my loading block, stopwatch, scorebook, pencil, wind chart, score card, and ammo box. I then place the number of rounds I will need in my loading block. I keep the record rounds and sighter rounds in a different part of the block. I place them where I can easily reach them while firing. By this time, the 3-minute ready period has started and I will dry fire a few rounds to settle both the rifle and myself.

While all this is going on I try to keep an eye on the weather conditions. I then make sure I have a scorekeeper and give my card to him or her. I tell the scorekeeper to call out the number of and the value of each shot so I can hear it. I also warn then that I tend to shoot very fast. I shoot so fast that if they drift off for even a second they could miss a shot.

Now it is time to dope the wind for the first sighter. I have already set the sights for the correct elevation and zero wind before I brought my gear to the line. I now double-check my elevation and decide what to use for wind. I change my windage knob to my best guess and write both it and my starting elevation in my scorebook.

When the fire command is given I double-check my best guess, and if conditions are bad, I wait until a few good shooters have fired. Then I study where their rounds have hit. When I am sure I have the best possible guess on the rifle, I let fly and immediately remove the fired round from the chamber and lay another round in the loading port. While doing this I try to remember to look at the flags and I look through the scope at the mirage. By this time (hopefully), the target has come up with an X. I listen to hear if the scorekeeper has seen the shot and called out the value. If this is my first sighter, I quickly plot it for future use, close the bolt, make a decision on the next shot and let fly. From this point on I attempt to get a rhythm going between me, the conditions, and the target puller to enable me to finish my string as quickly as possible.

Whenever the target comes up I have my hand on the bolt knob, ready to close it as soon as I can see where the last shot went. I make an instantaneous correction and shoot the next round. All the while I try to analyze the mirage and flags to keep the shots in the middle. The fewer changes I have to deal with, the better I like it. Oh yes, please don't forget to announce to the scorer when you are going for record!

If you are prepared for your first F-Class relay, I am sure you will enjoy it as much as I did my first one.

Sighters

It is important you know where your sighting shots are going to hit from both a clean and a fouled barrel. Let's say you only have two sighting shots, your first one out of a very (RemClean) clean barrel hits in the 8-ring at 7 o'clock.It would be of interest to know that the second one will move back up to the middle of the X-ring, without any sight changes. Knowing where your sighters will turn up will allow you to get centered up in the middle of the X-ring much faster —and the middle is where you want to be!

How you clean your barrel can have a profound affect on where your first round hits after cleaning. With my normal cleaning procedure I always had a low, left nine or eight at 800 yards from a clean bore. When I started using two dry patches after my Koil oil instead of one that problem went away. Two patches and the first shot is dead on. You will have to experiment to find out what works for you.

Shooting Strategies

There are many strategies a shooter can use to overcome the varying atmospheric conditions that affect our scores at long range. The British Commonwealth shooters and coaches will tell you that you must learn to read the flags, grass, mirage, etc. They say you must plot every shot and write down all of your sight changes. Of course, they shoot two or three shooters to a firing point (or mound as they term it) and have a lot more time to plot this information before it is their time to shoot another shot. Given their style of shooting, this is without a doubt the best way to achieve a good result.

However, it takes the average shooter a very long time to become competent at this. I am not the least bit competent, even though I have been shooting long-range off and on for 30 years. I always forget to look at all the indicators of wind conditions. I am forever getting wrapped up in the mirage that I normally pay close attention to and thus ignore all else. Since I am primarily a mirage doper or mirage reader (if you can say I can dope or read any condition), I am at a total loss when there is no mirage to be seen.

For the novice USA F-Class shooter, I am of the firm belief that the best policy is to plot very little, if any, information in your scorebook. Don't forget to make notes in your book after you finish firing (this is my biggest failing). Spend your time watching the mirage and/or the wind flags, grass, etc. As soon as your target comes out of the pits with your shot marker on it, make an instantaneous evaluation of what change, if any, you need to make for the next shot, and put the target frame back down in the pits! I have pointed out to a number of shooters, both old and new, the fact that while they had their noses in the scorebook the weather conditions were changing. The fewer changes you shoot through the better. If I can finish my 15- to 20-record shots in half the time you take, most of the time I am going to

beat you hands down.

Let me give you an example. We are both shooting at 1,000 yards, the wind is from the right, worth about three minutes (or 30 inches), and our last sighters were both pinwheel X's. You stop to plot that X in your scorebook. I fire my first record shot, reload for my second record and start looking through my scope as the target comes up. I notice the mirage is starting to let off even though I have another pinwheel X. I hold out into the 10-ring on the left side and fire just as you let go with your first record shot. My target comes back up with my second record shot as another X.

Since you were writing in your scorebook, you did not notice the subtle change in the mirage (it's hard to remember what the mirage looked like on the last shot when you have been plotting your elevation, windage, and shot hit for 30 seconds). You fire your first record shot and because of the letoff you get a 10-ring at 3 o'clock. I fired my third shot just after your first; since the mirage was picking back up and I *saw* it, I didn't hold off as much (left edge of the X-ring) and got another mid-X.

Remember, my eye is not out of the scope for more than a couple of seconds during the reload. Meanwhile, you are over there looking at your target through your scope and shaking your head wondering what is going on. You do your plot thing again, and while you are doing that the wind does a complete switch, and starts coming from the left.

I have been lying there watching the mirage

Left to right: Bill Wylde & Dick Vesy.

let up and then reverse. *This means it is coming from the left!* I hold up on firing and watch as you finally roll over. You load your rifle and take a quick look at the mirage (Forgot to look at the flags? Too upset?), the mirage intensity looks the same as last time so you hold out in the 10-ring at 9 o'clock. The target goes down, stays there for a while (always a bad indicator), and comes back up with a miss indicated. Now you are really PO'ed! "That can't be", you mumble, but I'm here to tell you, it can.

A few years back, I made this very mistake shooting iron sights at Raton, during the Rocky Mountain Palma© Matches. My buddy, Lyn Chowning, shot next to me, finished in half the time, and was off the firing line when the switch came through. Needless to say, Lyn doesn't let me forget it, and I am glad he reminds me, otherwise, I might forget the valuable lesson I learned that day.

The method of shooting F-Class I am advocating is usually called **"chasing the spotter."** *Bear in mind that I do watch the flags and mirage and, on some occasions, any other indicator such as the grass and dust to the best of my ability.* In F-Class you can, in some conditions, watch the trace of the bullet go into the target if your rifle does not recoil too much. I do not spend any time writing in a scorebook. I note the time, weather conditions, firing point, sight settings, etc., before I start shooting. I plot where my sighter shots go to help me learn what to start out with in the future. I also write down my sight settings and my score when I finish. I note any unusual happenings that occurred while I shot.

Most of the long range-shooters I have conversed with, and this includes those I "speak with" via the Internet, say that you should not hold outside the 10-ring or, at the very most, outside the black or bull while shooting in a match. These people click their scope knobs just like an iron sight shooter clicks his rear sight. I can never remember where I'm at, and hate to take the time to write down what I am doing. Also, since I am required to wear bifocals, I have a hard time seeing the knobs to read them anyway. Picking up a magnifying glass to read them just slows me up. In the American style of string shooting, any delay can mean death to a good score.

I, however, am pretty comfortable holding anywhere on the target or even off the target on occasion. If the conditions are changing in large and variable amounts and I feel that I can stay up with them, rather than holding up and waiting for a condition to come back I will hold off large amounts. I have on a few occasions in Raton, and in Mineral Wells held over on the next target frame. I do this when I am chasing the spotter and the changing conditions. I watch where the spotting disk is placed for each shot and correlate that with what I see in the mirage and wind flags and "follow" the previous shot. I seem to do this when I am "in the zone," and it comes naturally. When I hold up because of changing conditions, I have lived to regret it in almost every case. I suspect this has a lot to do with my shooting style and impatient attitude and may not work very well for someone else. Every shooter must learn what works well for himself.

Thoughts on Wind Drift and Doping

One of the factors in long-range high-power shooting that we often overlook is that we compensate for what the wind is and mirage does to a large degree. What this amounts to is a negation of the effect of the wind on the bullet flight.

If you and I shoot at the same time and your rifle caliber has an inherent wind drift less than mine, you would think that you would win hands down. But this is often not the case! Have you ever considered why?

The main reason, I believe, is what I stated back in the first sentence of this section, "we compensate for what the wind is and mirage does to a large degree." If I compensate better than you, I win; if not, you win. Luck does play a small factor in this equation, but we'll discuss that another time. The inherent wind drift of the two cartridges enters into the equation, *but to a very large degree is negated by our individual wind doping skills.*

During the RMPM at Raton, in June of 2000, I lost 4 points at 1,000 yards on the second day due to not reading the wind well enough. These points were the only points I lost in 4 days of shooting). I got to thinking that J.J. Conway's 6 Vais, with a 430-fps advantage over my 6 Norma BR, was going to kick my butt in the aggregate. We were both using 107-grain Sierra 6mm bullets. However, J.J lost a point at 900 that day, three at 1,000 on the third day and another point at 1,000 yards on the final day. I finished the three Palma(matches with a 1346-102x to J.J.'s 1344-88x. You see what I mean? Less wind drift does not mean you are going to win matches, it just means it may be easier for you to win. This is not to say that a round with much less wind drift is not an advantage. What I am trying to get across is that it may not be as big a factor as many shooters feel it is.

Other factors also come into the equation. If my cartridge is more inherently accurate than yours, I'll have an advantage that will tend to take away some of the wind drift advantage you have.

If my rifle recoils much less than yours, I may be able to shoot more accurately than you, particularly in the long term. My chances of jerking the trigger or hunching my shoulder into a shot are reduced to a large degree.

When you consider all these mitigating factors clinically (without emotion), it should become more apparent why the 6 Norma BR, 6-250 and cartridges of this ilk are becoming so popular. These small calibers and cases perform completely out of proportion to what their diminutive size would indicate.

Mirage

Mirage or visible heat waves can be an excellent indicator of what the wind is doing. I use it more than any other item to dope the wind. Of course I live and have lived for most of my shooting life in the southwestern United States. The mirage may be so bad at times that the target bull becomes all but indistinguishable through our target scopes. Do not let this get to you. Just keep in mind what it looked like on the last shot and adjust according to what happened.

Many times you won't be able to see the scoring rings. I hate when this happens and I have a hard time visualizing (i.e., remembering) where I held for the last shot. Memory loss is a terrible affliction for a rifleman, but at least I remember which end the bullet comes out!

Wind Drift

You can get a good idea of how much your bullet drifts in a given amount of wind by referring to the ballistic charts in the back of many reloading books or by using a ballistic program on your personal computer, which is what I use most of the time.

Long-range riflemen must put up with wind drifts of enormous proportions, which seem to change with every blink of an eye. Wind drift is a factor of bullet speed and the bullet's BC. The faster the bullet velocity and/or the higher its BC, the less drift it will have.

Bullets for use in F-Class must have high BCs for their caliber. Various manufacturers figure their BCs in different ways, and it is easy to become overloaded with the numbers. High-level high-power shooters I trust have told me they have experimented at 1,000 yards and found there is not much difference between the various manufacturers bullets when it comes to the retained velocity at 1,000 yards.

I believe if you have two match bullets of about the same weight, and both have boattails and reasonable metplates, you could shoot either one and not have any appreciable difference in wind drift.

The Sierra 6mm 107-grain bullet I use in my 6BR at 2,930-fps has a BC of 0.527. This gives me a drift at 1,000 yards of 39.55 inches in a 5-mph wind from 90 degrees. This compares very well with the Sierra 190-grain MatchKing .30 caliber's 0.533 BC.

A .30-caliber magnum loaded with a 190-grain MatchKing traveling at 3,000 fps has 37.29 inches of drift. Even if you move upscale to the

Wife—Beverly at DCRA.

hotrod 6.5/284 Winchester, the cartridge of choice for a lot of long-range champions is loaded with a 142-grain MatchKing (BC = 0.595) at a velocity of 3,000 fps and would have a drift of 33.38 inches. You can see from this the 6BR has more drift. I don't dispute this fact. In fact, the 6.17 inches difference between the 6.5/284 and the 6BR would move the bullet from the very center of the X-ring to the 10/9-ring line on the Palma® target. *However*, for this to happen *both* shooters, the 6BR and 6.5/284 rifleman/riflewoman (rifleperson?) *would have to misjudge the wind to exactly the same degree.* A 15- or 16-percent difference in a 5-mph wind is very hard to read when shooting at 1,000 yards. We are *only* talking 0.75 mph here!

Changes to Targets

It has been suggested that USA F-Class shooters should change to a target with smaller scoring rings. At this point in time, I truly believe this would be a mistake.

Both F-Class and Palma® type shooters benefit from shooting together. This is only possible if we use the same target. There are not enough long-range matches held as it is. If we try and complicate things by tossing in an additional target or separating the F-Class people from the Palma® types, we will only lose participation. While a few F-class shooters have cleaned the Palma® course, so have a number of Palma® competitors cleaned the F-Class course. Nancy Tompkins-Gallagher and Tom Whitaker immediately come to mind, as iron-sighted rifle people who shoot like machine rests.

The highest F-Class score I have any knowledge of (after exhaustive research) is a 450-39x out of 450-45x. There has been some discussion about starting an F-Class 450 club. This came up as a joke because one of the best F-Class shooters in the USA, (who has shot in the Canadian Nationals a number of times), has never cleaned the Palma® target. The F-Class competitors at the 2000 RMPM were ribbing him about it!

I believe the targets are fine the way they are, so long as we don't start having to have shootoffs because more than one shooter has a 450-45x clean. Most people have no idea how hard it is to keep 45 shots in a 20-inch circle at 800, 900, and 1,000 yards, much less all of them in a 10-inch X-ring!

It may be prudent to start collecting F-Class scores in the USA and devise a classification system. Not everyone, no matter how hard they try, can shoot a 450. Most of these people just enjoy shooting and deserve a chance to receive some form of recognition for their efforts in the form of trophies and awards.

In this regard I have noticed that for at least the last two years, the organizers of the RMPM in Raton have given awards to the top three shooters, only for the aggregate. The rest of the awards were presented for yard lines, daily matches, and were given to the highest shooters *who were not aggregate winners*. This gives shooters an incentive to continue coming back.

Canada 2000

I am writing this paragraph on August 30, 2000. I returned last night from the DCRA's 118th Canadian Fullbore Rifle Championships at the Connaught ranges just outside Ottawa. After 9 days of shooting I am done in!

This was the first time I have attended the DCRA Championships, but I am sure it will not be my last. Fifty-eight shooters from the US attended the CFRC this year. Of the seven F-Class US shooters who where able to stay for the entire 9 days of shooting, four finished in the top ten in the Aggregate for the 21st Century. In fact, Bill Wylde, Dick Vesy and myself finished 1,2,3.

I would like to mention at this point that two German shooters attended the matches as F-Class competitors. They were Wolfgang Scholze and Harold Potker. These two riflemen shot extremely well and would have been up in the top of the Aggregate for the 21st Century if they had shot all the matches required for that Aggregate. Wolfgang did win the F-Class Farquharson Trophy for being high F-Class shooter in the MacDonald Steward Grand Aggregate. Both of these gentlemen fired 6 BR's.

Bill Wylde shot a 22-250 out though 600 yards and a 6.5-284 at 700,800 and 900 meters. Dick Vesy fired a 6 BR at the short ranges and a 6.5-284 at long range. I used my trusty old 6BR all the way. If I go back I will consider a separate rifle for long range, if only to have a back up rifle. J.J. Conway had his 6BR go south on him and had to switch to his 6 Vais, however, he did not have enough ammo on hand to shoot all the matches he would have like to have used it in.

These matches are very different from anything I have shot in the past and I have shot a lot of different competitive shooting games in a number of countries.

The major difference affecting a US shooter is they shoot in pairs up north. One shooter shoots a shot and the other scores it. The second shooter then shoots and the first scores his shot. Each shooter has 45 seconds to fire his shot once the target comes out of the pits. This goes on until the match is complete. This style of shooting puts a premium on wind reading skills. It is much harder or next to impossible to chase the spotter. Your score can also be affected by who you are paired with. If your point partner shoots very slowly it is harder for a US shooter to stay up with conditions. Many Commonwealth shooters plot every shot and all the conditions after every shot. Make sure they score your shot after you fire. They are not used to fast shooters and can miss seeing you shoot. I had one partner who was always asking me if I had shot already.

The matches are by and large shorter than ours. All matches have 2 sighters, but vary in length from 7 or 10, to 15 or 20 shots.

We shot at 300 yards, 300 meters, 500 yards, 600 yards, and 700, 800, 900 meters. The targets are the DCRA 5-V printed on white paper, not the light tan we use in the US.

For a first timer it was a confusing 10 days. The vast number of matches shot and the strange names of those can cause you to go around in circles if you are not careful. You must also be very careful when you submit your entry. One very good US shooter was unable to fire in the Long Range Challenge match due to a screw up in his entry. Be advised that you may have to enter more than one time, using more than one form depending on what you wish to shoot.

While an F-Class shooter can win a metal in any of the matches, the Championships is and has been for 118 years designed for Target Rifle (TR) shooters. These rifle men and women shoot iron sighted rifles prone using slings for support. It is a tough game and the scores shot by the winners are unbelievable in many cases. A number of times the high TR person outshot the F-class.

The number of junior shooters must be seen to be believed. The same goes for female competitors. A total of about 350 entries fired in the matches.

There are matches that are considered open and which the F-Classers can win outright. Among these are the "Long Range Challenge", which Bill Wylde won this year, with a 391.42v out of 400. The Long Range Challenge is 4

Unknown F-Class Rifle.

strings of 20 shots over two days fired at 900 meters. Bill also won the "Aggregate of the 21st Century", which is a type of Grand Aggregate shot over nine days.

Dick Vesy of Boardman, Ohio won the F-class/TR-O final match with a 149-14V. This match consists of 15 shots at 800 meters followed by 15 at 900 meters. Only the top 10 F-class shooters are allowed to shoot in this match. The top ten are based on scores fired to that point in the "Aggregate of the 21st Century Championships". The results of this match become the last stage of the 21st Aggregate.

The most fun I had in Ottawa was during the Lum Trophy (Coon Dawg) F-Class team match. The US squared off against two fine Canadian teams. The US team, the "Redneck Rifle Team", consisted of Bill Wylde, team captain and coach, with Skip Epp, Van Alstyne, Texas, acting as upwind flag reader. The shooters were, J.J. Conway, of San Antonio, Texas, John VanMarter, of Capitan, New Mexico, Dick Vesy, from Boardman, Ohio and myself.

The "Canada's Old F's" was staffed by Jim Thompson, Colin Brown, Van Varve, Dave Runbold and John Tetlow. This team finished a close second. The other Canadian team, "F-Gang", consisting of John Poulin, John Ingoldsby, Claude Pilon, and Daniel Chisholm finished third.

The match was 10 shots each at 800 and 900 meters. The winds were tricky, changing value and worth about four to six minutes on my 6 BR. I believe the wind picked up some after I finished firing. Bill did an outstanding job of keeping us in the 5 and V rings, with an able assist from Skip Epp. As I recall we dropped only two points at 800 and one at 900 meters. The winning score of 397-59V's was a new record for the match.

J.J. Conway fired his 6 Vais wildcat, Dick Vesy shot his 6.5-284, John VanMarter sent rounds into the V ring with his 6/250 and I used my 6 BR. An interesting discussion was held between 800 and 900, when we were trying to decide if J.J. should shoot his 6 Vais, since one of his shots had went a little high at 800. J.J. stuck with his rifle and fired a 50 with 10 V's! Remember J.J. is 76 years old.

When the match was over and the scores totaled, all retired to the verandah of the club house where the losers bought drinks for the winning team and Bill Wylde tried to blow the Charles Young bugle which is part of the tradition of this match.

6.5/08 F-Class Rifle, 29 lbs., belongs to Brian Slink, Baldwinsville, NY.

The Future—2001

Next year you ask? Well, Canada and DCRA Championships are calling. I can hear the United States F-Class Team Captain, Bill Wylde, playing reveille on *PS* contributor Charles Young's bugle. The US team is forming for another charge. The competition will be tougher than ever, with teams coming (we hope) from England, Germany and Australia, but I have every confidence that Bill will lead the way to victory for the USA once again.

CANADA 2002

The DCRA Executive Committee has decided "in principle" to support a World F-Class Championship at the Connaught Range in Ottawa, Canada, in August 2002. This match will be set up similar to the World Palma® Championships, which are held every 3 to 4 years in different countries around the world. The targets, course of fire (for both the individual and team matches), and team sizes have yet to be finalized. The match will be held directly after the 2002 CFRC.

2005?

At the time of publication, it is not known where the *second* World F-Class Championships will be held. To get back in sequence with the World Palma® Championships the second World F-Class Championships will be shot in 2005. A number of countries, including Great Britain, would like to host the matches. From my perspective (proximity), Raton, would be an outstanding location!

If the NRA would start supporting F-Class in the United States, especially in regards to rules (darn few I would hope), registering matches, and keeping national records, the sport will continue to grow.

Thomas J. Whitaker, D.D.S. well-known Palma® team member and National Long-Range champion, has just (August 2000) proposed to the NRA (USA) that they recognize a "full-range prone-course of fire. This course would include slow-fire prone shooting at ranges of 300 to 1,000 yards. Including categories for 'prone with optical sights (TRO)' allowing those with poor or failing eyesight to compete. TRO will also bring back shooters who have retired from the sport because of failing/poor eyesight. Those who wish to compete but cannot (or do not want to) shoot the prone position may compete using a rest and may use a high-performance caliber in the F-Class."

It is up to the NRA's High-Power Committee to act on this proposal!

In Closing

I would like to take this opportunity to invite all of you who read this to come out and try F-Class. Even if you have never fired a round at long range I am sure you will enjoy the experience and challenge of shooting beyond a half a mile.

Chapter 12

Bill Shehan Zeroes In
On 1,000-Yard Accuracy

by Dave Scott

The early days

For decades Bill Shehane was a shooter looking for a sport. After a childhood of plinking and small game hunting, the North Carolinian ventured into handgun silhouette. After 12 years of competition, he finally decided that splatting metal turkeys was for the birds. So he and his wife Diane acquired compound tournament bows and took a shot at indoor and field archery. But launching aluminum tubing failed to give them sufficient twannng for the buck.

Then Bill discovered short-range benchrest, and for the first time he felt he had come home. However after several seasons of assaulting mothballs practically under his nose, he found himself wistfully gazing past the 200-yard targets, yearning for something to challenge the long-range possibilities of his rifles.

He found a satisfying answer to his distant longings in sniping groundhogs, which offered targets as far as he could hit 'em. But in the beginning that just wasn't far enough, so he acquired a Remington 40-X and rebarreled it with a Hart tube chambered for the far-ranging 6-284. Now he found himself seriously equipped for the long-distance activity he craved. He also built an even more serious long-range competition rig, this one using a 32" long, 1.35"-diameter Lilja barrel chambered by Ken Rhyne in 6-284 and screwed into a Hart action. The metal was set in a laminated-wood benchrest stock with a 5" wide forend. It was with this rifle that

Bill won the first 1,000-yard benchrest match in North Carolina, with a 7.2" group. (Shoot a group like that today, and you won't even win your relay.)

From those groundhog beginnings, Bill made two important discoveries. First, he came to appreciate just how effective the 6-284 is in reaching distant pastures, particularly with hefty bullets weighing in at just over 100 grains. Second, much later he came to realize that his Hart-barreled 40-X vermin rig was nothing less than a once-in-a-lifetime gun. In competition this hunting rifle would soon soar to true Hummer status, elevating it to the role of Bill's competition rifle and eventually relegating the heavier competition rig to varmint hunting.

Bill with his only fiberglass-stocked 1,000-yard rifle, assembled specifically for the 16 1/2-pound class at Williamsport, Pa. and chambered for the 6-284 Shehane Short.

The start of 1,000-yard benchrest down South

Other local shooters besides Bill had cravings to try some long-range work. John Seamon and gunsmith Ken Rhyne envisioned the idea of starting long-range benchrest competition patterned after the 1,000-yard activities of the Williamsport, Pennsylvania club. John Seamon leased two adjoining farms in the northern part of North Carolina's Iredell County. Portable benches were positioned on one farm, and the targets were placed 1,000 yards away on the other. And so began the first informal 1,000-yard competition in North Carolina, or for that matter in the entire South.

The matches were a big and immediate success, but a little over a year later the long-rangers lost their leases. It was then that two of the regular shooters stepped forward with a more permanent plan. Mike McNeil owned a large chicken farm in Wilkes County, and he pledged to build a 1,000-yard range on his property, aided in the project by his friend Johnny Byers. In a way, the project echoed the fervent hope expressed in the movie "Field of Dreams". If we build it, they muttered nervously among themselves, shooters will come.

Two months later, Bill was invited to look over their efforts. He was delighted to find 10 covered benches and sturdy target holders the required distance downrange. But what to call it? As if by divine intervention, two hawks soared by, and taking the hint, Mike christened the fledgling facility Hawks Ridge, realizing that Hawks Ridge had a tad more sex appeal than the Chicken Farm.

And come, the shooters did. For a period of time, the group conducted renegade matches (not sanctioned by the IBS or NBRSA). Then the Hawks Ridge Gun Club, formally known as the North Carolina 1000 Yard Benchrest Association, joined forces with a new, like-minded group of long-rangers in Virginia for the purpose of approaching the Williamsport club to propose affiliation with one of the governing bodies, thereby standardizing the rules of competition. After considerable negotiations, in 1995 Hawks Ridge and the Virginia 1000 Yard Benchrest Association merged with the IBS. Williamsport declined, opting to continue under its own guidelines. Since then, 1,000-yard clubs in England and Australia have united with North Carolina and Virginia to make the IBS truly an international association.

The records begin falling

That first sanctioned year, Bill and his 40-X hunting rifle made an indelible impression on 1,000-yard competition. On a single June day he captured the North Carolina State Championship in Light Gun for both group and score, with a two-day group agg a bit over 4" and a 48.5 agg score, both of which still stand as state records. At the same time he shattered the IBS Light Gun Class world record with a 5.058" group and a perfect 50 score. To top it off, at year's end he was named 1995 winner of the IBS Light Gun Class 6-match group aggregate, with an average 6.229".

But the best was yet to come. The following year, on a beautiful North Carolina spring day, the Light Gun IBS world record, then held by Gary McGee, again tumbled when Bill touched off 5 shots that could have been recorded on an ordinary business card. Measuring an incredible 3.150", the group also achieved a perfect score of 50.

As the year came to an end, the IBS handed Bill still another prestigious award, this one the Light Gun 10-match group agg. In wind, rain, sun and sometimes snow he turned in a year-long average of 10.4577", yet another IBS world record.

That was the good news. The bad news was that the accuracy of his beloved Hart-barreled 40-X had begun fading in mid-season. In order to finish the year, he quickly persuaded gunsmith David Tooley to cut 1½" from the Hart's fat end and rechamber it once again for the 6-284. This, of course, was a desperate attempt to restore accuracy by moving the throat forward into what he and David hoped were sufficiently higher, less eroded lands. At the next match, this stop-gap measure appeared to be for naught, as accuracy was less than encouraging. But things turned around in a big way the following match, when Bill and his shortened barrel produced the record-breaking 3.150"/50.

As good as 1996 had been, '97 was in most respects the most rewarding, as Bill diversified into the Heavy Gun Class. For his efforts he captured the Virginia State Two-Gun Overall Championship and was the Heavy Gun winner in score. He capped the year by placing first in the IBS 1,000-Yard Two-Gun National Championship. He also posted two new Light Gun Class IBS world records, a 10-match group agg of 8.6355" and an equally impressive record-breaking score averaging 43.33. By accumulating 28 points for the year's effort, Bill reached the epitome of shooting accomplishment when he was named IBS 1,000-Yard Shooter of the Year for 1997.

Was Bill over the hill?

After scaling the pinnacle of 1,000-yard accomplishment, Bill suddenly and mysteriously disappeared from the winners' roster. What happened to the man who had abruptly stormed into the long-range game and for three years electrified it with his shooting skills? He explains his withdrawal from serious competition as a simple change in priorities. "Now, it's more thrilling to see my customers win and set records than me doing it myself," he said. But understanding exactly what it takes to win, he also admitted that staying on top took time, energy and dedication, and the demands of his flourishing business deprive him of all three.

The customers Bill cheers on are using his line of Tracker stocks. D&B Supply, owned and operated by Bill and his wife Diane, furnishes benchrest, hunting and sporter stocks made of the latest hi-tech innovation in stock material: wood. Indeed, we've finally arrived at where we began. And it was high time. After reigning supreme in 1,000-yard shooting for years in the Heavy Gun Class, laminated wood is now making inroads even in short-range benchrest. Move over, fiberglass. Take a hike, graphite.

Even if they are laminated wood, be assured that these D&B creations are not our fathers' stocks. Thinner laminations, modern glues and the right woods, including an extremely lightweight African wood called obeche, result in stocks that set new standards of lightness, strength and stability. But the changes go much further than wood and glue. The Shehane-designed Tracker benchrest stocks feature a low center of gravity and an extended forend for long, heavy barrels. Another desirable feature of the

benchrest styles is very little taper to the lower rear portion of the stock, which helps keep the gun on target during recoil. The hunting and sporter stocks are more conventional in design, except for an extended beavertail forend that rides the bags nicely.

These stocks were designed specifically to fill the needs Bill found wanting in competition and hunting. So are the scopes he stocks. He is one of the nation's top distributors of Nightforce scopes, having sold well over 300 last year alone. The Nightforce is, he contends, as essential to successful 1,000-yard shooting as a good barrel.

Given his extraordinary shooting accomplishments, plus his knowledge of stocks and other gun accessories, no in-depth compilation of 1,000-yard material would be complete without input from Bill Shehane. In response to 82 questions, here are his observations and opinions on virtually every aspect of 1,000-yard rifle accuracy.

What was special about the 40-X you mentioned?

My first four records for group and score were in the Light Gun Class. I used a 40-X action that Bob Brackney blueprinted for me and a 1.35"-diameter Hart barrel with six flutes. David Tooley chambered it for one of my favorite varmint rounds, the 6-284.

The stock was the standard wood 40-X stock. We cut the rail out from under the forend and cut the hole clean through to let air in from the bottom. David glued the receiver into the stock without pillars and left a .062" gap in the forend around the barrel for plenty of air movement. We wanted the forend to ride in a 3"-wide front BR-type bag, so David made what we call an "ash tray" and attached it to the forend. It was made of Delron, 3" wide and 5" long, and it transformed the stock into a true bag-rider.

Trouble was, it was now a bit too heavy at the muzzle, and I wanted to get the balance point just in front of the action—a place I figured would be good for the free-recoil type of shooting. I unscrewed the barrel after a match in Virginia and gave it to Clay Spencer, requesting that he give me six more flutes between the six flutes Hart had cut. While Clay was doing that I had David make an aluminum muzzle brake.

Once I'd installed the barrel with its muzzle brake, I put enough lead shot in the buttstock to bring the weight up to 17 pounds, balancing the rifle just in front of the action.

I also added an aluminum bar under the buttstock to take out some of the drop so I could keep the rifle on target during a fast string. The trigger was a Jewell, and the scope was a 24X Leupold mounted in Kelbly rings.

Actually that rig started out as my varmint hunting rifle, but it was transformed into what at that time was one of the best 1,000-yard rifles going. With it I shot more groups in the 3's in one season than any other rifle I've ever owned. It had to be the barrel. If a man is lucky enough to get a true Hummer barrel in his life, this 8" twist Hart barrel was mine.

After a season of breaking the group and score aggs, the barrel began to lose its edge. Dave Tooley cut off the shank and rechambered it so I could finish the season. Now, the original 28" barrel was only 26¹/₂". The first match I shot with the shortened barrel was nothing to get excited about—a 6" group and a 47 score. But at the next match I lowered the 5-shot group and score record with a 3.1" and 50.

Which stocks do you now prefer on your rifles?

On my Light Gun Class rifles I use only wood Tracker stocks. I do, however, have a fiberglass version I use with a tapered barrel to meet the muzzle rules at Williamsport, as well as the 16¹/₂-pound limit at the World Open, where I compete once a year. My two Heavy Gun Class rifles have an aluminum stock and a wood stock. I'm always trying something new. You never know if something is going to work until you try it, and I like to do my testing in match conditions. This drives my gunsmiths crazy, because they want to see me win matches, not conduct experiments. But I simply don't have the time any more to test before a match.

I feel that wood stocks are much easier to tune and keep tuned through the season than the stiffer glass stocks. My first Tracker prototype was a glass stock Alan Hall sent me. I hacked it up, Bondoed it and fixed it like I wanted it. It shot well—24 matches averaging about 7"—but I

never shot as many groups in the 3's as with my old wood-stocked 40-X. It seemed to me that with the glass stock it was easy to throw a shot by bad rifle handling during a fast string. In contrast, you could do anything to the wood stock, and it didn't seem to matter. Now, a lot of shooters will say it was the barrel, but I don't think so. It was a good barrel, but wood stocks just shoot better for me than glass stocks.

I believe we're seeing a resurgence of wood stocks. I was delivering a load of my Baby Trackers at the last Super Shoot in Ohio and counted 14 wood stocks in just one relay of 60 shooters. A few years ago, it would have been 100% fiberglass.

Dry-fire your glass-stocked rifle a few times on the mothball and then dry-fire a properly bedded wood-stocked rifle, and you be the judge. Almost every time the glass-stocked rifle will jiggle the crosshairs on the target. What does this mean? I don't have a clue, but something is going on before the bullet gets out of the barrel. I

Brandon McNeil, the first junior shooter to win the IBS Nationals, poses with Bill in 1996 after their victories at Hawks Ridge. Framed by trophies is Bill's remarkable Hart-barreled 40-X, the hunting gun that in 1995 and 1996 rocked 1,000-yard competition.

want my rifle not to move, and that's what I get with wood stocks. I believe wood helps tame the vibrations and recoil to a certain extent or I wouldn't be shooting it. Besides, I like the way wood feels. I also earn my living making wood stocks.

For 1,000-yard shooting, what's important in stock design?

I like a stock that's easy to handle when you have to shoot fast, one that will stay on the white square under recoil. We sight in on clay birds in North Carolina, and I like to see my bullet impact during the sight-in period under all flag/wind conditions. My stock needs to be long enough in the forend to handle the 28" to 30" barrels and balance about 1" in front of the barrel/action junction. This seems to ride the bags best for me with a free-recoil hold. I have Light Guns that shoot best holding them tight, but most have shot best free-recoil. But remember, the Light Guns I shoot are 6mm and 6.5mm calibers. Not .30 caliber.

For Heavy Guns I've developed the Maxi-Tracker, an aluminum stock with stainless rails precisely cut on a CNC mill with a 60" bed. This rail will track just like the rail guns we use in 100- and 200-yard benchrest. When the bags are set up correctly you can put the dot on the X and shoot ten .30 caliber magnum rounds, and the dot will return to the X every time without any mechanical adjustments. This is a big improvement over when we had to fight with a gun to get it back on target quickly before the conditions changed.

Ten shots in 15 to 20 seconds will **always** beat 10 shots in a minute if the conditions are changing fast.

By using aluminum and stainless steel milled with modern CNC equipment, all surfaces are flat and precise, so the complete package has no other choice but to track back and forth the same way every time. This can be accomplished with laminated wood, but it's just easier with billet aluminum and stainless rails.

Do you have a favorite type of bedding?

I use both receiver and barrel-block bedding. Most of my Light Guns are receiver bedded, but if the barrel is 30" or longer or if it's straight

1.250" without flutes, I go to barrel blocks.

Which method of receiver bedding is best?

I've shot both glue-ins and pillar bedding, and I like the glue-in better. I'm trying a rifle now that's pillar bedded, but I don't know how it's going to work out. If done correctly, either method works well.

Any actions you particularly like?

That question can get me into a lot of trouble. There are more good actions out there than there ever has been. Seems like every week someone new is making an action. That's good for the game, but where do you go to make a good choice? Surely not to me. I like them all. I still own my first custom action. It's a Shilen DGA, and damn good it was and still is today. *(Ed Shilen labeled his actions DGA as an abbreviation for Damn Good Accuracy.)* Alan Hall, who at that time was working for Shilen, barreled it for the 6mm Rem. Imp. in 1976. The action is a bit heavy for the shooter wanting to use a 5-pound, 8-ounce barrel, but it's as good as anything you can buy today. I've sold and swapped a lot of actions in my day, but not that one. It's staying with me for the day my grandson Will gets the urge to bust one on the next hill. I'll put a fresh barrel on it in a few years and pass it on to my son for Will when he's ready.

Bruce Thom at BAT Machine and Glen Harrison at Nesika Bay are both making top-notch actions and are doing the most innovating. Still, Jim and George Kelbly probably sell more custom actions than anyone else. In BAT's early days I worked with Bruce to help him come up with the ideal 1,000-yard Heavy Gun action. Since then BAT has probably become the premiere 1,000-yard action. I'm currently working with Jerry Stiller of Stiller's Precision on his new Python action that will be targeted toward Light Gun 1,000-yard shooters. Right now I'm trying a right bolt, left port, right ejection action by Stiller, another by BAT and one by Kelbly. I'll know how they do after a few matches.

What are the most important features of a good

1,000-yard action?

First, I like one with plenty of primary and secondary extraction so you can break loose a case and get it out fast without upsetting the rifle. Then I like a loading port big enough to throw the big magnum rounds in fast. I also want a cone bolt so the round doesn't hit the back of the barrel when you're trying to run fast. I tend to lean toward a short action and bolt and a stiff receiver. For one thing, I think the lock time is faster with a short bolt. But quite frankly, I don't know if that makes a hill of beans difference. You also need a good bedding area and enough threads in the shank-tenon area of the barrel and receiver to hang the long, heavy barrels on.

Do you like tight-fitting bolts?

I like a bolt that's tight enough not to have any play side to side and up and down when it's in the fired position. But it also needs to be loose enough that I can run fast when I need to. Working with Bruce at BAT machine in the earlier days, I noticed that he was machining the bolts much too tight to work very fast. Since then, he has started leaving a bit more clearance, and I have him diamond flute my bolts to help keep them from binding when I run fast. We all know about the "Borden bumps" that Jim Borden designed for the Nesika actions. They help make the Nesika one of the finest on the market today.

Do you use lightweight firing pins with special springs?

Nope. I have in the past, but no more.

When you use barrel blocks, does this then make the precision of an action less important?

They say it does, but I think it's hogwash. I want the best action behind the barrel block I can get. And since I now lean toward a right bolt, left port, that makes it a custom action.

What brand of barrels do you prefer?

I prefer any brand that hummmms. I know it sounds like a cop-out, but I shoot them all. Today we have the very best barrelmakers turning out the best barrels we've ever had, and the steelmakers are supplying them with the best steels. I've set more records with Hart barrels, but I've had good results with Lilja, Krieger, Shilen, Spencer and BlackStar.

I believe the Hart on my original 40-X 6-284 was my once-in-a-lifetime Hummer barrel. I could shoot it in almost any condition and win. Too bad I was so dumb to have shot it out instead of saving it for the big ones. But you live and learn, and I'm still learning.

Is there an ideal barrel length?

My 6mms are no longer than 28". I've shot up to 32" but see no need for the extra length in a case as small as the 6-284. My .338 Yogi is 46" long and fixing to go under the cutoff wheel. I've been trying that long barrel with a tension tube, and it has almost beaten me to death. It's time to drop back and do what I know works.

Do you use muzzle brakes?

All my Light guns in the last six years have had muzzle brakes. I'm using three rifles now without brakes to see if they really do make a difference at 1,000 yards. But as I said before, I'm shooting 6mm's and 6.5mm's in Light Gun Class, and the recoil is not as bad as the .30 calibers.

The smaller calibers with brakes are much easier to get back on target and therefore are easier to shoot, and that has to affect the *shooter's* accuracy. But I'm not convinced a brake makes a *gun* more accurate, and in fact I tend to believe the brake actually harms accuracy. Time will tell if this is true.

Any preferences in muzzle brakes?

I've used them all, but the ones that Dave Tooley and George Vais made for me seem to work best. Neither of them blow my hat off, and both seem to control recoil very well.

Is there a best muzzle crown?

I like the recessed BR crown, but I shoot whatever the gunsmith I'm working with likes to do. Ever tried to get a stone mason to lay concrete block? My point is, if a crown is clean, indexed and done correctly, any one will work, and I want whatever my gunsmith does BEST.

Do you re-crown now and then?

I have in the past, but now I think it's another waste of time. Of course, if you bang it up or round it off with JB by running patches in and out the muzzle a bunch of times, which was one of my earlier sins, then you have to cut 1" off and re-crown or she ain't gonna work.

What's your break-in procedure for barrels?

Starting with a new barrel, *and before I ever fire a shot*, I run one patch wet with Bore-Tech, Hoppe's, Shooter's Choice or Butch's through. Right now I'm trying BR Gold, but I've used them all. While some are faster than others, all work fine. Next I take a new bronze brush and pass it back and forth about 10 times. I let the bore soak while I clean the brush with a degreaser and set it aside to dry. I then push a tight, clean patch through and wipe the muzzle clean. I follow that with another wet patch and 10 more passes with the brush. While I clean the brush, I let the barrel soak for about 15 minutes before running another clean patch through. If the patch appears dirty, I run another wet patch through and let it set another 15 minutes, followed by two dry patches. I believe all this is necessary to get the lapping compound used in barrel manufacturing out. Now I'm ready to start breaking-in the barrel.

With a clean, dry barrel I start by running through a patch wet with a drop of Kroil. The Kroil stain on the patch should be about the size of a dime. This is just enough to make sure the surface has some lube and is not scratchy dry. I know this goes against two different break-in methods, but I like it best. Some, including barrel manufacturers, recommend the bore be completely dry, while others suggest a heavier grease-type lube. I've tried all three methods and find that it takes less time with the same results doing it the way I'm describing. So I'll stick with it until something better comes along.

After firing the first bullet, which is usually a fire-forming round with the bullet making good

contact with the rifling, I run a wet patch of solvent through, make 10 passes with a clean brush and let it soak for 10 minutes. While I'm waiting, I clean the brush and then use 0000 steel wool to polish the inside and outside of the neck of the case I just fired. This utilizes my bench time instead of me sitting there looking at my watch and waiting for the solvent to work. I also usually have my equipment so I can size my fired brass, square up the primer pockets using an electric screwdriver and re-prime. When the 10 minutes are up, I run a clean patch through and save it for comparison purposes. I repeat this procedure for five shots, but after the fifth shot I run an additional clean patch or two through to make sure all the solvent is gone and that the bore is completely DRY.

That done, I take the rifle off the bags, lay the bolt on the bench and walk out from under the shooting shed. I then set the rifle butt on top of my foot with the muzzle up and tilted at a slight angle and insert a clean, white q-tip just inside the barrel. The reflected sunlight enables me to see any copper fouling very well as I rotate the barrel. Almost every time at this stage all fouling is gone.

If I do see copper, I continue cleaning, this time by applying a patch wet with Bore-Tech Copper Remover. I follow this with another wet patch, working this one slowly back and forth in 1" strokes to make sure the bore is soaked. After

Measuring 3.150", this Shehane-fired Light Gun Class 5-shot group held the IBS record for two years. To gauge the accelerating progress in 1,000-yard accuracy, consider that the IBS record now stands at just 1.996".

the solvent has worked for no longer than 15 minutes, I run a clean patch through, knowing it's going to come out green for sure. I save that patch. I again apply the Copper Remover as just described, let it work for about 15 minutes and patch it out. This patch should be much whiter than the first, but if not, repeat the process once more, which should do it. But don't expect any patch to come out nice and white or you'll be there cleaning all day.

With the barrel squeaky clean and dry, I lubricate it again with a bit of Kroil and go to shooting 3-shot groups for the next 15 rounds or so, testing for pressures as I go. I clean and then lubricate with Kroil between every three shots. After about 20 total rounds, I figure the barrel is broken-in, and I'm ready to set the bullet-seating depth and powder charge and head to a match to see what she's got.

By the way, I have a new gadget that every serious shooter should have. It's a Hawkeye Bore Scope. All of the gunsmiths I've dealt with over the years have had bore scopes, and I really never thought much about owning my own. But I'll never be without one now. Besides knowing for sure that you have all the copper out, all the way down the barrel, you can keep up with the throat erosion. Mine has a 45-degree eyepiece, and that makes it much easier to make a fast check before the shoot-off.

In competition, how often do you clean your barrels?

I clean after each record group, letting the barrel soak until I have to shoot again, hopefully in the shoot-off. I never take a dirty rifle back to the shop. But even so, at the shop I have a rack with a little muzzle tilt where I soak my barrels in Bore-Tech Benchrest Blend for 12 to16 hours before patching it out. I do this repeatedly until the patches come out WHITE, usually in two to three days.

I believe carbon build-up is the reason some good-shooting barrels go bad after a few hundred rounds. I never let that happen anymore. Every 50 to 60 rounds I apply JB to a tight patch wrapped around the jag. I short-stroke this patch about 20 to 30 times from the beginning of the throat to about 6" down the barrel. I finish by

stroking the JB farther down the barrel about 10 times, each time stopping just short of the muzzle and never allowing the patch to exit the barrel. This keeps carbon from building up in front of the throat, smoothes out the bore and removes any traces of copper. After the JB, I clean the barrel in the usual way to remove the abrasive and lubricate the bore.

Are you shooting moly-coated bullets?

Right now I'm not shooting moly bullets in competition, but I do use them in my long-range varmint and big game rifles. Kinda crazy, don't you think? I've shot some pretty good groups and scores with moly, and in fact some of my records were shot with moly bullets. But this is what I've learned from years of working with moly and the chronograph: To shoot good 1,000-yard groups you have to have a barrel that will stay virtually the same throughout 16 to 18 rounds fired in a minute or so. If the barrel does not have hidden copper under the moly, and if it has a good moly surface it will shoot good groups and give low velocity deviations. But to have a barrel in the condition I just described you'd need to clean with JB or some other kind of mild abrasive in addition to your regular cleaning method. Problem is, with that clean barrel it might take 18 to 20 rounds and sometimes more for the barrel to re-coat itself and settle down so it once again produces velocity spreads in the single digits. This is not a good situation when you have limited barrel life.

Do you think moly bullets have an effect on accuracy, either good or bad?

No.

Do you have reason to believe that moly bullets extend barrel accuracy life?

I don't believe so.

Do you think moly bullets have reduced your barrel fouling?

No.

Have you observed moly-coated bullets shooting flatter due to an increase in ballistic coefficient?

No.

What is the typical accuracy life of your barrels?

It depends on the caliber. My 6mm barrels usually will go 600 to 800 rounds before I see the accuracy get worse. I used to rechamber and re-crown at that point, but that was a waste of time and money. I have some .30 caliber barrels that have shot-out as quickly as 6mm's, but usually around 1,800 to 2,000 rounds is when a .30 caliber's match-winning accuracy goes. When match barrels play out, I use them to shoot groundhogs. After that, they make good tomato plant stakes. So you can see I'm really into this recycling thing.

In a barrel's accuracy life, is there an "accuracy plateau" when it shoots its very best?

I think a barrel shoots best at around 150 to 300 rounds if it's going to be a Hummer. I have had 6mm barrels shoot their best in less than that, but unfortunately by 600 rounds those barrels were gone.

Have you noticed any difference in break-in requirements between button-rifled and cut-rifled barrels?

I used to believe that cut barrels took longer to break-in, but that's hogwash. The final hand-lapping is the difference today. Don't believe it? Look through a borescope at both. The interior finish is almost the same. Five or six years ago the cut barrel would have looked much rougher, but the K&P and Krieger cut barrels I use take no longer to break-in than my button barrels.

Any difference in accuracy between cut and buttoned barrels?

The throat goes just as fast in either, and I've seen no difference in accuracy. A good barrel will shoot well, right out of the gate, and a bad barrel won't. It doesn't make any difference whether it was cut or buttoned.

Do you use cryogenically treated barrels?

Yes, I do. I believe in cryogenics for my barrels. In fact, the first one I tried lowered the 5-shot IBS group record and also the score record—both the same day. Back then, there were a lot of skeptics, and I suppose there still are today. But my feeling is this: If the freezing is done correctly I believe the deep hole drill has a better chance of getting the hole in the center of the barrel without all that jumping around when the drill hits a hard spot. I know for a fact that gunsmiths tell me that barrels chamber different-ly and the threads are a bit smoother in treated barrels. I know that in almost every case a frozen barrel is easier to clean than an untreated barrel.

I realize that freezing a bad barrel will not make it shoot any better, but if done correctly it also won't hurt it. In short, I believe that with a frozen barrel, the improved drilling, machining and ease of cleaning give you a better chance to get the most out of that barrel.

Have you used barrel-tuning devices?

I have never tried a tuner, but I did get as far as having one made for one of my Heavy Guns. Then when Williamsport banned them, I dropped it and never tried the tuner in IBS shooting. I believe the device will work on longer barrels, and a few of my friends at Williamsport have had great success with them.

What cartridges do you shoot in 1,000-yard competition?

At present I'm shooting cartridges of my own design in the Light Gun Class—the 6-284 Shehane, 6-284 Shehane Short and the 6.5-284 Shehane. These are based on the new Norma .284 brass. The body taper is .008" per inch, and the throat is dimensioned so the pressure ring on 105- to 107-grain bullets seats .020" north of the "dreaded donut" at the juncture of the shoulder and neck. On my 6-284 Short, the chambering reamer is run in .250" short, making the powder capacity about 95% of the .243 Ackley Imp. By the way, the body taper extracts very well when running fast, and in the full-length version adds about three grains more powder capacity.

In Heavy Gun Class I'm shooting the .338 Yogi. This is a .338 Lapua that Dave Tooley blew out to add more capacity. It holds about 105 grains of stick powder and is a super round if I can ever get my tube guns to stop the vertical stringing they've exhibited from the very beginning. The barrel is 46" long and is bedded with two barrel blocks. *(A tube gun uses a tube over the barrel, plus a nut and threaded barrel section to exert lateral barrel tension as a tuning measure.)*

What clearance in the neck do you like between a loaded round and the chamber?

I like to have .002" total, which means .001" per side. It releases the bullet just fine and is easy to keep up with. To check, I just take a loaded round and shove the bullet into the neck of a fired case. If the bullet goes in tight, the neck is too thick. It should only be very snug. Any problems can be detected early this way.

Is there anything unique about your chamber necks?

No.

Is there anything special about your chamber throating?

No. I've tried different leade angles, but have settled on the standard 1degree and 30 minutes. I couldn't tell any difference in any of them.

How do you establish the most accurate bullet-seating depth?

I always start against the lands, although not all my rifles will shoot that way. When I start on the lands, I want the lands to just make a mark on a bullet I've ringed with a magic marker. Starting low, I then increase the powder charge till I get to the point where I know the pressure is about right. I want a very small primer crater, no heavy bolt-lift and no flattened primers. Having reached the proper pressures, I go into the lands another .005" and shoot some 5-shot groups at

200 yards. If the pressures don't look too high and the accuracy is good, I go another .005" into the lands to see what that'll do. At about .020" of jam, the lands will begin pushing the bullet back into the case if the neck tension is right. Most of my 6mm's with VLD bullets like this better than anything else. The 107-grain Sierras either like that same seating or else will shoot best .005" off the lands.

My .338 Yogi has given me so much trouble I haven't been able to tweak this baby up with 300-grain Sierras or their new 250-grain MatchKings.

Do you prefer VLDs?

I like any bullet that'll shoot. I use the VLDs and the Sierra design because they've shot very well for me.

Are bullets a major concern?

You bet! Without good bullets you're not going to shoot good, consistent 1,000-yard groups, period. The ogive length must be within .002" of each other, the boattail must run true with the centerline of the body, and they all must weigh the same. Checking every bullet is a lot of trouble,

Backed by a trio of Australian shooting buddies, Bill exhibits one of his Heavy Guns, this one sporting a Shehane-designed laminated-wood Tracker stock and a 12-42X Nightforce scope. Standing, left to right, are Alan Peake, Tony Allison and Stuart Elliott.

but if you have any ambitions of winning a relay, much less a shoot-off, you better get used to it.

What degree of case neck grip on the bullet do you prefer?

I size .003" under the diameter of a loaded round, which gives the bullet grip I like.

Do inconsistencies in bullet grip make any difference at 1,000 yards?

All the difference in the world! Don't believe it? Carefully seat 20 bullets by hand and sort them out by the difference you feel in seating pressure. Shoot the tight ones over a chronograph, then the loose ones, and see what velocity spread you come up with. Then understand that every 25 fps of variation gives 2½" of vertical spread at 1,000 yards. And in our game, vertical kills you!

How little extreme velocity spread are you able to get?

I try to limit it to single digits, but that's not always possible, no matter what I do. Bruce Baer and I were discussing this, and he related a story about a 7mm he owned that was shooting like the proverbial house afire. He checked the velocity spread, and it was terrible. So he proceeded to work on neck tension, weighing his bullets and all the things he had learned about getting low spreads. That rifle never shot another good group until he went back to what he was originally doing. Still, it sure is nice to have in your mind that the spread is low, because it gives you confidence.

What brand of cases do you use?

I shot RWS brass for years in my .404 wildcats and still believe it to be the very best you can buy. I now use the new lot of Norma 6.5-284 cases in the Shehane cartridges and Lapua in the .338 Yogi. Although Norma has not got its act together yet on their 6.5-284 brass, Hornady and Lapua are just about ready to get their 6.5-284 brass ready. So hopefully between the three of them we'll have some good cases soon.

How do you prep your cases?

I lube and expand the necks with a neck mandrel .001" larger than my neck-turning mandrel. That done, I polish the inside of the necks with 0000 steel wool wrapped around a bronze brush; then trim the necks to the length of the shortest case in any group of brass.

Next, I outside-turn the necks to about ¾ of the total thickness I'll take them down, making sure I go .020" or so into the shoulder to avoid donut build-up. With my Neilson neck turner set to the final thickness, I then make the last cut. After uniforming the primer pockets and deburring the flash holes, I polish the necks inside and out with steel wool and degrease them with BreakClean. Now I'm ready to sort cases by weight. I don't know if this last step is really necessary, but it gives me confidence.

How long do cases last?

I'm still shooting some of my RWS brass after 20 firings or more, but I believe that now, more than ever before, brass wears out faster than we ever believed. I would say about 5 to 6 firings is all I get out of my serious match brass. After that they're used for sighters.

Do you re-turn necks at intervals during the life of a case?

Considering the short life of today's brass, not anymore.

Have you noticed that loaded-bullet runout makes any accuracy difference?

Yes, and I check every round to be used in competition with a NECO runout gauge.

What amount of loaded-bullet runout will you tolerate?

I want .0005", but .001" will do.

How do you accomplish so little runout?

It's important to prepare near-perfect necks and set-up the dies correctly. I also fire-form with the bullets jammed into the lands and the ejector plunger in the face of the bolt removed. Then if the gunsmith has done his chambering job correctly, runout ought to be within .001" every time.

What powders do you use?

I generally shoot Reloder 22 and 25, but I'm experimenting with Western ball powders, which run through a powder measure like water.

Do you weigh powder charges?

Yes. I want every one on the money, plus or minus ZERO. It's probably a waste of time, but I feel better about it.

Are some lots of powders more accurate than others?

I don't know if there's an accuracy difference, but some lots are much hotter than others. Once a powder shows real promise, I try and buy as much of that lot as I think will take me through a couple of seasons. Remember, if you *think* it's better, it probably is.

Is there a lack of powders suited for the larger magnum cases?

Maybe, but it's hard for me to tell. We shoot in conditions ranging from 10 degrees with no humidity to 100 degrees with 98% humidity. All we do is use more powder in the cold and less in the heat. Not very scientific, but it works for us. Reloder 25 and some of the VihtaVuori powders fill the large cases up, but 4831, Reloder 22 and Norma MPR still top the list of powders used today in 1,000-yard competition. Western ball powders are the new guy on the block, and the ones I have tested show definite promise in the larger cases. I hope they will work because they measure very well.

What powder loading density do you like?

That issue used to bug me a bunch, but I've seen rounds with 100% density that shot worse than rounds with 70%. I like to use as small a powder charge as possible and still get the velocity I need to do the job. If that's 100% density, so be it, but that's not necessarily what makes a load shoot.

In working up a 1,000-yard load, at what distances do you shoot?

I only have 200 yards, and it works fine for me. If a load won't shoot at 200, it ain't gonna shoot at 1,000. This stuff about a bullet going to sleep and finally settling down out there past 300 yards is so much bullhockey and makes me laugh.

What size groups do you shoot at 200?

My rifles must shoot .300" to .400" 5-shot groups at 200 yards to be competitive at 1,000. I like to see little, round circles with all the bullets touching for four or five test groups. One group doesn't mean anything. I need to see consistency.

What size groups win today's 1,000-yard matches?

Really small! Used to be, you could win a relay with a single-digit group. Now you better have a *small* single-digit group. I recently watched a fellow shoot a 6.236" 10-shot group with a 96 score, and he didn't even win his relay. This is the norm, not the extraordinary. In that relay were seven scores over 90 and nine groups under 7". And yes, I was in that relay and didn't even come close to winning.

We just finished the IBS 1,000-yard National Championship for the year 2000. In the Heavy Gun Class the top 20 shooters had a two-day average of 7.848", and the winner, Gray Durham from Wilkesboro, N.C., averaged 5.983" for the two days. In Light Gun the top 27 shooters averaged under 7" for the two days, and the winner, Liz Harris from South Boston, Va., averaged 4.997" for the two days. Now friends, that's what I mean when I say really small.

In load development do you use a chronograph?

I do when I get serious. I want to have extreme spreads in single digits if at all possible. I also want to see where the velocity starts falling off, even though I'm still going up on powder, and how it affects accuracy.

Are there velocity levels that are most accurate?

It depends on the twist of the barrel. My 6mm's with a 9" twist seem to like 3,200 to 3,300 fps. My 8" twists shoot better at 3,100. Rotational spin is the key here. Some bullets won't shoot that fast in my 6mm's, but Bergers and Sierras do fine for me at any of these speeds.

How do you know when a barrel begins to "shoot out"?

It quits shooting! It doesn't take many matches to see whether or not a barrel is going to shoot. When one starts shooting patterns and not putting three or four shots almost touching in a round group, I start looking for another barrel. In the meantime I'll chase the throat till the barrel quits shooting, but I've had some quit before the throat was completely gone. That's hard to figure, but it happens.

What sizing dies do you use?

I full-length everything with custom dies. Over the years I've found that full-length sizing gives less trouble when shooting fast, and the

The "big guns" of 1,000 yards, Bill (left) and Bruce Baer of Williamsport fame, clashed at the Super Shoot on Bruce's home turf at Williamsport, Pa. Unfortunately for Bruce, the year was 1997, when Bill won practically everything in sight, including $5 of Mr. Baer's disposable income.

rounds are exactly the same when the bolt drops. My custom dies only move the brass about .003" in the shoulder and .002" at the base. That makes for ease of extraction, but the brass is not over-worked as with factory full-length dies.

What bullet seater?

I use a Wilson die blank with my chambering reamer run into it. I like feeling the bullet slide down the neck, and this die lets me do that. If I have a tight or loose bullet I know it right then, and I can set aside that round to warm up the barrel or for a rough sighter.

Which primer seater do you like?

I have two, a Sinclair hand tool and an RCBS tray set-up I use on the .338 Yogi.

Any secrets to primer seating?

No secrets, just a little arithmetic. I want to make sure all the primers are seated to the same depth. I also want the seating step to crush the anvil .002", and the top of the primer should end up .002" below the case rim.

Do you weigh primers to look for inconsistencies?

I have in the past, but I now think that anything other than a visual inspection is a waste of time.

Do you avoid touching primers?

No.

What scopes do you prefer?

I use Nightforce exclusively. It's the only scope that allows me to see 6mm holes in the white at 1,000 yards. And because of the optical clarity, these scopes also help you see through mirage better, allowing the use of an additional 5 to 7 higher power. That's why in addition to using Nightforce scopes, I also sell them.

What power do you prefer?

I like the 8-32X, usually set on its highest power.

What reticle?

I'm a dot shooter, so it's a toss-up between the Double Dot—a 1/8" dot in the center and a 1/16" dot 8 moa below it—and the Ranging reticle, which has both dots and crosshairs.

What rings and bases do you use?

I use custom rings and bases made for me, and they've never failed on a customer's rifle or on mine.

Before mounting a scope, do you lap-in the rings or epoxy-bed the scope tube?

I always lap the rings. I've never epoxy-bedded a scope tube.

In competition, do you always "machine gun 'em" or do you sometimes shoot slowly?

I'll do either, depending on what Mother Nature deals me. As Tony Boyer once told me, the trick isn't how fast you shoot; it's how fast you can get stopped when the conditions change.

Do you watch wind flags or read the mirage, or both?

Both. I use one to test the other. I'd rather rely on the flags, but sometimes that's just not possible when the flags are going in four different directions. That's when I compare mirage against the flags.

Do you hold over for condition changes, or do you make scope adjustments?

I never change the scope when I start. I hold for changes.

Had you rather deal with tricky breezes or thick mirage?

Tricky breezes, for sure. I hate thick mirage.

How do you handle tricky breezes?

Most of the time they handle me. I just try to find a condition that holds 15 to 20 seconds on what I consider to be the dominant flag. Then when that condition comes back, I let 'er fly. By the way, more 1,000-yard shooters, including myself, get hurt in *letups* than in the apparent pushes.

How do you hold your rifles?

A little thumb pressure and nothing else. One exception is a rifle I made up to shoot at Williamsport. I have to hold it with a death grip to get it to shoot. I've never shot a group with that rifle any smaller than 4", and I'm sure it's because I can't possibly hold it that tight the same way for five shots.

Which front pedestal do you use?

I use a Bald Eagle 60-degree Deluxe Windage Rest for the Light Gun and a custom-made pedestal for the Heavy Gun.

On a crisp Easter Monday at the Shehane farm, young Bill #2 holds the variety of varmint that launched his dad's long-range career. The Easter Monday hunting trip has been a family tradition ever since the Shehane kids were old enough to shoot.

Do you use a forend stop?

Yes. I think it gives a more consistent return of the rifle when I'm shooting fast. I also seem to be able to shoot faster with the stop than without.

What rear bag do you like?

I like the Bald Eagle bag with a leather bottom and short bunny ears of cordura nylon. I use the three-seam type because it has a wider gap between the ears that accommodates the Tracker stock. The advantage of cordura is that it doesn't tend to stick to a stock on humid days.

Do you use any lubricant on the bags?

I use powdered flake graphite. It's dirty but very consistent.

Do you have a favorite trigger?

Jewell has long been my trigger of choice and in most cases has served me well. I do believe there will be another trigger maker coming along in the near future to give target shooters another choice. This will only serve to make triggers better for us all.

What trigger weight do you use?

I like two ounces because that's what I'm used to.

Among a glittering collection of shooting awards is the coveted Hart Trophy, center, presented to Bill as the 1997 IBS 1,000-Yard Shooter of the Year.

What's the biggest obstacle to even better 1,000-yard accuracy?

Bullet consistency, without a doubt. If our sport had 100 benchrest bulletmakers turning out heavy VLD bullets of the same quality as the match bullets for the PPC crowd, 1,000-yard records would fall. Yes, it's hard to make VLDs perform like flat-base match bullets, but if there was enough competition to urge improvement, that'd go a long way toward it.

Shooters also should do more practicing in bad conditions in order to learn the effects of wind and mirage. This would do as much as anything to improve the overall performance of 1,000-yard competitors.

Is there any new technology at hand that will soon enable 1,000-yarders to shrink their groups?

I don't see any new technology in the near future. What will shrink groups is the rapidly growing popularity of 1,000-yard shooting. As a result, the competitors will learn more about what makes 1,000-yard rifles work better. The shooters will in turn feed this information back to the suppliers and manufacturers, which will improve the equipment and supplies.

I think it will be a few more years before the sport is dominated by one round, like the 6PPC dominates 100- and 200-yard benchrest. There are a lot of good cartridges out there, and the shooters will find the best one.

What the sport needs most now are more ranges. The shooters are out there; they just need a place to shoot. The proof has been demonstrated at Hawks Ridge. In each of the last two IBS National Championships we hosted in '98 and 2000, more than 500 guns showed up. At the same time the number of vendors increased from 10 in '98 to 19 in 2000. If the sport weren't growing, the numbers would be going the other way.

Chapter 13

Handloading For Long Range Highpower Rifle Competition

by John Feamster

CAUTION: The methods, equipment and load data mentioned here appeared safe for use with the mentioned firearms, but they may not be safe in/with other rifles. No representation as to their safety regarding your rifle is given by either the author or the publisher. This chapter deals exclusively with the use of SMOKELESS POWDER, and black powder should never be dispensed or used with any equipment not specifically designed for its use, due to risk of fire/explosion. Shooting and handloading involve some inherent dangers, as do most other aspects of modern life, and the reader is advised that Precision Shooting Inc. and the author(s) disclaim all possible liability for damages, including actual, incidental and consequential, resulting from reader usage of information or advice contained in this book. Use data and advice at your own risk and with caution. Handling or discharging firearms and/or reloading components, ammunition or related chemicals may expose readers to lead or other substances/chemicals which are known to the state of California and/or other agencies to cause cancer, birth defects and other reproductive harm, whether through skin contact, inhalation or by other means. Read and obey all manufacturer's safety instructions and exercise caution during all phases of the shooting sports.

I. INTRODUCTION

Success in long range rifle competition requires an exacting blend of skill, art and science, and therein lies the fascination for its practitioners. Lying prone, using only a sling for support, and countering the effects of mirage and wind, plus variations in temperature, elevation and ambient light, to direct a few cents worth of copper and lead across 1000 yards and into a 10" X-ring is both challenging and rewarding. Most successful long range rifle competitors are handloaders, of necessity. Quite aside from avoiding the considerable expense of factory ammunition, the knowledgeable handloader may tune his ammunition to match his rifle's individual preferences. Thus, he extracts the maximum accuracy of which the rifle is capable, while keeping his ammunition consistent from lot to lot and

compensating for barrel wear through throat erosion. This chapter is intended for experienced handloaders who are already skilled at the fundamentals of centerfire rifle reloading. Those readers who are new to handloading are earnestly advised to read the "how to" section of any of the better reloading manuals, such as those sold by Speer or Sierra, and to seek guidance from an experienced, technically proficient handloader if needed. As always, readers should pay particular attention to all reloading safety precautions. Always wear safety glasses when handloading or shooting, exercise care and never eat, drink or smoke when handling potentially toxic chemicals or lead. Entire books can and have been devoted to the subject of handloading; shooters now have access to data in a type and quantity never before available. In order to best serve our readers in the space available, I will cite references periodically, in which more detailed information can be obtained. (NOTE: as a service to its readers, *Precision Shooting* magazine makes reprints of its articles available at nominal cost even when back-issues are no longer available.)

II. EQUIPMENT

In this section, I will make equipment recommendations based on over 25 years of handloading experience. During that time, I have found that it is not always necessary to spend large sums on gadgets in order to achieve excellent results. In fact, experiments I have conducted have demonstrated instances in which "standard" gear of decent quality out-performed "competition" gear costing three times as much! On the other hand, buying the cheapest tools available, without regard to their basic quality, is a sure recipe for frustration. Quite creditable handloading for long range competition can be done with high quality, standard reloading equipment such as that sold by RCBS and Redding, if the user is careful, meticulous and knowledgeable about setting up his gear. Of course, super-precise dies and other tools are, for many of us, a worthwhile investment; they can offer benefits of additional accuracy if used correctly. I would, however, state categorically that it is not necessary to spend your children's college fund on high-dollar reloading gear in order to be competitive in long-range shooting, so don't let "sticker shock" steer you away from competition!

Reloading Presses: Progressive or Single Stage?

Much of my competitive Highpower Rifle background has been in Service Rifle competition; serious SR shooters can burn up several thousand rounds of high-quality ammo in a single season. As such, in that arena, efficiency in the loading process becomes very important. I am a proponent of efficiency in handloading *as long as the reloader meets the required accuracy and safety goals.* I addressed efficiency at length in a chapter on reloading for gasguns in the *Precision Shooting Reloading Guide.* As an offshoot of work in this area, I later conducted extensive experiments at 250 yards using a scoped, custom Compass Lake Engineering

AR-15 service rifle, in calm conditions, with wind flags, firing several 10-shot groups per experimental condition. I tested the actual accuracy differences obtained when shooting ammunition progressively-loaded on a Dillon 550, vs. ammunition loaded using single-stage equipment. Also studied were accuracy differences obtained when metering powder charges (using Varget, a short-grained extruded powder) vs. weighing charges, differences between weighed, wall-thickness selected, neck-turned brass vs. unselected brass from the same lot, and also full-length sized vs. neck-sized cases. The goal was to help readers decide whether specialized loading techniques were sufficiently beneficial to accuracy, to justify the extra time involved, within the context of shooting at 200-600 yards. These experiments, reported in my book on AR-15 accuracy *(Black Magic: The Ultra-Accurate AR-15),* are far too detailed to summarize here, and should be considered within their original context—serious gasgun competition. Excellent ammunition can, and has been loaded on good-quality progressive presses, and I personally have fired good scores at 600 yards using progressively-loaded ammunition in my AR-15 service and match rifles.

However, long range competition does not typically involve expending nearly as much ammunition as across-the-course Highpower does. Matches are shorter, and opportunities to practice at 600 to 1000 yards are usually not as readily available, due to difficulty in accessing

Author's custom 6mm Ackley Improved—it works for long range competition and varmints!

full-distance firing ranges. Therefore, most long range shooters don't prepare, say, 3,000 to 4,000 cases for one season's competition, and the speed benefits of progressive handloading do not seem as relevant to long-rangers as they are to NRA Highpower Rifle competitors. The average, serious Highpower competitor may wish to weigh the merits of super-precise handloading techniques against the cost in terms of time involved, and determine whether the benefits are worth the time expenditure. However, long-range competition is a different animal in some respects; due to the lower volume of ammunition required, and the very exacting nature of shooting out to 1000 yards, I believe the average long-range shooters' needs can be well met with a good, single-stage press.

When it comes to single-stage presses, the RCBS Rockchucker has been an industry standard for decades. I've used one for many years with excellent results. While the theoretically-minded may ponder the differences in strength offered by different frame configurations ("C" vs. "O" frame, for example), basically, any strongly-built, good-quality press by big-name companies such as RCBS, Redding or Lyman should suffice. If you're buying a new press, I'd pick an "O" frame press, such as the Rockchucker, rather than an open-frame press, for preference. Heavy-duty presses resist the tendency to "spring" as stresses are placed on them when resizing or reforming large-caliber brass, keeping cartridge headspace more consistent; if buying an older or well-used press, check for excess play or wear in the fit of the ram to the frame and also in the handle linkage. Handloaders with a background in benchrest-style reloading are likely familiar with the arbor presses typically used with hand-type dies. Properly-made, these dies can offer great precision in keeping cases and seated bullets concentric (on which, more later) but they are not fool-proof. Arbor presses are convenient for low-volume neck-sizing and bullet seating, particularly when handloading on the range to speed the load-development process. However, I have found that excess neck-tension can induce significant error in seated-bullet straightness (concentricity). The shooter who has an arbor press and dies and wants to use them can obtain excellent results with due care, but I personally prefer a standard, single-stage press for my long-range ammunition.

Powder Measures

Bullet velocity variations that would not induce noticeable dispersion at 100 or 200 yards, can become significant at 600 yards and downright critical at 1000! As such, the serious long-range competitor is wise to weigh each powder charge in order to minimize velocity variations! The choice of powder measures is somewhat complicated by the tendency of many long-range competitors to rely on extruded type gunpowder, which is more difficult to meter uniformly than ball or flake type propellants. High-quality powder measures that dispense extruded powders reasonably well can speed up the process, but all charges should be weighed to ensure minimal variation. I have used an inexpensive RCBS Uniflow measure for years, finding it to actually work better with extruded powders than some others, including a very expensive custom benchrest measure, which frequently bridged powder charges when using even short-grain extruded powders such as RL-15 and Varget. I have also been well pleased with the excellent Redding BR-30 benchrest measure. It dispenses many extruded powders accurately, and offers quick adjustment via a micrometer-type screw. However, shooters using large-capacity cases will likely find its small powder reservoir an inconvenience. *Uniform technique is critical to metering charges accurately.* An internal powder baffle helps reduce variation as well; these may be purchased separately or can be easily constructed if your measure is not already so-equipped.

Scales

At the risk of sounding like a shill for RCBS, I should note that 25 years ago, I purchased an inexpensive RCBS balance-beam type scale, which performed well for many years. I later upgraded to an RCBS 10-10 (balance-beam type) in order to be able to weigh larger objects, and I have been very pleased with it. Several good mechanical scales are available, and while just about the last item I would skimp on would be a powder scale, most any from the better makers should suffice. High-quality scales are typically rated at +/- 0.1 gr. accuracy; physicist/engineer Matt Egloff's article on the theoretical accuracy of balance-type and electronic scales offers some interesting background information on this issue ("Measuring Stuff," *Precision Shooting Special*

Edition #4, v.1, p. 3.) Periodically using a set of scale calibration weights to check the accuracy of your scale is a good practice, both from a standpoint of turning out ammunition which is consistent from lot to lot, and for safety reasons. Most folks start with balance beam type scales, and consequently, many (including yours truly) continue to use them for their long-range Highpower reloading. They work well, but may be slower than some (not all!) electronic scales, and some may have little quirks to which the user should be attuned.

Of course, quirks are by no means limited to powder scales; for example, when loading rifle ammo progressively on my Dillon 550, I find that with an identical powder measure setting, my charges may be 0.2 to 0.3 gr. heavier when uniforming case-necks with a neck size die in the press, than when using it to just prime, dispense powder and seat bullets into previously-sized brass. The extra jarring of the press caused by the expander ball in the case neck seems to cause the powder to settle a bit more, dispensing a slightly heavier charge, which is consistent from round to round as long as the sizer is used. Along similar lines, when loading single-stage, I take care to tap the beam of my RCBS 10-10 scale after trickling a powder charge up to the desired weight. By doing so, I disturbed the beam and let it return to center. Why? Well, long ago, I learned that occasionally, when I trickled powder charges slowly to weight, if I subsequently tapped the beam and allowed it to re-settle, the powder charge would weigh 0.1-0.2 gr. heavier than it had indicated before the beam was tapped. My *THEORY* is that this may be due to the scale's magnetic damping feature. I am a careful, conservative handloader who doesn't load at maximum pressures, so I have a safety-margin built-in to my ammo. A variation of 0.1 to 0.3 gr. in powder charge between *lots* of ammunition loaded doesn't concern me nearly as much as the notion of variation of 0.1 to 0.3 gr. between *individual rounds*, as at long range, velocity variation induces significant vertical dispersion. This quirk of my scale doesn't bother me; I quickly learned to cope with it. I simply tap the balance once each time after weighing a powder charge, and verify that the reading is the same. It doesn't take long, and my results as verified over the chronograph have

been excellent. The lesson here is to pay attention to your equipment's idiosyncrasies and preferences, and learn to work with them.

Electronic scales have become increasingly available and affordable in recent years, and they can offer an outstanding savings of time, particularly for chores such as weighing brass. Precision on these units can vary from decidedly ho-hum, to downright excellent. I have an older electronic scale that has a hard time making up its mind; it frequently hovers between 0.1 gr. increments, and the case that shows 179.6 gr. right now may be considered to weigh 179.7 gr. on the next try. When weighing brass, such imprecision is acceptable, and the time savings over my old 10-10 is invaluable. However, this scale doesn't exactly inspire confidence when weighing powder charges for long-range competition, so I reserve it for less demanding applications. Still another step up the gadgetry food chain involves pairing scales with automatic powder dispensers which trickle powder charges for you—just press the button and step back! One such unit which has been praised for its speed and accuracy is the RCBS Electronic Powder Dispensing System (McPherson, *Precision Shooting, 9/97, p. 39.*) Another interesting approach to the same problem is the Prometheus, which operates on purely mechanical principles to achieve dispensing rates of 6 or more rounds per minute (McPherson, *Precision Shooting, 10/99, p. 58.*)

Priming Tools

Sensitivity and consistency in seating primers is considered by many to be an aid to consistent ignition. Numerous good priming tools are available; bench mounted tools such as the RCBS Automatic Priming Tool offer reasonable "feel" combined with excellent speed, while hand tools offer the reloader increased precision and consistency. Both RCBS and Lee make low-cost hand tools which are well-regarded, while the ne plus ultra is Sinclair International's benchrest-quality unit, if you're feeling particularly flush, but spending big money here is certainly not necessary, in my view.

Case Trimmers

High volume methods of case trimming are less necessary for the long-range competitor than for traditional Highpower shooters, but both hand and powered methods will be discussed here. Most long range competitors will be well served by the superb Wilson hand case trimmer. This gem offers unparalleled precision, and is also much faster and easier to operate than most traditional collet-type case trimmers. The fact that it is also less expensive than many inferior units makes it an even better bargain!! The Wilson uses a cylindrical shell holder to squarely support the case, and it is very easy to adjust to the exact length desired. It requires very little effort to operate, and is flexible, in that case neck turners and inside neck reamers are available as add-on accessories. As hand trimmers go, I consider it the one to beat!!

None the less, for pure volume reloading, power case trimmers win top honors, hands-down. The Gracey trimmer (Match Prep, tel: 805-822-5383) is very well-regarded; in an early test shortly after their debut, I processed 588 rounds of .223 brass in one hour, with excellent precision!! The Gracey trimmer uses sized brass; cases are inserted mouth-first into a shellholder until their shoulder contacts it, and the blades simultaneously cut and lightly chamfer/deburr the case mouth. Once the cutting stops, the user then gives the case a quick twist to ensure the mouth is cut absolutely square. Trim length is easily adjusted by screwing the shellholder closer to or further from the cutting blades, and the unit is both portable and very quiet in operation. In my experience, the Gracey trims cases with near-benchrest precision. About the only aspect of this system which is in any way time-consuming is that changing case neck *diameters*, say, from .223 to .308, requires adjusting 2 blades in the cutting head to produce a smooth, chamfered neck. I am not exactly Joe Mechanical Genius, and I mastered the process quickly and easily, but aftermarket carbide cutters which are effortless to adjust are also available from Bob Jones Lens Systems (tel: 602-840-2176). Wearing gloves can help prevent blisters from holding cases against the cutter blades in long reloading sessions. Years ago, I tested a Dillon (tel: 1-800-762-3845) power case trimmer, which mounts on the reloading press and sizes the cartridge simultaneously while trimming. The individual specimen I tested did not cut cases as square or as uniformly as the Gracey, but I know several other reloaders who use Dillon trimmers with satisfaction. One advantage of the Dillon is its ability to trim large cases with minimal effort. The Dillon trimmer/sizing die does not have an expander ball, so adjustments to the neck diameter (and thus, case neck tension on the bullet) can either be made by polishing the die to the desired internal diameter, or by using an expander die (such as a Lyman "M" die) as an additional step after trimming and chamfering. A variety of other power case trimmers is available, including kits which convert standard, collet-type hand trimmers for use with drills or electric screwdrivers.

Measuring Tools

I've said it before, and I'll say it again: *Don't skimp here!!* Buying the best measuring gear you can afford is a wise investment, as the precision it engenders will affect your handloading for many, many years to come. Quality measuring tools will last a lifetime and will contribute both to your precision and your level of confidence in your handloading. Once you get these beauties, take care of 'em—keep them clean and stored in their original boxes when not in actual use, to prevent damage. (Voice of experience: it is astonishing what havoc a small chip of brass or particle of grit can wreak with the working of a dial caliper if it gets into the right spot!) Stainless steel dial calipers reading to 0.001" are a must. Shooters who will turn case necks will also need a micrometer reading to 0.0001" for best preci-

Author competing in 1000-yard any-sight match with his Wylde Thing.

sion. I have used NSK, Starrett and Mitutoyo calipers and micrometers for years with excellent results. Another tool which I use regularly is the RCBS Precision Mic, which assists the handloader in determining the headspace of brass fired in his particular chamber, and also in setting up his sizing dies to provide consistent, optimum cartridge headspace for his exact rifle. While cartridge case gauges, such as those made by L.E. Wilson, Inc. can be used to check the shoulder to case head sizing dimension, the Precision Mic offers superior speed, accuracy and ease of use, in my experience. Other manufacturers, such as Stoney Point (tel: 507-354-3360) offer a different approach to the same task, by attaching fittings to the jaws of a 0.001" dial caliper, to measure cartridge case headspace. This tool may be combined with nose pieces that act as bullet seating depth comparators as well.

The relationship of the seated bullet to the origin of the rifling is critical to accuracy, and measuring it precisely helps the shooter quickly develop, and repeatably produce, accurate ammunition tailored to his specific barrel. While the RCBS Precision Mic is very useful for measuring headspace, the dummy bullet supplied with this tool for measuring seating depth to the lands does not appear particularly accurate. The most accurate measurements of the bullet-to-rifling relationship are obtained by using a sample bullet of the actual manufacture and style you will be reloading; whenever you switch bullet styles, new measurements should be taken. I use the Stoney Point Chamber-All OAL gauge, which inserts a cartridge case containing a sample bullet into the rifle's chamber. Once the case is inserted, a flexible rod pushes the bullet into contact with the rifling, and a set screw records this measurement. The OAL gauge is then withdrawn, the bullet reinserted into the gauge, and a measurement is made from the cartridge case head to the bullet tip or bearing surface. As bullet tips vary in length up to 0.030" or more (even within the same box), error can be minimized by using a bullet comparator, such as the Sinclair or Stoney Point, rather than by measuring cartridge OAL from case head to bullet tip. The comparator is placed on the bullet to read on its bearing surface, and this significantly improves precision.

While this tool is very convenient to use,

some variation in measurements will be found, even when using a bullet comparator. For example, in one experiment, I tested three Sierra MatchKings for three trials each, seated to the lands in a National Match M1 Garand. Using the OAL method (measuring to the bullet tip), maximum variance noted was 0.031". Using the comparator method, this was reduced to a maximum of 0.007" variance for three trials with three separate bullets. A similar experiment using a match AR-15 and 80 gr. Sierra MatchKings yielded a maximum of 0.014" variance with the OAL method, vs. 0.008" for the comparator method. Notice that even when using the comparator, some variation was observed; thus, I recommend taking several measurements for best accuracy. I view measurements such as these as a relative starting point for load development, rather than an absolute number accurate to 0.001"; one may choose to use either the average comparator length, or perhaps the longest length recorded, as his tentative cartridge length to lands.

Concentricity gauges are increasing in popularity among serious Highpower Rifle competitors. Several models are available, and they allow shooters to measure different aspects of ammunition and components. The primary use is to measure loaded ammunition concentricity, and, if problems are detected, to help diagnose the source of error and take corrective action to improve the "straightness" of the ammo. Delivering the bullet straight into the rifle's throat, rather than starting it at an angle, is believed to help reduce bullet distortion upon firing which can cause imbalance and reduce accuracy. Depending on the model's versatility, handloaders may also measure the straightness of the cartridge case body, case wall thickness variation, and case neck thickness variation. I have used the NECO (tel: 510-450-0420) Concentricity, Wall Thickness and Runout Gauge with excellent results; this high-quality tool allows measuring seated bullet concentricity, case neck and body runout, squareness of the case head, and case wall thickness variation. (It does not offer a means of measuring case neck thickness variation; specialized 0.0001" micrometers are best for this function.) Adjusting handloading gear to reduce cartridge concentricity errors will be discussed below. Readers who wish to study the wide variety of specialized measuring and accuracy-handloading tools available should consider obtaining a catalog from Sinclair International (tel: 219-493-1858); this fine firm offers one-stop shopping, excellent customer service, and experienced, knowledgeable hand-loaders on staff to help answer any questions.

Specialized Case Preparation Tools

Uniform bullet velocity is critical to accuracy at extreme range, and this starts with uniform ignition. As such, reaming primer pockets to identical depths, and deburring flash holes to improve consistency of primer spark are recommended. The operation only needs to be done once in a cases' lifetime, and when using relatively small quantities of brass, this doesn't take too long to accomplish. Flash hole deburring tools are available from a variety of sources, and I have used both the K&M and Sinclair models with excellent results. Another popular flash hole tool is the RCBS, which features an adjustable stop that indexes off the case mouth. I also use and recommend the Sinclair carbide primer pocket uniformer; when paired with a variable speed electric drill, this speeds up an otherwise onerous chore immensely. Some competitors will use custom, tight-necked chambers that require cartridge case neck turning. Turning case necks typically involves sizing the necks to provide a close fit on a mandrel, setting a cutter blade to shave off any brass over a certain dimension, and then turning the case onto the mandrel, slicing excess brass away from the case neck as it passes under the cutting blade. This thins the case neck walls by removing the high points and ensuring equal neck wall thickness. It also reduces the loaded cartridge's neck diameter to a specified dimension based on the individual chambering reamer used. This allows a close fit of cartridge case to chamber in the neck area, helps improve sized case and seated bullet concentricity, and thus helps ensure that the bullet starts into the rifle's throat as straight as possible. However, TIGHT NECK CHAMBERS AND CUSTOM FITTED AMMUNITION SHOULD ONLY BE USED BY EXPERIENCED AND METICULOUS HANDLOADERS WHO FULLY UNDERSTAND THE THEORY AND MEASUREMENT TECHNIQUES NEEDED TO ENSURE SAFETY. (A detailed, "how-to" description of the neck turning process is provided in Chapter One of the *Precision Shooting Reloading Guide*, and won't be repeated here.)

By way of example, in a custom 7mm chamber reamed with a 0.314" diameter neck, I use cartridge cases which have been neck-turned to a neck wall thickness of 0.013". Upon seating a 0.284" diameter bullet, the resultant loaded cartridge neck diameter is 0.310." Firing such a cartridge in my chamber allows neck expansion of 0.004" total, which, while safe, minimizes case neck stretch and work hardening, and helps the bullet gain a straighter entry into the rifling as it leaves the case neck. IT IS ESSENTIAL TO ALLOW ADEQUATE NECK CLEARANCE FOR PROPER BULLET RELEASE UPON FIRING, IN ORDER TO PREVENT DANGEROUS INCREASES IN PRESSURE. While some highly-experienced benchrest competitors fit their case necks to allow less clearance in a chambered cartridge, I recommend a minimum clearance of 0.004" total (0.002" per side) as noted in the example above, for safety purposes. Other handloaders may use standard (not tight-neck) chambers, but turn case necks in order to ensure consistent neck wall thickness. This helps case necks expand or contract more concentrically when sizing or firing and can help improve seated bullet concentricity. When turning case necks for use in a standard chamber, it is important to avoid thinning the case necks more than the minimum required to shave off the high spots, as excessive case neck clearance can reduce accuracy and over-work your brass. One way to do this when turning necks for standard chambers is to leave about 30% of the case neck surface (i.e., the "low spots") *unturned*, which will reduce neck thickness variation without excessively thinning case necks. I use a Sinclair "Phase I" neck turning tool, which is relatively economical and very precise. It lacks gauges to adjust the cutting blade, which necessitates using a "cut and try" method of adjustment. None the less, I find that by making very small adjustments, I can usually reach the desired neck wall thickness with little difficulty. Tools which allow mounting of a 0.0001" dial indicator are also available, and these can help speed up the initial adjustment process.

Reloading Dies

Gone are the days when a shooter's big die choices were between Redding, RCBS and Lyman standard, press-mounted full length or neck-sizing dies!! These days, there is an almost bewildering variety of dies available, and some allow the handloader to make separate adjustments to the neck diameter, case head-to-shoulder length (case headspace), and body diameter at will. Before delving into a detailed description of the various die types, I should note one thing: it is possible to load accurate ammunition with most any well-made dies from a quality manufacturer, regardless of type. Moreover, just because a die set costs big bucks and says "competition", does not mean that it will produce superior results!! For example, I conducted experiments some years back to compare results with a set of RCBS standard full length (FL) reloading dies against those obtained using RCBS Competition Dies in the same caliber. I measured seated-bullet concentricity (total indicator runout, or TIR) of ammunition produced using both sets of dies, and by using careful adjustment techniques (of which, more later), I was able to achieve superior results using the standard dies, at one-third the cost of the Competition dies!! That is, 92% of the cartridges produced on the standard dies measured under 0.002" TIR, while only 76% of those loaded on the Competition dies met this standard. That is not to say that specialized, competition dies don't make achieving precise results easier; some do, as I'll describe below. Standard, full-length dies offer the benefit of economy, and well-made specimens can produce good, straight ammo if used carefully and correctly. However, as they have a fixed neck diameter, they are limited in their ability to adjust case neck tension. Typically, these type dies are designed to size anybody's brass to work in anybody's chamber and produce durable ammunition which will stand up to rough handling in the hunting field. Translation: They tend to size case necks down to a tighter dimension than is needed, in order to ensure compatibility with all the various types of brass on the market; they then typically use an expander ball to open the heavily-sized case neck back *up* to a desired dimension that will produce adequate case neck tension for any use. The

expander balls tend to introduce concentricity error into the neck area of the case, as they are pulling on the case when it is unsupported; polishing them reduces this tendency, but whenever reloading for precision, avoiding the use of expander balls is a good thing.

While standard, FL dies can turn out excellent ammo, their flexibility is limited, to say the least. For example, using the aforementioned custom 7mm rifle with a 0.314" diameter chamber neck and 0.310" loaded cartridge neck diameter, my initial approach was to size my brass in a standard RCBS FL die without an expander ball. I checked the concentricity of my cases after sizing using this method, and all were concentric to less than 0.0015" runout. Great!! (Or, so I thought...) Because my turned necks were thinner than standard brass, the entire case neck would be sized to 0.306" by the die, and upon seating a bullet, the necks would expand 0.004", which would produce firm neck tension. However, I learned that seating bullets in this brass using a well-made Wilson straight-line

Redding Competition neck-size die offers flexibility and precision in sizing.

seating die and arbor press resulted in significantly excessive runout *simply due to the relatively heavy neck tension* induced by the sizing die. I subsequently reduced case neck tension by moving to a Wilson bushing-type sizer that sized my case necks to give 0.003" expansion for about 1/2 the length of the neck, and my excess seated bullet runout went away. Subsequent lots of ammo showed 100% of cartridges having TIR of less than 0.0015", with virtually all giving runout of less than 0.001". Rather than buying specialized dies, I could have had a gunsmith polish out the neck of my FL die to achieve a similar result, but then the die would work only with brass turned to those specs. Further, as the brass work-hardened through use, the polished factory FL die would not allow adjustment to increase neck tension— hence, the popularity of sizing dies with interchangeable neck bushings!! In addition to helping control TIR, it appears that being able to adjust case neck tension offers other benefits. The U.S. Army Marksmanship Unit's Handloading Shop considers the amount of case neck tension to

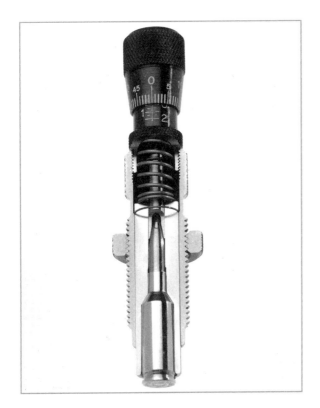

Author has had excellent results using Redding's Competition seater.

be an important factor in the accuracy of their ammunition. Using a fixture which measures case neck tension, they adjust their dies to set lots of ammo within pre-established neck-tension specs for each load they've developed. During extensive interviews with USAMU Handloading Shop personnel, I was informed that significantly excess case neck tension, in and of itself, had been demonstrated to significantly reduce accuracy.

Straight-line, bushing-type neck sizing and seating dies have been used by benchrest shooters for decades to obtain positively awesome accuracy; here, the industry standard has long been the products of L.E. Wilson, Inc., although others offer super-precise semi-custom and custom dies as well. Wilson-type bushing dies are flexible; the shooter can adjust neck tension in 0.001" increments simply by interchanging bushings, and as noted above, they can produce incredibly straight ammunition when used carefully. Wilson dies are not threaded for use in standard presses; they may be used with either a wooden mallet or an arbor press, which is a quickly-portable setup that allows benchresters to handload on the range. I occasionally handload using this type setup, but in honesty, I find well-made, threaded dies in my Rockchucker press to be faster and more convenient. One limitation of these neck-sizing only dies is that they do not allow the shooter to size the cartridge case shoulder, setting it back to allow smooth, effortless chambering. Beware of using cartridges with heavy neck tension in this type setup; as noted above, this can induce massive seated bullet concentricity error.

I frequently use Redding's press-mounted Competition Neck Size and Seating dies, and have had excellent results. These dies employ springs to put tension on their internal bushings and sleeves, and are held to close tolerances. The neck sizer die allows the use of Wilson-style neck bushings, and is equipped with a micrometer knob that allows adjusting the *length* of the cartridge case neck portion to be sized. In conjunction with these dies, Redding also offers a separate body sizing die. This acts as a full length sizer/shoulder bump die, but does not affect the case neck tension, thus giving the reloader excellent control over separate aspects of his cartridge case dimensions. The seating die offers a micrometer seating-depth knob that makes rapid, precise adjustments a breeze. In testing the Redding Competition Neck Size/Seating dies against a well-made set of standard dies, I found that 94% of cartridges loaded using the Redding dies indicated under 0.002" TIR, while only 46% of those produced on the normal dies met this standard. Further, the *worst* cartridges produced by the Reddings (6%) had runout of 0.002" to 0.003", while the worst (10%) produced on the standard dies had 0.004"-0.006" TIR! Interestingly enough, using brass sized on the standard, FL die from the reference set, but seating bullets using the Redding Competition die sharply increased the concentricity of the ammunition—raising the percentage of ammo with less than 0.002" TIR from 46% to 76%. Thus, the individual contribution to concentricity of both the Redding Competition NS and Seater dies was easy to determine. Finally, top-quality custom riflesmiths often offer dies for rifles they build, which give an optimally close fit of brass to that exact chamber; while not inexpensive, they make achieving extremely straight ammunition almost a no-brainer!

III. RELOADING COMPONENT SELECTION

In this section, we will briefly examine aspects of primers, powders, bullets and brass which are of interest to the precision handloader. The readers of this book are likely experienced shooters and reloaders, and no doubt, we have all formed opinions based on our experiences. I will offer mine, with supporting measurements where possible. It is important to remember, however, that, just as individual lots of factory ammunition vary in quality and accuracy, so do the lots of components from which they are assembled. Thus, just because Lot A of Brand X brass in your chosen caliber showed excellent wall thickness or weight consistency, that does not guarantee that Lot D from the same maker will do likewise. The next time you buy brass, the available lot of Brand Y's brass might offer better consistency, so by all means—keep an open mind!!

Cartridge Cases

Over the years, I have measured the weight uniformity and case wall thickness variation of numerous lots of brass. There is a body of research which holds that case-head squareness is affected throughout the functional life of a cartridge by the cases' wall thickness variation. Those cases which have minimal wall thickness variation (as measured just forward of the case head) are considered more likely to remain straight and retain square case heads over several reloadings, which may reduce the incidence of "fliers." Some handloaders select cartridge cases by wall thickness runout, with those exhibiting 0.001" to 0.002" considered to be premium, match grade fare while cases with 0.003" to 0.004" variation are considered marginal. Any cases exhibiting wall thickness runout over 0.004" are likely to be used as guinea pigs when setting up case neck turners, reserved for plinking, varminting and pressure-testing, etc. Quite frankly, hard, scientific data on the actual contributions of this technique to accuracy can be a bit hard to come by. One pioneer in this area was the late Creighton Audette, whose experiments were described in *Precision Shooting* years ago (*PS, 10/93; 11/93*). While anecdotal accounts appear from time to time, usually the people who are most interested in conducting this type research lack the facilities or budget to develop indisputable scientific proof in the matter. Confounding variables when conducting this type research can include the heat treatment and material quality of the individual lot of brass under study (some lots are simply better than others), and the action stiffness, plus squareness and fitting of the rifle barrel, chamber and bolt face/locking lugs of the individual rifle used. Given all the variables involved and the difficulty of locating definitive research, some specialized techniques are probably performed as much with the idea of leaving as little to chance as possible, as they are done because of a well-founded belief in their actual, demonstrable benefit to accuracy.

Personally, I tailor the precision of my handloading to the task at hand. For example, when I crank out 1000 rounds of .223 service rifle 100/200 yard practice ammo, I use mixed years of Lake City surplus brass, loaded on a Dillon progressive press, without any specialized preparation or selection whatsoever. How well does that stuff shoot? Well, by way of example, a while back I fired a series of six, 5-shot groups at 100 yards using a match-grade AR-15 which averaged 0.433", with a smallest group of 0.131". Switching to new, commercial Winchester brass, shrank the average of this recipe only minimally, to 0.355"! Obviously, the accuracy was up to the standard required. On the other hand, I believe that any beneficial effect of specialized case preparation techniques *should* be most apparent at long range. Thus, my 600 yard service rifle ammo is loaded in a batch of commercial Winchester brass, with primer pockets uniformed, flash holes deburred and wall thickness selected for 0.001" to 0.002" runout maximum. The longest range I can typically use for accuracy testing is 250 yards, so my 600/1000 yard testing is generally done under "match conditions!" I can't statistically prove that my 600 yard SR ammo shoots materially better because of the extra brass selection techniques employed, but my confidence is greater knowing I have left very little to chance, and greater confidence in one's equipment can help improve shooter's performance, in and of itself. Along similar lines, in my brass preparation for long range bolt-gun shooting, I weigh cases and segregate by no more than 0.7 grain increments, neck turn, uniform primer pockets and deburr flash holes; heck, I'd probably go to New Orleans and have a voodoo spell cast on my brass, if I really thought it would help!!

That said, my best results with American made cases have generally come with Winchester brass, both in terms of wall thickness runout, weight uniformity and durability. European brass from makers such as Sako, Norma and Lapua is very popular among many high-tech accuracy shooters; flash holes are generally drilled, not punched, so burrs are minimal, and the case walls can run amazingly true, depending on the individual lot. There can be no doubt that much of it is of jewel-like quality when compared to the mass-produced US fare. It should be; typically, European Wunder-brass costs up to twice (or more) the tariff charged for American brass! Nice though the Euro-brass can be, it is certainly not infallible. Years ago, I purchased a spendy batch of 200 Sako 7x57 cases, only to find that they developed pinhole leaks in the necks within 3

reloadings!! The relatively low volume of ammunition loaded for long-range competition reduces the sticker shock of high-dollar brass enough that those shooters who like it tend to use it; many report excellent results with the ultra-precise imported brass, but again, scientifically valid, comparative accuracy data can be hard to come by.

Primers

Primers are a surprisingly important component for the long-range shooter. Reducing vertical spread by attaining minimum velocity variation is critical to long-range shooting success, and primers are one key to this. Even when weighing cases, tuning neck tension to be highly consistent, and carefully weighing powder charges, it is possible to obtain excessive velocity variation in otherwise accurate ammo; simply changing primers can often reduce this greatly. As a rule, the milder the primer, the better, as it offers less disturbance upon ignition, although magnum shooters should be careful to select primers that will give safe, uniform ignition of their large powder charges. As an example of the benefits of selecting primers, my primary rifle for 600/1000 yard competition is a custom 6mm Remington Ackley Improved, in which I launch moly coated 107 gr. Sierra MatchKings fueled by RL-22. In my early load development, I compared Federal Match primers with Federal Match Magnum primers, using hand-weighed powder charges in weighed cases. The velocity extreme spread with Federal Match primers was 29 fps (highest to lowest velocity within a sample of 10 rounds), while with the Magnum version, it was **72 fps!!** Sierra's ballistics tables indicate that, at 1000 yards, the theoretical vertical spread due solely to velocity variation would be about 13.5" using the magnum Match primers, and only about 5.5" using the standard Match primers!! Competitive shooters have long held Federal Match primers in high regard, and many have also reported excellent results using RWS primers in their long range ammunition. I have found that different powders seem to like particular primers; for example, in the .223 cartridge, when using Varget, CCI-BR4 primers have often given me better long range accuracy and reduced velocity variation than others I have tried. In the final analysis, the best way to determine what primers your rifle and load will like, is to experiment with them, using a chronograph as well as accuracy-testing.

Powder Choices

Over the years, certain choices of gunpowder have become well-accepted favorites for specific applications. When choosing powders for accurate handloading, several attributes are desirable. A burning rate closely matched to the cartridge case capacity and bullet weight is a primary consideration; after that, powders which fill the cartridge case with little left-over air space can reduce variations in ignition, pressure and velocity, contributing to accuracy. It might be tempting to ask just how one is supposed to know the relative loading density of various powders in your caliber of choice, if you have not worked with the

powders in question. Certainly, buying a pound of each of several powders, weighing out representative charges and dropping them into cases to observe their load density is possible, but there is a better way! Nosler Bullet's reloading manual lists load density data for all powder charges they reference... which is very handy, indeed! (I just wish *all* the reloading manuals offered this convenience!)

Yet another attribute worthy of attention is a powder's uniformity of performance over a wide temperature range. It has long been accepted that, as ambient temperature increases, so do the pressure and velocity generated by most gunpowder upon firing. Obviously, developing your long range load at 60 degrees in the early season, only to compete with it at 105 degrees in the height of summer, can lead to some unwanted surprises!!

Chart A: Pressure/Velocity Changes by Temperature
(Data courtesy of Hornady Manufacturing Company)
NOTE: **THIS DATA PROVIDED FOR INFORMATION ONLY.
DO NOT USE AS RELOADING DATA IN YOUR RIFLE!**

Cartridge: .223 Remington   **Bullet:** Hornady 68 gr. BTHP
Powder: 25.5 gr. RL-15

Temperature (Degrees Fahrenheit)

	-5F	+70F	+140F
Velocity:	2945 fps	3039 fps	3206 fps
Pressure:	48,000 PSI	52,000 PSI	60,200 PSI

Cartridge: .243 Winchester   **Bullet:** Hornady 58 gr. VMAX
Powder: 43.2 gr. Vihtavuori N-150

Temperature (Degrees Fahrenheit)

	-5F	+70F	+140F
Velocity:	3754 fps	3756 fps	3772 fps
Pressure:	58,200 PSI	57,700 PSI	58,600 PSI

Cartridge: .308 Winchester   **Bullet:** Hornady 178 gr. BTHP
Powder: 43.5 gr. Vihtavouri N-150

Temperature (Degrees Fahrenheit)

	-5F	+70F	+140F
Velocity:	2543 fps	2594 fps	2598 fps
Pressure:	52,100 PSI	57,000 PSI	57,800 PSI

Considering that your rifle's *chamber* will be much warmer than the ambient temperature after a few rounds have been fired, this aspect of powder performance becomes even more interesting!! (This effect is just one of the reasons why it is unwise to exceed manufacturer's recommended load data, which takes such variations into account.) Powders which have been formulated to maintain extreme ballistic consistency across a wide range of temperatures are becoming increasingly available as this is written. In conducting research for this chapter, I contacted several well-known powder manufacturers and importers, requesting detailed temperature-testing information regarding powders of interest to long range shooters. Unfortunately, this type information can be rather difficult to obtain.

In discussing this issue with Dave Emary, Chief Ballistics Scientist at Hornady Manufacturing Co., he noted that, while there are many variables to take into account, in general, single base powders tend to perform more uniformly over temperature changes than double base powders. He supplied some interesting figures (see Chart A); for example, in the .223 Remington/RL-15 load tested, pressures varied 12,200 PSI, and velocity changed by 261 fps, while in the .243 Winchester/Vihtavuori N150 load, pressures varied only 400 PSI, and velocity was amazingly consistent at only 18 fps change!! Vihtavouri Oy's single-base propellants have earned a popular following due to their stability during temperature changes, and another powder line which is coming on like gangbusters is Hodgdon's "Extreme" series. These powders, engineered from the ground up for superior lot-to-lot consistency and stability over temperature changes, are rapidly gaining in popularity among accuracy-oriented shooters. In addition to their ballistic qualities, the Extreme series powders have been formulated with shorter grains than many traditional extruded powders, in order to facilitate easier metering. The first such powder introduced in the U.S. was Varget, which I have used for several years with excellent results in a variety of AR-15 match and service rifles. Varget has earned an enviable reputation for accuracy in the popular .223 Remington and .308 Winchester cartridges, among others, and paved the way for introduction of several new "Extreme" powders

ranging in burning rates from H4198 to H50BMG. Chart B gives data published by Hodgdon which compares the relative uniformity of Extreme series powders with that of other popular powders in .308 and .300 Winchester Magnum cartridges.

Bullets

If you are blessed with a well-built rifle, and stuff its cartridge cases with most any appropriate powder and a *good* bullet, you are quite likely to obtain accuracy ranging from at least good, to downright outstanding. However, take the same well-built rifle, choose an optimal powder for your application, and use poor bullets, and the result WILL be poor accuracy. The bullets you use in rifle competition can be considered analogous to the tires on Richard Petty's race car—the whole car's performance depends ultimately on the tires. That said, it becomes obvious that choosing well-made bullets with an optimal ballistic coefficient is a critical aspect of your rifle's overall performance. Top quality bullets are available both from old-line, major players such as Sierra, Hornady and Nosler, and, increasingly, from smaller accuracy specialists like Berger Bullets (tel: 602-842-4001) and JLK (tel: 501-331-4194). It is fair to say that Sierra Bullets has built an enviable reputation for consistent accuracy and outstanding lot-to-lot uniformity; they are incredibly popular among serious Highpower competitors, and a list of their national and international championship wins could probably fill this chapter! Nosler's Ballistic Tip hunting bullets and Hornady's Match and AMAX line have also earned followings among accuracy-oriented shooters, as well. Berger and JLK are smaller companies selling essentially hand-made bullets, specializing in the high-tech "Very Low Drag," or VLD configuration.

What defines a VLD bullet? Designed back around 1985 by famed ballistician and engineer William C. Davis, Jr., these extremely efficient projectiles are purpose-built to produce the lowest possible aerodynamic drag, within the design limitations imposed by accuracy concerns. The original VLD1 bullet, developed for 300 meter International competition, was a 6mm, 105 gr. bullet, 5 calibers in length and with 9.0 degree boattail angle and a 15 caliber radius to the ogival curve. The design has become popular in other calibers as well, especially with Highpower competitors using the .223 caliber AR-15, where it has done wonders to bring the "mousegun" into parity with the .308's. Once seen, VLD bullets are unforget-

table, as they are quite long and slender for their caliber, looking almost like little icepicks. Moreover, they *work*—they *do* minimize winddrift. Unfortunately, due to their rather specialized design, with minimal bearing surface for their length, they can be a bit tricky to get to shoot with great accuracy. Due to their great

---

Chart B: Pressure/Velocity Changes by Temperature
(Data courtesy of Hodgdon Powder Co., Inc.)
NOTE: **THIS DATA PROVIDED FOR INFORMATION ONLY.**
DO NOT USE AS RELOADING DATA IN YOUR RIFLE!

Cartridge: .308   Case: W-W   Primer: WLR   Bullet: 168 gr. Sierra BTHP
(All pressures measured in CUP; velocities given in FPS.)

POWDER:	VARGET	WIN 748	RL-15	VIT N140	IMR 4064	A2520
70 Deg. F						
Pressure	51,100	50,200	50,300	49,600	51,100	49,900
Velocity	2771	2724	2715	2665	2686	2805
125 Deg. F						
Pressure	51,500	51,100	47,300	51,000	49,700	52,600
Velocity	2779	2769	2705	2679	2697	2844
0 Deg. F						
Pressure	51,200	47,300	48,700	47,500	51,300	50,500
Velocity	2778	2655	2665	2629	2651	2781

Cartridge: .300 Win. Mag.   Case: W-W   Primer: WLRM   Bullet: 180 gr. Sierra BTSP

POWDER:	H4831SC	AA3100	IMR4831	VIT N560	RL-22
70 Deg. F					
Pressure	54,000	51,800	51,000	52,400	53,000
Velocity	2985	3050	3012	3009	3087
125 Deg. F					
Pressure	52,800	54,300	54,400	57,000	55,100
Velocity	2995	3113	3080	3101	3142
0 Deg. F					
Pressure	53,200	51,500	49,400	51,800	52,700
Velocity	2986	3000	2953	2980	3067

length relative to their weight, they typically require a faster-twist rifling rate than usually found in factory barrels (e.g., my 6mm Remington Ackley Improved was purpose-built for VLD's and has a 1:8" twist barrel, rather than the standard 1:9".) This can contribute to core-slipping problems if soft-cored VLD's are pushed too fast in a quick-twist barrel. Most shooters report they perform best when seated near the lands. Walt Berger, famed benchrester and bulletmaker who produced the first VLD's for use in International competition, has stated "It is ESSENTIAL to assemble VLD bulleted cartridges so that the JUMP is not more than 0.020", and better if it is 0.005" or even less, but the bullet should not be jammed [into the rifling]...." He further cautioned that all true VLDs require significantly more precision in adjusting seating lengths than standard bullets *(PS, Young, 6/95, p.56.)* VLD bullets have much to offer the competitor; they can significantly reduce wind deflection in any given cartridge for which they are available, and they handily meet their original goal—providing excellent wind performance *with cartridges giving minimum recoil.* Less recoil means less shooter fatigue, which is a good thing.

Just how effective *are* long, skinny bullets in the wind? Well, I recently shot a local 1000 yard prone match with serious long-range shark, MSGT Bill Walter of the U.S. Air Force Rifle Team; I had my 6mm Ackley, and Bill was using his heavy "thumper," a custom .300 Winchester Magnum with 240 gr. Sierra MatchKings. Bill came off the line after having produced a pretty durn sporty score, even in fairly tricky wind conditions, and then it was my turn to shoot. In order to get on paper a bit faster, I asked Bill how much wind he was using in his Magnum. "Three and a half minutes," he replied, so I dutifully cranked on 3.5 MOA right windage, to start... and my first sighter ripped through the ten-ring. Needless to say, that got my attention—and while Bill's choice is a bit more effective in the wind than mine, I personally prefer the light recoil and superb accuracy of a highly-efficient 107 gr. 6mm bullet at 3100 fps, to the .300's massive 240 grain hunka hunka burnin' lead!! *(With apologies to Elvis Presley, of course!)* The obvious caution here, of course, is the VLD shooter will need to

monitor his throat wear carefully, and make periodic adjustments as needed, to keep his VLD's where they like to be in relation to the lands as throat erosion takes its toll on his barrel.

And, now, a word about ballistic coefficients, which, in layman's terms, are a numerical expression of a bullet's ballistic efficiency expressed relative to a standard, theoretical bullet. Higher numbers mean greater efficiency, or retained velocity and resistance to wind deflection, given equal muzzle velocities. However, BC's are not cast in stone; *your actual mileage may vary.* Out to about 600 yards or so, using computer models to predict the wind deflection of a particular bullet design is relatively easy. Go much past that, however, and results of the various computer programs start to diverge—sometimes sharply. All sorts of factors can and do affect accurate measurement of ballistic coefficient, including individual differences in rifles, atmospheric conditions/altitude, and even the powder charge used. (I.e., excessively high peak chamber pressures can cause the bullet ogive to slump and significantly reduce the bullet's BC, as can too slow a rifling twist that causes excessive bullet yaw!) What does all this tell us? Well, first off—stay within the pressure limits recommended by reloading component manufacturers. Stuffing your case with rocket fuel to blast your bullets out at just under light speed is likely to cause all sorts of problems, and just one of them can be a significant degradation of *both the accuracy and ballistic efficiency* of your bullet! Secondly, BC's are perhaps best viewed as a rough guide to bullet performance, not as the final word. Let's take an example to show what kind of variations you might encounter. Let's say you are one of those intrepid souls who shoots an AR-15 Match Rifle at 1000 yards, and that you use an 80 gr. Sierra MatchKing at 2800 fps. Using 3 popular computer ballistics programs set for standard atmospheric conditions, I specified Sierra's given BC for this bullet at speeds of over 2200 fps. Out to 600 yards, the wind deflection data given by all three programs was fairly close; in a 10 mph full-value wind, the difference between the program predicting the most deflection and the one predicting the least deflection was only 2.07". However, at 1000 yards, in the same wind conditions, the three programs varied significantly. Here, the difference between the least and most predicted wind deflection was 14.51"! Sierra's data is derived from carefully-controlled firing tests, and interestingly enough, their wind-deflection estimate was squarely in the middle between the highest and lowest of the three programs!

And, what of moly? Coating bullets with "moly", or molybdenum disulfide, has been a hot topic among highpower shooters for several years. In the early days, ardent proponents of moly made all sorts of claims, including decreased fouling with resultant increase in optimum accuracy duration (i.e., shoot more, clean less), longer barrel life, higher velocities at equal pressures, and even improved ballistics at extreme range due to less bullet distortion. Well, it's some years later, and overall, shooters seem fairly well divided between two camps, concerning moly. Some believe it is manna from Heaven, and others lump it in the same category with Brooklyn Bridge sales pitches and a certain President's carefully choreographed, finger-wagging protestations of "innocence". Over the years, I have seen a lot of fads come and go, so when moly first became popular, I took a "wait and see" attitude. Well, I waited and saw for about a year, and when several shooters whose technical expertise I respected reported good results using moly, I decided my professional education required that I give it a try. I promptly purchased an RCBS Sidewinder tumbler plus the necessary moly coating supplies from NECO, and set about learning to coat my own bullets. This came easily enough, and after firing a couple of thousand rounds of moly'ed .223's in my target AR-15's, I can definitely attest to the "greater ease of barrel cleaning" claim. I never pushed the issue of firing more rounds between cleanings, to see if accuracy would last longer; I continued to clean my .223 barrels every 80-110 rounds or so, but it took about half the effort to get them clean that was required with "naked" bullets. Unfortunately, my computer is located in my reloading room—and lacking a garage or work shed, that's where I did all my moly coating. Moly is an incredibly fine powder that is all-pervasive, and I found that, despite my best efforts, everything in my reloading room was starting to acquire a fine coating of the

stuff!!! I figured not having to replace a $2,500 computer will buy a lot of barrels, so I quickly coated my 6mm Ackley Improved's remaining bullets on hand, and sold off my moly gear. I switched back to plain bullets in most calibers, but continue to shoot moly'ed bullets in my 6 Ackley, as it is a relatively small-bore/high-capacity cartridge. In the 600/1000 yard matches, I don't get to clean between stages, so I still use moly in this rifle with an eye to reducing fouling and keeping accuracy at its peak. My 6 Ackley's Hart barrel is still too new to give data on barrel life; frankly, I don't expect any miracles, but I'll monitor it just the same, to see if it lasts unusually long. In the meantime, I now buy whatever moly'ed 6mm bullets I need pre-coated. Readers interested in contrasting viewpoints on the benefits of moly coating may want to read the following articles, both published in *Precision Shooting:* "Works For Me" (Dick Wright, 7/99), and "Moly: Son of Cryo Test" (Kevin Thomas, 1/99). One doesn't hear many of the early "magic" claims for moly, these days; my personal belief is that, if there is any benefit of relevance to the long range competitor, it is likely reduced fouling in long courses of fire.

IV. THE RELOADING PROCESS

Overall, our goal in handloading for long range competition is rather straightforward—to produce safe, consistent ammunition which is accurate in our rifles. There are any number of approaches to this, and various degrees of precision which shooters may choose, depending on their needs, their equipment, and their level of skill. Some consider 1000 yard highpower shooting to be primarily a wind-reading game, and thus consider any handload capable of sub-MOA accuracy to be entirely adequate; as long as their ammunition will reach that level of accuracy, any additional handloading steps are considered superfluous. Internationally-respected custom riflesmith Bill Wylde ascribes to this approach, and with obvious success—he routinely wins or places near the top at the Canadian national championships in long range "F class" competition. Shooters in "F class" events use rests but fire prone for score (as opposed to group shooting, as is done in benchrest), and shooting is done out to 900 meters—or, virtually 1000 yards. Bill has his own 500 yard range with machine rest facilities, etc. and tests his "F class" rigs at that distance. He considers ammunition that will produce 0.5 MOA groups at 500 meters to be perfectly adequate. Years ago, Bill noted that deburring flash holes and uniforming primer pockets gave him an instant and significant accuracy improvement, so he routinely uses those techniques in his brass preparation. However, he doesn't bother with turning necks for cases that are fired in standard necked chambers, considering that to give minimal benefit for the time involved. Bill notes that, in score-type shooting, standard, US made brass gives adequate accuracy, but that if he were shooting 1000-yard benchrest, he would likely move to more expensive/consistent Norma brass for his 6.5-.284, and adopt more stringent case preparation techniques, such as neck turning and weighing cases. Bill is nothing if not an innovator who likes to experiment and challenge the established order of things... he is one of the bona-fide AR-15 accuracy pioneers, whose enhancements and experiments with these rifles in the early to mid-'80's did much to advance them to their current position of prominence in NRA Highpower. Obviously, he's not afraid to choose the path less trodden! As an experiment, he competed in—and won—the 1997 Canadian Long Range Challenge and shot the highest score in the McDonald-Stewart Grand Aggregate (300-900 meters) *using metered charges, not weighed!*

On the other hand, some folks just feel better knowing they have taken every step possible to maximize the accuracy of their equipment, so that anytime a shot is off call, they can be sure it was their technique, and not the rifle or ammunition that was at fault. And, there is nothing wrong with that; shooter confidence is a worthwhile asset to good performance, in and of itself. The relatively low volume of brass preparation and handloading that long-range competition entails allows such thoroughness without wasting excessive amounts of time in the process. For example, I initially prepped 100 Winchester cases for my 6 Ackley, and they're still in use after two seasons of long-range competition; they've all been weighed, wall thickness selected, neck turned, flash hole deburred and had their primer pockets uniformed,

but doing this for only 100 cases, rather than, say, 1000, keeps the misery factor low. (Before you ask, yes, I have a big box of 500 new 6mm cases sitting next to my reloading bench for next year...) Your degree of precision in brass preparation is certainly an individual choice; excellent results can be obtained with relatively minor case preparation, or you may feel more confident going "whole hog." Hard, scientific data on the actual benefit of specialized, advanced case preparation techniques is hard to come by, but logic suggests that any benefit they do offer is most likely to be visible at long range, rather than short range. The one critical exception to this, as noted above, is that everything possible should be done to minimize velocity variations, due to their significant effect on vertical spread at long range.

Initial Case Preparation

Ok, so you've waited the required months or years for your custom long-range Wunder-boomer to arrive, and now it's time for brass preparation to begin. The detail-minded may choose to select cases by wall thickness variation using a NECO gauge or similar instrument; if so, start with new brass, and size it to round out any dents that the necks may have suffered in shipping. Be careful not to set back the case shoulders excessively for your rifle, particularly if you will be fire-forming cases later, such as with an Improved cartridge. Brass with only 0.001"-0.002" wall runout should be earmarked for competition and that with 0.003"-0.004" runout reserved for less demanding tasks. Brass

Custom 6 Ackley in 1000 yard load testing.

can be permanently marked to identify its runout category by adding a tiny notch to the case rim using a needle file or Dremel tool with cutoff wheel. I use one notch for 0.001"-0.002" runout and two notches for 0.003"-0.004" runout. Confession time: I have had no problem at all shooting High Master scores at 600/1000 yards in the local prone, any-sight matches using match-prepped, weighed, Winchester brass that showed 0.004"-0.005" wall thickness runout, even over the course of numerous reloadings!! However, this rifle was set up with a custom, benchrest action, on which the bolt body was sleeved to give a super-precise fit to the receiver, minimizing bolt movement upon firing. Great care was taken to ensure that the rifle's bolt lugs were in proper contact, and that its bolt face, action face, receiver threading, chamber and barrel shoulder were concentric and square as appropriate, plus it has a custom, tight chamber, all of which probably helps minimize any effect of less than perfect brass. If your plan is to select US-made brass for wall thickness and/or weight variation to produce a reasonable quantity of highly-uniform brass for competition, here's a hint: *buy a bunch more than you need!!* (As in, at least double the quantity you want to end up with, and all from the same lot number, of course!)

Neck turning is next, if your rifle requires it or if you just want the extra edge of precision. After neck turning, trim and chamfer as needed, then be sure to remove any leftover case neck lubricant and brass shavings from inside the case. (I use Q-tips for this.) Now it's time to move on to flash hole deburring and primer pocket uniforming. While neck turning is optional in rifles with standard chambers, I personally recommend these last two steps, as they may impact the consistency of ignition of your ammo, and can help reduce velocity variation. Weighing cases goes fairly quickly if you have an electronic scale. The plastic trays that come in factory pistol ammo boxes are great for this—they are compact, cheap and plentiful at the local range. Small cases such as .223 can use the 9mm/.38 Special size trays, and larger cases such as .308/.30-'06 use the .45 ACP size trays. I mark them with the various weight ranges I am looking for, and stuff the cases into them as they come off the scale. What weight

variation is acceptable? Well, of course it depends on the size of your case. A 1-grain variation in .22 Hornet brass might be significant, but it means nothing if you're working with the .50 BMG!! When working with long-range brass for the .223, I like to segregate cases into lots based on about 0.6-0.7 gr. increments. That is less than a 1% variation in total case weight (most .223 cases tend to run about 92 grains on average), and it allows getting a reasonable number of matched cases per batch out of any given lot of brass. In heavier cases, such as 6.5-.284, you can use a correspondingly larger case-weight spread if needed, but if you start with a large amount of brass, you'll likely have plenty that fall within 0.5 gr. deviation or even less. For example, my 6mm Ackley's dedicated 1000-yard (only) cases are consistent to within only 0.2 gr. maximum deviation!! That was not due to a special requirement for such precision on my part; it just happened that the best 30 cases out of 100 fell in that group, so I reserved them just for use at 1000 yards.

Case Lubrication and Sizing

Lubricating cases involves more than just getting them slippery enough to go into and out of your sizing die without sticking. Uneven case lubrication can and will affect the headspace of your brass during sizing. The old-time method of rolling cases on a case lube pad is messy and time-consuming, and years ago I switched over to Dillon spray case lubricant. There are many variations on the spray-lube theme, and most work fine; the key here is to get the lube *lightly and evenly* applied to your brass. Using adequate, but not excessive lube prevents shoulder dents, and keeping lubricant consistent will help minimize variations in case headspace. Dillon's spray lubricant is alcohol based; a light coating quickly flows over the cases if they are allowed to sit for a few minutes before sizing, and it tumbles off easily. However, I've learned that it's wise to clean one's sizing dies after using any aqueous-based lube, to prevent rust. (I just use a Q-tip moistened lightly with Hoppes #9, which removes the lube and provides good protection.) If you tumble cases to remove sizing lubricant, be sure to remove any bits of tumbling media from the flash holes or that could be stuck inside the cases; while tapping the case mouths on the reloading bench works fairly well, the by-now-inevitable Q-tip run around the case body ensures abrasive grit doesn't get blasted down your $400 custom barrel at 50,000 PSI! Another approach to this, of course, is to wash the case lube off, whether in a case tumbler designed for this, or by slipping your brass into an old pillow case and throwing it into the washing machine (NO BLEACH) when your significant other isn't looking. When processing large batches of brass, I tend to wash them, while I tumble small batches to avoid the delay spent waiting for my cases to dry.

For use in **BOLT-ACTION** rifles which will be single-loaded for long range competition, neck sizing offers several potential advantages (however, opinions vary on this issue; see interview with long-range legend, Middleton Tompkins below). Once your brass has been fired in your chamber with a full-power load, it is closely fitted to the chamber. Assuming a chamber which is concentric to the bore, and use of cartridges with minimal seated-bullet runout, sizing only the case neck allows the case body to retain the closest possible fit, minimizing chances for slop and helping to minimize risk of the bullet's entering the bore off-center. By minimizing end-play (excess cartridge headspace), you are working to maximize consistency of ignition, with (hopefully) corresponding reductions in velocity variation. Side-benefits of neck-sizing are reductions in case-body stretch and work-hardening of your brass from over-sizing. However, sooner or later, even neck-sized brass will likely stretch and need to have the shoulders set back somewhat, to reduce stress upon the bolt/locking lugs and allow smoother, easier chambering. [NOTE: this information pertains to bolt-action rifles only; ammunition to be used in semi-automatic rifles should be full-length sized to allow a smooth, friction-less fit in the chamber and adequate headspace for safe functioning. Use of tight-fitting brass in semi-automatic rifles is NOT RECOMMENDED as, either alone or in conjunction with other conditions such as high primers or mechanical wear to the rifle's mechanism, this can contribute to dangerous slam-fires. Readers desiring a detailed discussion of the safety issues and safe headspace clearances when handloading for semi-automatic rifles are strongly encouraged to read the author's

"Gasgun" reloading chapter in the *Precision Shooting Reloading Guide*. As always, readers should have a thorough understanding of the techniques and safety issues involved before attempting handloading, should comply with all safety precautions and assume all risks of handling firearms, shooting or handloading.]

When setting up your full-length sizing die, a little care and attention can go a long way to reducing seated bullet runout. As with most handloading operations, approaches to this vary, and several methods can give good results. Long ago, *Precision Shooting* columnist Todd Kindler noted the beneficial effects of installing a rubber O-ring between the sizer die lock ring and the top of the reloading press, in reducing TIR. In use, the die is screwed into the press *without* the bottom of the die contacting the shellholder, and an O-ring is placed under the lock ring. One then takes a lubricated case, sizes it, checks it with an RCBS Precision Mic or other instrument to measure the distance the shoulder is set back, and then screws the die down a bit more, sizing and measuring after each pass through the die until the desired case headspace is produced. Once you reach the desired headspace, *run the sized case back into the die* to keep the die under tension, and then screw the lock ring down to the top of the press to apply firm pressure on the O-ring against the press. Then tighten the lock ring's adjustment screw. It is important to leave enough clearance between the top of the press and the lock ring to let the die "float" slightly if you exert pressure on it with your hand. Upon removing the die from the press, the lock ring and O-ring are left in place, and in future reloading sessions, the die will be adjusted downward to give the desired headspace in increments as before, with the O-ring providing tension to center the die in the press threads. How much cartridge headspace (end-play) is desirable? I personally set the shoulders of my 6mm Ackley Improved brass back 0.002" from the fired dimension each time I size my cases, as I prefer the brass to chamber smoothly and without effort. I chose this dimension while taking into account that my brass and dies give very little variation in sized case headspace. If you find that, for whatever reason (to be addressed below) your sized brass varies significantly in headspace, you will need to consider this when setting your die, so that all cartridges will chamber smoothly and give safe headspace in your rifle. For example, if some of my brass's shoulders were only set back 0.001", I'd adjust my sizer die downward to set my shoulders back 0.001" more if needed to ensure that all cartridges would chamber freely. Forcefully chambering brass which fits very tightly in your rifle poses the risk of galling of the bolt lugs/action recesses, particularly if wind blows sand into your action.

Another approach, and one which may offer some advantages, is to use Redding's custom variable-headspace competition shellholder set. This set of 5 shellholders is graduated in 0.002" headspace-reduction increments, and allows full-length resizing with quick and easy headspace adjustments. In use, the shooter measures the headspace of several cases fired in his chamber using a Precision Mic, etc., and then installs the FL sizing die in his press to provide full contact with the +0.010" shellholder when the press ram is raised. Sizing a case and remeasuring will give a starting point, and from there adjustments are made by switching shellholders until the desired case clearance in the chamber is desired. It is always wise to double-check your measurements by chambering a clean, EMPTY, sized case in your rifle to verify that the bolt closes smoothly and without excess force. One theoretical benefit of this approach is that the shellholders contact the die bottom when the press ram is raised. Depending upon the rigidity of your press, this may help minimize case headspace variations due to possible press flex, etc., although using an RCBS Rockchucker and the O-ring method above, I have typically been able to maintain consistent sized case headspace.

While on the subject of sized case headspace, I should mention that all brass is definitely not created equal, and readers should not take case headspace measurements for granted! For example, when sizing Lake City .308 cases with my sizing die set to give 0.006" headspace clearance, I noted that, without changing the sizing die adjustment, the shoulders of my Federal .308 brass were set back **0.009!"** Individual lots of brass vary, even when purchasing from the same manufacturer. Moreover, the degree to which brass is sized using a given die setting can vary

during your cartridge cases' lifespan due to progressive work-hardening, so it is always wise and recommended to measure the headspace of cases you size, each time you reload. In addition, individual cartridge cases within the same lot can vary somewhat in headspace after sizing; for example, in .308 brass, I have seen cases from the same lot vary 0.003"-0.004" in headspace using the identical sizer die setting and uniform case lubrication. One batch of Lake City Match brass fired in my NM M1 varied 0.004" in headspace the first time I resized them, but in subsequent reloadings, the brass became more consistent (perhaps due to work-hardening), and headspace varied only 0.002" after the second and subsequent resizings. Belted magnums are a special case unto themselves. While these cartridges are intended to headspace on the belt, rather than the case shoulder, factory rifles and cartridges tend to exhibit quite a bit of case stretch upon initial firing—up to 0.030" at times, depending upon the individual rifle and ammunition!! Obviously, resizing these cartridge cases to their original dimension each time they are reloaded can and does lead to short case life due to head separations. Here, it is recommended to treat the belted magnum as though it were a standard, rimless cartridge and use the shoulder to control headspace, setting it back enough to ensure smooth, easy chambering. *(Readers interested in a more in-depth discussion of special issues pertaining to belted magnum cartridge reloading may wish to peruse the "Magnum" chapter of the* **P.S.** *Reloading Guide.)*

Priming and Powder Dispensing

After sizing, trimming, chamfering and cleaning your brass, you're ready to move on to priming. If using brass which has been fired before, be sure to remove any priming residue left in the primer pockets. As noted above, priming tools vary in their approaches; what's critical here is to seat primers uniformly to the bottom of the primer pocket. Primers are shipped from the factory with the anvil protruding a few thousandths of an inch above the cup walls. This is intended to let the anvil slightly compress the pellet upon seating, and thus sensitize the primer. Primers should be seated firmly enough to seat the anvils into the cup, but not so much that they are crushed or distorted. Moderate, uniform pressure is enough to do this—leave the strength training for your gym workouts! Primers should be seated slightly below flush with the case head; this is particularly important when working with auto-loaders, as high primers which protrude above the case head can contribute to slam-fires in which the rifle fires when the bolt runs forward.

When dispensing powder, I recommend weighing charges for all long-range loads (600/1000 yard shooting). This can be a somewhat time-consuming task, but is worthwhile to the serious long-range competitor. Automatic powder dispensing systems have been discussed above; for those who use a standard balance-beam or electronic scale to weigh powder charges, here is a tip that can speed things up. Gun writers have long advocated setting the powder measure to throw charges slightly lighter than the desired setting, and then trickling each charge to weight. My procedure is noticeably faster; I set the powder measure to throw charges to the desired weight, which results in a fair percentage of charges being thrown exactly right, depending on the type powder used. Those charges go straight into the case after check-weighing; those that are a bit light are trickled to weight, and those that are overweight simply go back into the powder can and another charge is thrown. When weighing powder charges, it is important to take some basic precautions to maximize the precision with which your equipment operates. All scales should be protected from drafts, and mounted on a level, sturdy bench in a temperature controlled room. Take care in using them; even breathing on the scale pan can influence your readings! Electronic scales should always be allowed to warm up for at least 15 minutes prior to use, to insure maximum consistency.

Bullet Seating

Seating your bullets is the final step in producing highly-accurate ammo. First things first: **don't crimp your cartridges!** In my experience, crimping bullets when loading precision rifle cartridges causes a lot more problems than it solves. Long-range competition typically involves single-loading cartridges, not feeding them from the magazine, and maintaining adequate case-neck tension for this type shooting

is easy with any normal dies, without crimping. That said, taking a little extra care in adjusting your standard seating dies can noticeably reduce the runout in your seated bullets. I've had good luck with the following approach: I first insert a sized, trimmed case in the shellholder, and raise the press ram all the way up. Next, I back the die's seating stem out, and screw the die down into the press until I feel it touch the case, whereupon I unscrew the die 1/4 turn to insure I won't inadvertently crimp my ammo. Then, I lower the press ram, remove the case, and insert a flat piece of steel between the shellholder and the bottom of the die. I raise the ram to put tension on the die and straighten it in the press, after which I lock the die in place using the lock ring. Finally, I insert a primed, charged case into the shellholder and adjust my seating depth to the desired OAL. During this step, I keep the seating stem's lock nut loosened; when I reach the proper OAL, I *leave the press ram raised, with the cartridge in the die to keep the seating stem centered and under tension*, and carefully tighten the seating stem's lock nut. After the seater is set, I double-check my OAL, and then check for potential excess runout before loading a large batch of ammo. Micrometer-type competition seaters, such as the Redding, are simpler to adjust; their different design eliminates the need to center the seating stem or lock it into place. Periodic checks for runout when loading large lots of long-range ammo can help you avoid unwanted surprises. A bit of excess moly/carnauba wax or other foreign matter in the wrong part of a competition seater die can increase TIR significantly!

As noted above, VLD type bullets tend to perform best when kept close to the lands, while conventional style bullets may be more forgiving of bullet jump. Some shooters prefer to start their load development seating bullets to touch the lands. This helps center the cartridge in the chamber, many rifles shoot well that way, and there is only one direction to move the bullet when experimenting to improve accuracy (away from the lands). Needless to say, all cautions about using published data, not exceeding recommended maximums, and working up your loads incrementally using the recommended starting loads and watching for pressure signs apply here! From a purely safety-oriented perspective, it is desireable to have

RCBS Precision Micrometer.

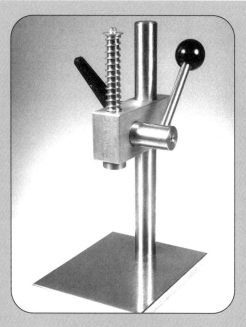

Sinclair Arbor Press.

RCBS Priming Tool.

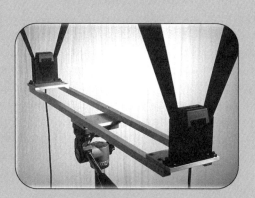

Sinclair Chronograph Skyscreens.

NECO Concentricity Gauge.

Sinclair Case Neck Micrometer.

0.005"-0.010" bullet jump to the rifling, particularly when using heavy bullets, as this can help keep peak pressures a bit lower. Still another approach to cartridge OAL is called "soft-seating," in which bullets are loaded a bit longer than needed to touch the lands while keeping case neck tension moderate. Thus, when the round is chambered and the bolt is closed, the bullet contacts the rifling and is pushed back into the case a bit as the locking lugs cam shut. This automatically compensates for any throat erosion and ensures the bullet will touch the rifling. Use caution with this technique, however; jamming bullets hard into the rifling, particularly when using only moderate case neck tension, can make removing a live round from the chamber a bit of a hassle. You may or may not have problems with this, depending on your chamber, bullets, case neck tension, etc. However, if you do, few things are more frustrating during a match than extracting a live round, only to have the bullet remain stuck in the barrel and a case full of powder dump into your action and locking-lug recesses. In rifle/cartridge combos prone to this problem, elevating the muzzle to a safe degree and *slowly, carefully* opening the bolt to extract the cartridge without spilling powder can prevent such misery. Finally, when conducting accuracy experiments to fine-tune your rifle, keep an open mind. Just because *many* rifles shoot best with bullets close to, or touching the lands, doesn't mean they *all* do. Occasionally, you may run across one that likes bullets to jump more than usual, perhaps even as much as 0.050" to 0.060!"

V. LOAD DEVELOPMENT STRATEGIES

Over recent years several different load-development strategies have become increasingly popular among rifle accuracy-buffs. I'll give a brief overview of the most popular. My personal approach is to do my homework as thoroughly as possible before attending a match, in order to avoid using a load that develops poor accuracy. Few things are more maddening than to drive to a match, pay your entry fee, and then get slammed by a load that doesn't shoot well! Be that as it may, many of the cartridges in use in long-range competition tend to have relatively short barrel lives. This is particularly true of magnums or high-intensity, small bore cartridges; if you're not careful, you could easily waste a significant chunk of your peak accuracy life just testing loads. Working up a *good* load without trying endless combinations of powder, bullet and seating depth makes a whole lot of sense. The cartridge component which will have the most dramatic effect on your accuracy results is the bullet; pick a good one, and test it with a powder carefully selected to give optimum results in your cartridge. If, with brief testing tuning powder charges and perhaps bullet jump, the bullet/powder combination doesn't give good results, you might try a different powder type. If that doesn't work, you may wish to move on to greener pastures, bullet-wise, as that is more likely to give a dramatic improvement than trying endless varieties of powder.

Long range shooting is as much a wind-reading game as anything; that said, assuming good accuracy, the more velocity you can *safely* achieve, the better, as this helps reduce wind deflection. Shooters using cartridges that are only marginally capable of staying supersonic at 1000 yards (e.g., .223 Remington, .308 Winchester) will need to take particular care when selecting bullets and powders, in order to maximize the chance that their bullets will not drop below the speed of sound before reaching the target. Some—but not all—bullets become less stable when they go subsonic, and when that happens, accuracy can deteriorate sharply. Most experienced long-range shooters have a ready fund of horror stories about scoring for shooters using a poor bullet/handload choice, that became unstable and went through the target *sideways* at 1000 yards!! A while back, I discussed this with Bill Davis, a nationally-renowned ballistician, who confirmed that some bullets, such as the 173 gr. .30 caliber GI Match FMJ, seem to tolerate going subsonic rather well, while others definitely do not. Thus, the .308 shooter may want to opt for the 190 gr. or the 175 gr. Sierra MatchKings, rather than Sierra's much-beloved 168, when working up loads for 1000 yard shooting, as they are much easier to keep supersonic at extreme range. (As Sierra's head ballistician, Kevin Thomas, puts it: "Friends don't let friends waste time even TRYING to shoot 168's at 1000!") Likewise, in the .223, JLK and Berger's 75 gr. VLD's have earned an informal reputation of shooting well even after going subsonic.

If at all possible, after doing your preliminary testing to develop an accurate load giving consistent velocities, *test your ammo at the distance you intend to use it.* Many shooters have a hard time getting access to 600 and 1000 yard ranges for testing, and resort to doing short-range load development, with the final testing done under match conditions! I must confess, I've been there and done that... and been bitten for it, as well! I typically do my initial load work at 100 to 250 yards, and with careful load testing and chronographing, this generally works well at long range. However, there are times when Murphy takes over. My most notable case was when using the .223 AR-15 in long range matches. While it is hard for some folks to imagine, the .223 Remington can be used with acceptable results out to 1000 yards, although it takes a savvy handloader to maximize the minuscule cartridge's potential at that range. I have fired 75 gr. JLK VLD's in a 20" barrelled AR-15 service rifle, which, while subsonic, shot well at 1000 yards and landed on call. The target crews reported nice, round bullet holes, and there was no reason to suspect anything was amiss. However, I then tried a good 600-yard load using 80 gr. Sierra MatchKings in an AR-15 spacegun (26" barrel) at 1000 yards and got a real eye-opener. While my load gave an extreme velocity spread (highest to lowest for 10 shots) of only 16 fps, my target showed much more vertical than I expected, based on calling my shots. The Sierras were subsonic upon their arrival at the target, and whether due to instability, an effect of barrel vibrations or both, accuracy was poor. The target crew reported slightly oblong bullet holes in this case. I later tested that load at 1000 yards shooting from a rest, using a 20X scope, and the 10-shot group stretched from the bottom of the X ring to the top of the 8-ring! Hence, the prescription to test loads at the actual distance they'll be used, whenever possible!

Chronographs are an essential tool for the long range competitor—so, get a good one, it's as simple as that. In a perfect world, you are trying to hold your maximum velocity spread to less than 20 fps in a 10-shot sample whenever possible; using an el-cheapo chronograph with a 2-foot screen spacing may actually influence the accuracy of your results. A six-foot screen spacing helps minimize inaccuracy of the chronograph, keeping readings correct to within 2-3 fps. One highly respected chronograph is the Oehler 35P, which offers a proof channel that compares two exit readings to one entrance reading. Any excessive difference between the initial reading and the two exit readings triggers a warning that the data for that particular shot may be suspect. Standard deviation is often quoted when shooters discuss the velocity variation of their ammunition; unfortunately, barrel life being at a premium, most shooters don't fire the 30-round samples that make this a useful statistic. For our purposes, the extreme spread (ES, or range of velocity from highest to lowest recorded in a 10 or 20-shot string) is sufficient. Just keep ES below about 25 and your vertical impact dispersion on target *due solely to velocity variation* should be acceptable.

I've found that when working with truly well-built custom rifles or the very-accurate factory rifle, it is generally easy to find a load that shoots well, when working with good bullets and a decent choice of powder. (It's the marginal rifles that seem to really require a lot of work and tuning to get to shoot well.) One traditional load development method is as follows, and especially when working with good rifles, it makes developing loads for long-range shooting relatively easy; just work your way up from the recommended starting load toward the maximum safe published powder charge, firing at least 3 cartridges at each of increasing 0.5 gr. powder increments. While doing so, it is important to chronograph and observe for signs of high pressure. At the first sign of high pressure, *reduce your powder charge at least one full grain, or possibly more if working with high-capacity cartridges.* Visual signs of high pressure include, but are not limited to, shiny ejector marks on the case head; loose primer pockets, gas leakage around the primer, flattened or heavily cratered primers, and difficulty opening the rifle bolt. Another indicator which requires use of a micrometer capable of reading to 0.0001", is to measure case head expansion and stop increasing powder charges when 0.0003" expansion is noted. NOTE: some cartridges, such as the Ackley Improved versions of standard cartridges, are less prone to show signs of high pressure, such as difficult extraction or ejector marks. The

Ackley Improved type cartridges have less body taper than standard cartridges, which reduces bolt thrust, and makes reading pressure signs more difficult. With Ackley Improved type cartridges, it is possible to be working at very high pressure before the standard pressure signs become obvious. These are NOT "magic cases" that are immune to high pressure, and loads must be kept at safe, sane levels; any wildcat or non-standard cartridges are best reserved for highly-knowledgeable, experienced and careful handloaders. There is no ballistic "free lunch"; individual barrels vary in the velocities they will achieve using a given set of components, but with a particular case, primer, powder, bullet and barrel length, it is safe to assume that velocity X equals pressure Y. This is just one reason why using a chronograph as you develop loads is so important; aside from giving you data on average velocity and velocity variation, the chronograph gives you an indirect indicator of the *pressure* your load is developing! Thus, if your reloading manual says that while using a particular set of components in a 26" barrel, their lab achieved a safe maximum of 2900 fps at 50,000 PSI, when you reach 2900 fps in *your* 26" barrel using the same components, *don't add more powder*, as you probably have reached 50,000 PSI, even if you are using less powder than the lab did! Excess pressure is not simply a safety concern; putting too much stress on your bullets can cause them to deform excessively in the rifling, the cores may strip, and/or the boattails may slump, any of which can wreck your accuracy. Once you have reached the optimal, safe velocity in your rifle, again not exceeding published reloading data, accuracy test your ammo. I recommend using 10-shot groups, as Highpower competition requires 10-shot strings of fire, and this gives you the most reliable predictor of your load's performance. For Highpower shooting, 3-shot test groups are worthless, and 5 shot groups are only slightly better. Initial testing may be done at 100/200 yards to reduce the effect of wind, but when you are confident you have a good load, it's time to move to the longest practical range for final testing. If the load shoots accurately and velocity variation is minimal, you're done!

Some accomplished Highpower shooters prefer to test their loads prone, using a sling, as they will be fired during competition. Shooters capable of a very consistent prone performance may well profit from this, as not only do they get to test the rifle in the exact configuration in which it will be used, they also get the benefit of extra practice! Many shooters, however, rely on a benchrest for testing ammunition. When load testing from the bench, a few rules apply. First, *let the sandbags do the work!* Use a high quality front rest, such as the Hart or Sinclair models, and a good rear sandbag that supports the toe of the stock. Lightweight, el-cheapo aluminum or plastic rests (I'm sure you've seen them—they tend to be orange) are best avoided, as they tend to move about on the benchtop excessively under recoil. The rifle should be pointed at the center of the target, when resting on the sandbags without your having to "steer" it significantly by exerting muscular tension. Adjust the rest and bag so that the rifle points naturally at the target, and then apply moderate, *consistent* pressure at the shoulder, cheek and pistol grip when firing. After each shot, return the rifle to the same place on the rest, ensuring it is again naturally aligned with the target. While benchrest shooters using small cartridges may successfully use the "free recoil" method (pulling the trigger without touching the rifle elsewhere, to allow it to slide freely on the rest and rear sandbag), rifles intended for long-range shooting typically require a different approach. Readers using rifles of medium recoil, such as the .308 or 6.5-.284, may very well find that holding the forend (forward of the rest) using light to moderate pressure from the non-firing hand, will reduce fliers, as this slows the rifle's jump off the sandbags. Magnum shooters may have to resort to a firm hold on the forend to accomplish the same thing. USE WIND FLAGS. They don't have to be fancy—just some florescent orange engineer tape will do, but you need something to let you see how the wind is running between you and the target. Particularly on days when there is little mirage, using flags will help you avoid gusts of wind that can leave you wondering about the accuracy of your ammo. I typically use 2-3 benchrest style wind flags when testing centerfires at 100 yards, and 4 flags when testing at 200-300 yards. There is a limit to the number of flags you can monitor, so place them in areas on the range where experience has shown that wind is likely to be channelled through (for example, where there are open spaces in berms or treelines). Wind closer to the shooter has more effect on the bullet than wind closer to the target, so be sure to put one flag about 15-20 yards in front of your bench. On my home range, shooters who have never used wind flags are consistently amazed when they see my wind flags showing the effect of significant wind downrange, while the air at the shooting bench is a flat calm!!

Another increasingly popular load development approach is that first proposed by a famous Highpower riflesmith and experimenter, Creighton Audette. Originally published years ago in volume III of the NRA's National Championship Training Clinics series (*Highpower Rifle Shooting*), Audette's method was clearly and thoroughly explained by Randolph Constantine in the *1997 Precision Shooting Annual*. Space limitations here prevent a detailed discussion of this method, but in essence, the shooter selects his powder, primer, case and bullet, and determines the working powder charge range for the propellant of interest. After determining the recommended, safe starting and maximum powder charges, the shooter then divides this range of powder charges into 20 increments, and loads *one* cartridge at each powder charge weight. For example, using 0.3 gr. increments and starting at 40.0 gr., twenty increments will lead to a highest powder charge of 45.7 grains. As Constantine notes, for medium to fairly large case capacity cartridges such as the .308 or .30-06, Audette used 0.3 gr. powder increments, while for really large cases, 0.5 gr. increments may be used. In smaller cartridges, 0.2 gr. increments are recommended. Precision is important, here; all powder charges must be weighed to within 0.1 gr! Naturally, your starting load MUST be safe for use with the powder you selected—for example, when using slow burning powders, one must never go below the manufacturer's minimum recommended charge, as this can cause catastrophic detonation (Secondary Explosion Effect, or S.E.E.) Marking the cases with the charge weight using a "Sharpie" or other marking pen before dispensing powder will help keep the cartridges organized, as the procedure calls for

firing each cartridge *in ascending order of powder charge increment.*

Once you arrive at the range, it is important to begin testing with a barrel fouled by firing several shots *using the powder you are studying*, in order to minimize any tendency for the barrel to throw shots due to its internal condition. Some barrels will sling the first few shots after switching powder types out of their normal group, which is known as the "settling effect." One fires the rifle at a single target, using a single aiming point throughout the test, and chronographs each shot; chronograph data can help later during the interpretation of the target. Testing at 300 yards is recommended, but this can be difficult as you will need to identify the location of each shot and plot it as it is fired; on ranges which feature target pits, having someone pull the target and mark each shot as it is fired can be very helpful. Firing at a large, white piece of paper or Birchwood Casey's Shoot-N-C visible indicator targets, with the group impacting above your aiming point can help also. The minimum recommended range for this type testing is 200 yards, in order to obtain meaningful results. After the 20-shot series has been fired, examine the target and compare it to your notes correlating powder charge with bullet location. Usually, the shots will land increasingly higher on target as the velocity increases; however, you will likely notice some clusters of several shots in a small group, despite the difference in powder charge. The goal is to find a succession of 5-6 *consecutive* shots that clustered together, as this indicates a "sweet spot" in which the barrel is insensitive to minor variations in powder charge. Once the sweet spot is identified, pick the powder charge in the middle of the range of charges forming that group. For example, if shots 12-18 land together in a cluster, and the charge weights forming that cluster are from 44.0-45.8 gr., the middle charge in that cluster would be 44.9 grains. In his excellent article, author Constantine offers explanations for factors causing this approach to work, citing an interaction between barrel time, recoil-induced elevation of the muzzle, and barrel vibration. The original intent of this approach was to develop loads which were insensitive to variations in powder charges when using a powder measure, but even when weighing each powder charge, it can't hurt to have barrel harmonics working for you, rather than against you!!

Highly-accomplished research scientist Harold Vaughn has undertaken numerous ballistics and accuracy experiments, and I heavily recommend reading his recent book, *Rifle Accuracy Facts* (Precision Shooting, Inc., 1998). This tome gives outstanding information on rifle accuracy, not only from a ballistics standpoint but also from studies of the mechanical aspects of rifles, that will be of interest to any serious accuracy buff. Mr. Vaughn advocates a somewhat-different long-range load development approach which also takes barrel vibrations into account *(Vaughn, PS, 10/98, p. 6; also see Rifle Accuracy Facts, Ch.4.)* Basically, he recommends the shooter fire groups of at least 4 shots at intervals of 50 fps muzzle velocity throughout the powder/velocity range one wishes to test. Using a grid target, one measures the distance of the center of the groups from the aiming point and plots them. In his article, Mr. Vaughn gives information on the effect of barrel vibration on vertical dispersion at long range, and shows how to pick powder charge/velocity ranges that are optimized for the vibration characteristics of one's individual barrel. He also details "sweet spots" occurring due to barrel vibration, and recommends shooting loads which print slightly to the right of a positive peak on the target grid, or slightly to the left of a negative peak on the grid.

CONCLUSION

Whew! As you can see, handloading for long-range competition can be as complicated and scientifically challenging as you'd like to make it! For some perspective, let's now see how a bona-fide long-range legend goes about handloading for competition. For this chapter, I interviewed Middleton Tompkins, who has the distinct honor of providing the ammo for not one, but *four* extremely talented long-range competitors—himself, his wife, Nancy Tompkins-Gallagher, and their daughters, Sherri and Michelle Gallagher. These four shooters have accounted for an astounding array of national-level long-range wins and national records over the years. Mid kindly agreed to discuss his loading procedure for the 6.5-.284, which he and his family have used with great success at Camp

Perry in recent years, and notes that at times, his load techniques are driven in part by the need for efficiency and economy, as he loads long range ammo in much larger quantities than most shooters. Mid does his own gunsmithing, and in working with the 6.5-.284, he found that his original reamer cut the back of the chamber oversize for optimal case life using Winchester brass; primer pockets expanded quickly, rendering the brass unusable. So, rather than switch to expensive imported brass, he had a reamer ground to fit the economical Winchester brass, specifying a 0.497" base instead of the previous reamer's 0.499". He then made his own dies to allow sizing to optimally close dimensions; however, Mid is not a proponent of neck-sizing. As he sees it, *all* chambers are by definition somewhat egg-shaped, and fired brass emerges slightly out-of-round. The best chambers are only microscopically eccentric, but matching an egg-shaped, neck-sized case to an egg-shaped chamber represents a theoretical nightmare. Ergo, Mid full-length sizes his brass, setting shoulders back 0.001". He believes that, when combined with seating bullets into the rifling, sizing cases smaller than the chamber helps the cartridge center itself upon chambering and gives the bullet its best chance at a straight entry into the throat. Mid is no fan of tight-neck chambers for Highpower. He turns his case necks to 0.012" to 0.0125" thickness which, when paired with his reamer, results in 0.002" neck clearance per side (0.004" total neck expansion upon firing.) He sizes his brass on a heavy-duty RCBS A-2 press, and also considers the RCBS Rockchucker a good, strong tool for minimizing any headspace variation due to press spring.

Mid sizes his brass using "Basic H," a soap/sizing lubricant, and then washes it in a tumbler with hot water and steel shot. This cleans the brass quickly and easily, and removes any priming residue so that he does not have to clean primer pockets. All cases are then trimmed to length. While he does not sort cases by wall thickness runout, he does weigh them on a highly-accurate metric scale in 0.1 GRAM increments. This equates to a weight spread of 1.5 grains per batch of cases. Cases are weight-sorted each time they are resized, as when dealing with 1000+ cases for four shooters, it is difficult to keep them sorted after firing. Mid does not deburr flash holes or uniform primer pockets;

he's not against these practices, but feels that given the amount of handloading he has to do, the accuracy gain is not worth the considerable investment of time it would require. He does, however, sort his bullets by weight, into ~0.5 grain increments. Mid shoots the 142 gr. Sierra MatchKing in his 6.5-.284's, and notes that lot-to-lot consistency and accuracy have been excellent. He seats his primers using the RCBS bench-mounted Automatic Priming Tool, and dispenses his powder charges using a transistorized-model Gunderson scale which he bought in 1954. The Gunderson is a little-known technological marvel that reaches speeds of about 250 charges per hour when holding tolerances to +/- 0.05 gr. (Mid's standard for 600/1000 yard ammo) and about 500 charges per hour when keeping tolerances of +/- 0.1 gr. (his standard for ammo to be used at 300 yards or less.) Before you get too excited, don't even think about getting one—they're old, they're out of production, they're rare as hen's teeth, and they only become available when a shooter goes to the Happy Hunting Ground...

Mid then seats his bullets using either a Wilson straight-line seater die or a Redding type "S" competition seater, both of which give him excellent results. While he does check runout initially to ensure that his dies are working properly, he does not select cartridges by seated bullet runout, preferring to rely on well-fitted barrels and top quality reloading dies to minimize TIR overall. Mid practices "soft-seating"—i.e., seating bullets further out than necessary to contact the lands, so that they will touch the lands and then be pushed into the case the requisite degree upon closing the bolt. He doesn't use moly, considering it just one more variable that he can do without, and nowadays, his powder choices run to Hodgdon's Australian imports (the "Extreme" series), particularly H-4350, due to their insensitivity to temperature changes. Mid uses Federal 210M match primers, and tests them by lot to ensure consistent velocities. When working up loads, his approach is simplicity itself—long experience has shown him that the 6.5-284 shoots best when running Sierra 142 gr. MatchKings at 3050-3100 fps., so he simply loads them to that velocity range, checks the velocity variation, and heads for the nearest match! I asked Mid for his thoughts on the popular scientific methods such as Creighton Audette's; while he is not opposed to them, he considers them to be a fair amount of work. He tests his loads in competition, and by matching his call to the shot's location, he can tell if everything is working as it should. During our interview, Mid volunteered that he has also found over the years that the 190 gr. Sierra MatchKing works best for him at about 2550 fps in the .308, while the 155 gr. Sierra Palma bullet's optimum speed in .308 is just under 3,000 fps. Mid uses 30" Krieger barrels in order to obtain maximum velocity for the powder burned.

In conclusion, there are many different approaches to handloading accurate ammo for long range competition. They vary in precision, in complexity, and in the time and effort involved; some aspects, such as maintaining excellent velocity consistency, are critical, while others are less so. Some techniques used by a low-volume shooter might require too much time and effort for the high-volume shooter. Moreover, some shooters feel better knowing they have done everything humanly possible to ensure the accuracy of their ammunition, while others load to a given, adequate accuracy standard and concentrate a bit more on the human element of the equation—i.e., "operator headspace." As always, the winner of any given rifle match will not necessarily be the shooter whose brass weighs precisely 174.3 grains, has 0.001" or less TIR and wall thickness runout, or which has been machined and massaged to within an inch of its life. The winner will be the superior marksman—an excellent shooter with good ammo will beat a marginal shooter with superior ammo, hands down. While good ammunition definitely helps competitors reach their full potential, most shooters will profit more through quality practice, than by spending countless hours fretting at the loading bench. Good luck, and good shooting!!